Impressionism for England

Impressionism for England

SAMUEL COURTAULD AS PATRON AND COLLECTOR

John House

with contributions by

John Murdoch, Andrew Stephenson,
William Bradford and Elizabeth Prettejohn

COURTAULD INSTITUTE GALLERIES
LONDON

Produced and distributed for The Courtauld Institute Galleries
by Yale University Press, New Haven and London

Designed by Gillian Malpass

Typeset by Servis Filmsetting Ltd, Manchester
Printed in Italy by Amilcare Pizzi, S.p.A., Milan

Library of Congress Catalog Card No. 94-60524
ISBN 0 300 06128 5
A catalogue record for this book is available from The British Library

CONTENTS

SPONSOR'S PREFACE

DIRECTOR'S PREFACE

In keeping with our forty-year commitment to supporting the arts, Cantor Fitzgerald is proud to sponsor 'Impressionism for England: Samuel Courtauld as Patron and Collector' at the Courtauld Institute Galleries. As one of Great Britain's most important benefactors, Samuel Courtauld helped shape the nation's visual culture with his generous bequests.

We extend our sincere congratulations to the Courtauld Institute Galleries for this magnificent exhibition which brings together the finest collection of French Impressionist and Post-Impressionist paintings ever formed in England.

Cantor Fitzgerald salutes the extraordinary patronage of Samuel Courtauld as well as the originality, quality and creativity evident in the works of these master painters.

B. Gerald Cantor
Chairman
Cantor Fitzgerald

This book is published to mark the opening of a special display of the paintings, drawings and prints of the Impressionist and Post-Impressionist schools collected by Samuel Courtauld to hang originally at his London house. These pictures, which formed the greater part of his personal collection, have acquired particular significance in the history of British visual culture in the twentieth century because he gave most of them to the Courtauld Institute, the school of the University of London that he financed in order to further the serious study and appreciation of art. A number of key pictures, however, he gave or bequeathed to close friends and to members of his family. They included such famous works as Monet's *Gare Saint-Lazare* (National Gallery, London), Manet's *The Road-Pavers, Rue Mosnier* (private collection) and the magical Renoir landscape *Spring (Chatou)* (private collection). In the display, we have sought to reassemble as many as possible of these 'lost' elements of Samuel Courtauld's collection, so that their relevance to the whole may be assessed, and the collection once again enjoyed virtually in its entirety.

The result makes clear the full magnificence of the collection, and confirms how good Courtauld's aesthetic judgement was in this field. It also suggests the extent to which the collection was formed according to rational principles, rather than simply by opportunism in the market-place. For within the collection as a whole, pictures complement and contrast with one another in their historical relationships and in their formal properties. We are able to see Renoir's *Place Clichy* (Fitzwilliam Museum, Cambridge) in apposition to our *La*

Loge, to turn from Monet's, *Argenteuil, the Bridge under Repair* (private collection) across the room to our *Autumn Effect at Argenteuil*, or from Picasso's *Child with a Pigeon* (private collection) to our Modigliani *Nude*. These visual relationships must have given Courtauld—his taste deeply influenced by Roger Fry's formalism—both intense pleasure and an invigorating insight into the nature of the Impressionist revolution. Some seventy years on, they also illuminate for us the way in which Impressionism was understood in England. Those particular juxtapositions are not normally available to visitors to our Galleries, and the fact they they can once again be experienced in the context of the whole Courtauld Collection is reason for gratitude to the lenders.

Impressive as it was in quality and range, however, Samuel Courtauld's private collection was not his only achievement as a discriminating purchaser of great pictures. For at the same time as he was buying pictures for himself, he was laying out money for the Courtauld Fund, which he had set up to enable the Trustees of the Tate and National galleries to acquire for the nation an equivalent collection of Impressionist and Post-Impressionist pictures. The 'public' collection now forms the nucleus of the National Gallery's representation of late nineteenth-century French art and includes such famous pictures as Degas's *Young Spartans*, Seurat's, *Une Baignade, Asnières* and the extraordinary group of van Goghs: *Sunflowers, The Chair and the Pipe* and *A Cornfield, with Cypresses*. Courtauld's intention was that the nation should obtain, before it was too late, as strong a representation as possible of the work of those painters who had launched 'modern' painting and made it as unmistakably great and exciting as the work of the Old Masters.

The two collections, private and public, were displayed together at the Tate Gallery in London in May 1948, as a memorial tribute to Courtauld shortly after his death, and they jointly form the subject of Douglas Cooper's monograph *The Courtauld Collection: A Catalogue and Introduction*, published by the University of London in 1954. It might have been fun to repeat the 1948 exhibition, but the fact is, the two collections were never intended as a single entity, were not intended to be seen together as such: the 'public' collection was, definitively, intended to transform and enrich the nation's premier public gallery (as it does), not to be transported around London for purely spectacular effect. Our intentions are more sober. In our display, we wish to explore the full significance of the 'private' collection, and in the book to deal also with the 'public' collection, considering it as an analogue rather than an extension of the private, and as its separate complement in relation to Courtauld's intervention in the visual culture of twentieth-century Britain. The National Gallery, by drawing attention to the Courtauld Fund pictures in its Impressionist rooms, makes it possible for visitors to both institutions to see the total effect of Courtauld's philanthropy, as he intended, in two sigificantly different places.

Our thanks, therefore, are due in the first instance to the Director and Trustees of the National Gallery for their instantaneous and enthusistic interest in the project, for lending to us pictures that once formed part of Courtauld's private collection, and for facilitating the loan of others. For Neil McGregor's warm support and for the ready help of Nicholas Penny and John Leighton we are extremely grateful. Latterly, Erika Langmuir has been characteristically energetic and inventive in developing with us a joint education programme and in making possible the video that accompanies the exhibition.

We owe a similar debt of gratitude to the Director and Syndics of the Fitzwilliam Museum: Simon Jervis and David Scrase have been active and thoughtful colleagues in the venture, which has led, in a happy gesture of reciprocity between sister academic galleries, to the loan of two major Impressionist paintings by us to Cambridge for the duration of the exhibition. It is more difficult to thank adequately those other lenders who, for understandable reasons, have felt they must remain anonymous; but without their generous support we shoud have missed many of the star pieces in the exhibition.

Happily, it is easier to thank those who have given equally generously of their knowledge and time to round out our account of Samuel Courtauld's background and circumstances. We are especially grateful to Sir Adam Butler and the Hon. Christopher McLaren for their help, and for their memories of Courtauld as a real person, not just as a businessman or collector. But without the business, there would have been no art, so the help of Professor Donald Coleman, the author of the standard history of the Courtauld companies, has been equally essential. We are grateful also to the Chairman and staff of the present company, Courtaulds p.l.c., the lenders of the splendid silver, made or sold by members of the Courtauld dynasty in the eighteenth century; to Shirley Rodden, company archivist at Coventry, and to Carol Fenton and Elizabeth Lay at the headquarters of the company in London, who have helped us to achieve in the exhibition at least some indication of the economic basis of Courtauld's collecting. Closer to home we wish to thank the many colleagues who have assisted in our research, in particular Jennifer Booth at the Tate Gallery Archive, Jacqui McComish at the National Gallery Archive, Nicholas Savage at the Royal Academy Library, Jacqueline Cox at the Twentieth-Century Archive, Kings College, Cambridge, Desmond Corcoran and Martin Summers of the Lefèvre Gallery, and, of course, our own colleagues in the Courtauld Institute Library. Gillian Malpass of Yale University Press has been the most supportive and understanding of editors.

Economically, the exhibition has been made possible by Cantor Fitzgerald, in particular by virtue of Mr Gerald Cantor's personal enthusiasm for the painting and sculpture of the Impressionists and Post-Impressionists. It has been a pleasure to work with Mr and Mrs Cantor, and with their representatives Philippa Polskin, Betsy Ennis and Steve Pagano in New York.

Finally, since this is a personal as well as a collective statement of gratitude, I should like to place on record my thanks for the generous energy poured into the project by John House, lead author and editor of this volume; and by William Bradford, Andrew Stephenson and Elizabeth Prettejohn. Their names appear on the title-page of this book, and they know how vital they have been in bringing our project to fruition. In addition, thanks are due to my colleague Gillian Kennedy, responsible for the personal and business section of the exhibition, and to the rest of those whose work has been vital: Ron Cobb, John Joseph, Philippa Alden, Madeleine Korn, Sarah Blain, William Clarke and Susan Blake, together with George Craig and his team, at the Galleries; and not forgetting Helen Braham in correspondence with Gregory Eades of the Government Indemnity Scheme for administering the loans—a demanding task, too often regarded as thankless.

John Murdoch
Director
21 March 1994

vii

IMPRESSIONISM AND ITS CONTEXTS

John House

AS A GROUP OF PAINTINGS, the Courtauld Collection is the product of a particular historical situation; but this moment in the history of art collecting in the twentieth century is quite distinct from the contexts in which the paintings themselves were made, in the later nineteenth century. The collection includes paintings of different types which would never have been exhibited together at the time of their making, and no single collector in the nineteenth century would have assembled paintings by all of the artists represented in it.

It is this twentieth-century history that meets present-day viewers in the Impressionist and Post-Impressionist galleries of great art museums. In a sense, of course, this is inevitable, since we are viewing them in the twentieth century, and with twentieth-century viewpoints and preconceptions. But this issue is more acute as far as Impressionism and Post-Impressionism are concerned than it is with any other movement from the art of the past, because they have, in the twentieth century, been so thoroughly dragged apart from their original contexts and presented as cornerstones of a seemingly organic cultural tradition—often simply described as 'modern art'. This tradition is itself a twentieth-century construction.

There are, then, two quite distinct histories of Impressionism and Post-Impressionism to be written: first, one that analyses the place that these works of art—their production, exhibition and sale (or non-sale)—occupied in the art practice of the later nineteenth century in France; and second, a history that describes the emergence of this retrospective 'modern' tradition in the twentieth century, and unravels its bases and the interests it serves. These two histories cannot be absorbed into a single unproblematic history, as has been done in some of the most celebrated accounts of the period;[1] for the values of a particular present position cannot be applied uncritically to the elucidation of the past.

In this essay, I want to outline some of the frameworks that seem to me to be central in the first of these histories: to consider the ways in which Impressionist and Post-Impressionist painting needs to be related to broader issues in the history of nineteenth-century painting. A number of recent studies have begun to tackle the art of the period from some of these viewpoints, and I indicate the most important of these in footnotes. At the end, I indicate briefly some of the key points in the second history, of Impressionism's emerging fame, and consider the moment at which the two histories converged, around the turn of the century. A second essay follows, which considers Samuel Courtauld's position as collector and patron in the London art world of the 1920s.

*　　*　　*

Fundamental to changes in French painting in the later nineteenth century were changing patterns of exhibition and sale. Increasingly professional and specialised art dealers were emerging, who sought to cater to the needs and tastes of an increasingly buoyant market for modern paintings among private collectors—not only French collectors, but an international phalanx of buyers who looked to the Parisian art market as the purveyor of artistic fashions. At the same time, the traditional dominance of the officially organised Salon came to be challenged, as artists found alternative means of exhibiting their pictures which better suited the smaller, more informal works that many buyers sought.

In discussions of Impressionism, much attention has been paid to the eight group exhibitions mounted between 1874 and 1886, at the first of which the painters were named the 'Impressionists'. But these exhibitions were only one symptom of the larger problem posed by the organisation of the Salon—a vast and multifarious exhibition, in which several thousand works were hung cheek by jowl in very large, tall spaces. Small pictures were at a disadvantage in these conditions: a few—but only the work of well-known artists—were hung low on the walls, beneath the large pictures; otherwise they were scattered high and wide wherever they could be fitted. The (admittedly fictional) story of the painter Claude Lantier in Zola's novel *L'Oeuvre* (1886), searching through the Salon halls for his small painting of his dead child, vividly dramatises this situation.

Thus an unknown painter could best attract attention with a large and insistent painting. Yet there was a growing feeling that the rhetoric of grand painting, and the repertoire of subjects from past history and ancient mythology that the Academy favoured, were inappropriate to the modern world. Moreover, such huge paintings could be bought only by the State or by a museum – few private residences could accommodate them. Smaller paintings, of traditionally less significant status, such as landscapes, everyday genre scenes and still life, stood little chance of making their author's reputation. It was such pictures that demanded smaller and more intimate exhibition spaces in order to gain notice. One such space was directed by Louis Martinet in the early 1860s; Manet showed many of his smaller paintings there, and in 1861 François Bonvin, specialist in genre scenes and still lifes, wrote to Martinet:

> Yet another good mark for your idea of holding a permanent exhibition! That picture I brought you a week ago has just brought me to the notice of the ministry. Placed in the big exhibition, this canvas would not, perhaps, have been noticed. *La peinture intime*, large or small, needs a setting like yours.[2]

The smaller spaces of the Impressionist group exhibitions likewise allowed such smaller works to be seen; at the first exhibition in 1874, the works were divided according to size, with all the smaller ones below the larger. However, such installations were a far cry from the spacious hanging we are accustomed to in modern museums and exhibitions. Although no images showing the installation of the group exhibitions have come to light, it is clear that pictures were still hung comparatively close to each other, and generally in at least two rows. Moreover, the works at the first show were hung on dull red material, which would have given an effect quite the opposite to that of the light-toned walls that until recently have dominated twentieth-century installations of Impressionist paintings. Dark, warm walls were the norm in the later nineteenth century, and the painters would thus have anticipated a light-toned or brightly coloured canvas standing out as the most vivid thing in its surroundings, whereas light walls tend to dull and deaden their effect.[3]

Concentration on the group exhibitions has tended to obscure the fact that, into the 1880s at least, the Salon remained by far the most significant outlet for modern art in Paris. Historians have sometimes been puzzled by Edouard Manet's refusal to join with his friends in the group exhibitions, yet his decision made absolute sense for two reasons: because he could reach a far larger public through the Salon, and because he continued to put his greatest efforts into a small number of ambitious pictures each year, works large enough in scale to be noticed at the Salon. The Courtauld Collection includes one of the last and most remarkable of these, *A Bar at the Folies-Bergère* (cat. no. 27), shown at the 1882 Salon; this is the only Salon painting in the collection and was thus designed to be seen in circumstances quite different from all the other paintings that now hang around it. When the critic Théodore Duret urged Camille Pissarro in 1874 not to join in the group exhibition, he was offering sound practical advice, which the comparative financial failure of the group exhibitions proved to be valid. He wrote:

> Among the 40,000 people who, I suppose, visit the Salon, you'll be seen by fifty dealers, patrons, critics who would never otherwise look you up and discover you. Even if you only achieve that, it would be enough. But you'll gain more, because you are now in a special position in a group that is being discussed and that is beginning to be accepted, although with reservations . . . I urge you to exhibit; you must succeed in making a noise, in defying and attracting criticism, coming face to face with the big public. You won't achieve all that except at the Salon.[4]

Recent research has shown that the group exhibitions were received far more positively by contemporary critics than has generally been acknowledged.[5] Many applauded the attempt to create an alternative forum to the Salon, and even the more critical accounts showed mostly a real understanding of what the painters were seeking. The satirical tone of some reviews, such as Louis Leroy's celebrated account of the 1874 show in which he named the painters the 'Impressionists', does not reveal a total hostility to their efforts. Such humour was often used to heighten the vivid, polemical tone of the best of nineteenth-century art criticism and to draw out the distinctive and novel qualities of the works under discussion. In order to see how these conventions of art criticism operated, the discussions of the group shows need to be analysed in relation to the patterns of contemporary writing about the Salon exhibitions.

The eight group exhibitions were presented as a single, numbered sequence, yet they were very varied, both in who took part and in the ways they were organised. The artists generally regarded as the core of the group – Monet, Renoir, Pissarro, Sisley, Degas, Morisot and Cézanne – appeared together only twice, in 1874 and 1877; and the sixth and eighth shows, in 1881 and 1886, were particularly remote from the first. The seventh, in 1882, brought many of the original group together again, but in another way it was crucially different from the rest, since it was virtually a dealer show – mounted and substantially selected by Paul Durand-Ruel.[6]

In another important respect, too, the exhibitions did not present a homogeneous image. From the start they showed paintings of varied status – occasional large pictures of a scale that suited the Salon, and mainly smaller pictures; but these smaller pictures included works of two quite distinct types: rapid and seemingly informal sketches, and more elaborated paintings, of the sort that by then was the stock-in-trade of art dealers such as Durand-Ruel. Both types were unsuitable for the Salon, but they had distinct histories, and the fact that they were brought together on the walls of the group exhibitions is of considerable importance for understanding the genesis of Impressionism.

Pictures painted for dealers were already a well-established commodity. In many artists' work in the 1850s and 1860s, there is a clear distinction between Salon paintings and smaller pictures intended to be sold through the trade to private collectors. This can be seen particularly clearly in the case of Millet, whose *Angelus* (later to become the icon of French peasant painting) was originally painted in 1857–9 for direct sale to a collector, not for immediate exhibition: it is smaller and less highly finished than his contemporary Salon pictures.[7] Among the associates of Monet in the 1860s, both Jongkind and Boudin were making their living from such pictures, sold mostly through dealers such as *père* Martin, and the canvases that Monet, Pissarro and Sisley sold to Durand-Ruel in the early 1870s fall into the same category. Renoir's *La Loge* (cat. no. 39), the only painting in the Courtauld Collection that was shown in the first group exhibition in 1874, is typical of these dealer pictures; Renoir sold it to Martin in 1875 for the comparatively high price of 425 francs.[8] Such pictures continued to appear in all the group shows. Indeed, it is probably no coincidence that the painters took the final decision to embark on their own shows at the moment that Durand-Ruel was forced by financial constraints to stop buying their work: they needed another outlet for such pictures once Durand-Ruel's extensive purchases of 1872–3 ceased.

All the early shows included also more informal sketches. Often these were subtitled *étude* (study) or *esquisse* (sketch), in order to indicate their status. The label *impression*, added by Monet to the title of his *Impression, Sunrise* at the 1874 exhibition, carried many of the same implications: the word *impression* was already in wide circulation among artists to refer to rapid notations of atmospheric effects. Though this title led to the naming of the group, the picture itself was untypical, and far sketchier than most of those shown in the exhibitions; however, the subsequent reputation and public image of Impressionist painting has viewed this canvas as the archetypal product of the group.

*   *   *

Such sketches belonged to a tradition with a long history. At least since the eighteenth century certain particularly 'artistic' collectors had favoured paintings of this type, as can be seen from the sale catalogue of Varanchan de Saint-Geniès of 1777:

> This collection would appear to be that of a rich artist with good taste rather than of a collector . . . Though finished paintings are more generally popular, a certain class of collector rejoices particularly in a simple sketch; he looks for the soul and the thoughts of the man of genius whom he can see and recognise.

In 1876, Duranty, a close associate of the group, described the Impressionists' decision to show sketches in their exhibitions in very much these terms; of the collections made by the principal early patrons of the group, those of Victor Chocquet and, particularly, their fellow painter Gustave Caillebotte fall into the category of 'artistic' collections of men who appreciated the immediacy and expressiveness of the sketch.[9]

All too often, though, such notions of immediacy and expressiveness, of sketches revealing 'the soul and the thoughts of the man of genius', have been taken at face value. But, of course, brushstrokes on canvas involve a complete imaginative transposition, and it is only on the basis of agreed conventions of representation that they can be seen as recreating an individual's experience of the world – let alone his or her 'soul and thoughts'.

No representation in paint is 'natural'; all alike demand historical analysis, to reveal the conventions that underlie them. This is most crucial with types of art such as Impressionism, which have come to be seen as direct, unmediated images of reality. At times, the Impressionist painters themselves fostered this idea: Monet declared that he would like to paint 'like the bird sings'. But such aspirations, too, have to be examined historically, as a rejection of the dominant artifice of Neo-Classical Salon painting in favour of a type of art whose technique evoked immediate experience. Moreover, their first viewers did not find their art 'natural'; it is only more recently that Impressionist visions of nature have come to be accepted as the norm for 'natural' vision in the west.

The unquestioning acceptance of their vision as natural has had a further implication, by disguising the polemical intent with which it was originally conceived. In its early years, the Impressionists' manner of painting, along with Manet's, was widely regarded as politically radical or subversive, since it challenged traditional hierarchies of representation. Their brushwork, according all objects in the scene approximately equal significance, challenged the centrality of the human figure in the world, and the groupings they chose often presented a complex interplay of elements which prevented any clear-cut reading of the relationships depicted. The uncertainties enshrined in the physical make-up of Manet's *A Bar at the Folies-Bergère* (cat. no. 27) are an important example of this.[10] The historian must examine the original contexts in which the pictures were seen, and their viewers' expectations, in order to understand the reasons for the initial shock they caused, rather than accepting their 'naturalness' uncritically.

It is here that a historical study of Impressionist painting technique becomes essential, both in relating the Impressionists' development of a sketch-like technique to a longer tradition that put a premium on such a sense of immediacy, and in studying in detail the ways in which their technique emerged, in relation to the accepted modes of representation at the time. It was in relation to the niceties of academic finish that their technique signalled their originality and their independence.[11] But, at the same time, the boldness of some of their paintings must be seen alongside the more tempered, carefully resolved treatment of the pictures they sought to put into the market through dealers; all their works alike need to be considered in relation to their potential public outlets.

Even Cézanne, whose private means largely freed him from the need to sell his work, needs to be considered in these terms; for it was his financial independence that allowed him to wrestle so unremittingly with the problem of transforming his experiences of nature into a resolved pictorial form, and also to develop a reputation as a mysterious genius whose works were known only to the chosen few. It was only at the very end of his life, and far more after his death, that this studiedly private art found a wider public and became for the twentieth century an archetype of solitary creative individualism.

Impressionist and Post-Impressionist art as a whole has become a paradigm of such individualism, but again this notion must be examined critically. The eighteenth-century promotion of paintings that expressed 'the soul and thoughts of the man of genius' must be related to changing notions of human (male) individualism at the time – notions that the Impressionist generation inherited; and our present-day glorification of these individuals – enshrined in collections like Courtauld's and in the galleries of great museums – demands analysis in relation to the very high premium put on individual human agency in modern western culture. These are matters for historical investigation, not unquestioning acceptance.

In recent years, much attention has been paid for the first time to the subjects the Impressionists depicted, and in particular to their fascination in the 1860s and 1870s with the changing landscapes of the environs of Paris.[12] This has served to emphasise their active engagement with the specifics of their surroundings and has quashed the myth that they just painted the scene nearest to hand. But, at the same time, it has proved difficult to pin down any real consistency in the visions they presented. Monet's depictions of Argenteuil are an example of this, for they show the place in many different guises, even in a single year. A small country town and agricultural centre about eight miles north-west of central Paris, it was being transformed by encroaching industrialisation and had also become a centre for recreational sailing.[13] Sometimes Monet emphasised one aspect of the place, sometimes another; sometimes modernity dominates (see cat. no. 30), while in other pictures, such as cat. no. 31, there is scarcely a hint of the changes in the place. Likewise, his friends showed varied facets of the place when they painted there, such as Manet in cat. no. 25.

Certainly, this diversity echoes the historical situation in the area around Paris, but the pictures cannot be seen simply as passive reflections of social reality. As paintings, they belonged in a specific context, on the walls of exhibitions or in the stock of dealers in Paris, and their original audiences would have received and classified them in relation to contemporary categories of landscape painting, not by reference to the 'facts of life' at Argenteuil itself, about which many who saw them would have known little. Thus they were primarily contributions to metropolitan debates about city, suburb and country, rather than historical documents about the places depicted. The information culled by the social historian must be complemented by analysis of the function of the pictures as representations – as images that themselves generated beliefs and opinions and orchestrated discussion.

The subjects the Impressionists chose cannot be discussed separately from the ways in which they treated them. Their unconventional and (by contemporary standards) very unpicturesque view of the world around them was inseparable from their sketchy, informal handling and their insistence on treating everything in a scene with equal focus. The interconnections between technique and world view were vividly evoked by Frédéric Chevalier in his review of the third group exhibition in 1877:

> The characteristics that distinguish the Impressionists – the brutal handling of paint, their down-to-earth subjects, the appearance of spontaneity that they seek above all else, the deliberate incoherence, the bold colouring, the contempt for form, the childish *naïveté* that they mix heedlessly with exquisite refinements – this disconcerting mixture of contradictory qualities and defects is not without analogy to the chaos of opposing forces that trouble our era.[14]

*   *   *

By the early 1880s, a major transformation had come over Impressionist landscape painting. Most of the original group had turned away from the landscapes of modernity of the Paris region, seemingly disillusioned with the possibility of producing an imagery of modern landscape. The painters moved in various directions – Pissarro to a more idealised, unspecific vision of peasant life, Renoir to a greater sense of tradition and classicism (e.g., cat. no. 43, a very late work), Sisley and especially Monet to a preoccupation with effects of weather and atmosphere. Monet's *Antibes* (cat. no. 34) is one example of this withdrawal, both in its focus on the dazzle of Mediterranean light and in its complete lack of any contemporary or human references.

Common to all of their positions was a search for some sort of unity, whether found in the subject depicted or in the atmospheric effect that cloaked it, in contrast to the diverse elements characteristic of many of their landscapes in the 1870s (e.g., cat. nos 36 and 58).

Even when Pissarro did paint urban subjects at Rouen in 1883 (cat. no. 37) and in Rouen and Paris in the 1890s, the whole scene is absorbed in a unifying light effect.[15]

There is no simple, clear-cut explanation for this change. It is certainly relevant that their dissatisfaction with modern imagery coincided with a degree of disillusionment with the results of their group exhibitions, and with a fresh attempt to find a steady market through art dealers. From 1880 onwards, Durand-Ruel was able to buy again, and bought extensively from Monet, Renoir, Pissarro and Sisley. His intervention certainly encouraged them to finish their canvases more fully,[16] and may have affected their choice of subjects. Many of Monet's pictures of the 1880s, in particular, show subjects that were becoming celebrated through tourism – Antibes, for instance, was already an expanding resort. In addition, all four were taken up by other dealers, too, and showed their work in the fashionable Expositions Internationales organised by the dealer Georges Petit.

However, such an explanation is not adequate in itself. The Impressionists' change of direction was only part of a wholesale reassessment during the 1880s of the position of avant-garde painting in France, and this needs to be explored from various angles. By 1880, overtly contemporary landscape subjects were playing a more prominent part in the Salon exhibitions, in the work of painters such as Antoine Guillemet and Luigi Loir, who were producing the large-scale tableaux of the modern scene that the Impressionists' friend and erstwhile supporter Emile Zola had long been advocating.

This was not, though, merely a shift in taste. Through most of the 1870s, in the aftermath of the Franco-Prussian War and the Commune of 1870–1, the government had operated a highly repressive regime, and the arts establishment had sought to foster a revival of traditional history painting. It was in this context that the Impressionists' contemporary subjects of the 1870s were seen as disconcerting and even disruptive. In 1879, however, with the presidency of Jules Grévy, a liberal Republican government took over, which removed most social and political controls and actively sponsored paintings of contemporary life scenes as reflecting the essence of modern France. In this context, the Impressionists' subject matter of the 1870s would no longer have been problematic; but all, in their different ways, resisted appropriation by the new regime and chose, instead, to develop their art in ways that highlighted their own individuality. In this they were encouraged by the rapid development of the art-dealer trade and the support of dealers such as Durand-Ruel and Georges Petit; this, by the 1890s, led the Impressionists, particularly Monet and Renoir, to increasing success and financial security.

However, the most significant development in the Paris exhibition world in the 1880s was the foundation in 1884 of an annual jury-free exhibition, organised by the Société des Indépendants, at which all submitted works were shown. It was here that Seurat and his fellow Neo-Impressionists, and also Vincent van Gogh, found an outlet for their work. Its importance was that it provided a forum for art of any sort whatsoever; before its institution, a self-taught amateur such as Henri Rousseau (e.g., cat. no. 44) would have had no chance at all of reaching an audience.

Broadly speaking, the aims of the Indépendants were anti-authoritarian and closely in line with the tenets of contemporary anarchist politics, which played a major part on the political left in

France in the 1880s and 1890s. In these years, the anarchists were not a marginal group, and their ideas provided a focus for many of the most crucial issues facing the artistic avant-gardes, about the role of art in modern society. Camille Pissarro was committed to a form of non-violent humanitarian anarchism, and many of Seurat's closest associates were anarchist sympathisers, though Seurat's own political position remains ambiguous.

In one sense, Seurat and his colleagues occupied the same position in the later 1880s as the Impressionist group had in the 1870s. Their technique, of treating the whole picture surface with equally weighted dots of colour, was viewed often as politically radical, since its homogeneity challenged the traditional focus on the human subject; and they espoused the imagery of modern Paris and its suburbs as the Impressionists had fifteen years before (see Seurat, cat. nos 47, 51 and 53). However, particularly in Seurat's later work, such as *Young Woman Powdering Herself* (cat. no. 53), there is a clear shift against the ostensible naturalism of Impressionist pictures such as Renoir's *La Loge* (cat. no. 39), in favour of a degree of schematisation which decisively sets the work of art apart from perceived reality. This change is in line with the tenets of the emerging Symbolist movement, with its rejection of naturalism in favour of types of art that sought to express the essence, or underlying idea, of the chosen subject.[17]

Seurat's position in the late 1880s makes a fascinating contrast with that of Gauguin. Gauguin, too, was evolving a technique that rejected the idea of naturalism, in order to extract some essential element in his subjects. But the two artists' paths diverged in two crucial ways. Gauguin refused to join the Indépendants, preferring to show in small and more select group shows; and he wholly rejected the imagery of contemporary life – not, like the Impressionists, in favour of a vision of light and atmosphere, but in pursuit of a notion of the primitive.

In his paintings of Brittany, Gauguin stressed the otherness of its inhabitants, presenting their life and labour as if they were hieratic ritual rather than real physical toil (e.g., cat. no. 19). By the time that Gauguin painted there, Brittany was expanding economically,[18] but it was in Paris that his images of the place had their currency; there, the place retained its image as a repository of traditional beliefs and folklore – of the values that urbanisation was putting under threat. Gauguin's evocations of Breton simplicity were the antithesis of the complexities and uncertainties of dominant city culture. Although expressed in a deliberately stylised pictorial language, they played on the same set of assumptions about life in Brittany which underpinned the paintings of Breton subjects that won great popularity in the Salon in the same years.[19]

Likewise, Gauguin's paintings of Tahiti from the 1890s played on standard western stereotypes of the 'primitive'. For many years it has been clear that these were not accurate images of South Sea island life, but rather visions created firmly within traditional notions of, and fantasies about, the primitive and the exotic.[20] *Nevermore* and *Te Rerioa* (cat. nos 20 and 21) both relate closely to the imagery of Orientalist painters of the mid-nineteenth century, translating into an Oceanic milieu the imagery of sensuous reverie and of awakening sensuality which had been the stock-in-trade of western images of the middle-eastern harem. Gauguin's trip to Tahiti, and the richness of his synthesis of a wide range of cultural traditions, reinvigorated this tradition, but its underlying dynamic remained largely unchanged, in its deployment of the image of non-western races to fuel debates about modern western society. To the western painter, as to the western viewer of his paintings, these images of indolence and sensuality presuppose the availability of these peoples – whether through economic or military domination – to satisfy western dreams of the 'other'.[21]

* * *

In general histories of the art of the 1880s, these changes have been described in terms of the replacement of Impressionism by 'Post-Impressionism' as the vanguard movement in Paris. But this formulation raises great problems. The term Impressionism itself had no clear unitary meaning at the time. As Henri Houssaye wrote in 1882: 'Impressionism receives every form of sarcasm when it takes the names Manet, Monet, Renoir, Caillebotte, Degas – every honour when it is called Bastien-Lepage, Duez, Gervex . . . or Dagnan-Bouveret.' In 1888, Van Gogh was able to say that he still considered himself an Impressionist 'because it professes nothing and binds you to nothing', though elsewhere he said that his own increasing preoccupation with expressive colour might not find favour with the Impressionists.[22] Indeed, the term Impressionist, loosely used, remained the most widely used broad category for modern French painting into the early years of the twentieth century. 'Post-Impressionist', by contrast, had no contemporary sanction, being the creation of a rather unconvinced Roger Fry, seeking a title for the exhibition he mounted in London in 1910. Its apparent homogeneity has always raised difficulties, given the diversity of the art it encompasses (Gauguin, van Gogh, Seurat and, at times, Cézanne, despite his presence in the early Impressionist exhibitions).

Certainly, the history of the use of the term 'Impressionist' has much to tell us about artistic debates in the 1880s, alongside the titles proposed at the time for alternative avant-garde groupings (Symbolist, Synthetist, Neo-Impressionist and so on), but these terms must be seen as focuses for discussion, in relation to which different groups negotiated and sought to establish their own positions, rather than as summing up any 'real' characteristics of the art under discussion.

The issues that I have so far raised seem important to the writing of a history of Impressionism and Post-Impressionism. The resulting history would not be a clear-cut sequential narrative of the development of artistic 'movements', but would focus on the varied relationships between the production of art and its exhibition, critical reception and sale. Such a history is only possible if notions of linear development in modern art, of one vanguard superseding another, are abandoned, in favour of a more wide-ranging analysis of the ways in which groupings of artists negotiated their positions within the dominant frameworks of the Parisian art world at the time. The historical significance of the Impressionists' group exhibitions, and of the works they showed there, can be understood only through a thorough analysis of the position of the Salon and of other institutions at the time.[23]

Much important work has recently been done in these areas, but the overall task is still impeded by the seminal role accorded to Impressionism and Post-Impressionism as cornerstones of the modern tradition. Two major recent exhibitions have proposed significant reassessments of the period, but both have failed to present the necessary wider perspective because of strong institutional pressures that they should be 'Impressionist' exhibitions, without the addition of the needed comparative material.[24]

*　　*　　*

The Courtauld Collection, of course, belongs to the same framework, since the collection itself is the product of this modern tradition, in its most exclusive form. It is here that we have to move from the first type of history of Impressionism to the second – to the emergence of the modern tradition in the twentieth century.

Only the briefest indication of this can be given here. There seem to be two distinct strands to the story, which only finally came together after the Second World War. The first of these was the gradual assimilation of Impressionism into the official French notion of the French artistic tradition; the second was the evolving modernist aesthetic, with its prime emphasis on essentially pictorial qualities as the defining characteristic of true modern(ist) painting.

Impressionist painting first found an accepting market in the United States, in the decade after the big exhibition mounted by Durand-Ruel in New York in 1886; it was largely through American buyers that prices for Impressionist paintings – initially primarily Monet and Renoir – boomed in Paris. But during the 1890s, French collectors and the French authorities began to take them more seriously. The French government bought an important recent painting from Renoir in 1892, but between 1894 and 1896 the acceptance of Caillebotte's bequest of his collection to the State still produced great controversy, before a large part of it entered the State's modern-art museum, the Musée du Luxembourg, in 1897.[25] Impressionist paintings were included in the French section of the 1900 Paris Exposition Universelle, but only after argument, and only in the retrospective section, not in the display of the art of the last ten years.

In the gradual emergence of Impressionist painting, the director of the Musée du Luxembourg, Léonce Bénédite, seems to have played a major part, both through his writings and through exhibitions he mounted. One little-known show that he put on at the Musée du Luxembourg may have been a significant step in this process of assimilation; this was the temporary exhibition of masterpieces by contemporary masters from private collections, under the aegis of the Society of Friends of the Luxembourg in spring 1904, in which even Manet's controversial *Nana* was shown, together with works by Monet, Renoir, Pissarro, Degas and Sisley, and leading academic masters of the period. It was shortly after this that the first book appeared that presented the development of modern art as a series of successive movements in which Impressionism played a decisive part; it even discussed the soon-to-be-named Post-Impressionists in a section titled 'Pantheist and Living Art'. This was André Fontainas's *Histoire de la peinture française au XIXme siècle* of 1906. In the same years, too, major retrospectives of van Gogh, Gauguin, Seurat and Cézanne, mounted by the Société des Indépendants and the recently formed Salon d'Automne, brought their art before a wider public. The writings of the much-translated German critic Julius Meier-Graefe also had a major influence on these changing views.

The comparatively late acceptance of Impressionism by French collectors produced an intriguing anomaly in the French national collections, in comparison with the major American museums. The American collectors, from the late 1880s onwards, bought mainly

very recent pictures; thus the residue of collections such as those of H.O. Havemeyer and Mrs Potter Palmer has left American museums particularly rich in later Impressionist pictures, of the 1880s and 1890s.[26] French collectors, though beginning to buy around a decade later, focused primarily on earlier paintings – paintings whose place in the French tradition was already comparatively secure. Of the few pioneer collections bought from the painters in the 1870s, only those of Gustave Caillebotte and Dr Paul Gachet were even in part given to the State; the other groups of pictures that contribute to the unique early Impressionist holdings of the Musée d'Orsay were assembled in retrospect, when the painters' stock was assured – they were mainly made, indeed, in the years in which Bénédite was promoting Impressionism so strongly.[27]

It was, again, early Impressionist painting that the French State primarily promoted in the years after the painters' deaths, for instance in the major series of retrospective exhibitions organised by the Musées Nationaux in the 1930s. This was particularly evident in the 1933 Renoir show, which gave scant notice to the painter's last works, which had aroused such interest among young artists when shown at the Salon d'Automne in 1920, shortly after Renoir's death.

However, during the same years, Impressionism's role in the modern movement was ambivalent. It was largely bypassed in the pioneering presentations of the modern tradition, from Roger Fry's *Manet and the Post-Impressionists* of 1910 to the formative policy of the Museum of Modern Art, New York, from 1929 onwards. The Impressionists' preoccupation with nature – with light and atmosphere – seemed to neglect painting's crucial concern with its own means, whereas Manet's concern with the *tache*, the patch of colour, could readily be assimilated into the modernist viewpoint. The genesis of this way of seeing paintings has to be traced back, through Maurice Denis's celebrated insistence on the primacy of the flat pictorial surface in 1890, to Zola's discussion of Manet's use of the *tache* in 1867. But, once again, the earlier writers cannot simply be subsumed within later priorities: both Denis and Zola demand to be discussed in relation to the debates current at the moment when their essays appeared, and in each case this highlights their distance from the mature 'modernist' position of the twentieth century.[28]

Courtauld's collection, largely formed in the 1920s and 1930s, occupies an intriguingly anomalous position between these two versions of the modern tradition; its balanced, yet notably diverse, group of fine and mainly early works by the principal Impressionists allies it with French official taste, whereas its outstanding Gauguins, Seurats and particularly Cézannes relate closely to the viewpoint that Roger Fry was propounding at the time; Courtauld knew Fry and his writings well (on Courtauld's collecting, see below, pp. 13–27).

These two strands of the modern tradition seem to have been finally brought together only in 1946, with the appearance of John Rewald's remarkable book *The History of Impressionism*, published by the Museum of Modern Art, New York, the prime promoter of the modernist tradition. It was in the late 1940s, too, that the writings of critics such as Clement Greenberg assimilated Monet's late paintings, notably his *Water Lilies*, into their presentation of this tradition. Rewald's book was followed by his *Post-Impressionism* in 1956; this marked the final acceptance of Fry's awkward term, which until then had not become firmly established. In Rewald's two books, both Impressionist and Post-Impressionist painters are presented as pioneers of a new vision, leading ever forward, while the contemporary contexts that gave their enterprises their point and significance are treated merely as the dead wood of reaction.[29]

This essay has described two histories of Impressionism that might be written. Closer analysis of these questions allows us to see more clearly what the Impressionists' art signified on its appearance in Paris in the 1860s and 1870s, and also how their paintings subsequently contributed to the emergence of the modern tradition. But we must not allow these two very different stories to be assimilated into a single, unproblematic account.

NOTES

A previous version of this essay was published in *Impressionist and Post-Impressionist Masterpieces: The Courtauld Collection*, New Haven and London (International Exhibitions Foundation) 1987.

1 Most notably, in John Rewald's *The History of Impressionism*, 1st edn, New York, 1946, and *Post-Impressionism*, New York, 1956; on these, see John House, 'Impressionism and History: The Rewald Legacy', *Art History*, September 1986.

2 Letter from Bonvin to Martinet, 22 April 1861, in E. Moreau-Nélaton, *Bonvin raconté par lui-même*, Paris, 1927, p. 58.

3 On the 1874 installation and the other group exhibitions, see Martha Ward, 'Impressionist Installations and Private Exhibitions', *Art Bulletin*, December 1991; and *The New Painting: Impressionism 1874–1886*, exhibition catalogue, The Fine Arts Museums of San Francisco, 1986.

4 Letter from Duret to Pissarro, 15 February 1874, in Rewald, *Impressionism*, 1973 edn, p. 310. The attendance figure mentioned, 40,000, is far below actual attendances recorded at the Salon – around 500,000 a year in the mid-1870s.

5 See *The New Painting* (cited in note 3); for reprints of the principal critical articles on the 1874 show, see *Centenaire de l'impressionnisme*, exhibition catalogue, Grand Palais, Paris, 1974 (English version, Metropolitan Museum of Art, New York, 1974).

6 Durand-Ruel also staged the 1876 show, but had little commercial involvement in it, in contrast to the situation in 1882; see *The New Painting* (cited in note 3).

7 See *Jean-François Millet*, exhibition catalogue by R.L. Herbert, Grand Palais, Paris, 1975–6, no. 66; the *Angelus* can be contrasted with the virtually contemporary *Woman Pasturing her Cow*, shown at the 1859 Salon (*Jean-François Millet*, 1975–6, no. 67).

8 For Jongkind's letters to Martin, see V. Hefting, *Jongkind d'après sa correspondance*, Utrecht 1969; for Durand-Ruel's reminiscences, see L. Venturi, *Les Archives de l'impressionnisme*, Paris, 1939, II; for the early history of *La Loge*, see *Renoir*, exhibition catalogue, Arts Council of Great Britain and Museum of Fine Arts, Boston, 1985–6, no. 26. The current monetary equivalents of nineteenth-century money are notoriously hard to estimate realistically. In relation to average salaries, one French franc of the 1870s is very roughly equivalent to £1.50–£2 (U.S. $2.50–$3) at 1994 values.

9 The Varanchan sale catalogue, quoted in J. Wilhelm, 'The Sketch in Eighteenth Century French Painting', *Apollo*, September 1962, p. 520. Duranty's essay *La Nouvelle Peinture*, reprinted and translated in *The New Painting* (cited in note 3), this passage p. 483 (translated on p. 46); much of Caillebotte's collection entered the Musée du Luxembourg and is now in the Musée d'Orsay, Paris (see note 25).

10 On the political associations of Impressionist painting, see the essays by Stephen Eisenman and Hollis Clayson in *The New Painting* (cited in note 3); for discussion of Manet in this context, see T.J. Clark, *The Painting of Modern Life*, London, 1985, and John House, 'Manet's Naïveté', in *The Hidden Face of Manet*, exhibition catalogue published in *Burlington Magazine*, April 1986, pp. 14–17.

11 For a valuable discussion of the 'technique of originality' see Richard Shiff, *Cézanne and the End of Impressionism*, Chicago, 1984; on the relationships of Impressionist technique to academic practice, see Albert Boime, *The Academy and French Painting in the Nineteenth Century*, London, 1971, though the links are somewhat oversimplified here, and John House, *Monet: Nature into Art*, New Haven and London, 1986, pp. 157–66.

12 For example, Robert L. Herbert, *Impressionism: Art, Leisure, and Parisian Society*, New Haven and London, 1988; Paul Tucker, *Monet at Argenteuil*, New Haven and London, 1982; *A Day in the Country*, exhibition catalogue, Los Angeles County Museum of Art, 1984; and Clark 1985 (cited in note 10).

13 See Tucker, 1982 (cited in note 12).

14 Frédéric Chevalier, 'Les Impressionnistes', *L'Artiste*, May 1877, p. 331.

15 See John House, 'Anarchist or Esthete? Pissarro in the City', *Art in America*, November 1993.

16 See, for instance, letter from Monet to Durand-Ruel, 3 November 1884, in Daniel Wildenstein, *Monet, biographie et catalogue raisonné*, II, Lausanne and Paris, 1979, letter no. 527. The implications of the relations between the Impressionist painters and their dealers need to be explored more fully.

17 See Paul Smith, 'Was Seurat's Art Wagnerian? And what if it was?', *Apollo*, July 1991.

18 See Fred Orton and Griselda Pollock, 'Les Données bretonnantes: la Prairie de la Représentation', *Art History*, September 1980.

19 See Michael Orwicz, 'Criticism and representations of Brittany in the early Third Republic', *Art Journal*, winter 1987.

20 See Bengt Danielsson, *Gauguin in the South Seas*, London, 1965.

21 For discussion of these stereotypes of the Orient, see Edward Said, *Orientalism*, New York, 1978, and Linda Nochlin, 'The Imaginary Orient', *Art in America*, May 1983. In relation to Gauguin, see Abigail Solomon-Godeau, 'Going native', *Art in America*, July 1989.

22 Houssaye, quoted Rewald, *Impressionism*, 1973 edn, p. 476; letters from Vincent van Gogh to Theo van Gogh, c.17 September and 11 August 1888, in *The Complete Letters of Vincent van Gogh*, London, 1958, letter nos 539 and 520.

23 From this point of view, the two most serious and far-reaching histories of French nineteenth-century painting were published in 1889 and 1931: C.H. Stranahan, *A History of French Painting*, London, 1889, and J.E. Blanche, *Les Arts plastiques, la troisieme république, 1870 à nos jours*, Paris 1931. The only book to discuss the Impressionists in the context of the contemporary art market remains H.C. and C.A. White, *Canvases and Careers: Institutional Change in the French Painting World*, New York, 1965.

24 *A Day in the Country* (cited in note 12) and *The New Painting* (cited in note 3); the arguments of both – the first about imagery, the second about exhibiting institutions – would have gained so much in historical insight if they had included discussion of the Salon and the works exhibited in it.

25 For the purchase of Renoir's *Young Girls at the Piano*, see *Renoir* (cited in note 8), nos 89–91; for the Caillebotte bequest, see Pierre Vaisse, 'Le Legs Caillebotte d'après les documents', and Marie Berhaut, 'Le Legs Caillebotte, Vérités et contre-vérités', both in *Bulletin de la Société de l'Histoire de l'Art Français*, 1983 (published 1985).

26 See Frances Weitzenhoffer, *The Havemeyers: Impressionism Comes to America*, New York, 1986; *Splendid Legacy: The Havemeyer Collection*, exhibition catalogue, Metropolitan Museum of Art, New York, 1993; for Mrs Potter Palmer, see Richard R. Brettell, 'Monet's Haystacks Reconsidered', *Museum Studies*, The Art Institute of Chicago, fall 1984, pp. 18–20.

27 For example, especially the collection of Etienne Moreau-Nélaton, comprising roughly equally early Impressionist canvases and works of Corot and his generation (see *De Corot aux Impressionnistes, donations Moreau-Nélaton*, exhibition catalogue, Grand Palais, Paris, 1991).

28 Maurice Denis, 'Définition du néo-traditionnisme' (1890; reprinted in *Théories*, Paris, 1910); Zola, 'Edouard Manet' (1867; reprinted in *Mon Salon, Manet, Ecrits sur l'art*, ed. A. Ehrard, Paris, 1970); on the latter, see House 1986 (cited in note 10), pp. 8, 14, 17.

29 For further discussion, see House, 1986 (cited in note 1).

MODERN FRENCH ART FOR THE NATION:
SAMUEL COURTAULD'S COLLECTION
AND PATRONAGE IN CONTEXT

John House

IN 1923, THE INDUSTRIALIST SAMUEL COURTAULD gave £50,000 for the purchase of Impressionist and Post-Impressionist paintings for the English national collections. The paintings bought over the next few years have become the core of the National Gallery's holdings in this area. During the same years, Courtauld was also amassing a major private collection. Some of this he presented to the Courtauld Institute of Art, the Institute founded in the University of London on the initiative of Courtauld and other benefactors in 1931; more of his collection was bequeathed to the Institute on his death.

In terms of what he collected, Courtauld was not a pioneer in Britain. By the time that he began to buy seriously, in 1922, many British collectors owned French Impressionist and Post-Impressionist paintings; and Courtauld's own collecting scarcely touched the art of the twentieth century. But the exceptional importance of his collecting and his other involvements with the arts was in his commitment to the public domain – to introducing the art in which he believed into the national collections, and to fostering the study of art in the English educational system.

Courtauld's determination that French Impressionist and Post-Impressionist paintings should be well represented in the national galleries needs to be seen in the context of the development of the galleries themselves, and the halting steps of their engagement with modern foreign art. Beyond this, Courtauld's activities involved a very particular view of art and its history, which set him in opposition to many of the entrenched interests in the English art world; and his commitments marked a wider belief that a taste for art and high culture should belong in a broad public domain, rather than be confined to a narrow élite. These issues will be explored in turn in this essay.

The Context

Before 1917, modern foreign art occupied an anomalous position in the national collections. The National Gallery was not allowed to collect work by living artists, and the National Gallery, Millbank (the Tate Gallery), founded in 1897, was able to include works by British artists only.

In the second half of the nineteenth century, information and knowledge about contemporary developments in the visual arts throughout the western world had spread dramatically, first through the sequence of international exhibitions and world's fairs held in major centres, and second through the rapid development of reproductive media – notably cheap wood engraving, and then photography. In the huge exhibitions, the canvases shown had for the most part been uncontroversial, falling broadly within the more widely accepted types of painting. As we have seen (pp. 1–3), Impressionist pictures were generally shown in independently organised shows and in dealers' galleries; they had quite regularly been shown in London, too, from the 1870s on, but primarily in smaller exhibitions which attracted a comparatively limited public.[1]

In France itself, the historical position of Impressionism became a subject of wider debate with the controversial display of Gustave Caillebotte's collection in the Musée du Luxembourg, the State modern-art museum, in 1897, followed by the inclusion of a significant group of earlier Impressionist paintings in the Paris Exposition Universelle in 1900. The Moreau-Nélaton bequest to the State in 1906, with its important early Impressionist pictures, consolidated Impressionism's position, and in 1911, with the Camondo bequest, the work of living Impressionist artists, Monet and Renoir, was for the first time hung in the Louvre itself.[2] Modern foreign art was also welcomed in French museums. The Musée du Luxembourg, particularly from the 1890s on, bought the work of non-French artists extensively, and by 1910 had a sizeable and varied holding of recent British painting.[3]

A range of factors forced the issue of modern foreign art to the top of the agenda in the English national museums in the early years of this century. There was greater public awareness of Impressionist and Post-Impressionist painting, through two exhibitions: the huge

2   Detail of van Gogh, *A Cornfield, with Cypresses* (fig. 11).

9

display at the Grafton Galleries in 1905, organised by the Paris dealer Durand-Ruel and including perhaps the most spectacular group of Impressionist canvases ever brought together, as well as ten works by Cézanne; and Roger Fry's *Manet and the Post-Impressionists* show, also at the Grafton Galleries, in 1910, with major groups of works by Cézanne, Gauguin and van Gogh.[4]

These exhibitions took place alongside broad discussions about the position of modern art as a whole in the national collections. The Tate Gallery had no separate purchase fund; the primary source of funds for the purchase of modern paintings for the nation was the Chantrey Bequest, a fund administered by the Royal Academy. By around 1900 the Chantrey purchases had become the butt of criticism for their mediocrity and conservatism, and in 1904 a Select Committee of the House of Lords, appointed to investigate the Chantrey Trust, published a damning report, arguing that the Academy had used the fund simply to support its own members. The report also pointed out that according to the terms of Chantrey's will the fund could be used to buy works by foreign artists executed in England; in evidence, D.S. MacColl, Keeper of the Tate, drew the Committee's attention to Monet's recent views of the Thames: 'That painter, to use Mr. Sargent's phrase, is one of the marking influences of our time. I express no critical opinion as to where exactly he comes.' MacColl cited also Degas, Pissarro and Sisley among others whose work might have been bought.[5]

Modern French Paintings for Museums?

The story of the acquisition of modern French paintings for English museums begins in 1900, with the bequest of Constantine Ionides to the Victoria and Albert Museum. His very wide-ranging collection included many paintings of the Barbizon generation, including a remarkable Courbet seascape, and also one of the finest of Degas's earlier works, *The Ballet Scene from 'Robert le Diable'* of 1876. Presumably, its place in Ionides's collection as a whole, as well as its refined execution and sober colouring, made this acquisition unproblematic.[6]

In 1905, inspired by the Grafton Galleries Impressionist exhibition, the critic Frank Rutter had launched the French Impressionist Fund to buy for the nation a painting by Monet, *Snow Effect at Vétheuil* (fig. 3; see below, texts nos 1 and 2, pp. 225–7). However, Rutter was given to understand that the National Gallery Trustees would not accept a Monet, and in the end only a painting by Boudin (died 1898) was bought, and presented to the National Gallery in 1906.[7] According to Rutter, too, the National Gallery Trustees refused the offer of a fine picture by Degas around 1905.[8]

The National Art-Collections Fund, founded in 1903, had as its brief the raising of funds for the purchase of significant works of art for museum collections, but concerned itself primarily with art of earlier periods. However, Rutter, when launching his plan to buy the Monet in 1905, asked the Fund to organise the appeal. Its committee, though declaring itself sympathetic to his aims, decided to concentrate its efforts on buying another recent work, Whistler's *Nocturne in Blue and Silver*, which was duly presented to the National Gallery. Ironically, when Rutter finally purchased the Boudin, he used the Fund as his intermediary in presenting it to the National Gallery.[9]

At the Fund's Annual General Meeting in 1909, Sidney Colvin, then Keeper of Prints and Drawings at the British Museum, made a plea that the Fund should buy one of the canvases from Monet's recent London series: 'Of his Thames pictures, two or three are still on the market which, without the more puzzling exaggerations of his manner, bring home in a new and thrilling light to Englishmen the pictorial interest and wonder of our great city and river.'[10] The Fund did not respond to his call; in 1913, however, it was the Fund that bought the cast of Rodin's *Burghers of Calais* now in Victoria Tower Gardens.

In 1910, the Contemporary Art Society was established, 'for the acquisition of works of modern art for loan or gift to public galleries', deliberately concentrating on an area with which the National Art-Collections Fund was little concerned.[11] Among its committee members were Fry, MacColl and Clive Bell. Although focusing chiefly on British art, the society planned to set up a fund for works by foreign artists, and considered buying a work by Puvis de Chavannes; in 1912 it set aside £50 'towards the purchase of an approved picture by Matisse'.[12] Nothing immediate came of these plans, but on Fry's initiative the Society did buy an unfinished painting by Gauguin exhibited in the *Manet and the Post-Impressionists* show.

The National Gallery's Board of Trustees registered the need for a gallery for modern foreign art in 1905 and 1912.[13] The gallery received its first significant group of French nineteenth-century landscapes with the Salting Bequest in 1910, but these were all by painters of the Barbizon generation, notably Corot and Daubigny, and thus were uncontroversial, as well as all by dead artists. However, the issues over the display of more recent French art came to the forefront in 1912–14, in two contexts: the controversy over the possible exhibition on loan of the collection of Sir Hugh Lane, and the preparation of a report by a committee of the National Gallery Trustees, chaired by Lord Curzon.

Lane first offered to lend his collection of modern continental pictures, which included a number of Impressionist works, to the National Gallery in 1907, but the Trustees promptly declined his offer.[14] In the summer of 1913, he made his offer again, and the Trustees initially agreed to exhibit the pictures once galleries were

3   Monet, *Lavacourt, Winter* ('*Snow Effect at Vétheuil*'), 1881, 59.5 × 81 cm., National Gallery, London (Lane Bequest).

ready for their display,[15] but in January 1914 the Gallery revised its position, briskly informing Lane that they would show only fifteen of his thirty-nine paintings: 'while some of these pictures are well worthy of temporary exhibition in the National Collection, there are others which hardly attain to the standard which would justify their inclusion'. Among those excluded were the canvases by Monet (fig. 3), Morisot and Pissarro, and Renoir's *Les Parapluies* (Degas was accepted, although the artist was still alive).[16] In making their selection, the National Gallery staff solicited the views of the painter John Singer Sargent and of D.S. MacColl, by then Director of the Wallace Collection, both of whom spoke very positively of most of the pictures, including some of those excluded.[17]

However, by the time the Gallery compiled its list, the staff were under pressure from a group of Trustees who had missed the previous summer's meeting, notably Lord Redesdale. The matter came to a head at the next board meeting, to which Redesdale submitted a startling memorandum, which, though presented in printed form, was shown to Sir Charles Holroyd, the Gallery's Director, only minutes before the meeting. Besides taking exception to the tone of Lane's understandably irritated reaction to the Gallery's change of heart, Redesdale launched an outspoken attack on the Gallery's chosen experts, MacColl and Sargent, and on modern French art as a whole:

> The National Gallery is—and should remain—a great Temple of Art. It should open its doors to what is highest and best: never to the productions of a degraded craze, which, it may be hoped, will be shortlived. I should as soon expect to hear of a Mormon service being conducted in St. Paul's Cathedral as to see an exhibition of the works of the modern French Art-rebels in the sacred precincts of Trafalgar Square.

(This remarkable document is reprinted below, text no. 3, pp. 227–8). Faced with this barrage, the Trustees accepted a motion that negotiations with Lane should cease, and that none of his collection should be exhibited.[18]

However, this backlash against modern French art misrepresented the Gallery's overall position. The Director, Holroyd, remained on civil terms with Lane throughout,[19] and Lord Curzon's Report, published in March 1914, presented a very different picture. The committee chaired by Curzon had taken evidence from a number of expert witnesses late in 1912 and had asked all of them their opinion on the idea of forming a Gallery of Modern Foreign Pictures and Sculpture. The final report came out strongly in favour of this:

> The evidence of our witnesses was strong to the effect that the formation of such a collection is not merely a duty imposed on us by the wise example of foreign countries, but is also essential to the artistic development of the nation. We have not in our mind any idea of experimentalising by rash purchase in the occasionally ill-disciplined productions of some contemporaneous continental schools, whose work might exercise a disturbing and even deleterious influence upon our younger painters. But the opposite theory that no foreign art of the present day is worthy of purchase is one which it is impossible to sustain . . .

The report suggested that a wing should be built behind the Tate Gallery for this purpose.[20]

As a supplement, the report included a list of significant artists unrepresented in the National Gallery. Redesdale must have been shocked to find that among the few listed in Class I, along with Dürer, Giotto and Masaccio, were Degas, Manet and Monet; in Class II appeared Pissarro, Renoir and Sisley, as well as such as Meissonier and Bastien-Lepage. The names of Cézanne, Gauguin, van Gogh and Seurat were nowhere to be seen.[21]

The committee clearly chose expert witnesses who were likely to support its viewpoint. Of those interviewed, only Sir Walter Armstrong, veteran conservative critic and Director of the National Gallery of Ireland, came out firmly against this position, from the standpoint of cultural nationalism:

> I think art, to be interesting, must be national, and it must be sincere, and nationally sincere, if possible. I think you do not want to have too much machinery to throw your own young men into lines which are not national.[22]

The only artist questioned, the octogenarian President of the Royal Academy, Sir Edward Poynter, said nothing about the modern foreign gallery, but declared that Whistler 'is a man who, in my opinion, is as much over-rated now, as he may have been underrated at the time'.[23] The other witnesses, among them Sir Sidney Colvin, MacColl and Roger Fry, strongly supported the creation of the foreign gallery.

Two other elements in the report are important for our subject. First, it vigorously renewed the attack against the administration of the Chantrey Bequest: 'many of the Chantrey pictures . . . are a discredit to the walls of the gallery'. And second, it recommended the creation of a separate Board of Trustees for the Tate Gallery, previously run by the National Gallery Board.[24]

The Beginnings of the Modern Foreign Gallery

The outbreak of war delayed the implementation of the Curzon Report. But during the war, three key developments took place which transformed the position of modern foreign art in the national collections. First, Lane was drowned in the wreck of the *Lusitania* in 1915, and, despite the heated public debates about his will, the National Gallery initially concluded that it was the rightful owner of his collection; the pictures were put on exhibition there in January 1917 (see below, texts nos 4–7, pp. 228–32). Second, in 1916, the art dealer Sir Joseph Duveen offered to pay for the building of a gallery for modern foreign art—behind the Tate, as suggested in the 1914 Report (see below, text no. 8, p. 232). And third, in 1916, the National Gallery Board took up the recommendation that a separate Board should be set up for the Tate; this was endorsed by the Treasury, and the new Tate Board met for the first time on 3 April 1917.

So, as economic and cultural life was gradually rebuilt after the war, there was the embryo of a modern foreign collection and the promise of a building to house it. But the creation of a separate Tate Board was perhaps the most significant development; for it meant that decisions about the acquisition of modern art for the nation were no longer subject to the prejudices of the establishment 'old guard' whose views Redesdale had represented so eloquently in 1914. As for the new Trustees, the Treasury recommended 'that a selection should be made of gentlemen with a knowledge of and an interest in modern and contemporary art'.[25] The question of who these should be raised broad questions about the cultural politics of the period, which will be discussed below (pp. 27–8).

The two boards quickly established that decisions about acquisitions for the projected modern foreign gallery should be the province of the Tate Board.[26] The new Board during the next few years made regular efforts to extend its collections of modern French painting, but with the immediate handicap that it had no purchase funds for the purpose; any acquisition had to be a gift, or financed by outside donation or appeal. Before the Tate reopened after the war, it was decided to devote one gallery in it to modern foreign pictures, showing as much as possible, including loans, so as to attract future gifts.[27] The Lane pictures were moved to the Tate when it reopened in 1920–1, and, in the years before the new galleries financed by Duveen were opened in 1926, other significant pictures, including much of the collection of William Burrell, were put on view there as loans.

The discussions and decisions of the Board during these years shed revealing light on the equivocal status of Impressionist and Post-Impressionist painting in the Gallery's thinking before Courtauld made his gift in 1923. The three artists who seem to have most concerned the Trustees were Gauguin, Degas and Cézanne.

The attention of the new Board focused initially on Gauguin. In summer 1917, the Contemporary Art Society gave the Gallery the unfinished *Tahitian Scene* that it had bought through Roger Fry in 1911, but clearly the Tate sought a more significant work. Late in 1917, a Paris dealer offered the Gallery Gauguin's great late masterpiece, *D'où venons-nous?*, for £6,000. After consulting Roger Fry, the Tate sought to raise the sum from private donors; the money was not forthcoming, and, a year later, the Director, Charles Aitken, had to report that the painting had been sold to a Danish collector.[28] Meanwhile, the Gallery pursued other possible Gauguins. *Nevermore*, owned by the composer Frederick Delius, was offered to the Tate for £2,000, but another canvas, owned by Michael Sadler, probably *Manao Tupapau* (now Albright-Knox Gallery, Buffalo), was preferred by the Trustees.[29] In the end, neither was acquired. *Nevermore* (cat. no. 20) later passed into Samuel Courtauld's private collection. However, Duveen, who had offered £2,000 towards *D'où venons-nous?*, in 1919 bought and presented to the Gallery a smaller late decorative canvas by Gauguin, *Faa Iheihe*.[30]

Another Gauguin was acquired for the collection in 1918, *Bouquet de fleurs*, bought at the sale of Degas's private collection in 1918. The purchases from this sale are a fascinating illustration of the ways in which knowledge about, and taste for, recent French art were disseminated in these years. Duncan Grant saw a catalogue of the sale in Roger Fry's studio, and persuaded John Maynard Keynes, then working as an adviser in the Treasury, to seek a Treasury grant for the purchase of pictures from the sale for the nation. Despite the war, £20,000 was allotted, and Charles Holmes, the new Director of the National Gallery, attended the sale with Keynes. Although he spent little more than half of the allotted sum, Holmes acquired for the nation a remarkable group of paintings, including fine works by Ingres, Delacroix and Corot, and, more relevantly for us, the Gauguin still life and works by Manet, including the magnificent fragments of the *Execution of the Emperor Maximilian*. But, despite the promptings of Keynes, urged on by Grant, Fry and Vanessa Bell, Holmes would not buy anything by Cézanne.[31]

However, Keynes did buy for himself a small oil by Cézanne – the

4 Cézanne, *Still Life, Apples*, c.1879, 19 × 27 cm., on loan to the Fitzwilliam Museum, Cambridge, by kind permission of the Provost and Scholars of King's College, Cambridge.

remarkable still life of seven apples (fig. 4) which became very much a talisman for the Bloomsbury group's theories about 'pure painting'. Virginia Woolf eloquently described the responses of Fry and Vanessa Bell to it:

> To Roger and Nessa . . . it was a question of pure paint or mixed; if pure which colour: emerald or veridian [*sic*]; and then the laying on of the paint; and the time he'd spent, and how he'd altered it, and why, and when he'd painted it . . .

Six years later, Samuel Courtauld told Lydia Lopokova, soon to marry Keynes, to tell Keynes 'that he [Courtauld] is jealous over your Cézanne, he used to admire even the photograph'.[32]

The work of Degas himself was the other focus of interest. When the studio sale of his own work came up, two months after the sale of his collection of works by other artists, responsibility had passed to the Tate Board, who were offered only £3,000 to spend there, less than half what Holmes had left unspent of the original sum. They sought some of the most important paintings in the sale, but were unable to make any satisfactory purchase.[33] During the same years, three works by Degas were acquired, none of them wholly characteristic,[34] but they failed to buy the more significant *Woman at a Window*, briefly on offer to them from the collection of Sickert's former wife, Mrs Cobden-Sanderson.[35] Samuel Courtauld later acquired this (cat. no. 16) for his private collection.

In contrast to Degas and Gauguin, Cézanne remained very controversial in England into the 1920s. Holmes's reluctance to buy his work at the Degas sale was echoed by the refusal of the Trustees in 1921 to accept the offer of the loan of two Cézannes from Gwendoline Davies. A vigorous press debate ensued, passing from the *Observer* to the *Burlington Magazine* and the *Saturday Review*. Initially Aitken claimed that there was not adequate room to display the pictures, but it quickly became apparent that it was Cézanne himself who was on trial (see below, texts nos 9–14, pp. 232–5).[36]

The situation changed the next year. In May 1922, the prestigious Burlington Fine Arts Club mounted an ambitious loan exhibition, *The French School of the Last Hundred Years*; Roger Fry was a leading member of the organising committee. In this, all three of the Davies

Cézannes were included; MacColl, one of the Tate Trustees, revised his view of the landscape, *Mountains, L'Estaque* (fig. 5), that they had been offered on loan the year before, and Fry sang its praises in the most eloquent terms (see below, texts nos 15–18, pp. 235–8). After the show closed, the Tate reversed its decision of the previous year and accepted it as a loan 'with a view to ultimate bequest'. The Davies Cézannes, though, did not end up in the Tate; the remarkable collection was bequeathed to the National Museum of Wales in Cardiff.[37] *Mountains, L'Estaque* was the first Cézanne to appear on the walls of a British public collection. However, the Tate Trustees would not consider buying the Cézannes that were proposed to them for purchase (admittedly at very high prices) during the later part of 1922.[38]

The Burlington Fine Arts Club show marked a significant shift in the status of Impressionist and Post-Impressionist art, from the domain of the dealer show or the exhibition organised by a minority group to that of a long-established and élitist institution which had organised a succession of major old-master loan exhibitions;

5 Cézanne, *Mountains in Provence* (*Mountains, L'Estaque*), c.1880, 54 × 73 cm., National Museum of Wales, Cardiff (Davies Collection).

admission to its shows was by invitation only. For our story, the particular importance of the show was that it was here that Samuel Courtauld was 'converted' to the art of Cézanne.[39] Indeed, it seems likely that this display of the holdings of private collections triggered the beginning of Courtauld's private collection of modern French painting: his first purchases, a Marchand and a Renoir (cat. nos 28 and 43), were made in September 1922.

The Courtauld Gift

Work on constructing the modern foreign galleries behind the Tate Gallery, funded by Duveen, was delayed in the after-war situation, and finally began in 1923. Although this gallery was envisaged to include art back to the early nineteenth century, it was evident that the existing holdings could not adequately fill the planned spaces. This seems to have been the catalyst for Samuel Courtauld's gift of £50,000, accepted by the Tate Board in June 1923, but only formally

announced in January 1924 when legal arrangements had been completed (see below, texts nos 19–20, pp. 238–9).

The initial letters that Courtauld wrote announcing his proposed gift were characteristically modest, even apologetic, in tone,[40] but the terms of the gift itself, submitted in draft with the initial proposal, show that Courtauld was determined that it should be administered very much on his terms, and that he himself should play a central role in choosing the paintings to be bought; the Tate Board enthusiastically accepted the offer in all essentials on his terms.[41]

The gift was administered not by the Tate Gallery's Board, but by a separate Board of Trustees, comprising Courtauld himself as Chairman, Sir Charles Holmes and Charles Aitken, the Directors of the National and Tate galleries, Lord Henry Bentinck, Courtauld's choice as representative from the Tate Board, and Michael Sadler, a leading collector of modern French art and Courtauld's choice as outsider on the Board (as we have seen, the Tate had considered trying to buy one of Sadler's Gauguins). Cheques for purchases were to be signed by Courtauld and either Holmes or Aitken; the Tate Board was asked to accept purchases that were essentially a *fait accompli*.[42]

Precisely specified, too, were the artists whose work might be bought. Accompanying the terms of the gift was a list of names, 'representing the modern movement from its inception to the present time'; names could be added only with Courtauld's formal consent. Frustratingly, no copy of Courtauld's list has yet come to light, but, in his initial letter to Aitken, he indicated, 'In my own mind the central men of the movement are Manet, Renoir, Degas, Cézanne, Monet, Van Gogh and Gauguin.'[43] The implications of the list, and of Courtauld's definition of the 'modern movement', will be discussed below (pp. 22–7).

At its first meeting, the Courtauld Trust agreed that it needed to meet only when 'there was business of importance to discuss', and the surviving minute-book contains minutes of just this initial meeting.[44] In practice, decisions were taken in a far more *ad hoc* way, between Courtauld and whichever of the Trustees he chose, or was able, to consult. He, in turn, sought advice from a range of contacts in the London art world. At the outset, he 'called on Sir Joseph Duveen . . . and found him very interesting and illuminating on the subject of picture-buying'. Soon afterwards, he agreed with Aitken's 'idea of making a kind of "left wing" and asking Roger Fry to scout for us. We might get some 20th century masterpieces for a tenth part of the money.'[45] Otherwise, Courtauld and the other Trustees reacted to approaches and suggestions from dealers and other contacts. Wherever possible, the Trustees examined the pictures and negotiated favourable prices; but on other occasions, decisions might have to be taken in great haste.

Two of the early transactions show how this worked in practice. From the van Gogh exhibition at the Leicester Galleries late in 1923, the Trustees agreed to buy two pictures, *The Chair and the Pipe* (fig. 6) and a portrait of the postman Roulin. In addition, Madame van Gogh-Bonger, widow of van Gogh's brother Theo and owner of the artist's residue, agreed to lend three more pictures, *The Artist's Bedroom*, *The House at Arles* and *Sunflowers*, to be exhibited at the Tate early in 1924 with the initial Courtauld purchases. However, Courtauld had second thoughts about the Roulin portrait, and the Trustees agreed to ask Madame van Gogh-Bonger to exchange it for one of the pictures she was lending. She had initially insisted, 'The

6 Van Gogh, *The Chair and the Pipe*, 1888–9, 92 × 73 cm., National Gallery, London (Courtauld Fund).

7 Van Gogh, *Sunflowers*, 1888, 92.1 × 73 cm., National Gallery, London (Courtauld Fund).

sunflowers are not for sale, never; they belong in our family, like Vincent's bedroom and his house at Arles'; but faced with Aitken's eloquent appeal to replace the Roulin portrait with the *Sunflowers* (fig. 7), she at last agreed: 'I felt as if I could not bear to separate from the picture I had looked on every day for more than thirty years . . . it is a sacrifice for the sake of Vincent's glory.'[46]

By contrast, the decision to buy Seurat's *Une Baignade, Asnières* (fig. 8) had to be made on the spot. Lucien Pissarro had apparently drawn the Trustees' attention to the fact that Félix Fénéon, Seurat's close associate from the 1880s, might sell the picture, and Fry, it seems, encouraged the purchase.[47] The dealer Percy Moore Turner of the Independent Gallery, perhaps Courtauld's most trusted adviser (see below, pp. 22–3), went to Paris to explore the situation and reported that Fénéon insisted on an instant decision; Courtauld, trusting Turner's judgement, agreed to what was perhaps his most spectacular purchase for the nation without even consulting his fellow trustees. Aitken's personal reservations about the deal may be sensed from his very cool statement of thanks to Fénéon: 'The painting will be an interesting addition to the Modern Foreign Collection in England.'[48]

More than half of the Fund had been spent before the details of the Trust were finalised. The two most expensive purchases of the Fund's history came first: Manet's *La Servante de bocks* (fig. 9) for £10,000, and Renoir's *La Première sortie* (fig. 10) for £7,500, both

bought from Messrs Knoedler for considerably less than the initial asking prices. These were followed by van Gogh's *A Cornfield, with Cypresses* (fig. 11) for £3,300 from Turner's Independent Gallery, and Degas's *Jeunes spartiates s'exerçant à la lutte* (fig. 12), at £1,200 very inexpensive, since it was seen as an uncharacteristic early work. With the two van Goghs from Madame van Gogh-Bonger, bought at the very modest price of £2,000 for the pair, the Trust was able to present six major purchases at the same time as the Fund itself was formally announced to the public.

A full chronological list of the Fund's purchases will be found below (pp. 221–4), dovetailed with a listing of the pictures that Courtauld bought for his private collection. A sketch is given here of the overall patterns of the Fund's purchases, and of what we can reconstruct of the discussions behind them. Courtauld realised from the start that the Fund would not be adequate to include every artist on his original list[49] and clearly decided that the group of pictures bought should be very varied, covering as wide a range as possible of the 'modern movement' as he saw it. In this sense, it cannot be seen as a collection in its own right, but needs to be understood in the terms in which Courtauld envisioned it—as a complement to the Lane pictures and the embryo of what he hoped (justifiably, in the long run) would become a larger and more comprehensive collection.

The purchases, too, were inevitably conditioned by what appeared on the market. From the start, Courtauld realised that any group of pictures bought was provisional and might be improved: hence the clause in the gift that pictures from it could be resold and the money spent on upgrading the collection. This option was most directly exercised with Sisley's *Le Pont de Moret*; this was accepted in 1925 with the understanding that it might be resold, and it was replaced in 1926 by a far finer Sisley, *The Watering Place at Marly* (fig. 13).[50]

In the end, some painters were not represented by their most characteristic works. Monet appears only with a small 1870 figure sketch and an 1899 lily-pond picture (figs 14 and 15), Pissarro with a late Paris scene, a night effect (fig. 16). Van Gogh, with four major works, is, by contrast, particularly well represented, and it must be a source of relief that, when buying van Gogh's *Long Grass with Butterflies* (fig. 17) in 1926, the Fund did not then sell the van Gogh *Chair* (fig. 6), as they first intended, feeling that 'we ought not to have too many Van Goghs'.[51]

The initial idea that Fry might instigate some remarkable twentieth-century purchases was not realised. Among younger generation artists, only Bonnard and Utrillo figure. Bonnard's spectacular *The Table* (fig. 20) of 1925, bought early in 1926, was in some ways the most far-sighted purchase of all those made by the Fund, and marks a confidence in dealing with the most recent art; we

do not know who was the prime mover in its acquisition. By contrast, the decision to buy Utrillo's *La Place du Tertre* (fig. 18) was explicitly Courtauld's; Aitken was unenthusiastic, thinking Utrillo 'not a first rate man', but agreed to Courtauld's wishes since the price was 'not exorbitant'.[52]

Predictably, given the past history of the modern foreign-paintings collection, it seems to have been Cézanne who aroused the strongest feelings among the Fund's Trustees. The Fund bought a first Cézanne, the *Self-Portrait* (fig. 21), in December 1925. A letter from Aitken to Holmes in December 1925, when the Fund's money was running low, is very revealing about their views of Cézanne and about the workings of the Fund in general:

Sadler says he will make a point of being here on Friday. It will be a good thing for the Courtauld trustees actually to meet for once.[53] Courtauld wants to have the Cézanne Rochers sent down for them to see. I think Blanche's Degas would really be a more valuable asset for the concluding 'big bang'.[54] We have no typical Degas, and Blanche's is that even if a little dull superficially, and probably as good a one as could be got now. I have asked Blanche if he can fix a price for consideration. As to Cézanne — we shall *probably* eventually inherit Miss Davies's 'Landscape', and, I

8 Seurat, *Une Baignade, Asnières*, 1883–4, 201 × 301.5 cm., National Gallery, London (Courtauld Fund).

suppose, those in Courtauld's private collection – one is a fine one – and possibly Mr Coleman's 'landscape' and 'still-life', so that Cézanne is really less pressing.

However, Courtauld seems keen and if he insists, we get it for very little of the fund money. He would have to pay most of it extra as the fund is nearly exhausted . . .[55]

The tone of this letter suggests that both Aitken and Holmes still did not share Courtauld's unequivocal belief in Cézanne's art. In the event, the Cézanne *Rocky Landscape* (fig. 19) was bought, with extra funds from Courtauld.

In the end, the 'big bang' that used up most of the residue of the fund was not another Degas, to complement the *Young Spartans* (fig. 12) and *La La at the Cirque Fernando*, bought in October 1925 (fig. 22); rather, the Fund's Trustees decided to buy another van Gogh, *Long Grass with Butterflies* (fig. 17), which was acquired in April 1926, along with two further, less significant works by Degas (figs 23 and 24), both bought with extra funds from Courtauld, and neither from Jacques-Emile Blanche.[56]

Pictures bought by the Fund had been displayed relatively informally, as space allowed. But, with the Fund nearly exhausted, it was decided to exhibit all its purchases together at the Tate; the opening of this display, in January 1926, with a brief catalogue of the pictures, offered the press and public their first chance to assess the collection and consider its implications. In a sense it also acted as a

10   Renoir, *The Café-Concert* ('*La Première sortie*'), *c*.1876/7, 65 × 51 cm., National Gallery, London (Courtauld Fund).

trailer for the opening of the new modern foreign-painting galleries, then nearing completion alongside the existing Tate buildings.

Press comment on the Courtauld Gift in January 1926 was overwhelmingly favourable (see below, texts nos 25–8, pp. 243–6). Courtauld's generosity was celebrated, as was his providence in allowing for the sale of pictures from the Gift if finer examples became available. Fry in the *Nation* joined in the panegyrics (see below, text no. 27, pp. 244–5): 'It is a matter for the greatest satisfaction that we should possess two first-rate Cézannes and perhaps the finest Seurat in the world. And these after all are the two great pioneers of modern art.' But, like some other reviewers, he criticised the installation, taking the Tate to task for showing the pictures, including the huge Seurat, 'in one of those small dark-rooms at the Tate Gallery so admirably suited for the development of photographic plates'.[57] At the same time, Fry wrote Aitken a characteristically splenetic letter:

> . . . I quite know that there are often practical difficulties to be overcome in the matter of exhibition but I cannot help thinking that it was a matter of importance in the policy of our national museums to give a rather exceptionally splendid welcome to so munificent a gift. I do know that Mr. Courtauld feels discouraged and I can't wonder . . .[58]

Courtauld himself, whatever he thought privately, was quick to

9   Manet, *The Waitress* (*La Servante de bocks*), 1878 or 1879, 97.5 × 77.5 cm., National Gallery, London (Courtauld Fund).

11   Van Gogh, *A Cornfield, with Cypresses*, 1889, 72.1 × 90.9 cm., National Gallery, London (Courtauld Fund)

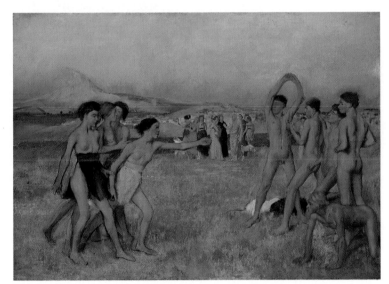

12   Degas, *Young Spartans (Jeunes spartiates s'exerçant à la lutte)*, c.1860, 109 × 154.5 cm., National Gallery, London (Courtauld Fund).

Personally I think that the little show has been very successful.

I certainly must share the blame (if any) incurred in choosing the little room; and I think I should make the same choice again . . .[59]

The modern foreign galleries opened in June 1926 with a major loan exhibition of French painting from about 1850 to 1925, presented with the existing permanent collection in a single integrated hang (see below, text no. 29, p. 246).[60] Interestingly, Courtauld lent only one, comparatively minor, picture from his private collection to this show, Marchand's *Saint-Paul* (cat. no. 28). He explained in a letter to Aitken that he could offer no more, since he was in the process of installing the collection in his new home,

13   Sisley, *The Watering Place at Marly*, 1875, 49.5 × 65.5 cm., National Gallery, London (Courtauld Fund).

14   Monet, *The Beach at Trouville*, 1870, 37.5 × 45.7 cm., National Gallery, London (Courtauld Fund).

disassociate himself with characteristic tact and modesty from Fry's views:

. . . I am awfully sorry that you should have been distressed by Fry's article.

I thought myself when I read it that all the first part [about the installation] was extremely childish, and that he must have been particularly fractious when he wrote it.

He always must have a dig at our public galleries: now that we have a Cézanne he has lost his past grievance, and as he couldn't find much fault with the pictures, he was reduced to blaming the arrangements.

I should like you to realise that I feel nothing but pleasure when I think of all the thought & work that you have put in to make our scheme a success, & I know that you could not have done more.

17

15 Monet, *The Water-Lily Pond*, 1899, 88.2 × 92 cm., National Gallery, London (Courtauld Fund).

17 Van Gogh, *Long Grass with Butterflies*, 1890, 64.5 × 80.7 cm., National Gallery, London (Courtauld Fund).

Home House, 20 Portman Square;[61] but we may surmise that he also felt that further, more spectacular loans from the private collection would dilute the impact of the pictures in the Gift. When, after the opening exhibition, the permanent collection of modern foreign pictures was installed in the new wing, it included not only pictures of the 'modern movement', but the whole of the nation's holdings of non-British art from 1800 on, beginning with Ingres, Delacroix and Goya.

18 Utrillo, *La Place du Tertre*, c. 1910, 50 × 73 cm., Tate Gallery, London (Courtauld Fund).

16 Camille Pissarro, *Paris, The Boulevard Montmartre at Night*, 1897, 53.5 × 65 cm., National Gallery, London (Courtauld Fund).

Inevitably, the impetus for acquisitions slackened when the Courtauld Fund was spent; but the Gallery was able to make further acquisitions in the later 1920s, including two Monets from the National Art-Collections Fund, given to commemorate the opening of the Modern Foreign Gallery in June 1926, and Pissarro's monumental *Côte des boeufs*, given by C.S. Carstairs through the National Art-Collections Fund in September 1926. But, at the same time, in 1926 the Tate Trustees declined the offer from Sir Joseph Duveen of the possible gift of Monet's remarkable *La Japonaise*, a huge painting of 1875–6 of a woman in a Japanese dress (now Museum of Fine Arts, Boston).[62] We have no indication of the Tate Board's reasons for refusing this offer, or whether Courtauld had any informal say in the matter. But this spectacular image, which Monet himself late in life described as a 'saleté', would have been quite out of key with the comparatively spare and clean-cut paintings that predominate in the purchases made by the Courtauld Fund.

19 Cézanne, *Rocky Landscape* (*Mountains in Provence*), *c.*1885, 63.5 × 79.4 cm., National Gallery, London (Courtauld Fund).

20 Bonnard, *The Table*, 1925, 103 × 74 cm., Tate Gallery, London (Courtauld Fund).

21 Cézanne, *Self-Portrait*, *c.*1880, 33.6 × 26 cm., National Gallery, London (Courtauld Fund).

At the same time as administering the Courtauld Fund, Courtauld became involved with the Contemporary Art Society. Over the years since the Society's creation in 1910, Roger Fry had sought to persuade it to begin to buy foreign art seriously. In 1922 and 1923, he regularly threatened to resign from its committee, arguing in 1923 that his membership 'had proved only a waste of time' and that 'he had been for nearly 10 years in a minority of one'.[63] However, in 1923 they at last launched a significant project to create a foreign-picture fund, and appointed Fry as buyer for the Society for 1924. In June 1924, a loan exhibition of living foreign artists was mounted at Colnaghi's Gallery to launch this fund (see below, texts nos 22–3, pp. 240–1), and on 30 May, *The Times* published a letter announcing the project (reprinted below, text no. 21, p. 239) from the Society's committee, including Fry and also Courtauld, who had been invited to join the committee earlier that month and had himself contributed to the new fund.[64] This letter explicitly stated that the new fund was meant to complement the Courtauld Fund, by buying strictly contemporary works. Fry and Courtauld first coincided at a committee meeting on 17 June 1925; this is their first documented meeting, though we can assume that they met a year or two earlier.[65] Fry, with Vanessa Bell and Duncan Grant, was also among the artists sponsored by the London Artists' Association, set up under the sponsorship of Courtauld, J.M. Keynes and others in 1926.[66]

*   *   *

22 Degas, *La La at the Cirque Fernando, Paris*, 1879, 117 × 77.5 cm., National Gallery, London (Courtauld Fund).

Cézanne Accepted

By the early 1930s, the cause for which Courtauld had made his gift was essentially won. Although the national collections had no funds to extend their collections in this area, the pictures they already owned had effectively crushed the opposition in England to the French 'modern movement' of the later nineteenth century. In the late 1920s, too, Courtauld had broadened the scope of his support of the national galleries, giving a large sum, for instance, towards the National Gallery's purchase of the Wilton Diptych and Titian's *The Vendramin Family* in 1929. Shortly before this, he had written to the Keeper of the National Gallery:

> Will you please remember that I shall be happy to help . . . whenever you next find a difficulty in securing an outstanding work for the nation – that is, of course, if I am still in a position to do so. There is nothing that would give me more satisfaction.[67]

At the same time, the controversial area for the Tate authorities shifted to the art of the early twentieth century. Two Braque still lifes

of the 1920s, both Cézannist in structure but with some Cubist traits, were accepted as gifts in 1926 and 1928, but in 1929 the Trustees refused the gift of Matisse's seemingly uncontroversial *Liseuse à l'ombrelle* from the Contemporary Art Society – it was finally accepted in 1938.[68] In 1927, the Trustees turned down also the offer of the loan of a Matisse *Interior of a Studio* from the Gargoyle Club.[69] The artists of this generation gained a firm footing in the Tate only with the bequest of C. Frank Stoop in 1933, but the more hermetic early Cubism had to wait until after the Second World War.

Two events can act as markers for the shift around 1930. First, in 1932, the Royal Academy of Arts devoted its regular winter exhibition to French Art 1200–1900. Courtauld was a member of the British Executive Committee for the show, together with Roger Fry and eight Royal Academicians. The show included a very fine representation of fifteen Cézannes, and major groups of paintings by Gauguin, Seurat and the painters of the Impressionist generation (see below, texts nos 32–5, pp. 249–52). Fifteen oils and six drawings in all were lent from Courtauld's private collection, including four of the Cézannes. As notable was the total omission from the show, apart from a handful of portraits of celebrities, of the academic painters of the later nineteenth century. In his review of the show, Tancred Borenius stressed the remarkable change in the status of modern French painting in England since Fry's *Manet and the Post-Impressionists* show:

23 Degas, *Elena Carafa*, 1873/4, 69.8 × 54.6 cm., National Gallery, London (Courtauld Fund).

This was but little more than twenty years ago, and yet I think it is almost completely forgotten with what volleys of hostile criticism that exhibition was received . . . Today the battle is won – triumphantly won . . . Considerations such as these throw a very vivid light on the ever-fresh problem of the attitude of the public towards the contemporary artist. May one hope that the promotion of Cézanne to rank, uncontestedly, among the great and permanent glories of French art will serve as a forcible reminder of that necessity of an unprejudiced vision, without which no art can thrive and flourish at any period?[70]

Second, two years later, Courtauld offered to lend two key works from his private collection, Manet's *A Bar at the Folies-Bergère* (cat. no. 27) and Cézanne's *La Montagne Sainte-Victoire* (cat. no. 8), to the National Gallery (both were by then in the possession of the Courtauld Institute). Sir William Llewellyn, President of the Royal Academy, was absent from the board meeting at which the loan was approved, and Kenneth Clark, recently appointed Director of the National Gallery, wrote to clear the decision with him. Llewellyn answered: 'I consider the acquisition of Cézanne's important work . . . a piece of good fortune.' Clark sent Courtauld a copy of Llewellyn's letter with the comment: 'The collapse of this last stronghold of academic art is rather surprising and I suppose must be explained by the President's genuine public spiritedness and tolerance.'[71] In response to Clark's grateful acceptance of the offered loans (seemingly, this was the first Cézanne to be exhibited in the National Gallery), Courtauld responded:

I thought I had a pretty good idea of your tastes, but I had no notion that Cézanne meant quite so much to you, and I am delighted that you should find a personal pleasure in receiving my picture at the Gallery. For my part, I am pleased to help in getting official recognition for Cézanne in England.[72]

The Relationship between Courtauld's Private Collection and the Gift

One final issue about Courtauld's activities as patron and collector needs to be raised – the relationship between the acquisition of paintings for the Courtauld Gift and his purchases for his own private collection (for a chronological listing of all his acquisitions, both public and private, see below, pp. 221–4).

On one level, the two facets of Courtauld's collecting were kept strictly separate. There is no evidence that he bought any picture for his private collection that was being considered by the Fund, and he evidently sought out pictures for the Fund which he might well have wished to acquire for himself. On only one occasion, as far as can be seen, did he buy pictures for both collections from the same source at the same time: in June 1926 Percy Moore Turner sold him a Degas for the Fund and a Sisley for himself (fig. 24 and cat. no. 57).[73]

Only one canvas brought to the attention of the Fund's Trustees was finally acquired for the private collection; in 1925 H.S. Ede, Assistant Keeper at the Tate, suggested to Holmes that the Fund might consider the small version of Manet's *Déjeuner sur l'herbe* (cat. no. 24); evidently nothing came of this. In 1927, after the Fund was virtually exhausted, the National Art-Collections Fund turned down the offer of the picture for £12,000; Courtauld bought it for £10,000 in 1928.[74]

24 Degas, *Dancers*, c.1880?, 72.4 × 73 cm., National Gallery, London (Courtauld Fund).

However, looking down the list of purchases for the two collections, Courtauld must, throughout the duration of the Fund, have been faced with choices between the two destinations. Pictures were repeatedly bought from the same sources for both collections, and prospective sellers would have well known that both were being made along very similar lines at the same time. Percy Moore Turner of the Independent Gallery, in particular, played a central role in acquisitions for both (see pp. 22–3).

Certainly, many of the most spectacular pictures in the private collection were acquired while the Fund was in existence. When the Fund pictures were put on view in 1926, one critic, in the *Morning Post*, pointedly noted that the Renoir and the Cézanne on show (figs 10 and 19) were lesser works than *La Loge* (cat. no. 39) and *The Montagne Sainte-Victoire* (cat. no. 8) in the private collection (reprinted below, text no. 25, p. 243). It may have been comments such as this that led Courtauld not to lend any major paintings to the opening exhibition of the Modern Foreign Gallery in June 1926, for fear of diluting the impact of the pictures bought by the Fund (see above, pp. 17–18).

Courtauld clearly always saw his commitment to the Fund as finite. Although, as we have seen, he did add extra money for the purchase of the Cézanne landscape and two works by Degas in 1926, he clearly never considered substantially adding to his initial gift. He wanted to buy for the nation as representative a collection as possible, but realised from the start that 'the fund won't be large enough to secure examples' of all the artists on his original list.[75] With this in view, it becomes clear that he could well justify buying some of the most extravagant items for himself: Renoir's *La Loge* and Manet's *A Bar at the Folies-Bergère* would together have virtually used up the total original gift to the Fund.

One further factor must have lessened any tension he might have felt between the two interests: from an early stage, he clearly intended that much of the private collection would ultimately enter the public domain. The dealer Ambroise Vollard, thanking him for payment for Renoir's *Portrait of Ambroise Vollard* (cat. no. 42) in 1927, said that he was delighted to learn that his French pictures were to go to the National Gallery;[76] Kenneth Clark later recalled that the National Gallery had been their original intended destination, and regretted that Lord Lee had led him to change his mind.[77] The catalyst for the change was the project, conceived by Lord Lee and others with Courtauld's moral and financial support, to create an art-historical institute in London University. It was Lee, Clark remembered, who had persuaded Courtauld to give the collection to the institute – to be named the Courtauld Institute of Art.

After this change of plan, Courtauld made the position clear to Lee, in his capacity as Chairman of the National Gallery Board of Trustees:

> As you know, it is my intention to make over my collection of XIXth century French paintings to the Trustees of the new 'Courtauld Institute'; part in the immediate future and the remainder at my death. The Collection is to become their absolute property.[78]

Beyond this, though, he offered certain key pictures on extended loan to the National Gallery, where Manet's *A Bar at the Folies-Bergère*, Cézanne's *The Montagne Sainte-Victoire* and Renoir's *La Loge* spent many years on view.

After the Institute was located in Courtauld's previous home, Home House in Portman Square, the first group of pictures to be given were installed there (figs 35 and 36);[79] the remainder, apart from the pictures included in private bequests, followed after Courtauld's death in 1947. At Home House, the pictures were visible by arrangement, but Courtauld made a gift of £70,000 for the construction of a permanent public gallery for the collection, which in the event was built only after his death and was opened in 1958.[80]

The Patterns of Courtauld's Collecting

At first sight, Courtauld may seem to have set out quite straightforward terms of reference for the Courtauld Fund, in specifying that it should limit itself to works 'representing the modern movement from its inception to the present time'. However, this seemingly bland description made some very significant assumptions, and also obscured a set of vigorous debates about the nature of 'modern' art and the values for which it stood.

First, it implied a break at the beginning of the 'modern movement' – a break marked by Manet, according to Courtauld's list of 'central men of the movement'. Second, it implied a continuity from Impressionists to Post-Impressionists – from Monet and Renoir to Cézanne, Gauguin and van Gogh. And third, it treated the 'modern movement' as continuing to the 'present time', although Courtauld's own purchases, for the Fund and for his own collection, stopped short of Fauvism and Cubism.

The next section places this notion of modern art in the context of recent and contemporary critical and historical debate. But first, a few comments are needed about the collections themselves. As we

have seen, the pictures bought with the Fund represented an attempt to make the basis of an evenly spread collection across the whole planned field. The broad terms of reference of the private collection were evidently similar, with Daumier added as the lone representative of the generation before Manet, and only Marchand, Utrillo, Modigliani and a very early Picasso representing the twentieth century. However, the private collection had certain distinctive points.

The initial purchase of two pictures in September 1922 were in some ways markedly different from those that followed, beginning in January 1923. The first two were very recent works, Renoir's *Woman at her Toilet* and Marchand's *Saint-Paul* (cat. nos 43 and 28), and both were prime examples of the types of Neo-Classicism so much in vogue after the war, although one was the work of an aged master, the other of a young follower of Cézanne. Both, too, were closely in line with the taste and writings of Roger Fry – eloquent chapters on both had appeared in his *Vision and Design* in 1920.

Looking more broadly at the core collection, as Courtauld accumulated it between 1922 and 1929, his shared interests with Fry are clear, in the paramount places given to Cézanne and Seurat – the latter a comparatively recent enthusiasm of Fry's. But there is another major group of pictures in which Fry would have had far less interest – the 'high Impressionist' canvases of the 1870s, and particularly Monet's *Autumn Effect at Argenteuil* (cat. no. 31) and the sequence of four Renoirs (it was the later, more classicising Renoir that appealed to Fry). Certainly, like the pictures bought by the Fund, the private collection did seek some sort of coverage of the key figures in the period; but its particular emphases coincided with no single position in the aesthetic debates of the time.

We know frustratingly little about the types of advice Courtauld took in his purchases. The vast majority of the purchases, as far as we can see, were made from dealers; a very few seem to have been from private collectors. Courtauld seems never to have bought at auction; this suggests that he valued the privacy that purchase from a dealer offered him, and that he felt the need of the advice and assurances of trusted dealers; buying through dealers also generally allowed him, as he wished whenever possible, to view paintings at leisure in his own home.

All the available evidence suggests that his principal adviser was Percy Moore Turner, who ran the Independent Gallery. It was Turner who arranged the hang of pictures when Courtauld moved to Home House in 1926.[81] Courtauld purchased the Renoir and the Marchand from Turner in 1922, but there is no evidence that they particularly represented his taste; indeed, the one picture that Turner lent to the Burlington Fine Arts Club exhibition in 1922 suggests that his real enthusiasm lay elsewhere: this was Renoir's early *Spring (Chatou)* that Courtauld was to buy from Turner in 1927 (cat. no. 38).

Many of the purchases for the Fund and particularly for Courtauld's private collection were made from or through Turner. On occasion, and most notably for Courtauld's two most expensive purchases, Renoir's *La Loge* in 1925 and Manet's *A Bar at the Folies-Bergère* in 1926, Turner explicitly acted as intermediary and was paid a sizeable commission; but his role was very probably that of agent or intermediary for many of the other purchases, which were, on paper at least, made by direct purchase from him at the Independent Gallery. Further investigation of Turner's activities and contacts will without doubt yield significant insights into the making of Courtauld's collection.

As far as we can tell, he was not regularly seeking Fry's advice through the 1920s. Although, as we have seen, they were acquainted, Fry seems not to have presented Courtauld with a copy of his book on Cézanne in 1927;[82] and it was only in January 1929, nearly three years after Courtauld moved into Home House, that Fry noted the address in his appointment diary.[83] Three eloquent letters from Fry to Courtauld later in 1929 survive: in these Fry urged him to buy Gauguin's *Te Rerioa* (cat. no. 21) 'which is I suspect *the* masterpiece of Gauguin', but was more equivocal about a Cézanne view of Gardanne that Courtauld in the end decided not to buy.[84] But it seems most unlikely that Courtauld regularly used Fry as a sounding-board for his projected purchases.

After Fry's death, though, Courtauld acknowledged his impact: 'He was unique in the world of art, & his views on art seemed to me more & more to illuminate life & thought in general.'[85] When the National Gallery launched a subscription to buy a Cézanne in Fry's memory, the Director, Kenneth Clark, wrote to prospective subscribers:

> everyone who has formed a collection of 19th century French painting and derived immense pleasure from it, will remember that we all owe the greater part of our interest in this period and school to Roger Fry. It was Mr. Courtauld who put this point of view to me . . .[86]

However, it would be misleading to imply that the collections simply represented a combination of Turner's advice and Fry's taste. It is clear, too, that he did not take good advice over all his early purchases: in May 1923 he bought a particularly crude Seurat forgery, a painting of a female nude, from the Barbazanges Gallery in Paris.[87] However, this seems to have been his only major mistake. In general, the final decision about a purchase seems to have been very much his, and his alone. Courtauld spent much time examining pictures in dealers' galleries in London, Paris, New York and

26 Gauguin, *Martinique Landscape*, 1887, 115.5 × 89 cm., National Gallery of Scotland, Edinburgh, formerly Samuel Courtauld Collection.

25 Gauguin, *Bathing Women, Tahiti*, 1897, 73 × 92 cm., Barber Institute, Birmingham, formerly Samuel Courtauld Collection.

elsewhere, and, whenever possible, in his own home, evidently placing a central significance on his own empathetic, subjective reactions to the pictures with which he lived. There are many testimonies to the intensity of his responses to paintings.

He was also prepared to admit that he had made a wrong decision. During these years, he also sold a number of pictures from his collection, including two Gauguins, two Cézanne portraits, both of his wife, a Degas pastel and a Matisse. He presumably felt that Gauguin's *Bathing Women, Tahiti* (fig. 25), bought in 1923, and Degas's late pastel *Two Dancers* (fig. 27), bought in 1924, were made superfluous by the later purchase of cat. nos 21 and 18; he bought the Matisse *Dancer* (fig. 28) in 1928 and resold it a year later;[88] it is not one of Matisse's strongest works, and was clearly out of line with the bulk of Courtauld's purchases in these years.

However, his other three traced sales were pictures that, in retrospect, would have adorned the collection: by 1929, he owned two of Cézanne's portraits of Madame Cézanne, one a key picture of the mid-1870s (figs 30 and 31); and in 1928, he bought Gauguin's *Martinique Landscape* of 1887 (fig. 26). When the Gauguin was exhibited in the 1932 Royal Academy French Art exhibition, loaned by Ewan Charteris, the catalogue gave no indication that Courtauld had so recently owned it – he may have wanted to conceal the fact that he was making sales. We do not, though, know when or why he

sold these last three pictures. There is no sign that he was in financial difficulties either before or after the crash of autumn 1929, and it seems more likely that in some way they did not meet his tastes; with the Cézannes, the austerity and detachment of the painter's view of his wife may have troubled him in a way that Cézanne's very comparable vision of male peasant figures clearly did not (see cat. nos 10 and 11).

Courtauld's buying stopped abruptly in 1929. We have no direct evidence for the reasons for this, but three distinct factors were probably important. First, the crash of autumn 1929 may have made him reluctant to undertake major capital expenditure, though there is no evidence that he experienced any serious personal financial insecurity at any point during the Depression. Second, his buying ceased around the time of the onset of the illness of his wife, Elizabeth, which led to her death in December 1931. Their involvement in the collection was evidently shared, and he may well have felt it inappropriate to continue alone. And third, once he had decided to divide up the collection during his own lifetime and to give a large part of it to the Courtauld Institute, he may have felt less impetus to go on accumulating paintings. The most significant of his acquisitions when he resumed buying in 1936–7 were all intended as private bequests. Between 1929 and 1936, he made just one odd and unexplained purchase – James Tissot's *The Gallery of H.M.S. Calcutta (Portsmouth)* (fig. 29), which he bought in 1933 and presented to the Tate Gallery in 1936.

* * *

Critical Perspectives on Modern French Art

The patterns of Courtauld's collecting must now be located in the context of the discussions about 'modern art', and specifically about modern French art, which dominated English art criticism throughout these years. The first thorough exploration of these issues in England had been in the polemics that accompanied the key exhibitions in London before 1914 – the Grafton Galleries Impressionist exhibition of 1905, and Roger Fry's two Post-Impressionist exhibitions of 1910 and 1912.[89] However, the situation was different in two significant ways when Courtauld launched the Fund. First, the work of the painters he was fostering was no longer novel to the London art public; and second, he was presenting it, through the Fund, not as the latest foreign fad, but as an art for the permanent collections of the national galleries, and thus as an integral part of the artistic 'tradition' that the galleries represented. Whereas before 1914 discussion had focused primarily on the question of whether these paintings should be seen as art *at all*, and on the sanity of their authors, the later discussions approached them in a wider and more historical perspective.

In its broad outline, Courtauld's notion of the 'modern movement' corresponded to that put forward in Julius Meier-Graefe's *Modern Art*, published in English in 1908. Meier-Graefe saw French art as the origin of recent developments, and saw as the 'pillars of modern painting' Courbet (seemingly omitted by Courtauld),

31   Cézanne, *Madame Cézanne in a Striped Skirt*, c.1876, 72.5 × 56 cm., Museum of Fine Arts, Boston (Bequest of Robert Treat Paine, 2nd), formerly Samuel Courtauld Collection.

30   Cézanne, *Madame Cézanne*, c.1890/2, 61.9 × 51.1 cm., Philadelphia Museum of Art (The Henry P. McIlhenny Collection in memory of Francis P. McIlhenny), formerly Samuel Courtauld Collection.

Manet, Cézanne, Degas and Renoir; Monet and Seurat represented the fullest development of colour, and Gauguin the development of composition. There is no evidence that Courtauld engaged with the complexities of Meier-Graefe's theoretical arguments, but he does seem to have shared his belief that the diversity of the work of these central figures could be encompassed within some overall notion of 'modern art'.

It is this that marks Courtauld's position out from that of Roger Fry. In contrast to Courtauld's list of 'the central men of the movement' as 'Manet, Renoir, Degas, Cézanne, Monet, Van Gogh and Gauguin', Fry placed the crucial break after Impressionism, with Manet as the solitary precursor of the Post-Impressionists' concern with expressive form, rather than with mere appearances. Elsewhere, admittedly, Fry modified the hard-and-fast distinctions in his 1910 preface to the *Manet and the Post-Impressionists* exhibition catalogue, and accepted that Degas and in particular Renoir, in his later work, had also revealed these formal concerns;[90] but his view of the development of modern art always excluded Impressionist landscape from the central role that Courtauld gave to it.[91]

Many English writers broadly shared Fry's view. Charles Marriott, for instance, in *Modern Movements in Painting* (1920) began his account with Impressionism, but only so as to show what it was that the Post-Impressionists had reacted against; and many other commentators treated Impressionism, with its supposed preoccupation with surface appearance alone, as an aside to the significant steps in the development of modern art.[92] In 1922, Frank Rutter noted that Impressionism had never really been popular in England: 'By one generation it has been thought to be slovenly; by another it has been thought to be mechanical.'[93]

In the context of the acceptability of modern French painting in the national galleries, the central problem was to reconcile the notion of 'tradition', for which the museums were supposed to stand, with the idea that French nineteenth century painting, at some point in its development, had witnessed a radical break with the past. In the writings of the pre-war critics of Impressionism and Post-Impressionism, the break had been viewed in two distinct ways. First, it was often seen as a loss of practical skill, either in terms of the inability to finish a painting in the traditional sense, or as the breakdown of training and discipline in drawing. Second, it represented a rejection of higher ideals and morality in art, in favour of an exclusive concern with surface appearances or formal qualities.

The inadequacies of the Impressionists' sketch-like handling had, of course, been central in the criticism of their art since its first appearance. By the 1920s, this particular sort of virtuosity was generally appreciated; but questions might still be raised as to whether such skill was art in the fullest sense. Sickert, reviewing the Burlington Fine Arts Club show in 1922, insisted on the distinction between sketchers and architects of pictures, setting Manet's inadequacies against the completeness of Ingres's work.[94] Even Charles Holmes, Director of the National Gallery, remained uncertain of the value of the small oil sketch. His 1927 volume on the National Gallery's collections of French and English art included sympathetic discussion of the pictures in the Courtauld Gift, including Monet's little *Beach at Trouville* (fig. 14); but in his introduction, he lamented the current vogue for 'small oil sketches and studies', preferring watercolour as a medium for small, informal works: 'The fashion for [oil sketches] has very strong Continental backing; yet even this can hardly prevail for ever, when their inherent disadvantages . . . are so numerous and so manifest.'[95]

The issues of finish and drawing were brought together in 1922 in an essay by S. Magee on Degas. Magee readily condemned the deadness of recent academic painting, in contrast to the vivacity of Degas's drawing, but lamented that Degas had lost any sense of communication with his public through his inability to take his art beyond the sketch and the fragment; his art, for Magee, had become a private reverie, not a complete, public statement.[96]

However, the prime focus of debates about drawing was Cézanne. In 1917, Fry's argument that Cézanne was 'a supreme master of formal design' without being 'a master of line in the sense that Ingres was' elicited an outburst from Ralph Curtis, a painter and friend of John Singer Sargent, against his 'pathetic lack of technical education' and 'the bloated monsters he longed to make decorative', with an aside against the 'fantastic fame of Renoir, who scumbles round, woolly contours with diluted currant-jelly'.[97]

In 1922, the *Burlington Magazine* elicited a further round of correspondence about Cézanne's drawing by publishing two very different analyses of a single Cézanne sketch, *Les Jeux*. D.S. MacColl condemned out of hand Cézanne's inadequate memory and failures in perspective and anatomy, insisting: 'The deformations described are not deliberate or subtly instinctive modifications of known forms

to enhance expression, solidity or pattern: they are fumbling shots at something insecurely seen.' R.R. Tatlock, the magazine's editor, argued, by contrast, that Cézanne's drawing should be understood in the terms of 'three-dimensional design', and that it was comparable with the work of El Greco or Rembrandt as the record of 'inward visions'. The letters in response were broadly in favour of Tatlock (and Cézanne) and included an outspoken attack by Fry against MacColl and his taste.[98] By the mid-1920s, Cézanne and Renoir were increasingly paired as the two painters who had lent substance to the legacy of Impressionism; Clive Bell wrote:

> Only twenty years ago admirers of Cézanne quarrelling with admirers of Renoir would have learnt with surprise that in 1926 they would all be agreeing to dwell on a family likeness, would all be delightedly discovering that Cézanne was more and Renoir less of an Impressionist than they had supposed.[99]

The issue of the moral dimension of art had been a cornerstone of the traditionalists' attack on Impressionism on its first appearance.[100] Although their paintings did not continue to be discussed in such overtly moralistic terms, the question emerged in criticisms of the vulgarity of their art and their subjects. For Sir Claude Phillips in 1917, Manet's *La Musique aux Tuileries* in the Lane Collection 'lacked vision of the higher truth which soars above the literal', while Renoir's *Les Parapluies* was 'a piece of jog-trot vulgarity' (reprinted below, text no. 5, p. 229).

In a wider sense, the moral question was reflected in long-running discussions about the status of anecdotal and literary content in painting. Here, the opposition between Gauguin and Cézanne was often made. As we have seen, the Trustees of the Tate Gallery were eager to acquire a major Gauguin before 1920, and the apparent literariness of his subjects, combined with his decorative use of colour, seems to have made him more immediately acceptable in England. By contrast, his reputation waned after 1920, as Cézanne's stock rose. For J.F. Holms in 1924, Cézanne was 'an incomparably better painter than Gauguin':

> [Gauguin's] was a vision that overflowed his artistic capacity in every direction, petrifying when it did so into illustrative symbols or sentimental captions which, so far from pointing, run the risk of obscuring altogether the truth he sought to convey.[101]

W. McCance's verdict was very similar: 'Gauguin has appealed chiefly because of his subject-matter . . . when considered as a constructive artist, he becomes of very little significance and cannot be compared with either Van Gogh or Cézanne'.[102]

Besides the work of Gauguin, the debates about literariness had another crucial focus, the contrasts often drawn between British and French art and taste – between the British love of extraneous content and the French concern for pure form. The two sides of the argument emerged vividly in a single issue of the *Burlington Magazine* in 1917. Charles Aitken, Director of the Tate, welcomed the recent display of the Lane Collection, but emphasised the French concern with external appearances and neglect of 'the psychological intricacies of individual character', in contrast to the works of the Pre-Raphaelites in the adjacent gallery:

> They probe into the human soul with sincere and personal insight, and they do manage to express new revelations – somehow.

After all we are human beings, and the human mind is our only register for art, so that to exclude the individual human soul and its emotions from the purview of art would seem to be an unwisely self-denying ordinance.[103]

By contrast, Clive Bell, writing on 'Contemporary Art in England', launched a savage attack on English artists for their insularity and ignorance of French developments, and their dependence on literature:

English painting . . . has been left high and dry, and our younger men either imitate their teachers . . . or, in revolt, set up for themselves as independent, hedgerow geniuses, ignorant, half-trained, and swollen by their prodigious cenceit to such monsters as vastly astonish all those who can remember them as children.[104]

As the project to create a gallery for modern foreign art developed, opinion was in general strongly in favour of bringing French art before the London public. In 1918, when Duveen's gift was formally announced, *The Times* argued that such a gallery would rescue England from ignorance and be of great educational value to artists (reprinted below, text no. 8, p. 232). However, even in 1932, an English artist, Robert Anning Bell, could utterly repudiate French Post-Impressionist art as representing 'senile decay' in its rejection of historic truth and the study of Nature; happily, he declared, young English artists worked on unaffected by this, 'as their fathers did before them' (reprinted below, text no. 35, pp. 251–2).

In validating recent French painting as worthy of the museums, the most recurrent rhetorical device was to evoke its links and continuity with some notion of tradition, whatever rupture might seem to have intervened in the development of this tradition. Such apparent ruptures might be reconciled with the idea of tradition in two ways, first by viewing history in terms of recurrent cycles, and second by invoking the notion of a return to basic, first principles. Charles Holmes combined both strategies in 1923, positing an alternation between mimetic imitation and the childlike simplicity of expression that he saw as characteristic of recent painting.[105] However, this return to basics might be located at different moments in the development of recent art; indeed, Holmes characterised both Cézanne and Cubism as marking such a return to first principles in the same book in 1927.[106]

However, more often than these modes of explaining historical discontinuities we find direct links drawn between recent and past art. Frequently, these were made in strictly nationalistic terms, by invoking a 'French' tradition. In 1926, Philip Hendy, later Director of the National Gallery, could even view French painting from Ingres to Braque as a seamless continuity, if in the vaguest terms;[107] and in 1931, Fry in a broadcast could elaborate this line of argument by positing two French traditions that had existed side by side through the ages, on the one side an intense interest in everyday things, on the other 'a passion for austere, almost abstract beauty'.[108] Following an argument such as this, of course, almost anything could be invoked in support of the notion of an essential 'Frenchness'; but the significance of the argument was its timing. The broadcast was given immediately before the Royal Academy's French Art exhibition of 1932, of which Fry was a member of the Executive Committee; he was thus seeking to disarm any residual conservative opposition to the central role that the exhibition gave to later nineteenth-century French art. Reviewing the exhibition itself, *The Times* critic Charles Marriott made a great point of tying Impressionism and Post-Impressionism into the strands of continuity that he saw running throughout French art: 'a working towards light and colour, and the emancipation of the picture as an object from social entanglements' (extracts reprinted below, texts nos 32–3, pp. 249–50).

The other type of invocation of the past linked specific recent works with particular moments in the past. At times, this involved making direct historical links, for instance between late Renoir and Titian,[109] or between Gauguin and Ingres.[110] In other instances, comparisons might have no claims to historical accuracy, but rather sought to validate the new in terms of the old: as well as citing Ingres in comparison with Gauguin, the same review invoked Botticelli's *Mars and Venus*. Such comparisons were used in a particularly self-conscious way in a pair of articles on Impressionism in 1908. An editorial in the *Burlington Magazine* compared Impressionism's fresh approach to nature with the art of fifteenth-century Florence, but sought to damn late Impressionism by reference to 'now forgotten Flemish and Italian eclectics'. In response, Roger Fry mocked the historical ineptness of these comparisons and proposed his own pairing – Impressionism with Roman Imperial painting, and Neo-Impressionism, Gauguin and Cézanne (what two years later he was to name Post-Impressionism) with the art of Byzantium.[111]

Such examples show that we should not be seeking historical analysis in texts such as these. The arguments that we have been examining, which sought to establish the historical place of Impressionist and Post-Impressionist painting, were all, in their different ways, polemical texts, staking out their positions within the patterns of current debates. In this context, Courtauld's invocation of 'the modern movement from its inception to the present time' may, from one point of view, look like an evasion of all the problems of definition and validation that were so troubling his contemporaries. But the very blandness of his formula may better be seen as a calculated strategy to disarm potential criticism, by seeming to deny the controversy that he feared might surround his enterprise. The warmth with which the Courtauld Gift was received, for all the reservations expressed about individual pictures, shows how effective this strategy was.

Interest Groups

Courtauld's activities and these critical debates are part of a wider story, the story of a struggle between different artistic groupings for ascendancy in the modern-art world. These questions are discussed in a broader perspective in Andrew Stephenson's essay (pp. 35–46). Here, only an indication can be given of the points at which these issues became most directly involved in the histories that we have been exploring. Three moments will be briefly examined: the formation of the new Tate Gallery Board of Trustees; the emergence of Courtauld as a patron and the creation of the Fund; and the foundation of the Courtauld Institute of Art.

As we have seen, the formation of a separate Board for the Tate took its activities out of the sphere of influence of an entrenched interest group on the Board of the National Gallery, whose views were most eloquently expressed by Lord Redesdale's memorandum on the Lane loan in 1914. However, the newly created Board met immediate opposition from another group of great influence – the Royal Academy. Immediately after the announcement of the composition of the new Board, the Academy's Council met to discuss it; at this meeting, one member, Sir Arthur Cope, declared that the new Board was not only part of the attack against the administration of the Chantrey Bequest, but also 'part of a larger design to take control of art and all matters relating to it out of the hands of professional artists and to place it in those of journalists and dealers'.[112] Although, after Arthur Blomfield had written a report on the position, the final tone of the Academy's response was more conciliatory, the presidents of many artists' bodies published an 'Artists' Memorial to the Treasury' in the press in July 1917.[113]

The core of the objections was that no artists had a seat on the new Board. In a sense, this was the result of an unfortunate accident, since John Singer Sargent had originally been nominated, but had declined to serve; Sargent, though, would not have been a reassuring choice for the Academy's old guard, since, although a full Academician, he was seen as representing an Impressionist position. However, the objections ignored the fact that two serving members of the Board were – or had been – artists; both Charles Holmes, ex-officio member as Director of the National Gallery, and D.S. MacColl, one of the appointed members, had been members of the New English Art Club.[114]

This was the nub of the matter. As Cope's protest shows, the Academy saw itself as representing all 'professional' artists; but this position had long been under challenge, most notably by the New English Art Club and the International Society. In response to the 'Artists' Memorial to the Treasury', the Observer pointed out that the 'Memorial' had not been signed by the presidents of either the New English Art Club or the International Society, 'the leading bodies of modern independents', and summed up the situation: 'Hence all the trouble which resolves itself into another feud between "official" and "independent" art.'[115]

The following spring, in a letter to Walter Lamb, Secretary of the Royal Academy, Charles Aitken, Director of the Tate, spelt out particularly clearly the Tate's own constituency as he saw it: 'I believe that a preponderating majority of the art "intelligenza" – critics, collectors, connoisseurs, the more intelligent and enterprising dealers, would take our view.'[116]

However, three years later, the Royal Academy's protests were answered by the appointment of four artists, all Academicians, to the Tate Board. It was, though, made clear that they were appointed 'in a personal capacity, and not an official or representative capacity'.[117] It was presumably their presence on the Board that contributed to the decision to give such autonomy to the Board set up to administer the Courtauld Gift (see above, p. 13 and note 42).

Concurrently with the formation of the Tate Board, a debate about many of the same issues was taking place in the Connoisseur, where Alexander Finberg voiced a position closer to that of the old guard on the National Gallery Board, with an added strand of fierce nationalism. He argued strenuously against plans to shift all British painting to the Tate, and the magazine imprudently printed a postscript by the author to his article:

Since this article was set in type, a separate Board of Trustees for the Tate Gallery has been constituted. Mr. MacColl is one of the

members of this Board, and other members appointed by the Treasury are known to share in his preferences for types of British art which are neither sane nor healthy.[118]

Although the magazine quickly withdrew this, MacColl's detailed refutation of Finberg's arguments was given an extra barb by the disclosure to him of the original wording of Finberg's postscript: '. . . other members appointed by the Treasury are known to sympathise with [MacColl] in his vendetta against all the sane and healthy branches of modern British art'.[119]

Finberg set out his wider position most clearly in a further reply:

I regard the full and complete representation of our national art in our own National Gallery as a matter of vital importance, not only to the welfare of British art, not only to the welfare of the nation, but to the welfare of the whole empire. That gallery has become an institution merely for the dilettanti and the cognoscenti: it stands for art connoisseurship in general, divested of all national and local requirements. I want to see it transformed into a great national institution which shall play a worthy part in the future by strengthening those ties of common feeling and imagination which bind the English-speaking peoples into one mighty empire.'[120]

The next moment that brings these questions into focus is the Courtauld Gift. As we have seen, the 1922 Burlington Fine Arts Club exhibition of French nineteenth-century art shifted Impressionist and Post-Impressionist art as a whole, and Cézanne in particular, from a minority sphere into mainstream high culture; it was here that Courtauld was 'converted' to Cézanne. One favourable review acknowledged the previous marginal status of the art by using the title '"Anarchists" in Painting' (reprinted below, text no. 15, p. 235). This clearly picks up on the pre-war reputation of Fry's 'Post-Impressionist' exhibitions, as representing socialist or anarchist tendencies in art.[121] It was presumably in this context that Aitken and Courtauld could talk of using Fry as 'a kind of "left wing"' in seeking twentieth-century paintings for the Gift (see above, p. 13).

The Burlington exhibition, of which Fry was a principal organiser, and the Courtauld Gift represented a sort of identity crisis for the Bloomsbury group. Such public endorsement of their taste, and of Cézanne in particular, threatened their position as a self-appointed élite. Some of this emerges from the condescending comments about Courtauld and his ambitions made by Bloomsburyites in the mid-1920s. The feeling was widespread that he had bought himself into the art world; in a sense, of course, this was true – not surprisingly, the establishment of the Courtauld Gift made him much in demand in artistic circles, and he very rapidly found a place on many influential committees.

However, there was an evident snobbism in some of the responses, presumably based on Courtauld's wealth and involvement in industry. For Vera Bowen, close friend of Lydia Lopokova and John Maynard Keynes, Courtauld was a social climber; the Gift was 'an occult scheme of social advancement' aimed at a peerage.[122] Keynes wrote to Lopokova about all the appeals made to Courtauld for financial support: 'Sam will soon be the most famous milking-cow in England! and will be made a Lord; but I think his udders must be sore with so much pulling by strange hands.' Lopokova, on very warm terms with Courtauld, replied in her inimitable English:

'While you tell me about Sam, Vera reads to me Sam's letter to her about the same famous lunch [at the opening of a new wing at the Fitzwilliam Museum]; the only Sam's sorrow that he is not entitled to a red gown, but his face would do instead. What a swift carrière he has made for himself!'[123] In 1937, Courtauld was to refuse a peerage.[124]

At the same time as these private comments among members of the Bloomsbury set, the public view of the Courtauld Gift went out of its way to stress its public-spiritedness. The editorial in *The Times* on the Gift contrasted Courtauld to previous great donors to the national collections, by stressing that his was explicitly 'directed to a special need' – to remedy a crucial gap in the existing public holdings, rather than being a gift of a pre-existing private collection (reprinted below, text no. 20, p. 239).

In 1927, Charles Holmes analysed more broadly the reasons for the poor standing of fine art in England and held up France as the pre-eminent country in terms of art. The reasons for this, he argued, were that in France there were no schisms within the art world. The success of painting and literature was fully supported both by its marketing – both the art market and broader cultural propaganda – and by French intellectuals. The position in England, with group working against group, was far less hopeful.[125]

These issues came into focus again with the foundation of the Courtauld Institute of Art in 1931. Before this, England had no university department of the history of art; evidently, in these circumstances, there was no agreement about the appropriate qualifications for posts such as curatorships in museums and galleries: should they be given to men from well-educated, artistic backgrounds – a hereditary élite – or to painters, whose credentials lay in hands-on experience, or to art critics, whose qualifications were wholly unclear?

In Lord Lee's initial announcement of the creation of the Institute, he stated that it would be 'for the systematic education of students in the History of Art or for the training of art critics and museum experts'. He challenged the English mistrust of 'highbrows' and insisted on 'the value of a knowledge of art as a means to happiness and well-being'; but the principal thrust of his argument was that museum professionals needed a professional training.[126]

Roger Fry gave the project his warm support in the *Burlington Magazine*. He explicitly challenged the notion that the best authorities were those who 'had some initial advantages by the accident of birth and previous training', and that the relevant aptitude was 'providentially distributed only to the sons of wealthy parents'. He mocked the idea 'that the understanding of art is a heaven-descended gift which comes by the grace of God and not by study': 'A fine and discriminating taste in works of art is of course a natural gift, but its effectiveness depends largely upon the extent to which it has been trained by constant exercise.'[127]

Yet, support was not universal. In the *Architectural Review* the young John Betjeman published a vigorous warning. He feared that the planned institute

seems but remotely concerned with artists, and more closely related to the antique trade. Nor is it related to the antique trade alone. The Institute may set up an atmosphere of pedantry and donnery about the remote artists of the past . . . Pale young men in horn-rimmed spectacles, arrogant old soothsayers on ever-

changing criteria, will flop about monumental Queen Anne passages and gibber in a rapidly accumulating collection of books.

His fear was that it would lead to a new form of academicism, replacing the Royal Academy, when it ought to engage directly with the present and the future of art itself: 'The Institute must keep our artists busy and turn for ever the pale young critics from its ferro-concrete threshold.'[128] In part, this was an attack against the association of art with commerce, but it also challenged Fry's link between taste and training.

In his own responses to art, Courtauld was 'a subjective – & sentimental – romantic, and . . . I love every kind of beauty'.[129] Late in his life, he argued that the Institute was concerned with more than 'history alone': 'What we endeavour to teach there is art appreciation.'[130] In announcing the foundation of the Institute, Lord Lee, after spelling out the practical, professional needs that it would fulfil, had concluded: 'the promoters of the scheme . . . have also been animated by the belief that in these hard and unlovely times too much attention is perhaps being concentrated on material things and too little on the spirit.'[131]

Conclusion

There are fascinating parallels between Courtauld's activities as collector and patron and those of Albert C. Barnes, the manufacturer of patent medicines who, during the same years, built up the remarkable collection of modern French painting that became the core of the Barnes Foundation in Merion, Pennsylvania. Both Courtauld and Barnes were buying Impressionist and Post-Impressionist paintings on the international market at substantial prices, and both acquired some of the key masterpieces of the period. Both, too, were committed to very much the same notion of 'modern art'; both were centrally committed to the art of Cézanne, and Barnes, like Courtauld, avoided true Cubist paintings, though his taste did extend to Matisse. Similar, too, was both men's commitment to art education: an educational scheme was fundamental to the conception of the Barnes Foundation.[132]

There, though, the parallels cease. Barnes's educational courses were open only to those who were prepared to give unquestioning adherence to his educational ideas; and he waged a lifelong war against the art expert and the art historian; many were the famous visitors turned away from his doors and denied access to his paintings. Courtauld, by contrast, was unequivocally committed to the public domain. All of his acts of generosity were enabling, not prescriptive, and none was designed to create a permanent monument to his generosity or his taste. The pictures in the Gift became an immediate part of the national collections and were never intended to be seen as a distinct collection in themselves; his private collection reached the public through the Courtauld Institute of Art, and no restrictions were placed on the teaching of the Institute at its foundation. As part of the University of London, it was from the start a part of the State higher-educational system.

One picture bought by the Fund, Renoir's 1888 *Bathing Woman* (fig. 32), was sold in 1944, and part of the proceeds were used in 1949, after Courtauld's death, to buy Picasso's *Seated Female Nude* of 1909–10 (fig. 33). Although Courtauld's own taste did not stretch this far, we can, I think, assume that he would have felt that this important

32 Renoir, *Bathing Woman*, 1888, 80 × 64 cm., present whereabouts unknown, formerly Tate Gallery, London (Courtauld Fund).

33 Picasso, *Seated Female Nude*, 1909–10, 92 × 73 cm., Tate Gallery, London (part purchased from Courtauld Fund). © DACS 1994

purchase, the first high Cubist work to enter the Tate's collections, was fully in the spirit of his Gift.

1949, too, marked perhaps the final flourish of the hostility to modern foreign art in England against which Courtauld had fought. At that year's Royal Academy banquet, Sir Alfred Munnings, shortly to retire as President of the Royal Academy, delivered a remarkable, rambling homily against modern art, to the evident amusement of many of his audience and the exasperation of some. Among his other targets, he mocked Anthony Blunt, by then Director of the Courtauld Institute, for claiming that Picasso was greater than Reynolds. Unabashed at the responses to his virtuoso impromptu performance, Munnings published almost all of his speech, very much as delivered (though without the pauses and slurrings) in the final volume of his autobiography.[133] One brief

passage, however, was omitted, although, he wrote, it caused 'the most prolonged laughter of the evening'. Happily, it was caught by the BBC:

> on my left I have the famous newly elected extraordinary member of the Royal Academy – Winston Churchill. He, too, is with me because once he said to me, 'Alfred, if you met Picasso coming down the street, would you join with me in kicking his something something something . . .?' I said, 'yes, sir, I would!'

It is easy to assume that we have now learned our lesson. But the public responses to Carl André's *Equivalent VIII* (the Bricks) in the 1970s and to Rachel Whiteread's *House* in 1993 should give us pause for thought.

NOTES

I am indebted to Elizabeth Prettejohn for gathering the dossier of press comment and criticism used in this essay, and to the Archives of the National Gallery (and particularly Jacqui McComish), the Tate Gallery (and particularly Jennifer Booth), Kings College, Cambridge, and the Royal Academy of Arts. I have made use of the valuable discussions of aspects of the subject in the following: National Gallery Millbank, *A Record of Ten Years 1917–1927*, London and Glasgow, 1927; Douglas Cooper, *The Courtauld Collection*, London, 1954; John

Ingamells, *The Davies Collection of French Art*, Cardiff (National Museum of Wales), 1967; and Ronald Alley, *The Tate Gallery's Collection of Modern Art other than Works by British Artists*, London, 1981.

1. During the 1870s, at exhibitions organised by the Paris dealer Paul Durand-Ruel in Bond Street between 1870 and 1875; for a chronology of exhibitions in London including Impressionist and Post-Impressionist paintings between 1880 and 1912, see *Post-Impressionism*, exhibition catalogue, Royal Academy of Arts, London, 1979–80, pp. 281–97.

2. The bequest of Etienne Moreau-Nélaton was initially hung in the Musée des Arts Décoratifs in 1907 and transferred to the Louvre only in 1934. The first artist whose work entered the Louvre against the museum's official regulations excluding living artists was the landscapist Félix Ziem, some of whose Venetian views were in the Chauchard bequest of 1909, shortly before the painter's death at the age of ninety, in 1911. The works by Monet and Renoir in the bequest of Comte Isaac de Camondo in 1911 challenged the rules far more obviously, since both artists were still active and the works bequeathed included some of their most recent paintings.

3. A list of the British artists represented in the Luxembourg was included in the *Report of the National Gallery Committee*, 1914, p.25, in order to highlight the inadequacy of English provisions for modern foreign art.

4. For photographs of the installation of the 1905 show, see John Rewald, 'Jours sombres de l'impressionnisme: Paul Durand-Ruel et l'exposition des impressionnistes, à Londres, en 1905', *L'Oeil*, February 1974. For valuable anthologies of the critical responses to these exhibitions, see Kate Flint (ed.), *Impressionists in England: The Critical Reception*, London, 1984, and J.B. Bullen (ed.), *Post-Impressionists in England: The Critical Reception*, London, 1988.

5. *Report from the Select Committee of the House of Lords on the Chantrey Trust*, London, 1904, pp. vii, 75; see also Theo Cowdell, 'The Chantrey Bequest', in Clyde Binfield (ed.), *Sir Francis Chantrey, Sculptor to an Age, 1781–1841*, Sheffield, 1981, pp. 85ff.

6. See C.M. Kauffmann, *Victoria and Albert Museum: Catalogue of Foreign Paintings, II: 1800–1900*, London, 1973, pp. viii–ix and 24–5.

7. See Frank Rutter, *Since I was Twenty-Five*, London, 1927, pp. 153–8. The Boudin is *Entre les jetées, Trouville* of 1888; the Monet that Rutter wanted to buy, *Snow Effect at Vétheuil*, was subsequently bought by Hugh Lane, and thus entered the National Gallery with Lane's collection in 1917 (see below; it is now titled *Lavacourt, Winter*).

8. Frank Rutter, *Since I was Twenty-Five*, London, 1927, p. 154. This refusal is not recorded in the National Gallery Board Minutes; however, the Trustees had decided on 14 March 1899 that rejected offers should not be recorded in the minutes, although in practice many such cases were.

9. National Art-Collections Fund, Executive Committee Minutes, 14 April 1905, 30 October, 13 November 1906.

10. *National Art-Collections Fund, Annual Report*, 1909, pp. 13–14.

11. Early publicity material for the Contemporary Art Society stated that it was founded in 1909. In the Society's Committee Minutes (Tate Gallery Archives), no year is given for the first two meetings, on 9 and 26 April, but there is no evidence of a year elapsing before the third meeting, dated 11 May 1910.

12. Contemporary Art Society, Minutes, 17 November 1910, 5 December 1912. It is possible that the Puvis that the Society considered in November 1910 was the cartoon bought by the National Art-Collections Fund the following year and presented to the Victoria and Albert Museum (*National Art-Collections Fund, Annual Report*, 1911)

13. In 1905 a modern continental gallery was one of the needs that the Keeper specified in a request to the government for extra gallery space. The Trustees reiterated the need in May 1912, on the occasion of the temporary display in the Gallery of a loaned portrait by Giovanni Boldini: the picture was taken down when it was pointed out in the House of Commons that Boldini was still living. National Gallery, Board Minutes, 27 June 1905, 14 May 1912.

14. National Gallery, Board Minutes, 19 February 1907.

15. National Gallery, Board Minutes, 5 August 1913; letter from Hawes Turner, Keeper of the National Gallery, to Lane, 12 August 1913 (copy in National Gallery Archives).

16. National Gallery, Board Minutes, 13 January 1913; letter from Hawes Turner to Lane, 15 January 1914 (copy in National Gallery Archives). The Monet was the canvas that Rutter had wanted to buy in 1905–6 with the French Impressionist Fund.

17. National Gallery Archives. MacColl's comments were an extensive memorandum, Sargent's a brief letter (24 January 1914) and annotations on a list of the collection, already annotated by one of the National Gallery's keepers. Sargent praised particularly highly the work of Antonio Mancini: 'It is possible that only artists at present realise what a wonderful painter he is and what a high rank he will hold one of these days.'

18. National Gallery, Board Minutes, 24 February 1914; letter from Lane to Hawes Turner, 12 February 1914; memorandum from Lord Redesdale to the Board of Trustees; MS notes by Holroyd on his response to the memorandum; letter from Hawes Turner to Lane, 28 February 1914 (all National Gallery Archives).

19. Letter from Lane to Holroyd, 13 February 1914; letter from MacColl to Lord Curzon, 6 March 1914 (National Gallery Archives).

20. *Report of the National Gallery Committee*, 1914, pp. 24–6. The members of the Committee were Lord Curzon (Chairman), Sir Edgar Vincent, R.H. Benson, Sir Charles Holroyd (Director of the National Gallery) and Robert C. Witt (Secretary of the Committee). The National Gallery Board welcomed the report, and its conclusion about the modern foreign gallery, on 10 March 1914 – the next meeting after Redesdale's strike against Lane.

21. *Ibid.*, pp. 148–9.

22. *Ibid.*, p. 112.

23. *Ibid.*, p. 133.

24. *Ibid.*, pp. 28–9, 29–31.

25. Treasury Minute, 24 March 1917, on the formation of the Tate Gallery Board (Tate Gallery Archives).

26. Tate Gallery, Board Minutes, 19 June 1917.

27. Tate Gallery, Board Minutes, 15 October and 3 December 1918.

28. Tate Gallery, Board Minutes, 22 October and 27 November 1917; 15 January, 19 February and 3 December 1918.

29. *Nevermore* was finally refused, at the reduced price of £1,800, in March 1921; Tate Gallery, Board Minutes, 19 February, 15 October 1918; 21 January 1919; 17 January and 9 March 1921. Michael Sadler owned several important Gauguins, including (as well as *Manao Tupapau*), *Poèmes barbares*, *Christ in the Garden of Olives* and *Vision after the Sermon*; the National Gallery of Scotland bought the last of these from him in 1925 – arguably a bolder purchase than any made by the Courtauld Fund during the same years.

30. Tate Gallery, Board Minutes, 18 March and 30 April 1919. The Executive Committee Minutes of the National Art-Collections Fund, 4 July 1918, discuss a sum of £2,000 that Duveen had offered for the purchase of pictures for the Modern Foreign Gallery at the Tate through the NACF, but it is unclear whether this is the same sum subsequently spent on the Gauguin.

31. See National Gallery, Board Minutes, 16 April 1918; R.F. Harrod, *The Life of John Maynard Keynes*, London, 1951, pp. 225–6; Richard Shone with Duncan Grant, 'The Picture Collector', in Milo Keynes (ed.), *Essays on John Maynard Keynes*, London, 1975, pp. 282–4; C.J. Holmes, *Self and Partners (Mostly Self)*, London, 1936, pp. 335–43.

32. Woolf, quoted in Frances Spalding, *Roger Fry: Art and Life*, London, 1980, p. 220; Lopokova, in Polly Hill and Richard Keynes (eds), *Lydia and Maynard: Letters between Lydia Lopokova and John Maynard Keynes*, London, 1989, p. 260, letter of 22 November 1924.

33. Tate Gallery, Board Minutes, 3 May and 16 July 1918. The works they particularly sought were *Portrait de famille* (the Bellelli family portrait, bought at the sale by the Musée du Luxembourg and now in the Musée d'Orsay), *Mlle Fiocre* (now in the Brooklyn Museum), *Au Foyer* (now in Ny Carlsberg Glyptotek, Copenhagen), and *Portrait of Duranty* (later bought by William Burrell, loaned to the Tate in the 1920s and now in the Burrell Collection, Glasgow). Although the Tate did not have the resources to buy any of these, the list shows how serious their ambitions were that Degas's work should be significantly represented in the collection.

34. *Sketch of Pellegrini*, given by the National Art-Collections Fund with £350 given by Duveen in 1916 (National Gallery, Board Minutes, 14 November 1916; *National Art-Collections Fund, Annual Report*, 1916); *Portrait of Princesse Pauline de Metternich*, bought by the National Art-Collections Fund for £526 12s 2d at the Degas Sale, and presented in 1918; *Head of a Woman*, presented by Viscount D'Abernon and Duveen in 1919 (Tate Gallery, Board Minutes, 15 October and 3 December 1918, 18 March 1919); on the first and last, see Ronald Alley, *The Tate Gallery's Collection of Modern Art other than Works by British Artists*, London, 1981, pp. 145–8; on the Metternich portrait, see Martin Davies, etc., *National Gallery Catalogues: French School, Early 19th century, Impressionists, Post-Impression-*

ists, etc., London, 1970, pp. 47–8.

35. Tate Gallery, Board Minutes, 15 October and 3 December 1918, 18 March 1919.

36. On this, see John Ingamells, 'Cézanne and the Tate Gallery Loans', in *The Davies Collection of French Art*, Cardiff (National Museum of Wales), 1967, pp. 28–30. The initial refusal, conveyed on 11 March 1921 by Aitken to Hugh Blaker, Miss Davies's agent, does not appear in the Tate Board Minutes for 9 March 1921, though presumably the offer was discussed then (on the National Gallery's policy of not recording refused offers, see note 8).

37. Ingamells, 1967 (cited in note 36), pp. 29–30. Tate Gallery, Board Minutes, 20 June 1922.

38. Tate Gallery, Board Minutes, 17 January, 2 May and 20 June 1922.

39. See Anthony Blunt, 'Samuel Courtauld as Collector and Benefactor', in Douglas Cooper, *The Courtauld Collection*, London, 1954, pp. 3–4.

40. Letters from Samuel Courtauld to (?)Lord D'Abernon, Chairman of the Trustees, and to Charles Aitken, 25 June 1923 (Tate Gallery Archives).

41. The draft contract for the gift is in Tate Gallery, Board Minutes, 27 June 1923.

42. Holmes strongly emphasised the distinctness of the two boards in a letter to Aitken on 3 January 1923, just before arrangements were finalised (Tate Gallery Archives): 'The Tate Board are not parties to the Courtauld Trust, though as a matter of courtesy it is to be shown to them before formal submission . . . It is not for instance pertinent if an R.A. challenges the schedule of painters. You will understand how ridiculous such a discussion might become and how likely to alienate both present and future benefactors.' The implications of this, in relation to the presence of Royal Academicians on the Tate Board, will be discussed below, p. 28.

43. Letter from Courtauld to Charles Aitken, 25 June 1925 (Tate Gallery Archives).

44. Courtauld Trust Minutes, in Tate Gallery Archives, meeting of 18 January 1924, when the legal terms of the gift had been finalised.

45. Letters from Courtauld to Aitken, 24 July and 12 August 1923 (Tate Gallery Archives).

46. See especially letters from Madame van Gogh-Bonger to H.S. Ede, 18 October 1923, and to Aitken, 3 December 1923, 16 January and 24 January 1924; letter from Courtauld to Aitken, 9 January 1924; Courtauld Trust, Minutes, 18 January 1924 (all Tate Gallery Archives).

47. W.S. Meadmore, *Lucien Pissarro: Un Coeur simple*, London, 1962, p. 184; letter from Lydia Lopokova to J.M. Keynes, 21 November 1924, in Hill and Keynes, 1989 (cited in note 32), pp. 259–60.

48. Letters from Fénéon to Turner, 1 March 1924, from Courtauld to Aitken, 2 March 1924, and from Aitken to Fénéon, 6 March 1924 (Tate Gallery Archives).

49. Letter from Courtauld to Aitken, 25 July 1923 (Tate Gallery Archives).

50. Tate Gallery, Board Minutes, 25 November 1925, 27 January 1926; *L'Abreuvoir* was in fact bought in December 1925, before the sale was completed, and the £1,200 raised by the sale was put towards the Monet *Water Lilies* in 1927. Sisley's *Le Pont de Moret*, *c.*1890, does not appear in François Daulte, *Sisley*, Paris, 1959 (photo in Archives of Lefèvre Gallery, London).

51. Letters from Aitken to Courtauld, 25 February 1926, and Holmes to Aitken, 1 March 1926; undated notes on a telephone call from Courtauld to J.B. Manson (Tate Gallery Archives).

52. Letter from Aitken to Holmes, 9 December 1925 (National Gallery Archives).

53. No minutes survive for any such meeting; see page 13.

54. Probably Degas's *The Rehearsal* of 1873–4, belonging to the painter Jacques-Emile Blanche, bought by Sir William Burrell in July 1926 (now Burrell Collection, Glasgow).

55. Letter from Aitken to Holmes, 12 December 1925 (National Gallery Archives).

56. Tate Gallery, Board Minutes, 27 January and 20 April 1926. Earlier in 1925 the Fund Trustees had considered buying Blanche's painting by Renoir, the 1887 *Baigneuses* now in the Philadelphia Museum of Art (letter from Aitken to Holmes, 13 March 1925, National Gallery Archives); Blanche apparently offered again to sell the picture to the Tate early in 1928 (letter from William Rothenstein to Lord D'Abernon, 1 May 1928, in William Rothenstein, *Since Fifty: Men and Memories, 1922–1938*, London, 1939, p. 66), though the rejection of this offer seems not to be recorded in the Tate Board Minutes. We do not know why and when negotiations for this and Blanche's Degas broke down; neither picture appeared among the loans in the opening exhibition of the Modern Foreign Gallery in June 1926.

57. Roger Fry, 'The Courtauld Fund', *The Nation and the Athenaeum*, 30 January 1926, pp. 613–14. The gallery in question was number X, one of the side-galleries intended originally for the Turner Collection.

58. Letter from Fry to Aitken, 29 January 1926 (Tate Gallery Archives).

59. Letter from Courtauld to Aitken, 3 February 1926 (Tate Gallery Archives)

60. Two separate catalogues were issued, of the permanent collection and the loans; reviews (e.g., T.W. Earp, 'Modern French Painting at the Tate Gallery', *Apollo*, August 1926, pp. 62–6) make it clear that all the pictures were hung as a single sequence, through the new galleries on the ground floor and in the basement.

61. Letter from Courtauld to Aitken, 27 March 1926 (Tate Gallery Archives).

62. Tate Gallery, Board Minutes, 9 June 1926.

63. Contemporary Art Society, Minutes, 13 November 1917, 15 July 1919, 2 June 1922, 14 March 1923. His criticisms were not wholly justified, for the Society's Prints and Drawings Fund, created in 1919, had in 1920 bought two Degas drawings, and in 1922 two by Gauguin and one by Picasso (Contemporary Art Society, *Report 1919–1924*)

64. Contemporary Art Society, Minutes, 8 May 1924. The Contemporary Art Society was always operating with far smaller funds than either the Courtauld Fund or the National Art-Collections Fund. In the first year of its foreign fund, it raised £680, matched by a further £680 from an anonymous donor (Contemporary Art Society, Minutes, 17 June 1925).

65. Contemporary Art Society, Minutes, 17 June 1925. Courtauld's address is noted in Fry's appointments diary for 21 March 1924, though without clear indication that he had an appointment to visit him (Fry Papers, XIV.4, Kings College, Cambridge).

66. See Robert Skidelsky, *John Maynard Keynes*, II, London 1992, pp. 243–4; J.B. Manson, preface to catalogue of the *London Artists' Association Retrospective Exhibition*, Cooling Galleries, London, March 1934. J.M. Keynes's extensive dossier on the London Artists' Association is File PP73 in the J.M. Keynes Collection, Kings College, Cambridge.

67. A few days earlier, Courtauld had drawn the Keeper Daniel's attention to a Bellini Madonna in Percy Moore Turner's Independent Gallery and had offered to help buy it, but willingly accepted Daniel's negative response to the picture (letters of 10, 14 and 22 November 1928, National Gallery Archives). The picture (reproduced *Burlington Magazine*, December 1928, opposite p. 269) is not now accepted as a Bellini.

68. On these, see Ronald Alley, *The Tate Gallery's Collection of Modern Art other than Works by British Artists*, London, 1981, pp. 78–80, 498. See also Richard Shone, 'Matisse in England and two English sitters', *Burlington Magazine*, July 1993, pp. 479–84.

69. Tate Gallery, Board Minutes, 18 October 1927.

70. Tancred Borenius, 'French Art at Burlington House', *Studio*, February 1932, pp. 77–8.

71. Letters from Clark to Llewellyn, 14 February 1934, from Llewellyn to Clark, 15 February 1934, from Clark to Courtauld, 19 February 1934 (all National Gallery Archives).

72. Letter from Courtauld to Clark, 15 February 1934 (National Gallery Archives).

73. The two appear on the same invoice, with a note in Courtauld's hand that the Degas was for the Tate (Courtauld Institute Archives).

74. Letter from H.S. Ede to Charles Holmes, 23 May 1925 (National Gallery Archives); National Art-Collections Fund, Minutes, 7 November 1927.

75. Letter from Courtauld to Aitken, 25 June 1923 (Tate Gallery Archives).

76. Letter from Ambroise Vollard to Courtauld, 23 June 1927 (Courtauld Institute Archives).

77. Kenneth Clark, *Another Part of the Wood*, London, 1974, p. 265.

78. Letter from Courtauld to Lord Lee, undated (copy in National Gallery Archives); the letter was considered by the National Gallery Board on 11 October 1932.

79. For further photographs of the installation, see Christopher Hussey, 'The Courtauld Institute of Art', I and II, *Country Life*, 15 and 22 October 1932.

80. On the formation of the Institute, see Blunt, 1954 (cited in note 39), pp. 5–7.

81. Letter from Courtauld to Aitken, 27 March 1926 (Tate Gallery Archives).

82. Courtauld bought a copy, along with Julius Meier-Graefe's book on Cézanne, from the Leicester Galleries in January 1928 (Courtauld Institute Archives).

83. Fry's appointments diary for 17 January 1929, with the time of an appointment to visit him (Fry Papers, XIV.4, Kings College, Cambridge).

84. Letters from Fry to Courtauld, 22 and 28 March, 31 July 1929 (Courtauld Institute Archives).

85. Letter from Courtauld to Christabel, Lady Aberconway, 19 September 1934 (British Library, Add. MSS 52432, quoted by Dennis Farr, 'Samuel Courtauld as a Collector and Founder of the Courtauld Institute', in *Impressionist and Post-Impressionist Masterpieces: The Courtauld Collection*, New Haven and London (International Exhibitions Foundation), 1987, p. 10).

86. Open letter from Kenneth Clark, December 1934, in the papers of Christabel, Lady Aberconway (British Library, Add. MSS 52432).

87. *Nu aux cheveux jaunes*, reproduced in César M. de Hauke, *Seurat et son oeuvre*, Paris, 1961, I, p. 303.

88. The pictures he sold are included in the chronological listing of his acquisitions below (pp. 221–4). I am indebted to Desmond Corcoran and Martin Summers of the Lefèvre Gallery for information from the gallery's records which helped to identify the pictures Courtauld sold.

89. For these debates, see Flint, 1984 and Bullen, 1988 (cited in note 4); for a valuable discussion of English art criticism between the wars, focusing on the critics of *The Times*, Arthur Clutton-Brock and Charles Marriott, see Nigel Halliday, *Craftsmanship and communication: a study of "The Times" art critics in the 1920s, Arthur Clutton-Brock and Charles Marriott*, Ph.D. thesis, Courtauld Institute of Art, 1987.

90. The 1910 preface, 'The Post-Impressionists', reprinted in Bullen, 1988 (cited in note 4), pp. 94–9 (there attributed to Desmond MacCarthy, who composed it from Fry's notes); on Degas and Renoir, see 'Retrospect (1920)' and 'Renoir' in *Vision and Design*, London 1920, 1961 edn, pp. 209–13 and 225–7, and 'The Last Works of Renoir', *Athenaeum*, 11 June 1920, pp. 771–2.

91. For example, Roger Fry, 'The Sir Hugh Lane Pictures at the National Gallery', *Burlington Magazine*, April 1917, p. 148 (reprinted below, text no. 7, pp. 230–2), and 'The French Exhibition–III', *New Statesman and Nation*, 23 January 1932, p. 93, lamenting the influence of Impressionism on Manet's later work.

92. For example, W.G. Constable, 'Renoir', *New Statesman*, 14 February 1920, pp. 554–6; Eric Maclagan, 'French Art at the Goupil Gallery', *New Statesman*, 17 July 1920, p. 420; Wyndham Lewis, 'Round the London Galleries, I', *Listener*, 10 June 1948, p. 944 (on the Courtauld Memorial Exhibition).

93. Frank Rutter, *Some Contemporary Artists*, London, 1922, p. 35.

94. Walter Sickert, 'French Art of the Nineteenth Century–London', *Burlington Magazine*, June 1922, pp. 260–71.

95. Sir Charles Holmes, *Old Masters and Modern Art: The National Gallery, France and England*, London 1927, pp. xxi, 125.

96. S. Magee, 'Degas and the Academicians', *New Statesman*, 14 January 1922, p. 420.

97. Roger Fry, '"Paul Cézanne" by Ambroise Vollard', and Ralph Curtis, 'Les Fauves', *Burlington Magazine*, August 1917, pp. 54–61, and September 1917, pp. 123–4.

98. D.S. MacColl and R.R. Tatlock, 'Cézanne's Sketch, *Landscape* and *Bacchanales*', *Burlington Magazine*, January 1922, pp. 42–3. Letters from F.H.S., Hugh Blaker and J.W.P., February 1922, p. 103; from MacColl, Fry and Edward Holroyd, March 1922, pp. 152–3.

99. Clive Bell, 'A Re-Formation of the English School', *Artwork*, summer 1926.

100. For a particularly virulent example, see Philip Burne-Jones, 'The Experiment of Impressionism', *The Nineteenth Century and After*, March 1905, pp. 433–5.

101. J.F. Holms, 'Gauguin', *New Statesman*, 9 August 1924, p. 522.

102. W. McCance, 'Gauguin at the Leicester Galleries', *Spectator*, 26 July 1926.

103. Charles Aitken, 'English 19th Century Art at the National Gallery', *Burlington Magazine*, July 1917, p. 10.

104. Clive Bell, 'Contemporary Art in England', *Burlington Magazine*, July 1917, pp. 30–7, quotation on p. 33.

105. Sir Charles Holmes, *Old Masters and Modern Art: The National Gallery, Italian Schools*, London, 1923, p. xxix.

106. Sir Charles Holmes, *Old Masters and Modern Art: The National Gallery, France and England*, London, 1927, pp. 127–8, xxii.

107. Philip Hendy, 'From Ingres to Picasso', *New Statesman*, 20 March 1926, p. 710.

108. Roger Fry, 'What France has Given to Art', *Listener*, 30 December 1931, pp. 1121–3.

109. Roger Fry, 'Renoir', *Athenaeum*, 20 February 1920, p. 247.

110. A. Clutton-Brock, '"Anarchists" in Painting: French Classics of the Last Century', *The Times*, 23 May 1922, p. 13, reprinted below, text no. 15, pp. 000–0.

111. Anon., 'The Last Phase of Impressionism', *Burlington Magazine*, February 1908, pp. 272–3; Roger Fry, Letter to the Editor, *Burlington Magazine*, March 1908, pp. 374–5.

112. Royal Academy of Arts, Council Minutes, 8 May 1917.

113. Royal Academy of Arts, Council Minutes, 13 June 1917; 'Artists' Memorial to the Treasury', published *Morning Post*, 17 July 1917, and elsewhere.

114. The other members of the Tate Board were the Earl of Plymouth (Chairman), Lord D'Abernon, R.C. Witt, Lord Henry Cavendish-Bentinck, Robert Ross, J.R. Holliday and Charles Aitken (ex officio as Director of the Tate).

115. *Observer*, 22 July 1917.

116. Letter from Aitken to Lamb, 6 March 1918 (Royal Academy Archives). The context of this letter involved also the continuing debates over the Chantrey Bequest.

117. National Gallery Millbank, *A Record of Ten Years 1917–1927*, London and Glasgow, 1927, p. 10. The four artist representatives were Sir Aston Webb, Sir D.Y. Cameron, Charles Sims and Muirhead Bone.

118. Alexander J. Finberg, 'Why banish the British School from the National Gallery?', *Connoisseur*, May 1917, pp. 3–6.

119. D.S. MacColl, 'Why banish Facts from Criticism?', *Connoisseur*, July 1917, pp. 123–5.

120. Alexander J. Finberg, 'Why banish the British School from the National Gallery? Reply to Mr. D.S. MacColl', *Connoisseur*, August 1917, p. 224.

121. See Bullen, 1988 (cited in note 4), pp. 14–16, and Stella Tillyard, *The Impact of Modernism 1900–1920: Early Modernism and the Arts and Crafts Movement in Edwardian England*, London, 1988, pp. 104–8.

122. Robert Skidelsky, *John Maynard Keynes*, II, London, 1992, p. 143.

123. Letter from Keynes to Lopokova, 13 June 1924, and from Lopokova to Keynes, 15 June 1924, in Hill and Keynes, 1989 (cited in note 32), pp. 220–1.

124. Letter from Courtauld to Christabel, Lady Aberconway, 25 May 1937 (British Library, Add. MSS 52432, cited by Farr, 1987 (cited in note 85), pp. 8–9).

125. Sir Charles Holmes, *Old Masters and Modern Art: The National Gallery, France and England*, London, 1927, pp. xviii–xix.

126. Lord Lee, 'Art and the Expert: A New Institute in London', *The Times*, 27 October 1930, pp. 13–14.

127. Roger Fry, 'Letter: The Courtauld Institute of Art', *Burlington Magazine*, December 1930, pp. 317–18.

128. John Betjeman, 'The New Chair of Art', *Architectural Review*, December 1930, p. 235; I owe this reference to Andrew Stephenson.

129. Letter from Courtauld to Lydia Lopokova, 23 December 1943 (LLK/5, J.M. Keynes Collection, Kings College, Cambridge)

130. Samuel Courtauld, 'Art Education' (1943), in *Ideals and Industry: War-Time Papers*, London, 1949, p. 56.

131. Lee, 1930 (cited in note 126), p. 14.

132. On Barnes, see Howard Greenfield, *The Devil and Dr. Barnes: Portrait of an American Art Collector*, New York, 1987, and *Great French Paintings from the Barnes Foundation*, Boston, Toronto and London, 1993.

133. Sir Alfred Munnings, *The Finish*, London, 1952, pp. 144–7; Munnings also included a very extensive selection of the responses–both favourable and critical–that he received for his outburst.

'AN ANATOMY OF TASTE':
SAMUEL COURTAULD AND DEBATES ABOUT
ART PATRONAGE AND MODERNISM IN
BRITAIN IN THE INTER-WAR YEARS

Andrew Stephenson

IN HIS BOOK *Ideals and Industry* (1949), a speech that Samuel Courtauld had given to the Association of Art Institutions in October 1943 was printed under the title 'Art Education'. Writing at the height of the war, the veteran art collector reaffirmed his belief in the timeless value of art as a 'civilising' influence', almost akin, in his evaluation, to religion. 'Art', he declared, 'is universal and eternal; it ties race to race, and epoch to epoch. It overleaps divisions and unites men in one all-embracing and disinterested and living pursuit.' However, unlike religion, in Courtauld's opinion, art had retained its aesthetic 'purity' because it had not been 'abused by . . . political power'.[1] Consequently, it remained untarnished by social concerns or debased by politics. Citing the 'remarkable attendances at art exhibitions and at classical concerts' during the war years, Courtauld interpreted these events as proof, at a moment of national crisis, 'of a new and almost universal groping after those spiritual values of which art rightly claims a share'.[2]

Against the elevated values of art, Courtauld contrasted the 'vulgar' culture of mass production and popular entertainment which depended upon the novel, fashionable and showy for its appeal and had 'nothing whatever to do with art and beauty'. Railing against 'commercialisation' and industrial exploitation for lowering national standards in art and design, Courtauld warned his audience of the urgency of educating the public against 'barbarous taste' and of the need to be vigilant in the future:

> Public standards of taste for many decades past have been set by the salesman and the advertiser, and I suggest that it is for those here to take this job out of their hands in future. In saying this I am not blaming the salesman and the advertiser; they have done what they have been paid to do, but so far as taste is concerned it has been a case of the blind leading the blind.[3]

Coming from a leading industrialist, these were thought-provoking, if not contradictory, sentiments. Courtauld had, after all, made a fortune out of the sale of artificial silk in the 1920s, and it was his acumen as a businessman that had allowed him to assemble his private art collection. By Courtauld's own account, however, culture and commerce, art and industry were uneasy partners. Where art patronage was concerned, it was evident that there were conflicts between private wealth and public interest which had to be carefully and sympathetically framed.

It is the aim of this essay to examine Courtauld's ideology of art patronage and his model of the discerning benefactor of the arts within the inter-war years. I shall suggest that Courtauld's simultaneous formation of public and private collections of modern art and his benevolence towards the Tate Gallery and the Courtauld Institute of Art can be seen as part of a wider desire to maintain historically proven standards of aesthetic judgement whilst at the same time promoting a belief in art education as a 'civilising' force, able to instil humanist values of responsible citizenship. In order to provide a historical context within which to evaluate these ideas, I shall focus on the period from 1917, when Courtauld's interest in modern art was stimulated by seeing the Hugh Lane Collection exhibited at the National Gallery, through to 1937 when he had largely stopped buying paintings. In addition, I shall examine the press criticism that Courtauld's patronage activities attracted and the ways in which his pro-French taste in modern art was discussed and characterised by different art audiences within these years.

*   *   *

At the beginning of his 'Art Education' speech, Courtauld had forewarned his audience that he came before them without 'real qualifications' for the job of 'President of the Association of Art Institutions'. He was neither practitioner nor theorist, neither teacher nor critic: 'I am not an artist – not even an amateur – nor am I an expert in art history, art criticism, or the laws of aesthetics; nor has my experience of art in relation to industry been particularly encouraging.'[4] Instead, Courtauld played up his role as a successful manufacturer of textiles whose involvement in art patronage was primarily a commitment to the enjoyment and appreciation of the arts as a 'civilising' force. The wealth generated from his business activities and investments had permitted him and his wife Elizabeth to collect works of art privately for their own satisfaction and pleasure. Simultaneously, such independent means had also allowed him to shower largesse upon the nation's art institutions by giving generously to the national collection of modern art at the Tate Gallery and to the Courtauld Institute's art collection (which by 1943 consisted largely of the Courtauld private collection donated to the Institute).

In some earlier notes entitled 'The Layman's Proper Part', which were made for a projected set of essays (and were quoted by Anthony Blunt in his memoir of Courtauld in 1954, but are now lost), Courtauld had reiterated his belief that any true love of art and understanding of beauty was not gained from occupying the position of the art expert and applying rational argument and learned theory; rather, it emerged from pursuing the path of an 'unadulterated amateur' and responding spontaneously to the pleasures of the work of art:

> if [the art lover] follows one line of study too exclusively he soon gets on to dangerous ground, and may end up losing the greatest rewards of the true amateur without ever becoming an acknowledged expert . . . therefore unless his initial impulse is spontaneous, or at any rate seems to come to him naturally if inspired by others, perhaps he had better leave pictures alone.[5]

Such veneration for the amateur as 'layman aesthete', the assertion of the importance of aesthetic pleasure over intellectual rigour and the belief in the act of looking at an work of art as a form of 'spiritual communion' was entirely in line with Bloomsbury art theories. Both Clive Bell and Roger Fry, the group's leading art writers, similarly sustained a commitment to the autonomous experience of art as a transcendant, almost metaphysical one. Courtauld's belief in a correspondence between the spiritual value of art and religion appears to be indebted to these convictions, and in particular to Bell's essay 'Art and Society' in his book *Art* (published in 1914 and the 'gospel' of Bloomsbury supporters throughout the early 1920s), in which Bell evangelised:

> Let everyone make himself an amateur, and lose the notion that art is something that lives in museums understood by the learned alone . . . If they acquire the sensibility to appreciate, even to some extent, the greatest art they will have found the new religion for which they have been looking.[6]

'Bloomsbury', as an informal network of artists, on art writers and intellectuals linked through family connections, education, friendship or shared taste, was highly influential, if unconventional, in its support of modern art.[7] Samuel and Elizabeth Courtauld moved in some of the same social circles, and Courtauld, through his support of the London Artists' Association from 1926, worked closely with John Maynard Keynes (see below, p. 41). Through the inter-war period, the importance that was credited to the aesthetic arguments and theoretical positions of the Bloomsbury critics fluctuated, but, in the first half of the 1920s especially, they commanded a great deal of respect across a wide variety of art audiences.[8]

Courtauld's model of the ideal patron of the arts is a revealing, if slightly curious and idiosyncratic, amalgam of aspects of Bloomsbury thinking. It interwove features of eighteenth-century English aristocratic philanthropy with the ethical aspirations of the Arts and Crafts movement, as they had been reformulated within the Bloomsbury brand of English modernism. Using a comment by Fry as a starting point for drawing such a comparison between artists and the conditions of patronage in the eighteenth and twentieth centuries, Courtauld recorded that

> Roger Fry said in one of his books that the English art patrons of the eighteenth century deserved better artists than they got. I should say that the reverse is true of the twentieth century, and that to-day artistic producers of all kinds deserve better patrons than they got. In the eighteenth century, of course, patrons of art belonged almost exclusively to the wealthy classes, whose artistic education was very good, on the whole, from traditions at home and travels abroad.
> . . . But we are not talking now about wealthy people who can buy old Masters . . . but about the great majority of the population, who have enough money, and ought to have the wish and opportunity, to envisage something – if only a little – beyond the bare necessities of existence.[9]

On the one hand, Courtauld's views were evidently marked by traces of a late nineteenth-century Arts and Crafts liberal idealism and social conscience as they had penetrated into early twentieth-century English modernism. These Arts and Crafts principles permeated Courtauld's vision of art education not merely as a transformation of an individual's knowledge about art, but, more significantly, as a contribution to an altered ethical attitude towards life. Within this vein, art patronage was viewed in redemptive terms, as simultaneously a public act of social responsibility and one of aesthetic faith.[10]

Such a conception underscored Courtauld's generosity to the Tate Gallery and his aspirations when setting up the Courtauld Institute of Art as a place to 'train young people for careers in connection with art'. More significantly, both were viewed as practical ways of 'raising the general level of public taste' and transforming attitudes towards modern French art. Following on from this, there were many remainders in Courtauld's speech of a way of thinking indebted at a distance to William Morris and the Arts and Crafts movement – in his assertion of the necessity of 'fitness to function' and of the importance of fundamentals over details, and in his concern with form before content and with an overriding purity of aesthetic conception and truth to nature.[11]

On the other hand, Courtauld's typology also carried within itself vestiges of pre-industrial aristocratic ideals. These were exemplified by the figure of the eighteenth-century connoisseur-collector: in his own words, a gentleman in whom 'dare-devil standards of conduct went hand in hand with genuine connoisseurship'.[12] On some level, Courtauld envisaged private patronage as upholding such a tradition of aristocratic munificence (tempered as I have indicated by a kind of social citizenship). The symbolic significance of this ideal was reflected in Courtauld's early preference for eighteenth-century English art and architecture. In 1921, when Courtauld became head of his family's rayon company, he had initially bought two Gainsborough portraits at a time when the artist's work in particular, and eighteenth-century portraiture and landscape painting in general, were exceptionally highly esteemed as a point of excellence in Britain's cultural achievement.[13]

The most emphatic parallels between Courtauld's patronage and earlier traditions of philanthropy were drawn at the time of the formal declaration of the Courtauld Gift to the Tate Gallery in January 1924. In its editorial (reprinted below, text no. 20, p. 239), *The Times* placed Courtauld within a stream of such gentleman connoisseurs 'who, prizing beauty, had the patriotism and the vision to contribute to our fund and heritage of art. It may be that Mr Courtauld's name will be held in esteem distinct from that in which we hold the names of George Beaumont, Wynn Ellis, Temple-West, Layard and Salting'. The main distinction intimated by the critic of *The Times* was that whilst the majority of these earlier patrons had bequeathed British art and 'Old Master' paintings to the state art collections (with the notable exception of Salting, who had given his collection of nineteenth-century French landscape paintings mainly of the Barbizon School), Courtauld had for his part established a trust fund to purchase modern French paintings. By pointing up the 'patriotic' nature of the gift and locating it within this earlier, respected tradition of philanthropy, questions raised by Courtauld's pro-French taste appeared less significant.

Courtauld's choice and restoration of the Adam-designed, Neo-Classical Home House in Portman Square as his London residence further reinforced such correspondences of taste between the eighteenth-century connoisseur and the modern collector. When it opened as the Courtauld Institute of Art with his collection of French art installed, writers were quick to highlight how the eighteenth-century interior decoration and the late nineteenth-century art collection were complementary aspects of refined, good taste (figs 35 and 36). Christopher Hussey in *Country Life* (October 1932) recorded that

> The conjuncture of Mr. Courtauld's famous collection of modern paintings with Adam's decorations might be expected to produce a discord. [However,] far from any disharmony resulting, the two

36   The Ètruscan room at 20 Portman Square, *c*.1931.

forms of art, at first sight so disparate, actually have a complementary effect upon each other.[14]

The reviewer of *The Times* praised Home House as a place where British scholarship, in that 'tradition of connoisseurship and appreciation fostered during the 18th century', and 'now in danger of being lost', could be 'found' and revitalized beneath Adam's classical decorations.[15]

Courtauld's belief, again indebted to Bloomsbury art theory, that art training should be primarily an aesthetic education experienced, as he put it, 'chiefly by the eye' through direct engagement with the artwork and not learned within the 'unwholesome atmosphere' of the public art gallery, appears to have been fulfilled by establishing the Institute within the collector's own home.[16] Whilst the public were not excluded, the Institute, nevertheless, retained the atmosphere of a private mansion. Its collection of modern French art was hung in a way that was not only enhanced by the elegant, decorative features of the rooms, but suggested a casual, enlightened fine taste (and which belied Courtauld's use of professional advice on hanging from the art dealer, Percy Moore Turner[17]). Taken as a whole, as an article in the *Listener* emphasized, the Institute's beautiful environment and magnificent collection provided the ideal atmosphere in which valuable works of art could be individually studied, a developed aesthetic sensibility fostered and the principles of Art History acquired.[18]

35   The front parlour at 20 Portman Square, *c*.1931.

*   *   *

Courtauld's activities as a patron of modern art and his public generosity to the nation's art institutions embroiled him within wider political debates about the relative responsibilities of state and private patronage. His preference for modern French art and for contemporary British paintings that displayed evidence of Anglo-French allegiances also involved him in arguments about Anglo-French rivalry in modern art. Within the complex cultural debates and pervasive nationalism of the inter-war years, each strand of discussion inflected back onto the other; both issues became entangled in the claims and counter-claims of rival art groupings and embedded within their respective conceptions of the role of art and art institutions within post-war society. At different historical moments through the period, Courtauld's motives and tastes were re-examined in the light of these concerns.

At the time of the opening of the Tate Gallery's extension in June 1926 which integrated Courtauld's gift with other loans of modern French art, these issues emerged within press reports. Many reviews like *The Times* article (reprinted below, text no. 29, p. 246) related Courtauld's benevolence as a donor back to questions of national prestige in modern art:

> With the opening of the new modern foreign section our reproach of seeming to ignore the most recent development of art outside of these islands is removed . . . The intention of the collection and its galleries is not so much to exalt foreign art at the possible expense of our own as to encourage in the public that broader view of art through which alone our native production can be rightly appreciated. Comparison there must be, but it is of kind rather than quality . . . In any case, the broader view cannot fail to stimulate interest in British art.

The King's speech at the opening, reprinted in *The Times*, similarly underlined the national importance of the extension of the Tate Gallery's modern collection and stressed its undoubted edifying effect:

> The establishment in London of a permanent collection of fine paintings by the great continental painters cannot fail in many ways to exercise a beneficial influence. And we may hope that visitors from abroad who come to study in our foreign collection, will be led to see and admire the work of the great British masters, too often but little known outside their own country.[19]

After commending the Board of the National Gallery of British Art for the speed with which it had acted to open these galleries (the Board was established only in April 1917 and Duveen's offer of financial support, though made in 1916, was officially announced only in 1918), the King then praised the liberality of those patrons who had made it possible: '[it] is almost entirely due to the munificence of the private benefactors and has incurred little or no expenditure of public money. This is a remarkable and inspiring achievement.,[20] Whilst many members of the British arts establishment, like the King, saw such benevolence to the nation's art collections as highly commendable, others were less convinced. Some interpreted art donations as the acts of social climbers and as part of 'an occult scheme of social advancement aimed at a peerage'.[21] And following the 1921 amendment of the Finance Act which allowed exemption from death duties if works of art were donated to the state, some critics wondered whether such tax incentives left the nation's museums open to being flooded by works of art of dubious value that exemplified the taste of the 'newly enriched'.[22]

In the face of an increasing dependence upon private donations by wealthy patrons such as Courtauld, this issue of how private and state funding to Britain's art galleries and museums should be balanced and how the artistic tastes of different and competing social groups were represented within national art institutions was a highly controversial one. Moreover, as the 1927 Royal Commission into Museums in London and Edinburgh later reported, the government's abdication of responsibility and lack of funding placed the nation's art galleries in a weak and vulnerable position. The Final Report warned that the expansion of national collections 'has been spasmodic' and 'as a result' required some serious attention. It concluded that 'In general it is true to say that the collections . . . once formed by the zeal of individuals, and thereafter bestowed or acquired by the state, have been maintained at the lowest possible cost . . . [displaying] a passive and mainly receptive attitude' on the part of the British government.[23]

This dependence upon private patronage also carried with it serious implications for the professional integrity of museum staff, who as custodians of the national heritage and upholders of artistic excellence were required to maintain proper standards in the face of such uncertain conditions. One area of concern expressed in the press was the qualifications of national museum boards to decide whether works should be accepted into the State's collections or not. And related to this, it was asked how appropriate it was for them to pass judgement on the donor's artistic taste in the first place.[24] In the light of the Hugh Lane affair, following his death on the *Lusitania* in 1915, and the refusal of the Davies loan of works by Cézanne in 1921 (see above, pp. 11–12), many national institutions realised that such decisions not only ran the risk of attracting adverse press attention and courting controversy, but could possibly 'alienate both present and future benefactors'.[25]

As a consequence, the acceptance of any private donation such as Courtauld's by the nation's art galleries required careful management, for it opened out onto conflicting sets of attitudes held by different art audiences towards private patronage, professional expertise and public standards of taste. To signal one instance of opposition to such developments, Clive Bell had railed in his *Art* against the rising influence of museum staff with their 'professional sensibility' and the vagaries of 'cultivated, middle class opinion'. Rallying Bloomsbury supporters behind him, he declared:

> The money that the State at present devotes to the discouragement of Art had better be given to the rich . . . It is unthinkable that any Government should ever buy what is best in the work of its own age . . . for though a State may have amongst its employés men who can recognise a fine work of art, provided it be sufficiently old, a modern State will be careful to thwart and stultify their dangerously good taste. [State patronage] can benefit no one except the dealers . . . As for contemporary art, official patronage is the surest method of encouraging in it all that is most stupid and pernicious . . .[26]

He continued:

The cultured . . . who expect in every picture at least some reference to a familiar masterpiece, create, unconsciously enough, a thoroughly unwholesome atmosphere. For they are rich and patronising and liberal. They are the very innocent but natural enemies of originality . . . To be frank, cultivated people are no fonder of art than the Philistines.[27]

From 1923 to 1924, this opposition on the part of Bloomsbury artists, critics and their supporters towards what Fry and Bell castigated as the tastes of 'trained professionalism' on the one hand and 'bourgeois commercialism' on the other, were to become more entrenched. In the face of rising market demand and growing speculative investment in modern art, particularly the amazing prices paid for modern French painting,[28] Fry's and Bell's assertion of the autonomy of art and the non-commercial and 'gratuitous' nature of 'authentic patronage' (as opposed to the financially motivated interest of 'indiscriminate patronage') appeared less and less sustainable. Their arguments came under increasing attack in the press from dissenting critics and from vociferous wider middle-class audiences whose attitudes towards private donations and artistic taste were at odds with the Bloomsbury stance.[29]

Against this background, Samuel and Elizabeth Courtauld's positions are revealing. From 1923, the pace of their acquisition of major works by French Impressionist and Post-Impressionist artists for their private collection quickened considerably, reaching its most intense pitch in 1926–8, when market values and critical estimation were at their height. These years also corresponded to increasing levels of profit for the Courtauld company: in 1928, it reached the apex of its inter-war stock-market valuation and gained a reputation as 'the stock exchange sensation of the year'.[30] In addition, Courtauld was alert to the fluctuations in the exchange rate between France and Britain, and prepared to take advantage of it when in his (or the nation's) favour.[31]

It was, however, John Maynard Keynes, in an article published in the *Nation and Athenaeum* in 1923 (reprinted below, text no. 19, pp. 238–9), who used the Courtauld Gift as an opportunity to refocus these debates about private patronage onto the imbalances that had resulted in the representation of work by British and foreign artists within the nation's museums. Whilst Keynes commended the Tate's acceptance of Courtauld's gift of French Impressionist and Post-Impressionist painting as a move in the right direction, and praised the benevolence of private collectors such as Courtauld, Lord Henry Bentinck and Michael Sadler for employing their own wealth (rather than state revenues) to fill 'the great and notorious gap in our national collections', he, nevertheless, drew attention to the inadequate view of modern European art history that British institutions gave. Highlighting the absence of examples of contemporary French painting in the Tate Gallery's collection, he argued that it was the responsibility of the National and Tate galleries to redress this situation. Speculating as to how this 'exclusion' had come about, and whether or not it was a case of financial cost, institutional mismanagement or conflicts of taste, Keynes urged:

Would it not be well to secure first-rate specimens of (for example) Derain, Picasso and Matisse, whilst they can still be purchased at a comparatively modest figure . . . ? . . . the position of these original geniuses in the development of European painting is already sufficiently secure to justify their representation in the National Museums.

In drawing attention to the lack of recent work (i.e., Cubist or post-Cubist works) by 'living' artists like Derain, Picasso and Matisse in any of the recent donations to the Tate, Keynes was underlining the drawbacks of too great a reliance upon private wealth and the limitations of its 'conservative' tastes in modern art. Whilst the boards of the National and Tate galleries had recently welcomed the Wertheimer and Courtauld donations of critically acclaimed, mainly late nineteenth-century British and French artists, they were hardly exemplars of daring patronage or avant-garde taste. As Keynes noted, the Courtauld Gift, for example, contained no Cubist or post-Cubist work. In the absence of increased government funding and faced with rising market prices, as Keynes was aware, the national institutions themselves were hardly in a financial position to be able to purchase such kinds of work even if they wanted to.[32]

This question of the shifting status of Cubism (as raised by Keynes and as demonstrated through its conspicuous absence in both Britain's major public collection and Courtauld's private collection) requires further attention and two features need to be underscored. First, as early as the second Post-Impressionist show organised by Fry and held in London in October 1912, there had been a reticence on the part of Fry to engage fully with the implications of Cubism as an artistic practice for Bloomsbury aesthetic theories. This exhibition, as Stella Tillyard has argued, signalled a crucial change in historical emphasis.[33] It marked a move away from Cézanne, van Gogh and Gauguin being accredited equal status in Post-Impressionist developments in France towards one in which the pre-eminence of Cézanne was asserted. This carried implications for the kinds of contemporary French art that were most enthusiastically endorsed by Bloomsbury in the post-war period, namely the work of Derain, Herbin, Marchand, Lhote and Matisse. With Cézanne's painting held up as formal exemplar, Bloomsbury art writers constructed a history of modern European art in which the importance of Cubist work was sidelined and criticised as 'formulaic'. As a result of these historiographical revisions, Cubism had not been comprehensively assimilated by the art writers and artists of Bloomsbury or their supporters. Nor had any adequate critical language been developed by Bloomsbury with which to evaluate Cubism's concerns beyond the version, modelled on the example of Cézanne's art, that Fry had earlier supplied.

Second, what also emerges within critical discourse in 1918–22 is that, apart from Bloomsbury support for its own artists and their brand of English Post-Impressionism, evidence of references to pre-war avant-garde subjects or vocabularies (such as Cubism, Futurism or Vorticism) was extensively attacked by a wide range of critics as retrograde and 'old-fashioned'.[34] As the *Sunday Daily Telegram* and *Drawing* critic declared, 'Futurism and Vorticism . . . have all gone under and we are in the full swing of a classical reaction, "Back to Ingres" [is] the watchword.'[35] For its part, *The World* drew attention to the fact that 'Cubist leaders [were] returning to the sober path of classicism'.[36] Christopher Nevinson's abandoning of his earlier Futurist-inspired machine aesthetic and his rejection of Cubist-informed spatial dislocations attracted extensive coverage in the press as an example of this 'return to academicism'. As the artist reportedly put it: 'I have now given up Futurism and am devoting my time to legitimate art.'[37]

Many of the other forums for contemporary art in Britain were also hesitant in their support for post-war Cubist-informed art, if not totally antagonistic to it. The Royal Academy was widely seen as a centre of entrenched conservatism and 'unaware of what [was] happening in the world around it'. Following the election of Sir Aston Webb as its president in 1919, artists and critics alike derided it for 'not only [being] dead, but deadening' and for 'being hopelessly out of touch with modern aspirations'.[38] Critics also rounded on art groups and exhibition societies which had been seen as dynamic and innovative in pre-war days, for their lack-lustre post-war performance. And depending upon the critic's particular standpoint and allegiance, exhibitors were condemned for being 'isolated from the rest of Europe . . . and a backwater' (the New English Art Club);[39] for upholding 'debilitated futurism . . . the graveyard of all the isms'(the Allied Artists Association);[40] as 'too often consciously imitating Cezanne's mannerisms' (the London Group),[41] or for producing 'well-worn novelties' (the Friday Club).[42]

The Bloomsbury group's continued post-war espousal of 'anglicised' forms of French Post-Impressionism and its 'cult of Cézanne' stood out against these trends of abandoning pre-war artistic positions and of artists distancing themselves from their earlier ethical commitments and aesthetic beliefs. As art galleries and art associations began to display more modern art, Bloomsbury supporters were active in promoting Post-Impressionism as 'very much alive' and still 'compelling our attention'.[43] Exemplified by the work of Duncan Grant and Vanessa Bell with its domestic English subject matter and informal 'conversational' portraits, a string of monographs, articles and reviews by Fry and Bell in the *New Statesman* and the *Studio* worked to reaffirm the artistic credentials and aesthetic merits of this on-going tradition of Anglo-French modernism. Similarly, Bell's *Art* and *Since Cézanne* (1922), and Fry's *Vision and Design* (1920) and *Transformations* (1926) mapped out the art-historical trajectory within which such work and its 'Anglo-Frenchness' was to be located and understood.[44]

When Courtauld first saw examples of Cézanne's work from the Davies collection in an exhibition entitled *The French School of the Last 100 Years* at the Burlington Fine Arts Club in 1922 and bought Marchand's *Saint-Paul* and Renoir's *Woman at her Toilet* (cat. nos 28 and 43) in September of that year, his approach to modern French painting had already been prepared by such ideas (probably Bell's essay 'The Debt to Cézanne' in *Art* and Fry's two essays 'Jean Marchand' and 'Renoir' in *Vision and Design*).[45] However, whilst Courtauld's change in taste embraced Degas, the 'Louvre' classicists and Italian 'old masters' (probably paralleling Fry's admiration for what he called early Italian 'primitives') as well as these modern French artists' work, it evidently did not extend to Cubist work (unlike Keynes who bought Braque's *Cubist design* in the same year).[46] Courtauld's purchase of Marchand's work needs to be set alongside the reading of his work given by Fry, who had characterised him as 'the most traditional of revolutionaries', and Fry's reservations about the value of Cubism: 'Cubism, like St Paul, has been all things to all men . . . To some it has been a doctrine and a revelation; to some it has been a convenient form of artistic journalism; to some it has been a quick road to notoriety; to some an aid to melodramatic effect.'[47] By the time Courtauld bought

Matisse's *Dancer* (fig. 28.) and Picasso's early *Child with a Pigeon* (cat. no. 35) in June and October 1928, even though Fry's evaluation of Cubism had not been substantially revised and he still castigated some of Matisse's work as 'decorative', Bloomsbury attitudes towards both artists work had shifted considerably, and their importance in the evolution of modern French painting had been established.[48]

*　　*　　*

Courtauld's endorsement of a cosmopolitan brand of Anglo-French modernism supported by Bloomsbury art writers and identified with the London Group and the London Artists' Association, drew him into art debates that expressed the fierce and complex national and cultural rivalries of the period. These reached their most vehement in the second half of the decade. There were accusations in the press, spearheaded by R.H. Wilenski amongst others, that the Anglo-French taste of Bloomsbury in general, and Fry's and Bell's promotion of French modernism in particular, worked against the interests of British art, and by implication was 'anti-patriotic'. In one such article in *Britannia* in 1928, Wilenski criticised the 'elite' Francophile taste of Bloomsbury and linked it to issues of French 'protectionism' in the arts and 'double-standards' on the part of the French government, which exported its own modern art, but discriminated against British artists and art dealers when exhibiting and selling British art in Paris:

> There is a prejudice in artistic circles . . . in favour of contemporary French art, or rather of the present day art that comes from Paris . . . No sensible man will wish to prevent the exhibition and sale here of the best or most interesting modern works of art from Paris . . . No man who respects art will protest if English collectors acquire works by [foreign] artists of distinction. But every fair-minded man must regret that no similar opportunities of increasing their fame and their bank-balances are habitually given to British artists in Paris.[49]

This outburst needs to be located in the context of a public debate that had been set in motion by Duveen at the beginning of January 1926. In a letter addressed to the Prime Minister, Stanley Baldwin, published in *The Times*, Duveen had launched a patriotic 'Campaign for the Support of British Art'. In summary, Duveen's letter argued that if the condition of Britain's art and the vitality of its art patronage were an 'infallible measure of national health', then urgent help was needed. In Britain, he commented, although artists were actively producing work, British buyers preferred to buy Old Masters at very high prices or to 'patronise foreign schools'. Thus the market for modern British art was in a dire state – a situation that contrasted starkly with the buoyant markets for modern art in France and the United States. Duveen, therefore, urged the British government to take action in ways similar to the French government, namely by commissioning decorative schemes financed by central and local government, by promoting British art in foreign markets and sponsoring art exhibitions and by encouraging an expanding art market through financial incentives. He then rounded on the British middle classes who, he stressed, could equally be held responsible for this state of affairs. In patriotic tones, Duveen called upon them to 'do their duty' as art patrons and, however limited in income, to 'encourage British art by every means in their power'.

In reply, the Prime Minister, although making reference to the work of the Fine Art Commission in supporting artists, refused to draw comparisons with France and America, and rejected the proposal of state intervention in the art market. Instead, he maintained that it was the responsibility of the artist and not the government to 'stimulate' the British public into buying his art.[50] This exchange of letters produced a huge amount of correspondence in the national press as artists, art writers and critics, government officials and museum directors, art dealers and collectors entered into the debate, using it as a benchmark to assess the success of the post-war transition from state-sponsored patronage of the arts to a free-market economy. This correspondence was summarised with additional responses, including a brief comment from Courtauld himself, in *Drawing and Design* in March 1926.[51]

The background to this, put briefly, was that the 1914–18 war had substantially disrupted the conventional educational and career patterns for artists and had broken up pre-war avant-garde group formations.[52] Under the auspices of government agencies such as the British War Memorials Scheme, Wellington House and the Imperial War Museum, many male artists had either volunteered or been conscripted into the armed forces. Those who worked as artists, illustrators or designers on propaganda projects for the Ministry of Information were subject to state-monitored censorship controls (operated under the Defence of the Realm Act). As a result, many artists were encouraged to adapt their pre-war artistic rhetorics and styles to the changed requirements.[53] Art critics judging the evidence of war-time and immediate post-war art exhibitions believed that such state interventionism had stunted artistic innovation and ossified creativity, producing work that 'tended to be toned down to official dullness in order to meet the requirements of military . . . etiquette'.[54]

Following demobilisation, the demand for patriotic commemorative designs – the 'war memorial business' – and local-authority commissions to revive public mural painting or decorative projects (such as the schemes for Leeds Town Hall or St Stephen's Hall, Westminster) had given a limited number of artists employment.[55] However, in the long term, the government had maintained that the return to a free-market economy for art was the most effective means of generating work for artists, 'kick starting' the art market and revitalising British art. High levels of unemployment amongst artists (most acute in 1921–4), fears about a 'culture drain' of works of art abroad (especially 'Old Masters' to the United States) and the assertion of the superiority of modern French art (conspicuously supported by Bloomsbury critics and by important London dealers) had raised doubts about the effectiveness of such a policy.

These anxieties resurfaced in a slightly different context, in a report on Britain's representation at the 1925 Paris International Exhibition of Industrial Art and its standards when set against the work of other nations 'in international rivalry'. Similar reservations about the inferior condition of British art, its conservative 'dullness' and 'absence of spirit' and the need for 'a searching self-examination' on the part of the government, were noted:

[H]ow far . . . do the qualities observed in the British section imply a degree of rigidity and ossification? . . . How far again is

the British reluctance to break with past practice a sign of the vigorous persistence of living tradition, or how far is it the mere clinging of a parasitic plant which has lost the power of independent growth of life? These are grave questions . . .[56]

It was against these fears about national artistic decline and competition from France that Courtauld's support for modern French painting had attracted such interest and his 'patriotism' had been brought into question.

Courtauld's brief response to Duveen's letter, published with other responses in *Drawing and Design* in March 1926, was that 'what [was] primarily needed was the education of the public taste'.[57] Among the other responses, two relate particularly closely to Courtauld's position. The first of these, from Roger Fry in a letter to *The Times*, argued that in order to promote British art, 'enlightened self-interest' practised by patrons of recognised good taste should be encouraged. Echoing Bell's sentiments (discussed earlier), Fry warned of the dire consequences of handing over the responsibility for art patronage either to the State and its museum professionals, or to the majority of the middle class public. He railed that such patronage 'by ignorant and self-satisfied patrons [was] worse than sheer indifference to art' for it 'choked' the museums of England with 'munificent purchases of . . . indiscriminate buying'. 'Preserve us', he concluded, 'from philanthropic generosity, Ministries of Fine Art, committees of taste and other such expensive machinery of state'.[58]

The second response, from the secretary to the London Artists' Association, R.A.W. Bicknell, drew attention to the formation the previous July of a group of influential collectors of modern pictures to lend financial support to British artists 'in whose talents and reputations they had faith'.[59] Courtauld, with Keynes, Hindley Smith and L.H. Myers, formed the committee members of this association. According to Keynes, the LAA was 'a small organisation formed on co-operative principles' whose chief aim was to 'get a better market in the long run' for British artists' work. Each artist received a guaranteed income of £150 per year and any sales attracted a commission, which was then ploughed back into the group's funds.[60] To generate public interest and finance its activities, the LAA regularly held three or four exhibitions each year. As a result, between 1925 and 1930, it sold more than seven hundred works, raising over £22,000. Whilst it priced its works modestly to attract a wider audience, the Association's most consistent patrons were all well-known British private collectors: Edward Marsh, Montague Shearman, Lord Ivor Churchill, Joseph Duveen, Sir Michael Sadler, Lord Henry Bentinck and the Earl of Sandwich, as well as Courtauld and Keynes.[61]

In many respects, Courtauld's involvement with the LAA gained him a public reputation as a 'patron' of British art and could be interpreted as an altruistic gesture designed on some level to offset allegations mentioned earlier of the 'unpatriotic' nature of his pro-French taste. Courtauld was also active within other ventures that supported contemporary British art. He was elected to the committee of the Contemporary Art Society from 1924 to 1948. With Hugh Walpole, Courtauld financially backed the *Daily Express* Young Artists' Exhibition in June 1927, and he acted as a financial advisor to the East London Art Group, an art society of 'East London working people' which held classes at Bow and

Bromley Commercial Institute, often with Sickert as a tutor, and which arranged open exhibitions at the Whitechapel Art Gallery in 1928 and the Alex. Reid and Lefèvre Galleries in 1929.[62]

Nevertheless, in comparison with the sums he spent on modern French painting, Courtauld's expenditure on modern British art was extremely modest. He bought works from LAA and London Group shows by Vanessa Bell, Duncan Grant, Keith Baynes and William Roberts, amongst others. He purchased also works by John Armstrong, Paul Nash, Winifred Nicholson, Glyn Philpot and Walter Sickert from leading London dealers such as the Leicester Galleries and the Independent Gallery in the 1920s. This choice of works signalled a preference for the work of Bloomsbury artists or for works by 'English Impressionists' such as Sickert which drew on late nineteenth-century French modernism.

Since all of the original artist-members of the LAA were associated with the pro-French Allied Artists' Association or the London Group, a predominantly Bloomsbury-backed group, and two of its leading artists, Vanessa Bell and Duncan Grant, like Keynes himself, were Bloomsbury members, it is hardly surprising that their exhibitions attracted attention as an important forum for Anglo-French modernism. A review by Bell in *Vogue* in 1926 commended the work of Bell, Grant, Fry, Baynes, Adeney, Porter and Dobson for 'plunging boldly into the European stream' and engaging with the work of Cézanne and 'the movement that derives from him'. Characterising such work as showing 'an inestimable superiority of not being provincial' by having been through a 'French apprenticeship', Bell then praised it for displaying a temperament 'unmistakably British'. From the evidence of the exhibition, he continued, it is clear that these 'are the children and grand children of Cézanne, but they form hands across a century with our national tradition'.[63]

This re-framing of Bloomsbury's 'Anglo-Frenchness' in a way to stress forcefully its allegiances to a 'patriotic British tradition' was further reinforced by Bell in a review of an LAA exhibition in *Artwork* in 1926. Evaluating the work of Grant, Bell and Fry, he wrote that 'the natural sincerity of these English painters has been confirmed and encouraged by the example of Cézanne and his disciples'. Then, drawing favourable comparisons between Bell and Constable, and between Grant and Gainsborough, he concluded:

these artists [of the LAA] are still accused by stupid and ignorant people of being Frenchified and exotic . . . they did turn [earlier in their careers] to the modern movement and to be sure that movement was essentially French . . . But they are adult now. They have found themselves. And themselves . . . are as you would have expected profoundly British. These artists have jumped the Slade and Pre-Raphaelite puddles to join hands with their ancestors – Hogarth, Gainsborough, Crome, Cotman and Constable. Wherefore if the English tradition exists anywhere, it exists in the London Association. Here is the nucleus of a modern British school![64]

For Courtauld, the stylistic internationalism displayed in LAA exhibitions with its indebtedness to the Bloomsbury brand of Anglo-French modernism and to French Post-Impressionism, marked out a set of artistic concerns on the part of British artists in the second half of the 1920s, which underscored not only the artistic prestige of his own collection and of the Courtauld gift to the nation,

but also registered the importance of his supportive role as both patron and collector of contemporary British art.

Although the Courtaulds continued to buy reasonably priced British works at a reduced rate after 1929, purchases of modern French painting were dramatically curtailed during the Depression. The impact of the Wall Street crash in October 1929 upon Courtauld's American investments and its negative consequences for the British economy through to 1933 meant that the 'great rayon boom' had ended.[65] Even though Courtauld's private wealth remained considerable, between the end of 1929 and 1936 (when Courtaulds' profit and share prices showed a sustained growth and sterling regained its pre-slump exchange level), few paintings were added to the collection. The death of Elizabeth Courtauld in December 1931 was another key factor. In addition, there was Courtauld's financial support in the setting up of the Courtauld Institute of Art, negotiations for which had commenced with London University in 1928; it opened in 1932 and in that year Courtauld donated £70,000 to it for the purpose of housing and maintaining his 'private' art collection.[66]

*   *   *

In April 1935, the art journal the *Studio* published an editorial entitled 'What next in Art?' which drew attention to the conservative shift in cultural attitudes that had occurred in Britain as a result of the Depression. Three features were identified as conspicuous and interrelated. First, there had been a decline in the importance of Paris as a leading centre for modern art. Making reference to an article by Clive Bell in the same issue, the editorial stated that 'It is becoming apparent that the phase of Twentieth century art called Post-Impressionism has run its course . . . Clive Bell tells us that the unquestioned supremacy of Paris is waning . . . and turns our eyes to America as the source from which a new revival may be hoped.'[67] It concluded that, as Bell had signalled, there was an urgent need to seek out a new artistic centre from which the refurbishment of modern art might come, particularly in the light of the exodus since 1933 of artists and intellectuals from Germany and Austria. Whilst some art writers promoted London's case as a dynamic arts centre, other British artists and writers saw these changes differently. They focused attention instead on the Soviet Union as a source of alternative artistic models, or, encouraged by the arrival of refugees from the Bauhaus, turned to the artistic and architectural inheritances of Weimar Germany as a means of revitalising their work.[68]

The second feature, linked to these redirections, was the reorientation of British art criticism away from French modernism as the yardstick of artistic and aesthetic standards. The pre-eminent position of Bloomsbury as the arbiter of 'advanced taste' in modern art declined as the serious impact of the slump upon artistic production was felt. Its negative effect upon artists' employment opportunities and the art market undermined the Bloomsbury claim that 'Art' was an autonomous sphere of activity distinct from and unaffected by wider social and economic factors.[69] Following the resignation of Grant, Bell and Baynes from the London Artists Association in 1931 (which had acrimonious consequences), Keynes's withdrawal of support for the group in October 1933 precipitated its closure. The loss of one of the most prestigious public platforms for the Bloomsbury position was compounded in 1934 by the death of Roger Fry, one of its most persuasive and energetic publicists.

A third feature of the Depression years was the diminishing number of wealthy connoisseur patrons active in the art market. As the *Listener* in February 1934 had noted, 'The private patron of art disappears like mist in a storm'.[70] In their place, there was a substantial growth in corporate patronage and the emergence of a new audience for modern art composed of younger, metropolitan middle-class buyers who purchased modern art primarily as decorations for the home.[71] This trend was spotlighted in a series of four articles published in the *Listener* in September 1935 under the title 'Patronage in Art Today'. In the first of these, Roger Hinks emphasized how the precarious financial positions of both artist and patron had had an impact upon the kinds of artwork currently being produced. He wrote that,

[J]ust as economists are now concerned above all with the problems of consumption, so those who reason about the nature of art are driven to devote more and more of their attention to the problem of patronage and its formative effect on the work of art . . . Above all, [the artist] must be abused of the notion that great works of art are produced by aesthetic emotion alone . . . [and] remain in immediate contact with everyday life and its immediate wants.[72]

In the final article in the series, Jack Beddington, the publicity manager for Shell-Mex and B.P. Limited, emphasized how 'collective or commercial patronage' of the arts by State or semi-public corporations had largely rendered the role formerly occupied by the 'grand private patron' redundant: 'The day of the grand private patron of the arts is over . . . in his place has come a patron, still private, but on a much smaller scale [who] buys (but rarely commissions) a few pictures (small) that he fancies will look well on the walls of the rooms of his flat.' Artists, he advised, would do well to study such shifts in patronage and changes in taste carefully, and to modify their work and expectations accordingly.[73] As the *Studio* had succinctly phrased it earlier, 'Britain is looking for British pictures of British people, of British landscapes . . . a thorough going nationalism'.[74]

Sandwiched between these texts, two articles by Osbert Sitwell and Edward Marsh, both distinguished private collectors, reviewed these trends from different perspectives. Whilst Marsh, predominantly a collector of modern British art, displayed a benevolent attitude towards the conservative tastes of the corporate patron and younger middle-class buyers,[75] Sitwell, who had written an eloquent article on Courtauld's private collection in 1925 (reprinted below, text no. 24, pp. 241–3), adopted a far less accommodating tone. Taking issue with Hinks, he regretted the dwindling status of the 'grand private patron', whose fine judgement could never be replicated by the new industrialists, arts administrators or professional broadcasters. When faced with precarious finances such as experienced during the Slump, Sitwell argued, what was the illustrious patron to do: donate his collection to the museum, 'as though it were the annex of his own house', where it would become like 'a limpet' cramped in 'arid corridors' incongruously alongside other collections, or sell through the 'gates of the Lefevre Gallery or of Bernheim Jeune' to the 'millionaire collectors?' The withering away of the connoisseur patron as custodian of standards of taste was,

for Sitwell, symptomatic of cultural degeneration and the invasiveness of 'middle-brow' taste. Turning to its implications for art patronage, Sitwell inveighed:

In future the happy artist will be obliged to depend, instead of upon the whim of a proud and often crotchety individual – upon for instance, Charles I, Horace Walpole, or the late all-consuming, Mr. Pierpont Morgan – on the informed taste of the Town Council, the Museums and the B.B.C. . . . I for one regret the change. Those bodies who, for the public good, intrude – no doubt rightly – upon the private ownership of land have invented a term to apply to the land which the owners agree to keep open in perpetuity for the use of the public: 'Will you agree to *sterilise* it?' they ask. And I find the term applicable too, to the works of art, many of them transcendent, which rot away in the galleries of museums and pinacothecas. Placed there they fail to fertilise the imagination . . . I would do almost anything, short of murder, to prevent any object I really loved from entering the sterilising precincts of a museum.[76]

It is against these debates about the demise of individualistic role models for the art patron that Courtauld's renewed activity in the art market in 1936–7 needs to be seen. Like a number of other private collectors, as Courtauld's financial circumstances improved (reflecting the growing recovery of corporate share prices and profits in Britain and the U.S.A.) and as advantage could be taken of the improved levels of currency exchange between sterling and the franc, works by late nineteenth century French artists such as Cézanne, Monet, Seurat and Pissarro with established critical reputations and rising market valuations were purchased.[77] Most of these later acquisitions for Courtauld's private collection were destined for private bequests, rather than the Institute's collection.

*　　*　　*

To return to the 1943 'Art and Education' speech with which this essay began, Courtauld concluded his remarks with a rhetorical flourish championing the cause of universal art education and increased accessibility to the arts as a means of breaking down social snobbery and class barriers: 'Moreover, the way to receive [Art's] gifts *can* be thrown open to all; it is not reserved for the wealthy, the idle and the learned . . .'[78]

Such a noble resolve anticipated the commitment to universal education that would be encapsulated in the 1944 Butler Education Act[79] and promoted a liberal-arts ethos that, in a different way, was to become embodied in the State-funded cultural agency, the Arts Council, established in 1946. Courtauld's greatest acts of benevolence to the nation, namely the gift of £50,000 to the Tate Gallery to establish a trust for the purchase of modern French paintings in 1923 and the founding of the Courtauld Institute of Art as part of the University of London in 1931, fell in line with these concerns. Both cases of generosity were made in order to encourage change in public attitudes towards art appreciation and art education (as Courtauld saw it, 'overcoming in Anglo-Saxon countries the idea that art is something effeminate' and not worthy of serious academic study) and to allow the general public greater access to modern art.[80]

And yet, Courtauld would not have wholeheartedly embraced the dominant post-war model of art patronage with its State management of the arts and increasing bureaucratisation either. For in his writings, he sustained very different attitudes towards art patronage from the Keynesian 'paternalistic' model of State-financing which was to become the dominant post-1945 form of art funding. Whilst seeming to approve of the aggrandizement of national institutions and expansion of art holdings through private donations, Courtauld was opposed to professionally administered artistic 'taste' supervised by 'art experts'.[81]

Paradoxically, Courtauld cherished a highly individualised form of cultivated amateurism, informed by Bloomsbury's cult of the amateur, which he identified with his own conception of the art patron as a 'layman' aesthete. As Courtauld's collection of predominantly Impressionist and Post-Impressionist paintings attests, such taste was most conspicuously identified with modern French painting before Cubism. To a lesser degree, it also accommodated works by British artists who sustained a commitment to that brand of 'Anglo-French' modernism that the London Artists' Association promoted and that corresponded to Bloomsbury support for artists such as Vanessa Bell, Duncan Grant and Keith Baynes, and embraced 'English Impressionist' painters such as Sickert.

As one reviewer of Courtauld's collection commented, 'every collection is a confession . . . a revelation of preferences and personal taste'.[82] In donating works to the Tate Gallery and, more particularly, in giving over his private collection and home in Portman Square to the Courtauld Institute, Courtauld opened up his 'private' artistic judgement and aesthetic values to public scrutiny. At different historical moments throughout the inter-war years and since, the appropriateness of Courtauld's 'layman' model for the art patron, the validity of his Anglo-French taste in modernism and the benefits that his donation has brought to the nation's art collections and its cultural life have come under examination. Whilst both collections divulge in different ways Courtauld's personal 'anatomy of taste', they are equally revealing about the wider historical and cultural forces that underpin changes in artistic judgement and frame public attitudes towards art patronage and art education. These factors continue to shape the content of our national collections and to condition our understanding of modern art and its histories in the 1990s.

NOTES

I am indebted to the Tate Gallery Archives, and particularly to Jennifer Booth, and to the Archives of the Whitechapel Art Gallery.

1. Samuel Courtauld, *Ideals and Industry: War-Time Papers*, Cambridge, 1949, p. 45.
2. *Ibid.*, p. 52.
3. *Ibid.*, p. 49.
4. *Ibid.*, p. 45.
5. Anthony Blunt, 'Samuel Courtauld as Collector and Benefactor', in Douglas Cooper, *The Courtauld Collection*, London, 1954, p. 6.
6. Clive Bell, *Art*, London 1914, reprint edited by J.B. Bullen, Oxford 1987, pp. 291.
7. For the complexities of examining 'Bloomsbury', see Raymond Williams, 'The Bloomsbury fraction', in *Problems in Materialism and Culture*, London, 1980, pp. 148–69.
8. For further analysis of the importance of Bloomsbury art writers in establishing the terms of aesthetic debates in the 1920s, see Simon Watney, 'The Connoisseur as Gourmet: The Aesthetics of Roger Fry and Clive Bell', in *Formations of Pleasure*, London, 1983, pp. 66–83.
9. Courtauld, 1949 (cited in note 1), p. 48.
10. For an extensive account of how 'Bloomsbury's' brand of English modernism was heavily indebted to Arts and Crafts ideology, see Stella Tillyard, *The Impact of Modernism 1900–20: Early Modernism and the Arts and Crafts Movement in Edwardian England*, London, 1988.
11. Courtauld, 1949 (cited in note 1), pp. 46, 51–2, 57.
12. *Ibid.*, p. 52.
13. The record prices paid for British 'Old Master' paintings attracted widespread press coverage in the early 1920s, particularly when an increasing number of country-house collections such as the Donaldson and Michelham collections (June 1925 and September 1926) achieved record prices at auction for works by Gainsborough, Reynolds, Romney and other eighteenth-century painters. When many works were exported abroad, mostly to the United States, concern about an 'art drain' led to calls for government controls on export licences to stem the flood. At the time of the transfer of the Leverhulme sale to New York in September 1925, further alarm was expressed that London dealers were no longer financially able to handle the large sums involved and thus that the lucrative 'Old Masters' market would move to New York (see 'Unparalleled in the Annals of English Auctions', *Illustrated London News*, 26 September 1925, pp. 576–7). The high prices of works by Gainsborough are noted in Bruce Arnold, *Orpen, Mirror to an Age*, London, 1981, p. 393. For a historical assessment of this type of connoisseur taste, see Christopher Hussey, *The Picturesque: Studies in a Point of View*, London, 1927.
14. Christopher Hussey, 'The Courtauld Institute of Art, 20 Portman Square', *Country Life*, 15 October 1932, pp. 428–33. Quotation from p. 433.
15. *The Times*, 27 October 1930, p. 13.
16. See Clive Bell, 'The Aesthetic Hypothesis', in Bell, 1914 (cited in note 6), pp. 3–37, especially pp. 6–7. For further discussion of Bloomsbury's system of personal aesthetics, see Watney, 1983 (cited in note 8), pp. 72–7, and Berel Lang, 'Significance or form: the Dilemma of Roger Fry's Aesthetic', *Journal of Aesthetics and Art Criticism*, winter 1962, pp. 167–76.
17. Courtauld, in a letter to Aitken, 27 March 1926 confirmed that P.M. Turner hung many of the pictures in Portman Square (Tate Gallery Archives).
18. 'Editorial', *Listener*, 23 March 1932, p. 409.
19. 'Opening of the Tate Gallery Extension by the King; Modern Foreign Art', *The Times*, 28 June 1926, p. 11.
20. *Ibid.*, p. 11.
21. This was the allegation made against Courtauld by Vera Bowen, as recorded in Harold Bowen's diary, 11, 17 June 1923. Quoted by Robert Skidelsky in *John Maynard Keynes*, II, London, 1992, p. 143. Samuel Courtauld's refusal of a peerage in 1937 Coronation Honours List refutes this interpretation, although he did accept an Honorary D.Litt. from London University in 1931 and was made an officer of the Légion d'honneur for his services to French art by the French government in 1933.
22. See Bell's attack on the artistic perspective of 'insular' art patrons in 'Wilcoxism', *New Republic*, 3 March 1920, pp. 21–3, and Fry's condemnation of 'new money' for approaching art like stock-market bonds in *Vision and Design*, London, 1920, reprint Oxford, 1981, p. 43.
23. 'The Final Report of the Commission on National Museums and Art Galleries', in *Parliamentary Papers*, (VI: *Reports from Commissioners, Inspectors and Others (1929/30)*, London, 1930, part 1, p. 10, quoted in Janet Minihan, *The Nationalization of Culture: The Development of Subsidies to the Arts in Great Britain*, London, 1977, p. 182.
24. In a series of exchanges in the *Morning Post* in January 1921 about the precarious state of modern 'Art in England', the professional integrity of the museum curator came under scrutiny. It was claimed that, alongside the art critic and dealer, museum directors were aiding speculative returns by encouraging patrons to buy 'foreign art' rather than work by British artists.

In 'Art and the Money Changers' (13 January 1921), the *Morning Post* critic alleged that by setting artistic fashions and legitimising taste, 'Public Art Gallery Directors and officials, [were] either acting as dealers on their own account or as commissioned touts for the "trade"'. He commented that 'Traffic of this nature still goes on, unfortunately, but it would be untrue to say that all Art Gallery Directors and officials were or are engaged in this pernicious habit of bartering'.

25. Letter from C.J. Holmes, Director of National Gallery, to Aitken, 3 January 1924 (Tate Gallery Archives).

26. Bell 1914 (cited in note 6), pp. 254–5.

27. *Ibid.*, pp. 270–2.

28. See 'The Amazing Sale', *Illustrated London News*, 1 August 1925, and Fry's 'A Sale at Christies', *Nation and Athenaeum*, 14 August 1926, p. 556.

29. See Fry, 1926 (cited in note 28), p. 556, on the relationship between artistic merit and market values, and the inadequacies of patronage practices of the 'newly enriched'.

30. *The Economist*, 25 February 1928, cited in D.C. Coleman, *Courtaulds: An Economic and Social History*, II, Oxford, 1969, p. 256.

31. A letter from Samuel Courtauld to Aitken dated 18 March 1924 about payment to Fénéon, signals his awareness of fluctuations in exchange rate between sterling and the franc, and its effect upon price levels for modern art (Tate Gallery Archives).

32. When the galleries of British art at the Tate Gallery were reopened after the war, in 1921, many critics acclaimed the collection as 'really modern' and 'up-to-date'. This judgement was based on the holdings of work by John, Orpen, Steer, Spencer, Nevinson and others. In the *Observer* (19 June 1921), P.G. Konody, whilst commending the efforts of the Contemporary Art Society, the Imperial War Museum and private lenders, drew attention to the problem that the 'Victorian academicism' of the Chantrey Bequest posed to such claims.

33. Tillyard, 1988, (cited in note 10), pp. 175–80.

34. For an example of this reassessment of pre-war radical art languages and their continued survival in post-war British art, see Percy Wyndham Lewis's article 'What Art now?', published in the *English Review*, April 1919, where he speculates that 'The war drove all the great pictures off the surface of the earth and into the cellars of the museums. And it drove all the arts underground. They now come up; a little wan and blinking some of them. What are they going to do now? we are asked. Have their houses been damaged and destroyed in the interim? If so, how are they going to rebuild them? Same architects as before?'(Reprinted in Paul Edwards (ed.), *Wyndham Lewis: Creatures of Habit and Creatures of Change; Essays on Art, Literature and Society 1914–56*, Santa Rosa, 1989, p. 46.)

35. *Sunday Evening Telegram*, 29 June 1919, reprinted in *Drawing*, August 1919. In October–November 1919, the exhibition *French Art 1914–19* at Heal's Mansard Gallery was acclaimed by art writers as the most representative show of modern French art in London since 1914. It gave critics an opportunity to draw parallels between French and British developments over the same period and to signal a shared 'return to neo-classicism' and academicism. For surveys of French art examining these changes, see: Christopher Green, *Cubism and its Enemies: Modern Movements and Reactions in French Art 1916–28*, New Haven and London, 1987; Kenneth Silver, *Esprit de Corps: The Art of the Parisian Avant-garde and the First World War, 1914–25*, London, 1989; and Elizabeth Cowling and Jennifer Mundy, *On Classic Ground: Picasso, Leger, de Chirico and the New Classicism 1910–30*, London (Tate Gallery), 1990.

36. Review in *The World*, 22 March 1919. Many critics argued that Cubist and Futurist languages were inappropriate for war paintings and that the vehemence of the war had 'subdued' progressive attitudes and art languages (notably ignoring the evidence of many works by Wyndham Lewis, William Roberts and Richard Nevinson). The 'failure' of the 'Group X' show at the Mansard Gallery in March–April 1920 was used to corroborate such claims about the collapse of the pre-war vorticist *avant-garde*. See Charles Harrison, *English Art and Modernism 1900–1939*, London, 1981, pp. 156–60.

37. Interview with Nevinson in the *Illustrated Chronicle*, 22 January 1919.

38. See Theo Cowdell, 'The Role of the Royal Academy in British Art 1918–30', unpublished Ph.D. thesis, University of London, 1980. Quotation from P.G. Konody, *Observer*, 1 May 1926, in Cowdell, p. 194.

39. Review of the New English Art Club exhibition, *Guardian* 6 June 1918.

40. Review of Allied Artists' Association exhibition, *The Truth*, 24 July 1918.

41. Review of the London Group exhibition by P.G. Konody, *Observer*, 3 November 1918.

42. Review of the Friday Club exhibition by P.G. Konody, *Observer*, 14 April 1918.

43. Frank Rutter, 'Modern French Painting', *The Sunday Times*, 10 August 1919.

44. For full list of Fry's publications in this period, see Donald A. Lang, *Roger Fry: An Annotated Bibliography of the Published Writings*, New York, 1979. For Bell, see Lang's 'A Checklist of the Published Writings of Clive Bell', in William G. Bywater, *Clive Bell's Eye*, Detroit, 1975. For Vanessa Bell, see Frances Spalding, *Vanessa Bell*, London, 1983; and for Grant, see Simon Watney, *The Art of Duncan Grant*, London, 1990. For a discussion of 'Bloomsbury' as a 'conversational community', see Lisa Tickner, 'The "Left-Handed Marriage", Vanessa Bell and Duncan Grant', in Whitney Chadwick and Isabelle de Courtivron (eds), *Significant Others: Creativity and Intimate Partnership*, London, 1993.

45. Bell, 1914 (cited in note 6), pp. 199–214, and Fry, 1920 (cited in note 22), pp. 195–8, 186–9.

46. Cooper, 1954 (cited in note 5), pp. 3–4.

47. Fry, 1920 (cited in note 22), pp. 195, 197.

48. It is important to distinguish between Fry's and Bell's approaches to Cubism in general and to Matisse's and Picasso's work in particular. Fry's writing drew upon his own changing practice as a painter, and this influenced his fluctuating attitudes towards the 'decorative' (especially in Matisse's work); whereas Bell's position as an art critic/journalist sustained a more entrenched attitude towards the division between 'art' and 'life', and drew upon his closer links with Picasso, Matisse and Derain when evaluating Cubism.

49. R.H. Wilenski, 'The Week Artistic', *Britannia*, 28 September 1928. See Wilenski's attack on Bell and his 'criterion of value' (and, by implication, on Bloomsbury's art theories and aesthetic judgements) in *The Modern Movement in Art*, London, 1927, pp. 150–2.

50. Duveen's earlier letter and the Prime Minister's reply were published in *The Times*, 22 January 1926.

51. 'A Campaign for the Support of British Art', *Drawing and Design*, March 1926, pp. 326–30.

52. This disruption extended not only to male artists enlisted into the Armed Forces, but to women artists drafted into the war effort at home and abroad. For an important study of the effect of such changes on women artists, their work and its reception, see Norwich Gallery, Norfolk Institute of Art and Design, *Ten Decades, Careers of Ten Women Artists born 1897–1906*, curated by Katy Deepwell, March–May 1992, and Deepwell's unpublished Ph.D. thesis, 'Women Artists in Britain between the Two World Wars', University of London, Birkbeck College, 1991, from which the exhibition catalogue draws its material.

53. For a broader examination of the effects of the war upon British art, see M. and S. Harries, *The War Artists: British Official War Art of the Twentieth Century*, London, 1983, and for its impact upon particular artists' work, see Sue Malvern, 'War as it is': The Art of Muirhead Bone, C.R.W. Nevinson and Paul Nash, 1916–17', *Art History*, December 1986, pp. 487–515.

54. *Daily Telegraph*, 4 May 1918.

55. For further discussion, see Cowdell, 1980 (cited in note 38), pp. 12–29.

56. Department of Overseas Trade, *Report on the Present Position and Tendencies of the Industrial Arts as indicated at the International Exhibition of Modern Decorators and Industrial Arts, Paris 1925*, London, 1925, pp. 37–8.

57. *Drawing and Design* (cited in note 51), p. 330.

58. Letter to *The Times*, 12 January 1926, p. 12.

59. *Drawing and Design* (cited in note 51), p. 327.

60. John Maynard Keynes, 'The London Artists' Association, its origins and aims', *The Studio*, November 1930, pp. 235–40. Quotation from p. 235.

61. The purchase accounts and stockbooks of the London Artists' Association are contained in the Keynes Library and Archive, King's College, Cambridge. For Keynes as a collector, see David Scrase and Peter Croft (eds), *Maynard Keynes, Collector of Pictures, Books and Manuscripts*, Cambridge (Fitzwilliam Museum), 1983.

62. For the activities of the Contemporary Art Society, see Contemporary Art Society, *British Contemporary Art 1910–1990*, London 1991; for Courtauld

and the *Daily Express* Young Artists' Exhibition, see the *Daily Express*, 10 June 1927, and for his involvement with the East London Art Group, *The Studio*, February 1929, p. 136. The catalogue to the group's first exhibition in December 1928 at the Whitechapel Art Gallery, London, lists Courtauld as a financial advisor. I am indebted to the Archive of the Whitechapel Art Gallery for this information.

63. Clive Bell, 'The Allied Artists' Exhibition at the Leicester Galleries', *Vogue*, late May 1926, pp. 64–6.

64. Clive Bell, 'A Reformation of the English School', *Artwork*, summer 1926, pp 1–5. Quotation from p. 5.

65. See Coleman, 1969 (cited in note 30), pp. 314–15.

66. See an earlier report on 'Art and the Expert', *The Times*, 27 October 1930, p. 13, which outlined the keen significance of Courtauld's generosity to British art-historical scholarship and to its international reputation. This article revealingly compared the Institute's future activities with the Fogg Institute at Harvard University and with the *Kunsthistoriches* institutes in Germany and Austria.

67. 'Editorial', *The Studio*, April 1935, p. 175, with article by Clive Bell on p. 176.

68. See Robert Radford, *Art for a Purpose: The Artists' International Association 1933–53*, Winchester, 1978, pp. 18ff.; Herbert Read's introduction to *Art and Industry: The Principles of Industrial Design*, London, 1935; and the essays in Betty Rea (ed.), *Five on Revolutionary Art*, London, 1935, as examples of these artistic and critical reorientations.

69. For a fuller account, see Andrew Stephenson, 'Strategies of Situation: British Modernism and the Slump *c.* 1929–34', *Oxford Art Journal*, XIV, no. 2, 1991, pp. 44–7.

70. Quoted in 'Help for American Artists', *Listener*, February 1934, which contrasted the Federal Arts Project in the United States with a lack of similar support from the British government for artists during the Depression.

71. See Jane Beckett, 'Circle: the theory and patronage of constructive art in the Thirties', in *Circle, Constructive Art in Britain 1934–40*, ed., Jeremy Lewison Cambridge (Kettle's Yard), 1982, pp. 12–15.

72. Roger Hinks, 'Patronage in Art Today' (Part 1), *Listener*, 4 September 1935, p. 385.

73. Jack Beddington, 'Patronage in Art Today' (Part 4), *Listener*, 25 September 1935, p. 527.

74. 'Editorial', *The Studio*, January–June 1932, p. 64.

75. Edward Marsh, 'Patronage in Art Today' (Part 3), *Listener*, 18 September 1935, pp. 487–8.

76. Osbert Sitwell 'Patronage in Art Today' (Part 2), *Listener*, 11 September 1935, pp. 419–21. Quoted from p. 419.

77. See Coleman, 1969 (cited in note 30), p. 315, for increased profitability of Courtaulds. For fluctuations in franc/sterling exchange rates, see S.N. Broadberry, *The British Economy between the Wars*, Oxford, 1976, p. 125.

78. Courtauld, 1949 (cited in note 1), p. 57.

79. R.A. Butler, the main instigator of the bill, was Courtauld's son-in-law.

80. Courtauld, 1949 (cited in note 1), pp. 46, 52.

81. For an interpretation of the Keynesian model and its application to the funding of the visual arts in post-war Britain, see Andrew Brighton, 'Art Currency', in *Current Affairs: British Sculpture and Painting in the 1980s*, Oxford (Museum of Modern Art), 1987, pp. 13–14.

82. Horace Shipp, 'The Courtauld Collection', *Apollo*, September 1947, p. 57.

THE COURTAULD FAMILY AND ITS MONEY

1594–1947

John Murdoch

DURING THE 1920s, SAMUEL COURTAULD[1] led a charmed life. In August 1921, he was elected Chairman of the long-established and prosperous family business, Courtaulds Ltd. He bought the lease of one of London's major town houses, 20 Portman Square (fig. 38), designed by Robert Adam, which soon became known for its 'socialite functions'.[2] He and his wife, Elizabeth (known familiarly as Lil), were much in demand for any public work that required the combination of enlightened views and great wealth. She was deeply involved at the Opera House, Covent Garden; he at the National Gallery and Tate Gallery.[3] He was an honoured familiar of politicians and of *bien-pensant* intellectuals and was known in London, Paris and New York as one of the truly formidable players in the international market for the best examples of recent French painting. By the end of the decade, his son-in-law, the young 'Rab' Butler who had married the Courtaulds' only daughter, Sydney, in 1926, was rising fast in the Conservative party. But also at the end of the decade, his wife became ill,[4] and she died on Christmas Day 1931. The economic outlook darkened as the Wall Street collapse was followed by recession and increasing protectionism world-wide. Though his public work and benefactions of all kinds continued, there is a sense in which that which had previously seemed miraculous had come to an end.

This narrative describes the background to the miraculous years of Samuel and Elizabeth Courtauld: how they happened and when they stopped; not – at least not in any profound sense – why they happened or stopped. There could be other narratives, about the intellectual and spiritual odyssey of Samuel, the scion of a refugee family, growing up against the background of the English Unitarian[5] connection of the nineteenth century; or, more speculatively, about the pain, loneliness and introspection of the widower in the 1930s. But Samuel was a private man, and there is little evidence to support a more personal account of him.[6] This, therefore, is an economic narrative, concentrating on the money that enabled Samuel, as a practical man, to make the impact he did on the history of British culture in the twentieth century.[7]

37 Samuel Courtauld IV, July 1936 (photo: Courtaulds p.l.c.).

47

38 20 Portman Square.

Early History: Huguenots.

The earliest ancestral record of the Courtaulds is in a document of 1594, referring to a Christophe Courtauld, 'marinier', who could not write and who signed his name with a mark. A resident of the Ile d'Oléron, one of the two islands that help to secure the entrance from the Atlantic to the important port city of La Rochelle, Christophe seems to have earned his livelihood from its sea-borne carrying trades.

Politically and economically, the date of Christophe's entry into the record coincides with a period of relative optimism and prosperity for La Rochelle after the violence of the religious wars in the 1560s and '70s. By this time the principal centre of the Reformation in France, the city had survived a long siege which followed the massacres of St Bartholomew's Day in 1572. The Protestant citizens had retained a measure of freedom of worship and, with the accession to the throne of France of the Protestant Henri IV in 1589, looked forward to a more general recovery of Protestant fortunes in Paris and the rest of France. But famously, Henri thought Paris 'worth a mass' and converted to Catholicism, and it was not until 1598 under heavy pressure from the Protestants of western France that he promulgated the Edict of Nantes, granting partial religious freedom, together with the civil rights to trade freely, inherit property and receive education, to Protestants throughout France.

These larger, national developments provide the background to an evident rise in the civic status and prosperity of the Courtaulds. Christophe's daughter Anne was married openly in a Protestant church in 1594, and his son Augustin[8] learnt to write. When Augustin's son, also Augustin,[9] married in 1619, the marriage contract was witnessed by four merchants, a lawyer and a judge. Wine and salt production were already by this date major businesses of western France, and La Rochelle, the safest port on the coast, was well placed to take advantage of the expanding trade with French Canada. In 1677, an inventory of the property of Sieur Pierre Courtauld,[10] shows that the family interests had expanded well beyond the marine carrying trade: the family was now landed, owning houses and a vineyard.

Despite the toleration extended to Protestants by the Edict of Nantes, the family's advance in status and fortune cannot have seemed secure. During the early part of the seventeenth century, La Rochelle remained the military bastion of Protestantism within France, a kingdom torn apart by religious civil wars. Privateers from La Rochelle attacked French commercial traffic, seized naval vessels and blockaded the Gironde. In 1627, Richelieu moved decisively against the city, cut off its commerce and forced its capitulation after a year's seige. Increasingly, the legally entrenched civil and religious rights of Protestants aroused the resentment of the Catholic majority, and from the middle years of the century a series of edicts and local regulations steadily eroded the position of the Protestants. Many emigrated, speeded by 'dragonnades', or attempts at forced conversion. Finally, on 18 October 1685, Louis XIV formally revoked the Edict of Nantes, offering to Protestants only the option of abjuring their beliefs to avoid further persecution.

It is said that some two hundred thousand Protestants – the Huguenots – fled, to the lasting enrichment of the states – Holland, Prussia, Switzerland and England – in which they settled. Pierre Courtauld, who was sixty five, was too old to flee and abjured, but his son Augustin,[11] having initially abjured also, took his young son and went to England. Possibly his hesitation was influenced by the illness of his first wife, Julie, the daughter of a local merchant-tailor whom he had married in 1677 and who died sometime between November 1685 and January 1687. In England in March 1689, he married another Protestant refugee, Esther Pothier, also from La Rochelle. Evidently bringing with him enough capital and experience of the trade, he established himself as a wine-cooper and vintner, but apprenticed his sons, Augustin[12] and Peter,[13] to the well-known Huguenot silversmith Simon Pantin.

Although Peter was admitted to the Goldsmiths Company in 1712, none of his silver survives. Augustin, on the other hand, who was admitted in 1708, was a highly successful businessman, working from premises in Church Street, off St Martin's Lane, with a distinguished clientele extending across Church and State. His work is in many ways typical of the best Huguenot silver.[14] It is massive, has the beauty and sophistication of finish associated with the French manufacture, but is austere in its avoidance of flamboyant *Régence* ornament. The series of presentation cups in the Courtauld Collection show Augustin perfectly attuned to an English market in which fine manners and 'breeding' were recognisable by their restraint, yet in which silver, displayed on formal occasions, functioned as an open statement of wealth and power (fig. 39). Augustin's son, Samuel,[15] was apprenticed to his father in 1734 and

39 Augustin Courtauld VI, The State Salt, 1730–1, Mansion House, London (photo: Goldsmith's Hall Library).

acquired or set up in 1782 just when the obsolescent and heavily regulated Spitalfields industry was coming under pressure from new producers using water- and steam-powered mills in areas of cheap labour. In 1785, he sold up and went to America, bought land and farmed it, manufactured pearl-ash, and on a brief trip back across the Atlantic, met his future wife Ruth Minton whom he married in New York in 1789. George remained in America, safe from a trade recession in which the silk mills of all his London correspondents stood idle; but soon after the birth of his son Samuel[20] in June 1793, he leased off his land and plant in America and returned to the silk business in England. By August 1794, he was working for another Huguenot silk throwster, Peter Nouaille, at his mills near Sevenoaks in Kent.

Nouaille is said to have been one of the pioneers of Italian-style crape production in England. George, with an eye to the increasing use of this crimped black crape for mourning, was much taken with the business, but the arrangement with Nouaille lasted for only three years. A convert to Unitarianism[21] and a passionate admirer of the Republican virtues as they seemed to be enshrined in the American Constitution and the French Revolution, George was out of step with the times in an England that was the paymaster of conservative Europe.

By 1799, after a brief spell in the paper business in London, he was back in silk, managing on behalf of a London firm, Witts and Co., a water-powered throwing mill at Pebmarsh in Essex. This lasted for some nine or ten years, during which protracted negotiations with Joseph Wilson, of the silk manufacturers Remington Wilson and Co. of Cheapside, were opened for the establishment of a throwing and crape-making business in Essex. Eventually, a site at Braintree was found, and a deed of partnership establishing the firm Wilson and Courtauld was signed in May 1809.

This stormy partnership, which was finally wound up in the Court of Chancery in 1818, led to the creation of a sizeable business, giving scope for all George's energies and inventiveness—in 1814, he patented a new double spindle for the production of 'organzine' yarn[22]—but also for some high-minded ineptitudes in managing the unskilled juvenile workforce. But, as a result of the Chancery battles of 1817–18, George's son, Samuel III, partner in a small throwing mill at Bocking near Braintree, emerged from his father's shadow, and fell in love with and married Ellen, the daughter of his cousin and partner Peter Taylor. With long-term capital from his father and with the assistance of his brother George,[23] he created over the next seven or so years a well-equipped steam-powered family business, Courtauld & Taylor, for the manufacture of silk yarn, together with machine shops for the production and sale of specialised throwing and twisting machinery.

Against the background of trade liberalisation in the later 1820s, companies that were suitably equipped to increase production grew rapidly. Between 1828, when the deed setting up Courtauld & Taylor was signed, and 1866 when Samuel III retired, the capital of the business rose from about £15,000 to over £350,000. The prosperity of the firm was increasingly based on the manufacture of mourning crape. Samuel's drive and energy, along with the technical inventiveness of George II, enabled the firm to displace older established competitors and take an increasing share of an exceptionally profitable and vigorously expansive market. In the 1840s, annual profits and interest on capital reached over £40,000.

admitted to the Goldsmiths in 1741. Coming into the business in the forties, he necessarily responded to the influence of the Rococo, but, at least in the examples in the Courtauld Collection, arguably lacked the highest skills of design and *facture* available in London in the mid-century.

At his death in 1765, the business was carried on by his widow, Louisa Perina,[16] at first on her account and then, from 1768–1777, in partnership with her husband's former apprentice, George Cowles, a nephew by marriage. During the seventies, and possibly under the influence of her son Samuel,[17] the house style responded powerfully to the Neo-Classical 'purification' of taste, and some superbly executed presentation cups, tea-wares and especially sauce-boats survive. As *objets-de-forme*, affirming the inherent beauty of the metal as they conceal the art of the smith, they represent the London trade at its day-to-day best, a trade in which numerous manufacturers were capable of production at this level of near mechanical perfection, and in which profitability necessarily suffered from competition.

In 1780, Samuel and his mother sold up. Louisa lived on in London until 1807. He emigrated to America and became 'a kind of itinerant merchant', in the words of his younger brother, George.[18] He died in 1821, 'low in pocket'. George thus became the senior representative of the family in London, but in a different line of business.

The Silk Business

Possibly because of the increasing competition in the silver industry, George had been apprenticed in 1775 to the silk throwster[19] of Spitalfields, Peter Merzau, a relation by marriage of his mother's family the Ogiers, who were Spitalfields weavers. In the 1770s, silk production in England was booming, sheltered by prohibitive rates of duty imposed on imports of finished French silks. But George, despite considerable entrepreneurial energy and a deep commitment to the idea of a better world, lacked basic managerial skills. His first enterprise was a horse-driven throwing mill in Spitalfields, which he

As the fashion for heavy and prolonged mourning was beginning to spread across European society, the crape business was already fulfilling the roseate hopes of George Courtauld I. By the mid century, Samuel Courtauld and Co., as the firm became generally known, had achieved a position of dominance in the market – and the best was yet to come.

In the next thirty years, the firm consolidated its prosperity, increasing its concentration on crape as its major, indeed virtually its only, product by the 1880s (fig. 40). These were the years of the boom in mourning, in which widows were expected to wear black from head to toe for a full two years, followed by at least six months of half-mourning. Mourning for a parent or child was twelve to fifteen months and for siblings, at least six months. Households wore mourning for both sides of the family, and those with a real or fancied connection to the Court observed also the passing of royals. At most of the stages of mourning, crape was required; death was inevitable, but the subject naturally of fears, so when the weeds were cast aside, superstition prevented their being kept for use again.[24]

A large market was thus endlessly renewing itself. In the early 1870s, the return on the partners' capital was over forty-eight per cent. In the peak year, the partners drew nearly £200,000 out of the firm, investing it in houses, land and securities, as successful industrialists have always done. But at the same time, the underlying financial position of the firm, in actual cash and security reserves, was immensely and prudentially strengthened.

It needed to be. The major trade depressions of the 1880s caused a collapse in profits, from over £100,000 in 1884 to a low point of £4,000 in 1894. Domestic, and increasingly international, competition in all branches of the silk industry put a premium on quality. In the 1880s, Courtauld & Co. had persistent problems of poor and uneven quality, and deficiencies emerged in the machinery, which continued, largely, to be made in the company's own machine shops. Furthermore, although the crape market as a whole grew marginally until the death of Queen Victoria in 1901, there were significant shifts in the pattern of demand. The cult of sport and outdoor pursuits, personal and domestic hygiene, dress reform and other social changes associated with Aestheticism in the last quarter of the century, reduced the demand for crape at the upper end of the market. The partners, now including members of families related to the Courtaulds, responded to these signs by restructuring the firm in 1891 as a private joint-stock company with limited liability. Ways of improving its products were sought – for example, by waterproofing the crape against rain – and of increasing productivity by the introduction of new looms imported from Switzerland. Most significantly for the future, it head-hunted from the great Bradford company of Lister and Co. the forty-two year old head of silk manufacturing at the Manningham Mills, Henry Greenwood Tetley (1851–1921).

Tetley's task on joining the company in 1893 was immediately to repair and reorganise its manufacturing capacity. But he was also sceptical of the long-term prospects for crape and was keen to diversify. Early the next year, he appointed on behalf of the Board another ex-Listers man, Thomas Paul Latham, then aged thirty-eight, as Sales Manager. Five years later, with new plant, improved productivity and new lines of coloured chiffon and crêpe de Chine, total sales had grown by seventy-five per cent. The immediate crisis had been survived, the crucial steps away from the doomed crape

FASHIONABLE CRAPE TRIMMED MOURNING

WE STOCK ALL QUALITIES IN SILK CRAPE

40 Advertisement for mourning crape, c.1908, from Courtauld's Halstead Mill (photo: The Braintree Heritage Trust Collection).

market had been taken, but the new professional management was aware that long-term trends in the silk industry, the rise of protectionism in international markets, and pressure on margins made further change essential.

The Viscose Patents

On 19 February 1904, Tetley paid a visit to a small experimental factory at Kew where artificial silk was being produced by the 'viscose process'.[25] He already knew that a French operation at Besançon was showing large profits in the production of artificial silk by the inherently more expensive Chardonnet process; what he, together with his chief chemist and head of production, saw at Kew convinced him that investment in the viscose process was the way to restore Samuel Courtauld & Co. to the high levels of profitability experienced at the height of the crape boom. Through that spring and summer he pressed his case to the Board, but the Board, predominantly composed of aged members of the extended Courtauld family, was cautious. Investment on the scale likely to be necessary to bring the new process into full and profitable production was in any case likely to be beyond the prudent capacity of a family-owned firm, so the outcome depended on another of Tetley's ventures that year, the flotation of the business as a public company.

The flotation took place in early July and was successful, providing a good margin of cash at the disposal of the new company. At its first Board meeting, Tetley, backed by his joint Managing Director, Latham, persuaded the other directors to go ahead with the new investment. The British patents and licences of the viscose process were bought for £25,000. Land and buildings in Coventry were acquired; chemists were hired; and an important technical collaboration agreement with the French licencees of the process was signed. It all took just over a year at Tetley's pace. On 15 August 1905, viscose operations were finally transferred from Kew to

Coventry. Over the next few years, the whole nature and balance of the company were irrevocably transformed. The Essex-based family firm of crape and silk fancy-goods manufacturers was turning into an international textile/chemical company, producing yarn for other manufacturers.

The main problems of the company were now of chemical-engineering rather than finance or management, for Tetley and his colleagues had initially underestimated the difficulty of achieving quality and consistency with the process they had bought. During the following years, collaborating with the French, the company struggled successfully with the technical problems, transforming both the chemical and the mechanical aspects of the process. By 1910, they were without doubt the most technologically advanced of the European and American producers, and profits began to fulfil and vastly exceed Tetley's predictions. In the most difficult of these years, 1907, the company paid a dividend to shareholders of 3%; in 1908 it was 9%, in 1910 it was 20%, and in 1912 it was 50%. At the same time, large reserves of cash and securities were once again accumulated and enormous bonuses paid to the senior managers.

So, spectacularly right and self-confident in his fundamental business judgement, Tetley was poised to take advantage of one of the great business opportunites of the twentieth century. While other members of the European industry were struggling with financial problems, John Read Pettit, the owner of the American rights of the viscose process, was compelled by a combination of technical and financial difficulties to open negotiations for entry to the consortium of European producers. In 1909, heavy tariff barriers were imposed on imports into the U.S.A., and it was obvious that only those with a production base inside the U.S.A. could in future hope to compete in this potentially vast market. Although Tetley had been appointed to represent the Europeans in negotiating with Pettit, he was now determined to seize the prize for Samuel Courtauld & Co., in any event the only company in a position financially to consider direct investment. So the Board invited Pettit to sail to England to discuss the sale of his American patents, and on 16 June 1909, at a Board meeting attended by Pettit, the sale was concluded at a price of $150,000 (about £31,000).

The company had thus acquired the monopoly of the successful process in an American market that was heavily protected against competition from imports. An American company called American Viscose Corporation (AVC) was founded, but with its capital and management wholly controlled by the parent company. With the benefit of the recent technical progress and production expertise gained at Coventry, a new factory was built at Marcus Hook, near Chester in Pennsylvania. Beginning production in early 1911, it was immediately and brilliantly successful. In 1912, net return on subscribed capital was nearly seventy-eight per cent, and by the end of 1915 the American company had overtaken its parent in yarn production. But with feeling running high in Congress against big business, especially when it was foreign-owned, AVC seemed to be making more money than was good for it. Consequently, there were successive reconstructions of the financial side of the business on both sides of the Atlantic. In 1913, to take some account of the income from America, the British company Samuel Courtauld & Co. was reorganised as Courtaulds Ltd, with a capital of £2,500,000. The Courtauld family alone owned thirty-two and a half per cent of the equity.

Despite shortages of raw materials and labour in the latter stages of the war, both the British and the American ends of the business entered 1919 on a strongly rising trend of production and profitability. Trading profits plus investment income of the total business that year reached £4.25m., and the effective rate of dividend was forty-three per cent. In 1919–20, the capital structure of the parent company was again reorganised, and a two-for-one bonus issue was made to shareholders in December 1920. This brought the ordinary share capital to £12m., but still heavily understated the value to the company of the American business. Even so, it showed a growth in shareholders' funds, over the years since the first purchases of the viscose rights, of some 5,900 per cent. The American business was now the largest producer of viscose yarn in the world, and the British was the largest in Europe.

Samuel Courtauld IV (1876–1947)

This achievement, remarkable in itself, put the company in a position to take advantage of the post-war economic boom and of further enormous growth in the international market for 'rayon', as viscose 'artificial silk' soon became known in England, following the American example. It was in large measure due to the entrepreneurial flair and immense personal drive of Henry Tetley as Managing Director and, since 1917, as Chairman of the company. On 21 August 1921, approaching his seventieth birthday, Tetley died. His successor was Samuel Courtauld IV, a former manager of the company's textile mills, who had been appointed to the Board in 1915 and had succeeded Tetley as joint Managing Director in 1917.

Samuel was the direct descendant not of his namesake Samuel III, the first great entrepreneur of the family, but of his younger brother, George II, the engineer. Samuel's father Sydney[26] followed George as head of the technical and engineering side of the business, passing on to his son not only a capacity for detailed attention to manufacturing technicalities, but a strong sense of the radical, Unitarian tradition of the family. Samuel was sent to preparatory school at Bingfield, near Southport, a school attended by the scions of other Nonconformist families prominent in business, and thence to Rugby,[27] where the Arnoldian bias of the curriculum towards the humanities may not at this stage have suited him. Instead of heading for Oxford and Cambridge with the sons of other Nonconformist families who were destined for the professions or for politics, Samuel was sent abroad to study the silk industry at Krefeld and Lyon. In 1898, he returned, joined the company and three years later, at the age of twenty-five, was appointed manager of the weaving mill at Halstead in Essex, employing some thousand workers.

He was evidently capable. Though the textile side of the business had been largely reorganized before he entered the company, continuous improvements to efficiency were none the less required, and Tetley was a restless, watchful Managing Director, alert to any falling off in performance. Courtauld had, at this stage in his life, the reputation of being an aggressive manager, hungry for detail and hard on junior staff.[28] In 1908, he was promoted to be general manager of textile manufacturing, followed by appointment to the Board in 1915.

His rise was thus entirely in the traditional, silk-manufacturing side of the company. Whether this was seen as a weakness or not is hard to say. Early in the century, the initial difficulties in producing usable viscose yarn had been overcome by the application of empirical, production-engineering solutions, rather than by the high scientific expertise of, for example, the German competitors. The company's experience and expertise as a textile manufacturer had helped greatly in making a practical success of the new viscose yarn. In electing Samuel Courtauld as the new Chairman, the Board may well have looked for a continuation of that tradition.[29] In truth, however, there was no other realistic internal candidate for the leadership of a £12m. international company.

The Board may also have felt that a period of consolidation was appropriate in the early 1920s, when the pace of growth in the established rayon business seemed to require only more of the same, rather than innovation. But in 1925, the basic viscose patents expired and there was intense global competition.

In the 'thirties, with even more difficult market conditions and the beginnings of research into non-cellulosic materials such as 'nylon', a more strategic approach was clearly needed.[30] Some limited changes at Board level were then made, aimed at introducing financial and technical expertise. Courtauld himself was certainly aware of the relative weakness of the company in basic research, telling his Board late in 1938 that, with the discovery of nylon in America, 'Our company, which was a pioneer in the early days, has, with its associates, rested too much on its laurels in recent years and competitors have got ahead of us in the race.'[31] Internally there was a clear recognition that the managerialist 'Coventry spirit', which had served the company so well before the First World War, was now also preventing its scientific and organisational development. Francis Rodd,[32] a merchant banker who joined the Board in 1935, observed in 1938: 'one of the main difficulties in which the company found itself was that of transition from a state in which the business had been built up and inevitably run by a few individuals to a state of a big public company with a board to direct its operations where individualism was no longer possible.'[33]

These comments came towards the end of a period in which Courtauld had been trying to reorganise the company, to set up a

42 Advertisement for stockings made from Courtaulds rayon, from *Picture Show*, 15 September 1934 (photo: Courtaulds p.l.c.).

department for basic research, to establish Board sub-committees for matters such as finance, and generally to counteract local intransigeance. But by this time Courtaulds was a very large and diversified multi-national company. Companies of similar size and diversity, such as Du Pont in the United States, were at this time developing decentralised divisional structures, with boards only minimally concerned in executive matters. But at Courtaulds, upward management from its plants was replaced (partially) by management downwards from the Board, sometimes even from its Chairman. At best, this undesirable situation meant that the Chairman's humane and increasingly liberal views in the 'thirties percolated to the shop-floor and helped to maintain the company's reputation for good industrial relations despite increasing labour problems in its core plants. But the weaknesses at Board level in understanding the trends of scientific possibilities, in developing the capacity for innovation and entrepreneurial risk, and in strategic direction on a global scale remained.

Lest this should seem too negative, it is necessary to stress the continuingly extraordinary performance and growth of the company during Samuel Courtauld's chairmanship. The output of viscose filament yarn increased five-fold between 1921 and 1928, and new ways of processing it for a variety of uses from women's stockings (fig. 42) to tyre cords were developed. Production of viscose staple[34] fibre increased eight and a half times; it provided the main growth area in the 1930s, increasing thirty-fold in the decade to 1939. The company, on the personal initiative of the Chairman, fought its way into the manufacture of the other main type of rayon, cellulose-acetate, to compete with the market leader 'Celanese'. In 1935, it set up a viscose film ('Cellophane') subsidiary, and just before the war joined ICI in setting up British Nylon Spinners to exploit the Du Pont discovery of nylon in Britain.

The company continued to expand in Europe, building factories and acquiring new subsidiaries. In America, progress, from a higher base than in Britain was almost as spectacular, at least in the 'twenties.

41 Main Works plant of Courtaulds Ltd at Foleshill Road, Coventry, in the 1930s (photo: Courtaulds p.l.c.).

Output of the basic yarn increased four-fold; between 1924 and 1928, there was heavy investment in new factories, some $50m. was added to reserves and $76m. paid out in dividends. AVC's massive contributions to the parent company helped to bring a leap in the net income[35] of the parent company from £3.3m. in 1923 to £5.6m. in 1928. Although UK investment remained high and reserves continued to accumulate, over £2m. a year was paid out in dividends between 1924 and 1928. In 1924, less than four years after the two-for-one bonus of December 1920, there was a further issue of two five per cent cumulative preference for every three ordinary shares; and in 1928, a one-for-one issue of ordinary shares. During this amazing period, the price of the £1 ordinary shares rose from 69s. 9d. to 182s. 6d.[36]

The End of the Boom

This was the high point. At the Annual General Meeting in March 1930, the Chairman reported on the collapse of Wall Street. The highest price of Courtaulds' £1 ordinary shares that year was 57s. 2d.;[37] by 1940, it was 39s. 10d.[38] Net company income fell from £4m. in 1929 to a low point of £100,000 in 1938, recovering to £1.5m. in 1940. Many companies, which had crowded into the market in the mid-1920s, went out of business as prices fell and margins were squeezed. Courtaulds, with its immense accumulation of financial strength, its tradition of incremental cost-saving on the shop-floor and its advantages of scale, survived. But overall profitability in the later 1930s was disproportionately dependent on staple fibre production, which took off in 1935, masking very poor results in the textile mills and in the foreign subsidiaries.

AVC, still the world's largest rayon producer, failed to maintain its competitive edge, its market share dropped catastrophically and, after 1929, profits began a steep decline, culminating in an actual loss in 1938. Local management and labour relations absorbed a great deal of main Board time, and although the acetate and viscose staple sectors began to contribute handsome profits from 1939, the company never regained the fabulous glitter of the 1920s. The eventual fate of AVC, which was compulsorily sold to American interests as part of the political price for the ratification of Lend-Lease in March 1941, was traumatic for the company. Itself symbolising some of the structural problems in the central direction of the company, the 'loss' of AVC overshadowed, at least financially, Samuel Courtauld's last five years as Chairman. But through its sale – and with substantial compensation from the British Treasury – the company entered the post-war period cash-rich, with strong businesses in staple fibre, tyre yarns and nylon to provide the basis for new ventures, new technologies and new sources of profit, if they could be found. It was a situation not, perhaps, unlike that which Tetley 'inherited' from the family in the 1890s.

In May 1946, Samuel Courtauld had a severe attack of pneumonia and on his recovery indicated to his colleagues that he wished to resign the Chairmanship. His chosen successor was John Hanbury-Williams (1892–1965), a very different character from Henry Tetley. Samuel Courtauld remained on the Board, but died shortly after, aged seventy-one, in December 1947.

His close friend the novelist Charles Morgan described him elegiacally in his last months, in semi-retirement at his country house Gatcombe Park:

43 A reeler at work in Courtauld's Main Works plant in Coventry, April 1928 (photo: Courtaulds p.l.c.).

He had come so near to death that he was aware, after his recovery, of having been outside his body, and the experience continued in his recollection, giving him, in the noblest sense, lightness of heart . . . During his last summer, when he and I were alone at Gatcombe, I knew, as we walked in the woods or beside the lake, or sat on the evening lawn that overlooked his valley, that he did not want to go. Earth held him by her beauties, life by her opportunities. He was still eager to try, to taste, to experiment, to test his powers. Pictures, newly bought, were arriving in packing-cases. Like a boy, he could not wait to uncover them, and we were soon on the floor with pliers and chisels. When the pictures were hung, he visited them continually, learning them, interpreting them, renewing himself in them, and among the last and the happiest of our many discussions was a discussion of the sonnet form, for he was writing a sonnet on one of his pictures, and every evening would show me a revision of it. He was happy; he did not want to go; and yet, knowing in his heart that he must go soon, was at peace.[39]

Charles Morgan's description is Galsworthian, doubtless correct in recording his friend's state of mind, but exaggerating the extent to which Courtauld's pleasure in existence was still expressed through buying pictures. The diagram in figure 44 compares three sets of figures,[40] the company income in the 1920s and '30s, the ordinary share price and Samuel Courtauld's annual spending on pictures for his private collection and for the nation. His spending on other cultural 'goods', such as music, on education or on other charities, is excluded. In addition, it should be remembered that there were three occasions during the period when major shareholders would have felt particularly well-off: after the bonus issues of 1920, 1924 and 1928. The shape assumed by all these factors on the graph is interesting, and it shows the extent to which Courtauld, fastidiously averse to the vulgarities that often accompany wealth, channelled the money that came to him in the 1920s into a highly focused campaign of picture buying; and then, for whatever reason, virtually stopped buying pictures and found other outlets for his wealth and benevolence.[41]

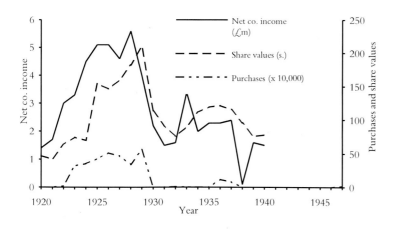

In 1928 the issued ordinary share capital of the company was doubled, so the values of the existing shares was halved: prices from 1928 onwards have therefore been approximately doubled in order to preserve notional comparability with the pre-1928 numbers.

44   Graph comparing the income of Courtaulds p.l.c., the ordinary share price, and Courtauld's annual spending on pictures in the 1920s and '30s.

Samuel Courtauld was, of course, an extremely wealthy man who did not need bonuses in order to afford his purchases. It would be wrong therefore to suppose that there was a simple causal relationship between his money and his picture-buying: money was the necessary condition – hence this narrative – but insufficient on its own. Furthermore, in the 1930s when the art market collapsed, there would have been excellent opportunities either to buy more Impressionist pictures, or to develop further in company

with Arthur Lee[42] his hesitant beginnings in buying Old Masters for the benefit of the collection that he already intended to support the teaching of the history of art at the Courtauld Institute, or for the national collection. We may therefore speculate that his picture-buying may have been part of a joint enterprise – the counterpart of Lil's musical patronage – until her death knocked the heart out of it. The diagram thus reminds us that wealth is a psychological as well as financial condition, and that art, as a possession, often functions to express social aspirations, or to represent feelings of achievement and power, that would otherwise be publicly indescribable. Despite his considerable output of poems and essays dating from the late 1930s and '40s, all carefully typed and bound,[43] it is difficult to believe that Samuel can have had much insight in this arena of the self. In his poetry, he attempted to express some of his 'very personal and emotional reaction to pictures',[44] and in one of his published speeches, he speaks of art as 'the most uniformly civilising influence which mankind has ever known'.[45] Later in life, he learnt more about himself, as we all do, under the pressure of relative adversity, and with the encouragement of Christabel, Lady Aberconway.[46] But he seems never to have been able to turn back analytically to that time when everything he and Lil touched seemed to turn, not just to more gold, but, magically, to Art.

That sudden start to his buying, the missionary fervour and concentration on one particular sort of art; then the sudden stop, and the feeling that the collection and the beautiful house that he and Lil had created, were now too painful for him to hold on to:[47] these suggest an episode of exceptional personal significance, probably unreachable in its nature by us as it was by him. All we see of it is the trace provided by those lines on the graph: they chart the euphoria, disclosing its economic and temporal location, but they leave its nature properly shrouded in mystery.

NOTES

1 IV, 1876–1947.

2 R.A. Butler, *The Art of the Possible, the Memoirs of Lord Butler K.G., C.H.*, London, 1971, p. 19.

3 He was twice Chairman of the Trustees of the National Gallery, and a Trustee of the Tate Gallery during the 1930s.

4 Of cancer: on holiday in Canada in, apparently, 1929, she suffered a fall and became conscious of an acute pain in her side. An exploratory operation after her return to London confirmed the existence of a tumour. Courtauld kept this news secret from all, except Christabel, Lady Aberconway (see note 46), who guessed it. His misery during the last two years of Lil's life is described briefly in his typed narrative, 'Tribute to Beauty' (ch. 9, pp. 45–6), which he bound and presented to Lady Aberconway in the 1940s. I am indebted to the Hon. Christopher McLaren for allowing me to see the volume.

5 Christian orthodoxy, both in the Catholic and Reformed traditions, is 'Trinitarian', that is, it postulates that God is three in one and one in three. Unitarians, who are heretics in both traditions and have been burnt for their beliefs, postulate a singular and indivisible God, and thus deny the deity of Jesus Christ and the theology of salvation. Unitarianism had a strong appeal to the economically and intellectually active middle class in the late eighteenth and early nineteenth centuries, encouraging in its members a belief in reason and human responsibility for the pursuit of happiness, and a reforming tendency in politics. For long excluded from the ancient universities, Unitarians were influential in the establishment of the new

educational foundations of the nineteenth century, such as University College in London, where the Unitarian tradition of rationalism coalesced institutionally with the philosophic radicalism of Bentham and Mill. On their admission to Cambridge towards the end of the third quarter of the century, sons and daughters of the old Dissenting families were among the highest-fliers, soaring far from their family backgrounds in business. It was almost certainly his encounter at the end of the First World War with beneficiaries of this process, such as Roger Fry and Maynard Keynes – men with whom he had so much in common except their university education – that changed the course of Samuel Courtauld's inner life in the 1920s. With Keynes, Courtauld also shared an admiration for the Russian ballerina Lydia Lopokova, subsequently Lydia, Lady Keynes, which developed into the most important of his emotional attachments during the 1920s. His account of 'Z' is given in chapter eight of 'Tribute to Beauty' (cited in note 4). The identification of 'Z' as Lydia Lopokova is made by Christabel, Lady Aberconway, in a manuscript note on page 36.

6 Several scholars have considered writing his life but have found the materials disappointing. The best accounts are by Professor Coleman in his history of the company (see below) and in the *Dictionary of Business Biography*.

7 The account that follows is based on D.C. Coleman, *Courtaulds: An Economic and Social History*, 3 vols, Oxford, 1969–80. Details of the family history will be found in S.L. Courtauld, *The Huguenot Family of Courtauld* (privately printed, 3 vols, London, 1957–67). I am grateful to Professor Coleman for his advice; and to him and Courtaulds p.l.c. for permission to quote from his admirable history of the company. I am also grateful to Dennis Farr, Sir

Adam Butler and the Hon. Christopher McLaren for their advice, information and memories concerning Samuel Courtauld.

8 I, died after 1619.

9 II, died c.1627.

10 II, died before 1700.

11 IV, 1655–1706.

12 VI, died 1751; his elder brother, Augustin V, had died before his christening in France.

13 D.1729; his son by his second wife.

14 On the silver, see J.F. Hayward, *The Courtauld Silver*, Sotheby's, London and New York, 1975.

15 I, 1720–65.

16 Born Ogier, 1729–1807.

17 II, 1752–1821.

18 I, 1761–1823.

19 Silk, being a continuous filament, is twisted, or 'thrown' into thread, rather than spun from short lengths like other textile fibres.

20 III, 1793–1881.

21 George was thus the founder of the family's Unitarianism, in which he was followed with particular enthusiasm by his son Samuel III. Samuel was one of the leaders of Dissenting protest against the civil disabilities of non-Anglicans in the mid-century. His particular battle was against the liability of Dissenters to pay Anglican church rates, in which he was successful, but during which he suffered some rough handling from the establishment.

22 Used for the warp threads of crape.

23 II, 1802–61.

24 Lou Taylor, *Mourning Dress. A Costume and Social History*, London, 1983. See also Ursula Priestley, 'Norwich and the Mourning Trade', *Costume*, no. 27, 1993, pp. 47–53.

25 This involved the treatment of cellulose, in the form of woodpulp, with caustic soda and carbon disulphide. The resulting viscose solution was then, like silk, drawn out in filaments and twisted into yarn.

26 1840–99; Samuel's only child, the daughter who married 'Rab' Butler, was given this name.

27 He was at Rugby in Cotton House between September 1890 and the end of the autumn term 1894. His strongest subject was 'science', at that time taught as an amalgam of physics, chemistry and biology, in which he was top in his final sixth-form year. During this time the school had a particularly active art department. I am grateful to Jenny Macrorie, archivist at Rugby School for this information.

28 Verbal communication from Professor Coleman, reporting an interview with R.A. Butler in the 1960s. Butler was discussing the reputed change in Courtauld's personality during the 1920s, from that of the early 'positive' manager to that of the Olympian chairman, increasingly introspective and moralistic in his habits of thought.

29 Tetley himself had come from a similar textile background at Manningham Mills, and he had evidently had his eye on Samuel Courtauld. Samuel may thus have seemed to combine Tetley's practical strengths with membership of the family and a more evidently 'blue-chip' personality.

30 In the 1920s the total world market for cellulosic fibres grew from some 35m. lb. to about 450m.; against this, Courtaulds' increase from 6.9m. lb. in 1921 to 31.8m. in 1928 looks cautious. In the 1930s, when the world market for artificial staple fibre took off, Courtaulds were held back by voices on the Board that claimed to 'see signs of a set-back'. In this competitive environment, Courtaulds' share of the U.K. cellulosic yarn market dropped from virtually 100% in 1920 to about 57% in 1940. In the U.S.A., the decline was even more marked, from about 98% in 1920 to about 27% in 1940. (Coleman, 1969–80 (cited in note 6), II, fig 40).

31 Coleman, 1969–80 (cited in note 6), II, p. 229.

32 1895–1978, who later succeeded his father as the 2nd Lord Rennell of Rodd.

33 Coleman, 1969–80 (cited in note 6), II, p. 236.

34 The viscose filament is converted into staple by cutting it into short lengths, like the natural fibres of wool or cotton, and then spinning it into threads. Suitably treated, it was used as a cheap substitute for natural fibres in clothing, and in many other applications. Especially in the command economies of Germany, Italy and Japan during the 1930s, domestic production of rayon staple was deliberately increased in order to suppress imports of relatively expensive wool and cotton, production of which remained depressingly flat throughout the inter-war years, contributing to extremely difficult conditions for the traditional raw-material producers, such as India, and for manufacturing areas in Britain, such as Lancashire. In the latter, conditions were rendered acute by Britain's return to the Gold Standard in 1925, and led to attempts at restructuring between 1926 and 1929 in which Samuel Courtauld's friend Maynard Keynes played a leading role. R.F. Harrod, *The Life of John Maynard Keynes*, London, 1951, 1972 edn, pp. 445–53.

35 That is, trading profits plus investment income minus tax and depreciation. The main source of investment income was, of course, the American company, but Courtaulds continued to build up financial assets in the U.K., which contributed to income.

36 Or 348.75 pence to 912.5 pence (decimal).

37 About 286 pence (decimal).

38 About 199 pence (decimal).

39 Samuel Courtauld, *Ideals and Industry: War-Time Papers*, Cambridge, 1949, preface, p. xiii.

40 The first two are from Coleman, 1969–80 (cited in note 6), II, tables 51 and 67 (net company income, i.e., trading profits plus investment income, less tax and depreciation, and highest stock exchange quotation for ordinary shares for the year). The share-price figures from 1929, when the one-for-one issue should in principle have halved the value of the pre-issue ordinary shares, have been adjusted (× 2) in order to preserve broad comparability with the pre-issue sequence. It should be remembered, incidentally, that the sequence as given here begins at the new price level established by the two-for-one bonus of 1920. The third, which is my own amateur invention, is derived from totalling the available invoices for his major acquisitions for the private and the public collections, less any sales (such as his Matisse). It is not a complete record, so no reliance should be placed on the precise figures, as distinct from the broad quantities.

41 In the 1930s, for example, he became keen on rural pursuits, such as hunting from his country house at Gatcombe Park. Gatcombe has since become famous as the house acquired by the British Royal Family for Princess Anne and her former husband, Captain Mark Phillips.

42 Viscount Lee of Fareham (1868–1947), who suggested to Samuel that he put up the money for the Courtauld Institute and whose own collection of Old Masters and historic British art subsequently joined Samuel's as one of the 'founding collections' of the Courtauld Institute Galleries. Earlier in life, he had formed a different, mixed collection of furniture and pictures at his house, Chequers, in Buckinghamshire, which, in 1921, he gave and endowed in trust as the official country residence of British Prime Ministers.

43 I am indebted to the Hon. Christopher McLaren for allowing me to see these volumes.

44 The phrase is Samuel's own, taken from the manuscript letter, dated November 1947, enclosed with the copy of his book, *Pictures in to Verse* (privately printed, 1947), which he sent to Anthony Blunt (now Courtauld Institute Library). It is dated from 12 North Audley Street and concludes: 'it is a good thing that you should know more about the tastes in matters of art of the man who is associated with you in a great art campaign. Yours very sincerely Sam. Courtauld.'

45 'Art Education', Presidential Address to the Association of Art Institutions, London, 20 October 1943, in *Ideals and Industry . . .*, 1949 (cited in note 37), p. 45.

46 Christabel Mary Melville McNaughten, born 12 December 1890; married 19 July 1910 Henry Duncan McLaren, 2nd Baron Aberconway; died 16 August 1974. Her private correspondence with Samuel is in the British Library (Add. MSS 52432–5; sections of it remain on restricted access). Together with the Butlers, Christabel and her family were bequeathed major paintings from Samuel's private collection.

47 Hence the gift of the remaining fifty years of the lease, the furniture and a first instalment of the pictures, to the Trustees of Home House for the benefit of the Courtauld Institute. Before he vacated the house, however, he recorded its interiors in a series of photographs, one set of which he had bound in an album for presentation to Christabel, Lady Aberconway, 30 September 1935. This copy, with Samuel's inscription, is now in the Library of the Courtauld Institute.

CATALOGUE

EXPLANATORY NOTE

ALL OF THE MODERN FRENCH PAINTINGS, sculptures and drawings in Samuel Courtauld's private collection are catalogued below, together with a checklist of his prints. The present ownership of the works is indicated in the head-notes.

The only works omitted are those that Courtauld himself sold from his collection, including two paintings by Cézanne, two by Gauguin and one by Matisse; we must assume that these were works that, in the end, did not satisfy him (on these, see pp. 23–4). However, these are included in the listing of the paintings he purchased, both for his own collection and for the Courtauld Fund, presented in chronological order of their acquisition (pp. 221–4).

The entries for the paintings are by John House, those for the sculpture, drawings and cat. no. 18 by William Bradford, who has also compiled the checklist of prints. The entries for the pictures included in the exhibition catalogue *Impressionist and Post-Impressionist Masterpieces: The Courtauld Collection* (United States, 1987–8) have been reworked from those published in that catalogue. Extensive use has been made of material published by Douglas Cooper in 1954 (Cooper, 1954) and by Dennis Farr in 1984 (Japan and Canberra, 1984). Caroline Villers of the Courtauld Institute's Department of Technology has contributed many detailed technical observations, and we are indebted to Robert Ratcliffe for information and advice about Cézanne.

Dimensions are given in centimetres, height before width. The references at the end of each entry are not comprehensive. Exhibition catalogues that include significant historical discussions of the work are cited in the exhibition listing only; other references to the work appear under 'Literature'. Standard reference books on individual artists are cited in full in the first entry for that artist, and thereafter in abbreviation.

The following publications relating to the Courtauld Collection are cited in abbreviation in the listings of exhibitions and literature in the individual entries.

French Art, Royal Academy, London, 1932
> *Exhibition of French Art 1200–1900*, Royal Academy of Arts, London, January–March 1932

Jamot-Turner
> Paul Jamot and Percy Moore Turner, *Collection de tableaux français, faite à Londres, 20 Portman Square, par Samuel et Elizabeth Courtauld, 1914–1931*, 50 copies, privately printed, London, 1934

Home House Catalogue
> *A Catalogue of the Pictures and Other Works of Art at Home House, 20 Portman Square, London*, published by the Home House Society Trustees, London, 1935

Tate Gallery, 1948
> *Catalogue of the Samuel Courtauld Memorial Exhibition*, Tate Gallery, London, May-June 1948

Cooper, 1954
> Douglas Cooper, *The Courtauld Collection: A Catalogue and Introduction*, with a memoir of Courtauld by Anthony Blunt, London, 1954

Orangerie, Paris, 1955
> *Impressionnistes de la Collection Courtauld de Londres*, exhibition catalogue, Musée de l'Orangerie, Paris, October 1955

Manchester, 1962
> *Master Drawings from the Witt and Courtauld Collections*, Whitworth Art Gallery, Manchester, October–December 1962

Nottingham University, 1969
> *Watercolours, Drawings and Engravings from the Courtauld*, Nottingham University, October–November 1969 (a selection of forty works without catalogue)

Courtauld Centenary, 1976
> *Samuel Courtauld's Collection of French 19th Century Paintings and Drawings*, catalogue of centenary exhibition to commemorate the birth of Samuel Courtauld, organised by the Courtauld Institute of Art and the Arts Council of Great Britain

Arts Council, 1977–9
> *Drawings from the Courtauld*, Arts Council travelling exhibition, Graves Art Gallery, Sheffield, October–December 1977, Wolverhampton Art Gallery, December 1977–January 1978, Bolton Museum and Art Gallery, February–March 1978, Laing Art Gallery, Newcastle-upon-Tyne, October–December 1978, Ferens Art Gallery, Hull, December 1978–January 1979, Portsmouth Museum and Art Gallery, February–March 1979

National Gallery, London, 1983
> *Paintings from the Courtauld*, National Gallery, London, February-March 1983 (no catalogue)

British Museum, 1983
> *Mantegna to Cézanne: Master Drawings from the Courtauld*, British Museum, London, January-June 1983

Japan and Canberra, 1984
> *The Impressionists and the Post-Impressionists from the Courtauld Collection*, University of London, Takashimaya, Tokyo, Kyoto and Osaka, 1984; *The Great Impressionists: Masterpieces from the Courtauld Collection of Impressionist and Post-Impressionist Paintings and Drawings*, Australian National Gallery, Canberra, 1984

United States, 1987–8
> *Impressionist and Post-Impressionist Masterpieces: The Courtauld Collection*, Cleveland Museum of Art, The Metropolitan Museum of Art, New York, The Kimbell Art Museum, Fort Worth, The Art Institute of Chicago and the Nelson-Atkins Museum of Art, Kansas City, 1987–8 (catalogue published by Yale University Press, New Haven and London, and the International Exhibitions Foundation, Washington, D.C.)

C.I.G., 1988
> *Impressionist, Post-Impressionist and Related Drawings from the Courtauld Collections*, Courtauld Institute Galleries, London, 1988

I BONNARD, PIERRE 1867–1947
The Blue Balcony 1910
Le Balcon bleu
Oil on canvas, 52.5 × 76
Signed, bottom left: 'Bonnard'
Courtauld Institute Galleries (The Samuel
Courtauld Trust)

The Blue Balcony shows the view from the
artist's house, *Ma Roulotte*, at Vernonnet, in the
Seine valley near Monet's home at Giverny. *Ma
Roulotte*, literally 'my gypsy caravan', was the
humorous name for this country villa;
Bonnard's friend Thadée Natanson described
the place:

> The upper floor of the 'Roulotte', with a
> wooden balcony, was on the same level as
> the road, and the small garden fell away
> steeply to the river bank where a boat was
> moored. The bedroom and bathroom were
> on the level of the road, with a garage which
> they had built on the other side of a little
> courtyard. They ate in the dining room, on
> the lower level, the ground floor, less often
> than they did in the local inn.

One of Bonnard's favourite themes in his
middle and later years was the relationship
between houses and gardens, which he
presented in many unexpected forms,
challenging the usual ways of depicting
buildings in landscape; he created instead a far
freer interplay between houses and their
surroundings. Here, the most active part of the
composition is relegated to the extreme left – the
structure of the house and balcony, and the
single small figure; but the gesture of this figure
remains unexplained, as she stoops towards we
know not what. The recession through the
centre of the picture leads only to a summarily
treated bank of trees, with a hint of a garden
table and chairs, and perhaps a figure in a red
skirt, at the end of the path.

The different elements in the composition are
all absorbed into an overall play of coloured
touches which creates scattered points of focus
all across the canvas; the figure and the tree-
trunks are no more crisply defined than the
patches of light on the path and between the
trees. Soft greens, blues and greys dominate the
composition, enlivened by a few accents of
sharper colour, such as the unexpected and
isolated red flowers at lower right.

PROVENANCE Bought from the artist by
Bernheim-Jeune, Paris, 1910; Hugo Nattan;
Bernheim-Jeune 1912; Paul Vallotton,
Lausanne; Galerie Druet, Paris, 1928; Percy
Moore Turner, London; bought by Courtauld,
1928, price unknown. Courtauld Gift 1932.

EXHIBITED *Oeuvres récentes (1910 et 1911) de
Bonnard*, Bernheim-Jeune, Paris, 1911 (14); Tate
Gallery, 1948 (2); *Bonnard*, Kunsthaus, Zürich,
1949 (90); Orangerie, Paris, 1955 (1); *Bonnard*,
Royal Academy, London, 1966 (92); Courtauld
Centenary, 1976 (1); National Gallery, London,
1983 (no catalogue); Japan and Canberra, 1984
(1); United States, 1987–8 (46).

LITERATURE Home House Catalogue, no. 50;
Cooper, 1954, no. 2; J. and H. Dauberville,
Bonnard: Catalogue raisonné de l'oeuvre peint, II,
1906–19, Paris, 1968, p. 209, no. 625.

2 BOUDIN, EUGÈNE 1824–98
   The Beach at Trouville 1875
   La Plage de Trouville
   Oil on panel, 12.5 × 24.5
   Signed, bottom left: 'E. Boudin'
   Courtauld Institute Galleries (The Samuel
      Courtauld Trust)

In 1862, Boudin began to paint fashionable
figures on the beaches of the celebrated holiday
resorts of Trouville and Deauville on the
Normandy coast. In his previous paintings, he
had explored the coastline around his home
town of Le Havre, just across the Seine estuary
from Trouville, but it was with this genre of
modern-life beach scene that he won a
reputation. In 1868, he wrote to his friend
M. Martin:

> These gentlemen congratulate me for having
> dared to put down on canvas the things and
> people of our own time, for having found
> the way to gain acceptance for men in great-
> coats and women in waterproofs . . . The
> peasants have their favoured painters . . . but
> the bourgeois who walk on the jetty towards
> the sunset, don't they have the right to be
> fixed on canvas, to be brought out into the
> light?

In this picture, Boudin adopted his
characteristic compositional arrangement, of
groups of figures loosely strung across an
elongated horizontal format. There is no clear
centre of attention, and the figures are treated
summarily and without any anecdotal detail,
though the slightly more solid forms of the
group on the left hold the attention first. The
eye scans the picture without focusing on any
group or incident; by this studied informality
Boudin could suggest the informal clusters of
holiday-makers gathered along the beach.
Boudin worked on the beaches in a variety of
media – in pencil and watercolours as well as
oils. His more elaborate paintings of such figure
subjects were presumably reworked, or indeed
entirely executed, in the studio, but small,
loosely handled panel paintings like this were
very probably painted on the spot. The
technique is nevertheless quite complex. Four
distinct stages in the painting process can be
discerned; these can be clearly seen in the area
of the head and shoulders of the woman on the
extreme left. Two layers of blue paint were
broadly and thinly applied and allowed to dry
before the figures were added. The ridges of the
brushstrokes of this blue underpainting can be
seen under the figures. The figures themselves
are swiftly painted, wet in wet. The sky was the
final stage in the painting, added around the
figures; small marks were scratched into the still
wet paint diagonal to the direction of the
brushwork, revealing the blue underpainting.

PROVENANCE Anon.; Louis de Wild, The
Hague; sold Hôtel Drouot, Paris, 29 May 1920
(lot 11); Knoedler, London and New York, by
1925–6; bought by Courtauld, July 1926, £50.
Courtauld Gift 1932.

EXHIBITED Tate Gallery, 1948 (3); Orangerie,
Paris, 1955 (2); Courtauld Centenary, 1976 (2);
Japan and Canberra, 1984 (4); United States,
1987–8 (19).

LITERATURE Jamot-Turner, no. 2; Home House
Catalogue, no. 20; Cooper, 1954, no. 4; R.
Schmit, *Eugène Boudin 1824–98*, Paris, 1973, I,
no. 1033.

3 BOUDIN, EUGÈNE 1824–98
   Deauville 1893
   Oil on canvas, 50.8 × 74.2
   Signed, bottom left: 'Deauville/E. Boudin
      93'
   Courtauld Institute Galleries (The Samuel
      Courtauld Trust)

In his later work, Boudin concentrated more on
the open panoramas of the Normandy beaches
than on the holiday-makers who peopled them
(contrast cat. no. 2). The figures here are rapidly
indicated – holiday-makers, it seems, over by the
water, working men with their cart and horses
on the left – so that we sense the varied uses of
the beach. But light and atmosphere form the
principal subject of the painting.

   Though Boudin had worked closely with
Monet in the 1860s and exhibited in the first
group exhibition in 1874, he never fully
adopted the broken touch and lavish
atmospheric colour of the Impressionists. His
brushwork remained rather tighter and more
graphic, suggesting forms and textures very
delicately, and his colour more restrained,
though nuances of blue and green are used here
to suggest the forms in the distance, and a
sequence of tiny red touches across the
background lends an almost subliminal
animation to the effect. In this sense, Boudin
remained faithful to the *peinture claire*, the
luminous, blond painting, of which he had been
a pioneer in the 1850s.

   By this refined touch and colour, Boudin
managed to evoke the vast scale of the beach
and sky, bearing witness to the skills that led
Corot to name him the 'king of skies'.
However, the execution of the canvas was a
more complex business than appears at first
sight. Where the primed canvas is visible in the
sky area, it shows a speckled worn surface,
indicating that it was rubbed or scraped down
in order to reduce an early paint layer, a blue
that shares signs of this abrasion, and the process
inevitably removed the upmost ridges of the
canvas weave. The present state of the sky, for
all its apparent freshness, is thus a thorough
revision of the painting's original effect and
exploits the partial retention of the underlying
blue layer.

PROVENANCE   Dr Delineau, Paris; Delineau
Sale, Hôtel Drouot, Paris, 1 February 1901 (lot
36); Devilder, Roubaix, France; Wildenstein,
Paris, London and New York; bought by
Courtauld, July 1936, £600. Courtauld Bequest
1948 (on loan to Lord (R.A.) Butler until 1983).

EXHIBITED   Tate Gallery, 1948 (4); Courtauld
Centenary, 1976 (3); Japan and Canberra, 1984
(5); United States, 1987–8 (20); *Boudin at
Trouville*, Glasgow and London, 1992–3 (46).

LITERATURE   Cooper, 1954, no. 5 (where
incorrectly dated 1883); R. Schmit, 1973, III,
no. 3150, as 'Deauville, la plage, marée basse';
R. Bruce-Gardner, G. Hedley and C. Villers,
'Impressions of Change', in United States,
1987–8, p. 23.

4 CÉZANNE, PAUL 1839–1906
The Etang des Soeurs, Osny c.1875
L'Etang des soeurs, Osny
Oil on canvas, 60 × 73.5
Unsigned
Courtauld Institute Galleries (The Samuel
    Courtauld Trust)

Osny is a village near Pontoise, north of Paris, where Pissarro lived in the 1870s; Cézanne worked with him there on several occasions during the decade. This painting has usually been dated to 1877, but was very probably painted in 1875; there is no record of his visiting Pontoise that year, but he was in the north of France, and a visit to Pissarro might well have passed unrecorded. Cézanne had initially worked with Pissarro in 1872–4 in order to learn the discipline of painting from closely observed natural effects (see cat. no. 36), but by around 1874 both men began to build up their paint surfaces with denser, more tightly structured zones of colour, and in several paintings dated 1875, Pissarro made extensive use of the palette knife. *The Etang des Soeurs, Osny* is one of a group of paintings by Cézanne that are closely comparable with these; by 1877, Cézanne, like Pissarro, was again working only with the brush, and with a far more broken touch.

The knife is used here to build up the composition in bold swathes of paint, particularly in the foliage of the trees. In some places, the paint is applied in denser blocks of colour, but the rhythm of the foliage is achieved by broad movements with the knife, creating a strong directional movement across the central area. Some sweeps of paint cover considerable areas of the picture with great simplicity, but others cover the underlying layers so thinly that they set up complex relationships with the colours seen through from below. The apparent breadth of this knifework belies the delicacy with which the knife is used. The brush is also employed on occasion, particularly in some of the narrower trunks and branches, but in the principal trunks, the paint is largely built up from complex, superimposed knife-strokes.

Green is the dominant colour of the picture: vivid yellow-greens appear in the sunlit foliage across the water, and strong clear greens are used in other areas, while the more shadowed zones are suggested in part by darker greens, in part by the mixture of blue with the colour, thus combining tonal and colouristic methods of modelling. Small, warm-hued accents enliven the composition, and at certain points, such as on the main tree-trunks and along the far edge of the water, rich juxtapositions of blue with warm oranges, reds and browns create a more elaborate effect.

We have no clear evidence of how far Cézanne worked out of doors on paintings such as this, but it is likely that it was, in part, executed in front of the subject. However, the forms are simplified and rather stylised, with the arcs of trunks and branches framing the broad sweeps of the foliage. By using the knife, Cézanne gave the surface an overall coherence through the breadth and flatness of the paint layers, but the movements of the knife also give the areas of foliage a strong directional rhythm, running across and down from left to right. Individual areas also acquire distinctive shapes of their own, rhyming with other similar shapes, most notably in the bands of dark leaves that lie over the sunlit foliage beyond.

By the early 1880s, Cézanne was working with the brush, in delicate parallel strokes of colour, but in the trees in cat. no. 6, for instance, these finer strokes are grouped so as to create rhythms and patterns whose overall effect is comparable to the foliage here. X-rays of the picture underline the similarity of handling: individual touches with the knife or brush can be clearly distinguished with characteristic accumulations of paint at the end of each stroke. In cat. no. 6, Cézanne must have used the brush to place the paint on the canvas in a way comparable to his use of the palette knife here.

The canvas is primed with a light cream tone, but the variations in the density of this ground around the cusped weave of the canvas edges indicate that it was applied when the painting was already stretched, and it is therefore likely to be the artist's own application. The areas of exposed brownish canvas, in a roughly vertical band a few inches in from the left edge of the picture, suggest that at some time it was stored unstretched with its edge crudely folded.

PROVENANCE Camille Pissarro, Paris; Alphonse Kann, Saint-Germain-en-Laye; with Galerie Barbazanges, Paris; Reininghaus, Vienna; Galerie Barbazanges, Paris; Alex. Reid, Glasgow; Agnew, London; bought by Courtauld, July 1923, £2,400. Courtauld Gift 1932.

EXHIBITED *Französische Kunst des 19. u. 20. Jahrhunderts*, Kunsthaus, Zürich, 1917 (19); *Masterpieces of French Art of the 19th Century*, Agnew, London, 1923 (3); *Cézanne*, Leicester Galleries, London, 1925 (15); Tate Gallery, 1948 (5); *Cézanne*, Edinburgh and London, 1954 (16); Orangerie, Paris, 1955 (3); Courtauld Centenary, 1976 (4); Japan and Canberra, 1984 (7); United States, 1987–8 (21).

LITERATURE Home House Catalogue, no. 74; L. Venturi, *Cézanne, son art, son oeuvre*, Paris, 1936, no. 174; Cooper, 1954, no. 6; W. Rubin (ed.), *Cézanne: The Late Work*, London and New York, 1977–8, pp. 5–6.

5   CÉZANNE, PAUL   1839–1906
Farm in Normandy: The Enclosure   1882?
Ferme en Normandie: le clos
Oil on canvas, 49.5 × 65.7
Unsigned
Private Collection, on extended loan to the
     Courtauld Institute Galleries

In 1882, Cézanne's principal patron, Victor
Chocquet, inherited a farm at Hattenville near
Yvetot in Normandy, and Cézanne very
probably visited him there that summer; this is
one of a group of four closely related paintings
of Normandy orchards, all of them originally in
Chocquet's collection, which presumably show
the place.

Though the picture is comparatively small
and not elaborately finished, Cézanne built up a
composition with a real monumentality, framed
by the arching branches from the left trees, and
structured by the rhythm of the background
trunks. The canvas was left off at a point when
some areas were more fully worked than others.
At the top left, the background is blocked in
with simple patches of colour, thinly applied,
and the grass is treated in broad sweeps of quite
uniform colour; but at certain points in the
foliage, the brushwork is far more broken and
rhythmic, in crisp parallel strokes which suggest
the texture of the foliage at the same time as
giving the painting a taut surface structure. This
type of brushwork, Cézanne's so-called
'constructive stroke', appears again in cat. no. 6.
The greens that dominate the composition
range from light and yellowish where the
foliage is caught by the light, to duller hues
with rich nuances of blue in the shadows;
against this play of cool colours are set
successions of warm touches–heightened red
accents that appear, seemingly without
naturalistic justification, on tree-trunks and
branches, and on the roof edge on the left.

The sticks or saplings on the meadow to the
right reveal most clearly Cézanne's process of
revising his compositions. Though this area is
not thickly painted, their placing was altered at
least twice. Both verticals are overpainted,
across the top of the area of open grass, with a
stroke of green, as if both were to be erased, or
perhaps their bases raised so that they seem to
stem from the hedge; moreover, the left vertical
was moved; its previous position can still be
seen, not fully covered by reworking, at the
same angle and about $\frac{3}{4}$ inch to the right of its
present position. Since Cézanne did not have to
sell his paintings in order to survive, he
abandoned many of them when different areas
of them were in different states of completion,
and certain parts were left unresolved. This
blatant rejection of traditional notions of 'finish'
in painting disconcerted the first viewers of
canvases such as this, but has fascinated later,
twentieth-century viewers, who have come to
see such visible evidence of the artist's working
methods as the direct expression of creative
genius.

PROVENANCE   Victor Chocquet, Paris;
Chocquet Sale, Paris, 1, 3 and 4 July 1899 (lot
11, as 'L'Eté'); Ambroise Vollard, Paris; with
Bignou, Paris; Reid and Lefèvre, London;
bought by Courtauld, July 1937, £2,500; Lady
Aberconway, 1948; private collection.

EXHIBITED   *Paintings from the Vollard Collection*,
Knoedler, New York and Detroit, 1933 (7);
Tate Gallery, 1948 (6); *Landscape in French Art*,
Royal Academy, London, 1949–50 (316);
Cézanne, Edinburgh and London, 1954 (30);
Orangerie, Paris, 1955 (4); *Impressionism*, Royal
Academy, London, 1974 (53); Courtauld
Centenary, 1976 (5); United States, 1987–8 (22).

LITERATURE   Venturi, 1936, no. 443; Cooper,
1954, no. 7; J. Rewald, 'Chocquet and Cézanne',
in *Studies in Impressionism*, London, 1985,
pp. 151–2, 165 and 184, n. 73.

6 CÉZANNE, PAUL 1839–1906
Tall Trees at the Jas de Bouffan c.1883
Grands arbres au Jas de Bouffan
Oil on canvas, 65 × 81
Unsigned
Courtauld Institute Galleries (The Samuel
Courtauld Trust)

The Jas de Bouffan was the house and estate owned since 1859 by the artist's father, Louis-Auguste Cézanne, a wealthy banker; it lies about a mile and a half west of the centre of Aix-en-Provence. Cézanne painted many views of the house and grounds from 1866 until he sold the estate in 1899, and found there the solitude that he needed in order to work, both in the garden and in his studio in the house.

Tall Trees at the Jas de Bouffan is a particularly clear illustration of Cézanne's painting technique at the period. Working from a light, creamy priming (still seen unpainted in places, for instance near the bottom right corner), he first laid on comparatively simple, flat layers of colour, such as those seen to bottom right, to lay out the essential planes of the composition. These were gradually refined by the addition of variegations of colour in crisper, more distinct brushstrokes; he did not work up the whole composition simultaneously, but focused on certain salient points, leaving other areas scantily painted. In its more highly worked parts, the resulting painting is covered with a network of rhythmic strokes, often running in sequences parallel to each other; their varied colour gives a shimmer and richness to the whole surface and a sense of light and atmosphere, but their ordered arrangement, and the simplified monumentality of the tree-trunks, give the painting a structure that transcends the mobile effects of light on foliage which were Cézanne's starting point. This treatment of the surface in sequences of parallel brushstrokes has been described as Cézanne's 'constructive stroke'; it can be compared with the evenly weighted, rhythmic handling adopted by his friend Pissarro in the same years (see cat.no. 37). Although quite elaborated in parts, Cézanne abandoned work on the picture when not all its forms were clearly indicated; we are left uncertain of the structure of the building or wall behind the trees on the left, and of the spatial position of the alternating planes of warm and cool colour that lead into distance on the right.

The colour in the picture is clear and rich, with strong reds and oranges set off against the dominant network of blues and greens; even the more subdued areas of the picture, such as the tree-trunks amid the foliage, are enlivened by accents of stronger, warmer colour. This heightened range of colours, adopted to evoke the rich, coloured light of southern France (see also cat.no. 7), is a contrast to the rather duller, denser greens of cat.no. 5, painted in Normandy in the same period.

The composition of the picture is very tautly structured, in part by the strongly articulated pattern of the tall tree-trunks, but also by the colour and lighting. The two principal sunlit areas – the view into distance on the right and the building beyond the trees at far left – frame the scene, while between these luminous, warm zones a single, stronger reddish accent, just below the bushes near the centre of the canvas, anchors the whole image.

PROVENANCE Ambroise Vollard, Paris; Paul Rosenberg, Paris; bought by Courtauld, May 1924, £4,500. Courtauld Bequest 1948.

EXHIBITED *Grands maîtres du 19me siècle*, Paul Rosenberg, Paris, 1922 (11); *Cézanne*, Leicester Galleries, London, 1925 (16); Tate Gallery, 1948 (11); *Cézanne*, Edinburgh and London, 1954 (33); Orangerie, Paris, 1955 (8); Courtauld Centenary, 1976 (7); Japan and Canberra, 1984 (8); United States, 1987–8 (23).

LITERATURE Jamot-Turner, no. 20; Venturi, 1936, no. 475; Cooper, 1954, no. 11.

7 CÉZANNE, PAUL 1839–1906
View over L'Estaque c.1885
Vue sur L'Estaque
Oil on canvas, 71 × 57.7
Unsigned
Private Collection, on loan to the
Fitzwilliam Museum, Cambridge

L'Estaque, on the Mediterranean coast west of Marseilles, was a favoured site for mid-nineteenth century Provençal painters; the view down over the bay to Marseilles itself, flanked by its hills, appeared in celebrated pictures by landscapists such as Emile Loubon (Musée des Beaux-Arts, Marseilles). Cézanne worked there on many occasions from around 1870 on; although the view over the bay was one of his principal motifs there, he was willing to include evidence of the changes that were taking place on the coast, and particularly the factory chimneys in L'Estaque. Both there and at Aix-en-Provence (see cat. no. 8), he included explicitly contemporary elements in his landscapes at a date when the other Impressionists had largely abandoned them (but see Pissarro cat. no. 37). By 1902, though, he considered the place ruined:

> I well remember the . . . once so picturesque coastline at L'Estaque. Unfortunately, what we call progress is nothing but the invasion of bipeds who do not rest until they have transformed everything into odious *quais* with gas lamps – and, what is still worse – with electric illumination. What times we live in!

The experience of painting in the south revealed to Cézanne the full potential of colour. In the early 1870s, Camille Pissarro had taught him to 'replace tonal modelling by the study of colours' and had justified this in naturalistic terms, but the implications of this became clear only when, in 1876 at L'Estaque, he began to paint a motif of red roofs against the blue sea. He wrote to Pissarro about this experience: 'The sunlight here is so intense that it seems to me that objects are silhouetted not only in black and white, but also in blue, red, brown and violet. I may be mistaken, but this seems to me to be the opposite of modelling.' The painting mentioned here is the first of a long sequence, including *View over L'Estaque*, in which Cézanne looked down from the hills above L'Estaque across the roofs of the village to the Bay of Marseilles, and used the contrast between the red-orange roofs and the blue sea as the pivot of his compositions.

At the end of his life, Cézanne told Maurice Denis, 'I was pleased when I made the discovery that sunlight cannot be reproduced, but that it must be represented by something else, by colour.' His paintings show the results of these lessons in two ways – in his use of bold, dominant colour contrasts, like the orange and blue here, and in the shifting colour nuances, or 'modulations', which he used to suggest relationships of small-scale forms and textures. These devices appeared particularly in his paintings of southern scenes, as they did in Monet's Mediterranean canvases of the 1880s (see cat. no. 34). Both artists found that the light of the south brought home to them the impossibility of imitating nature directly and forced them to think in terms of coloured paint as an independent means of conveying the effect of light.

The composition of *View over L'Estaque* is particularly tautly structured, with darker trees acting as *repoussoirs* framing the central coloured vista, and the edges of the tree at top centre framing the distant island (compare the tree and mountain in cat. no. 8). Parallels for this can be found in the work of Poussin and Claude, the French classicising landscapists of the seventeenth century. Cézanne's concern with such compositional devices seems to be an early stage in his search (as he is reported to have said in 1905) to 'revivify Poussin in front of nature'.

In principle, he sought to achieve the spatial structure of a picture such as this by relationships of colour alone. But in *View over L'Estaque*, as in very many of his other later canvases, he was forced to add small linear accents, late in the picture's execution, to help define spatial planes. Most obviously, this is seen here along the upper edge of the lit rocks at bottom centre; but elsewhere in the picture, too, small, crisp lines serve a similar function, sharpening the edges of certain roofs and areas of foliage.

PROVENANCE   Denys Cochin, Paris; Durand-Ruel, Paris; Galerie Matthiesen, Berlin; E. Goeritz, Berlin; Wildenstein, Paris and London; bought by Courtauld, November 1936, £8,000; Mrs R.A. Butler; private collection.

EXHIBITED   *Interprétations du Midi*, Libre Esthétique, Brussels, 1913 (50); *Cézanne*, Montross Gallery, New York, 1916 (3); *Cézanne*, Leicester Galleries, London, 1925 (7); *Cézanne*, Matthiesen, Berlin, 1927; *Homage to Paul Cézanne*, Wildenstein, London, 1939 (32); Tate Gallery, 1948 (8); *Landscape in French Art*, Royal Academy, London, 1949–50 (308); *Post-Impressionism*, Royal Academy, London, 1979–80 (42); *Cézanne and Poussin*, Edinburgh, 1990 (35).

LITERATURE   Venturi, 1936, no. 406.

8 CÉZANNE, PAUL 1839–1906
The Montagne Sainte-Victoire c.1887
La Montagne Sainte-Victoire
Oil on canvas, 66.8 × 92.3
Signed, bottom right: 'P. Cézanne'
Courtauld Institute Galleries (The Samuel
   Courtauld Trust)

The Montagne Sainte-Victoire lies to the east of
Cézanne's birthplace, Aix-en-Provence, and
from many points of view its broken silhouette
dominates the town. Cézanne painted it from
many viewpoints throughout his career, and it
was clearly a subject to which he attributed
great significance. In this composition, it is seen
from a vantage point to the west of Aix, near
Cézanne's family home, the Jas de Bouffan (see
cat. no. 6), with the valley of the Arc in the
foreground. The mountain peak lies about eight
miles from this viewpoint, but Cézanne, by
focusing on a comparatively small part of the
scene in front of him, gave the mountain its
dominant role in the composition. A variant of
this subject, including the trunk of another pine
tree on the right, is in the Phillips Collection,
Washington, D.C. Although we now tend to
see this scene as unspoiled and even timeless, the
presence of the prominent railway viaduct at
the far right would have been a strongly
contemporary reference for the picture's
original viewers.

When this painting, along with a *Champ de
blé*, was shown by invitation at the exhibition
of the Société des Amis des Arts at Aix (a
society of amateur artists) in 1895, it was
received with incomprehension, but it attracted
the admiration of the young poet Joachim
Gasquet, son of a childhood friend of Cézanne.
When Cézanne realised that the young man's
praise was sincere, he signed the picture and
presented it to him, initiating a friendship that
lasted until around 1904. It is one of the very
few paintings from after 1880 to which
Cézanne added his signature. In 1908, two years
after Cézanne's death, Gasquet sold it for the
very high price of 12,000 francs to the dealers
Bernheim-Jeune.

In comparison with *Tall Trees at the Jas de
Bouffan* (cat. no. 6), the picture shows a
simplification of Cézanne's painting technique.
Traces of his system of parallel brushstrokes
remain, particularly in some of the foliage, but
elsewhere the paint areas are flatter and less
variegated, with soft nuances of colour
introduced to suggest surface texture and the
play of light. In places the cream priming of the
canvas is left bare, and its luminosity contributes
to the overall tonality of the picture. Traces of
the initial underdrawing, in Prussian blue paint,
remain visible in the final state of the painting.
Infra-red photography reveals how extensive
this preparatory drawing was.

Recession into distance is suggested in two
ways, by colour and by line. There is a gradual
transition from the clearer greens and orange-
yellows of the foreground to the softer
atmospheric blues and pinks on the mountain,
but even the foreground foliage is repeatedly
tinged with blues; and pinks and reds – notably
on the branch silhouetted against the sky – knit
the foreground forms to the far mountain. The
placing of the branches, carefully framing the
contour of the mountain, enhances this surface
coherence (compare cat. no. 7). Small touches of
red were added in several parts of the
composition at a late stage in its execution in
order to emphasise these interconnections, most
conspicuously the crisp red stroke on the roof
of the tiny building about four inches above the
bottom centre of the canvas.

On the right side of this same roof, though,
there is a crisp dark blue stroke, emphatically
demarcating its edge. This is part of a network
of quite linear contours, suggesting fences, walls
and the edges of fields, which – along with the
shifts in colour – lead the eye into the distance;
on the mountain itself, a few distinct, slightly
cursive linear strokes reinforce the use of colour
contrasts in suggesting its form.

The treatment of the whole picture – zones of
cooler and warmer colour virtually alternating
as the eye moves up its surface and into space,
and the luminous space framed by tree-trunk
and branches – transforms the natural subject
into a composition of great order and
monumentality.

PROVENANCE Given by the artist in 1896 to
Joachim Gasquet, Aix-en-Provence; sold by
Gasquet to Bernheim-Jeune, Paris, 1908;
through Percy Moore Turner, London; bought
by Courtauld, April 1925, price unknown.
Courtauld Gift 1934.

EXHIBITED Société des Amis des Arts, Aix,
1895 (23); *Französische Kunst des 19. u. 20.
Jahrhunderts*, Kunsthaus, Zürich, 1917 (35);
Grands maîtres du 19me siècle, Paul Rosenberg,
Paris, 1922 (10); Centenary Exhibition,
Norwich, 1925 (63); *Cézanne*, Galerie Pigalle,
Paris, 1929 (6); *French Art*, Royal Academy,
London, 1932 (457); Tate Gallery, 1948 (10);
Cézanne, Art Institute of Chicago, and
Metropolitan Museum, New York, 1952 (52);
Cézanne, Edinburgh and London, 1954 (39);
Orangerie, Paris, 1955 (9); Courtauld
Centenary, 1976 (8); National Gallery, London,
1983 (no catalogue); Japan and Canberra, 1984
(9); United States, 1987–8 (24).

LITERATURE J. Gasquet, *Cézanne*, Paris, 1921,
pp. 54, 79; Home House Catalogue, no. 75;
Venturi, 1936, no. 454; J. Rewald, *The Ordeal of
Paul Cézanne*, London, 1950, pls 84–5; Cooper,
1954, no. 12; H. Perruchot, *Cézanne*, Paris,
1961, pp. 263–4; J. Rewald, *Cézanne, Geffroy et
Gasquet, suivi de souvenirs sur Cézanne de Louis
Aurenche et de lettres inédites*, Paris, 1960, pp. 20,
29, 39, 49, 50; E. Loran, *Cézanne's Composition*,
3rd edn, Berkeley, 1963, p. 60.

9 CÉZANNE, PAUL 1839–1906
Pot of Flowers and Pears c.1888–90
Pot de fleurs et poires
Oil on canvas, 46 × 56.2
Unsigned
Courtauld Institute Galleries (The Samuel
Courtauld Trust)

The apparent simplicity of this image of a plant in a pot, with three fruit and a plate, is deceptive. The primary subject and its surroundings are treated in a way that knits the whole image into a complex interplay of forms and colours; and, as the eye explores the picture, the configuration of shapes in the background becomes increasingly hard to read. Is the form on the right the chassis of a canvas seen from the back, leaning against the wall, or a painter's easel—as its shape might suggest, were it not for the beige canvas tone between its bars? And what is represented by the three strips of colour on the background wall, the one in the centre a clear red? X-rays reveal that Cézanne lowered the line of the table edge to the right of the pears so that it is no longer on a continuous level across the picture plane and more of the easel is seen.

These uncertainties prevent us from reading the image simply as the depiction of an actual space and force us rather to concentrate on the roles that the colours and shapes play in the overall composition. At the core of the composition, the lavish curves of the green plant are framed by the crisp bars beyond them, and their colour is set against the red bar seen through their leaves. Around the plant, the colouring is predominantly yellows and oranges alongside soft blues, variegated with great delicacy throughout. In places, the boundaries between forms are simply expressed by changes of colour, but elsewhere Cézanne added fine contour lines late in the execution of the picture, presumably feeling that a more emphatic demarcation was needed. These contours are carefully varied according to their position, with a mainly green outline separating the nearer fruit on the plate from the one beyond it, while a crisp deep blue line pulls the right side of the pear on the table forward from the flowerpot.

Though most of the canvas is quite fully covered, it is not particularly thickly painted; its brushwork is unemphatic, and Cézanne has given it no strong overall rhythm. This handling seems to fit a date at the end of the 1880s, not long after cat. no. 8.

PROVENANCE C. Hoogendijk, Amsterdam; Paul Rosenberg, Paris; Marquis de Rochecouste, Paris; Galerie Barbazanges, Paris; Bignou, Paris; Reid and Lefèvre, London; bought by Courtauld, January 1928, £5,000. Courtauld Bequest 1948.

EXHIBITED *Cézanne*, Bernheim-Jeune, Paris, 1926; *19th Century French Painters*, Knoedler, London, 1926 (21); de Hauke Gallery, New York, 1927; Tate Gallery, 1948 (12); *Cézanne*, Edinburgh and London, 1954 (40); Orangerie, Paris, 1955 (10); Courtauld Centenary, 1976 (9); Japan and Canberra, 1984 (10); United States, 1987–8 (25).

LITERATURE Jamot-Turner, no. 25; Venturi, 1936, no. 623; Cooper, 1954, no. 13; R. Bruce-Gardner, G. Hedley and C. Villers, 'Impressions of Change', in United States, 1987–8, p. 23.

10   CÉZANNE, PAUL   1839–1906
The Card Players   c.1892–5
Les Joueurs de cartes
Oil on canvas, 60 × 73
Unsigned
Courtauld Institute Galleries (The Samuel
   Courtauld Trust)

During the 1890s, Cézanne painted a long sequence of canvases of peasants from his home town of Aix-en-Provence. The most ambitious of these show groups of men playing cards. Two show three card players, with spectators (Metropolitan Museum of Art, New York, and Barnes Foundation, Merion, Pa.), and were probably painted first; in the other three, which differ in size but are very similar in detail, the subject is distilled into a simpler form, with two figures facing each other, seen in profile (one other version in Musée d'Orsay, Paris). The existence of a number of preparatory studies indicates the importance Cézanne attached to the theme.

The overall tonality of the present picture is quite subdued, but a wide range of subtly gradated colours is used to model the figures and their surroundings. A succession of warm accents revolves around the table-top, with a sharp red placed above the left figure at the top of the picture (it is hard to tell whether this suggests something on a background wall, or in a wider space beyond the figures). Against the warm hues are set the soft blues that suggest the atmosphere of the room, but these cool hues are also very varied, with a few sharper accents of clear green. The colour is simply and broadly brushed on to the canvas for the most part, but at certain points, particularly in the men's faces, crisper and very delicate accents are introduced in order to suggest their modelling more closely; elsewhere, for instance in the hands, small zones of unpainted cream-primed canvas suggest the play of light. Numerous adjustments, for example to the contours of the hats, cards and knees, are visible in a good light. Infra-red photography revealed extensive drawing in Prussian blue.

In the painting's final state, there are certain clear discrepancies with 'normal' natural vision: the verticals of the table lean to the left, and the knees of the left figure extend unduly far to the right. Such oddities were not, it seems, wilful and deliberate distortions, but rather emerged during the execution of the painting, as Cézanne concentrated on relationships of colour and tone at the expense of the literal representation of the depicted subject. When friends pointed out the oddities in his canvases, he used to laugh them off: 'I am a primitive, I've got a lazy eye,' he told Rivière and Schnerb in 1905, 'I presented myself to the Ecole [des Beaux-Arts], but I could never get the proportions right: a head interests me, and I make it too big.'

However, this preoccupation with the organisation of his canvases does not mean that Cézanne was unconcerned about his subject matter. In his later art, he sought a reconciliation between working from nature and old-master traditions; in the Card Players paintings he harnessed himself to a long tradition of images of figures seated round tables, perhaps in particular to the art of the French seventeenth-century painters of peasant subjects, the Le Nain brothers, of whom he spoke with admiration in the 1890s. At the same time, he worked closely from the observed model: apparently his peasant sitters posed for him at the Jas de Bouffan, probably one at a time, for the preparatory studies show single figures. He felt that peasant life enshrined the basic values of his local region, which he saw as threatened by contemporary urban fashions; at the end of his life, he told Jules Borély:

> Today everything has changed in reality, but not for me, I live in the town of my childhood, and it is with the eyes of the people of my own age that I see again the past. I love above all else the appearance of people who have grown old without breaking with old customs.

In this sense, the image of peasants seated still, concentrating on their game of cards, is the living counterpart to the landscapes of his home countryside, notably the Montagne Sainte-Victoire (see cat. no. 8), which held such significance for him.

PROVENANCE   With Paul Cassirer, Berlin; Dr Julius Elias, Berlin; J.B. Stang, Oslo; Alfred Gold, Berlin; bought by Courtauld, March 1929, £12,500. Courtauld Gift 1932.

EXHIBITED   *Cézanne*, Galerie Pigalle, Paris, 1929 (8); *French Art*, Royal Academy, London, 1932 (392); Royal Scottish Academy, Edinburgh, 1933 (142); *Chefs d'oeuvre de l'art français*, Paris 1937 (256); Tate Gallery, 1948 (13); *Cézanne*, Edinburgh and London, 1954 (52); Orangerie, Paris, 1955 (11); Courtauld Centenary, 1976 (10); Japan and Canberra, 1984 (11); United States, 1987–8 (26).

LITERATURE   Jamot-Turner, no. 23; Home House Catalogue, no. 1; Venturi, 1936, p. 59, no. 557; Cooper, 1954, no. 14; B. Dorival, *Cézanne*, Paris, 1948, pp. 62–5; K. Badt, *The Art of Cézanne*, London, 1965, pp. 87–130; T. Reff, 'Cézanne's "Cardplayers" and their Sources', *Arts Magazine*, November 1980, pp. 104–17.

11 CÉZANNE, PAUL 1839–1906
Man with a Pipe *c*.1892–5
L'Homme à la pipe
Oil on canvas, 73 × 60
Unsigned
Courtauld Institute Galleries (The Samuel
Courtauld Trust)

The model is the same as that for the left-hand figure in *The Card Players* (cat.no.10); he was a peasant gardener, apparently named *le père* Alexandre. The two paintings were probably painted at much the same date, since they are very similar in colour and handling. Here the man's face, the prime focus of the composition, is more elaborated than any part of *The Card Players*: parts of the face are treated with successions of diagonal strokes (here running from upper left to lower right), reminiscent of the 'constructive stroke' that Cézanne had employed a decade earlier (see cat.nos 5–7). Pivotal to the treatment of the face is the contrast between the dull blues of the shadow of the nose and the rich warm hues of its lit side; this contrast is heightened by two particularly crisp, bold strokes of red added down the ridge of the nose very late in the execution of the painting. Prussian blue is used here together with a red lake pigment to underdraw and subsequently redefine the forms.

Again, as in *The Card Players*, the simple, monumental form of the figure is used to suggest the timeless, traditional values that Cézanne attributed to the old peasants of the Aix region (see cat.no.10).

PROVENANCE Ambroise Vollard, Paris; Paul Gallimard, Paris; Galerie Barbazanges, Paris; Bignou, Paris; Reid and Lefèvre, London; bought by Courtauld, October 1927, £7,500. Courtauld Gift 1932.

EXHIBITED La Libre Esthétique, Brussels, 1904 (no number); *Cézanne*, Galerie Pigalle, Paris, 1929 (9); Tate Gallery, 1948 (14); *Cézanne*, Edinburgh and London, 1954 (51); Orangerie, Paris, 1955 (12); Courtauld Centenary, 1976 (11); National Gallery, London, 1983 (no catalogue); Japan and Canberra, 1984 (12); United States, 1987–8 (26).

LITERATURE Jamot-Turner, no.22; Home House Catalogue, no.9; Venturi, 1936, no.564; Cooper, 1954, no.15; R. Bruce-Gardner, G. Hedley and C. Villers, 'Impressions of Change', in United States, 1987–8, p.21.

12 CÉZANNE, PAUL 1839–1906
Still Life with Plaster Cupid c.1894
Nature morte avec l'amour en plâtre
Oil on paper, laid on board, 70.6 × 57.3
Unsigned
Courtauld Institute Galleries (The Samuel
Courtauld Trust)

Cézanne's still lifes perhaps reveal his changing preoccupations most fully, since still life gave him the freedom to choose and arrange the combinations of objects he wanted to depict. A witness described the complex business of setting up one such still-life subject:

> The cloth was arranged on the table, with innate taste. Then Cézanne arranged the fruits, contrasting the tones one against the other, making the complementaries vibrate, the greens against the reds, the yellows against the blues, tipping, turning, balancing the fruit as he wanted them to be, using coins of one or two sous for the purpose. He brought to this task the greatest care and many precautions; one guessed it was a feast for the eye to him.

Still Life with Plaster Cupid is one of the most complex of his late still lifes, both in its composition and through the inclusion of the cast and other works of art. The plaster cast of a Cupid (formerly attributed to Pierre Puget) still remains in Cézanne's studio at Aix, as does the cast of a flayed man which is seen in the painting at the top of the present picture. The Cupid cast is in reality eighteen inches high, and it appears larger than life in the painting. The same is true of the canvas that is shown leaning against the wall on the left, *Still Life with Peppermint Bottle* (National Gallery of Art, Washington, D.C.), which was painted at much the same time as this picture; the area of it that we see, which includes the red stripe and blue area at top left, is shown here larger than it is in the original canvas, although implicitly it is standing on the floor well beyond the foreground table. The far apple, apparently placed on the distant floor, appears as large as the fruit on the table.

There are ambiguities, too, in the relationships between the objects. The 'real' blue drapery at the bottom left merges with the painted still life in the picture on the left; the foliage of the 'real' onion fuses with the table leg in the same still life; and the back edge of the table-top virtually dissolves into the floor to the left of this onion. There is also real uncertainty about the arrangement of planes in the background, where the edges of the canvas depicting the flayed figure cannot be clearly determined.

The inconsistencies and paradoxes of the space are compounded by the paradoxes about the nature of the reality depicted which recur throughout the picture: between 'real' and painted fruit and drapery; between 'real' fruit on the table and the Cupid figure – a cast of a statue; and between this cast and the flayed man beyond – a painting of a cast of a statue. All of these devices seem to stress the artificiality of the picture itself – of its grouping and of its making; of all Cézanne's still lives, this one reveals most vividly the artificiality of the idea of *nature morte*, an assemblage of objects, arranged in order to be painted, and, beyond this, the artifice of the art of painting itself.

Some sketching, probably in pencil, is clearly seen in normal light as underdrawing for the apples, and infra-red photography revealed more underdrawing in the Cupid's face. There are other areas where no underdrawing is visible and the image is started and finished in paint. In one area, the apple on the lower edge, there is pencil drawing on top of the paint.

PROVENANCE Bernheim-Jeune, Paris; Dr G. Jebsen, Oslo; Paul Rosenberg, Paris; Alex. Reid, Glasgow; bought by Courtauld, May 1923, £2,850. Courtauld Bequest 1948.

EXHIBITED *Fransk Malerkonst d. 19 Jaarhonderts*, Copenhagen, 1914 (20); *Cézanne*, Montross Gallery, New York, 1916 (16); *Masterpieces of French Art of the 19th Century*, Agnew, Manchester, 1923 (5); Tate Gallery, 1948 (15); *Cézanne*, Edinburgh and London, 1954 (50); Orangerie, Paris, 1955 (13); Courtauld Centenary, 1976 (12); *Cézanne: The Late Work*, Museum of Modern Art, New York, Museum of Fine Arts, Houston, Grand Palais, Paris, 1977–8 (23); National Gallery, London, 1983 (no catalogue); Japan and Canberra, 1984 (13); United States, 1987–8 (28).

LITERATURE Jamot-Turner, no. 24; Venturi, 1936, no. 706; Cooper, 1954, no. 16; W. Rubin (ed.), *Cézanne: The Late Work*, New York and London, 1977–8, pp. 30–2; R. Bruce-Gardner, G. Hedley and C. Villers, 'Impressions of Change', in United States, 1987–8, p. 23.

13 CÉZANNE, PAUL 1839–1906
The Lac d'Annecy 1896
Le Lac d'Annecy
Oil on canvas, 65 × 81
Unsigned
Courtauld Institute Galleries (The Samuel
Courtauld Trust)

The Lac d'Annecy was painted while Cézanne
was on holiday at Talloires on the shores of this
lake in Haute-Savoie in July 1896; the view is
taken from the beach of Talloires, looking in a
southerly direction towards the Château de
Duingt, half hidden by trees on the far side of
the lake. Cézanne wrote in a letter to Gasquet
from Talloires:

> This is a temperate zone. The surrounding
> hills are quite lofty. The lake, which at this
> point narrows to a bottleneck, seems to lend
> itself to the line drawing exercises of young
> ladies. Certainly it is still a bit of nature, but a
> little like we've been taught to see it in the
> albums of young lady travellers.

In this canvas, with its vibrant colour and
monumental structure, Cézanne was clearly
determined to transcend this commonplace
picturesque.

The large part of the canvas is dominated by
a cool colour range of blues and greens,
sometimes quite deep and sonorous in tone, but
its principal focus is the succession of warm
accents that runs across it, where the early
morning sunshine strikes the objects in the
scene – the far hills, the left tree-trunk and the
buildings across the water. This warm-cool
contrast is brought into particularly sharp focus
on the left edge of the castle tower: a vertical
stroke of orange is set against the deep blues
beyond, but, between the two, there is an
extremely narrow band of canvas, only very
thinly painted with very pale hues so that the
building is lifted forward from its surroundings
both by the stroke of warm colouring and by
this thread of light. The decision not to
overpaint this fine streak at the point that he
added colour on either side of it shows how
tightly he controlled the colour effects he
achieved.

The whole picture is carefully structured,
with the massive bulk of the tree as a *repoussoir*
on the left and its branches enclosing the top
(compare *The Montagne Sainte-Victoire*,
cat. no. 8); the composition is anchored in the
centre by the tighter, more rectilinear forms of
the buildings and their elongated reflections. In
reality, the castle is about one mile away across
the water from Cézanne's viewpoint, but, by
narrowing his visual field and focusing closely
on it, he made it seem considerably closer
(compare the mountain in cat. no. 8). The
reflections are slightly distorted – like the table-
legs in *The Card Players* (cat. no. 10), they are
not exactly vertical; Cézanne often ignored
discrepancies of this sort as he concentrated on
the relationships of colour and form in his
canvases.

The brushwork across the background builds
up a sequence of planes of colour, which unite
the nearby foliage to the far hillsides; but, at
certain points, cursive, graphic arcs virtually
detach themselves from the foliage, and
accentuate the sense of formal rhythm and
pattern across the top of the canvas. These
means of giving a unified structure to the whole
surface became even more prominent in
Cézanne's last works, but it was not a means of
rejecting nature; rather he sought, he said, a
'harmony parallel to nature'; it was thus that he
hoped to make out of his experiences of the
visible world a lasting, coherent art.

PROVENANCE Purchased from the artist by
Ambroise Vollard, Paris (1897); C. Hoogendijk,
Amsterdam; Paul Rosenberg, Paris; Marcel
Kapferer, Paris; Bernheim-Jeune, Paris; Percy
Moore Turner; bought by Courtauld, January,
1926, £8,000. Courtauld Gift 1932.

EXHIBITED *Grands maîtres du 19me siècle*, Paul
Rosenberg, Paris, 1922 (14); *Les Grandes
Influences*, Paul Rosenberg, Paris, 1925 (14);
Cézanne, Galerie Pigalle, Paris, 1929 (7); *French
Art*, Royal Academy, London, 1932 (505); Tate
Gallery, 1948 (16); *Cézanne*, Edinburgh and
London, 1954 (55); Orangerie, Paris, 1955 (14);
Courtauld Centenary, 1976 (13); Japan and
Canberra, 1984 (14); United States, 1987–8 (29).

LITERATURE Jamot-Turner, no. 27; Home
House Catalogue, no. 8; Venturi, 1936, no. 762;
Cooper, 1954, no. 17; J. Rewald, *Cézanne,
Geffroy et Gasquet*, Paris, 1960, pp. 27, 28; W.
Rubin (ed.), *Cézanne, The Late Work*, New
York and London, 1977–8, pp. 26, 64; P.
Cézanne, *Correspondance*, ed. J. Rewald, Paris,
1978, p. 252.

14 DAUMIER, HONORÉ 1808–79
Rescue c.1860?
Sauvetage
Oil on canvas, 34.3 × 28
Unsigned
Private Collection

Daumier's activity as a painter was largely private: he exhibited a few canvases at the Salon around 1850 (including one Don Quixote subject), and one in 1861, but otherwise his paintings remained unseen by the public until, just before the artist's death, the dealer Durand-Ruel put on a major display of his paintings in 1878.

His 1861 Salon exhibit was a small canvas of laundresses beside the Seine in Paris, presented as a monumentalised group, set against a simplified backdrop of the buildings along the *quai*. In *Rescue* he adopts a very similar format. Moreover, the summary background of *Rescue* also represents the river banks; two other versions of the same composition show the setting in more detail.

Whereas the pictures of laundresses present an image of the harshness of the everyday life and work of women beside the river, *Rescue* focuses on a dramatic moment – the rescue of a child from the water. In mid-nineteenth century Paris, the Seine was a potent emblem in both literature and painting for the hardships and sufferings of the urban population; here, for once, a potential tragedy has been averted.

Despite the small format and summary execution, the figures in the painting are given rhetorical gestures more reminiscent of the expressive language of Mannerist or Baroque painting. The existence of versions of *Rescue* which set the figures in a wider setting and show the background in some detail suggests that Daumier may have considered working up the subject as an ambitious canvas on a larger scale. However, he seems never to have done so (for his problems in painting on a larger scale, see entry for cat. no. 15).

PROVENANCE Camentron, Paris; Eugène Blot, Paris; Blot Sale, Paris, 10 May 1906 (lot 23); Druet, Paris; Holzmann, Berlin; Galerie Matthiesen, Berlin; Bernheim-Jeune, Paris; through Percy Moore Turner; bought by Courtauld, November 1929, £3,200 plus commission of £320; Lady Aberconway; private collection; private collection.

EXHIBITED *Daumier*, Ecole des Beaux-Arts, Paris, 1901 (27); *Daumier*, Galerie E. Blot, Paris, 1908 (9); *Daumier*, Barbizon House, London, 1923 (1); *Daumier*, Matthiesen, Berlin, 1926 (52); *Corot and Daumier*, Museum of Modern Art, New York, 1930 (82); Tate Gallery, 1948 (19); *Daumier: Paintings and Drawings*, Arts Council at Tate Gallery, 1961 (16).

LITERATURE *Catalogue de la Vente E. Blot*, Paris, 1906, no. 23; E. Klossowski, *Honoré Daumier*, Munich, 1908, no. 316; E. Fuchs, *Der Maler Daumier*, Munich, 1927, no. 65; Jamot-Turner, no. 4; Cooper, 1954, no. 20; K.E. Maison, *Honoré Daumier, Catalogue Raisonné of the Paintings, Watercolours and Drawings*, London, 1968, I, no. 229.

15 DAUMIER, HONORÉ 1808–79
Don Quixote and Sancho Panza   *c.*1870?
Don Quichotte et Sancho Panza
Oil on canvas, 100 × 81
Unsigned
Courtauld Institute Galleries (The Samuel
    Courtauld Trust)

Themes from the Don Quixote story recur in
Daumier's painting; he was clearly fascinated by
the contrast between the gaunt elongated figure
of the Don and his roly-poly companion. His
first biographer, Arsène Alexandre, suggested
that the artist viewed his own artistic *persona* in
terms of both figures and the relationship
between them – between Quixote's visionary
idealism and Sancho Panza's down-to-earth,
peasant common sense. Here, unusually for
Daumier, the two are presented side by side, as
complementary equals.

His few more highly finished oils suggest that
he had great difficulty in completing paintings
on a larger scale. The vivid undulating line
which he could use to such effect in his
lithographic caricatures, by which he won his
fame, did not readily translate into oil paint and
on to a large scale, in a form that nineteenth-
century viewers would have regarded as
making a finished painting. In the nineteenth
century, certain connoisseurs of taste, and
fellow artists, had appreciated such rapid
sketches, seeing them as reflecting an artist's true
creativity, but the public celebration of rapidly
brushed, unfinished surfaces as the essential
form of artistic expression is a phenomenon of
the twentieth century. However, to twentieth-
century viewers these bold notations have had a
great appeal; Roger Fry spoke of the tragic
overtones of this painting, which he likened to
a work by Rembrandt, and regretted that
Daumier was forced to spend so much of his
creative activity in producing humorous
caricatures for journals like *Le Charivari*, instead
of being able to devote himself to painting.

His work in oils is notoriously hard to date,
but the present canvas, one of the largest and
grandest of all his oils, was probably executed
quite late in his life; in 1867 he had painted a
rough sketch of a Don Quixote subject as a
decoration for the house of his friend the
landscapist Daubigny at Auvers (now in the
Musée du Louvre, Paris), and the present
picture may have been painted soon after this.
The figures are treated as vivid silhouettes
against the hillside, with flowing ribbons of
grey paint beginning to suggest their forms
over the initial rapid brown underpainting.

PROVENANCE   Ambroise Vollard, Paris; Paul
Rosenberg, Paris; Bignou, Paris; Lefèvre and
Son, London; bought by Courtauld, May 1923,
£1,350. Courtauld Gift 1932.

EXHIBITED   *Daumier*, Ecole des Beaux-Arts,
Paris, 1901 (89); *Daumier*, Galerie Rosenberg,
Paris, 1907 (32); *Art français au 19me siècle*, Paul
Rosenberg, Paris, 1917 (20); *L'Art français*,
Basel, 1921 (52); *Grands maîtres du 19me siècle*,
Paul Rosenberg, Paris, 1922 (34); *Impressionist
School*, Lefèvre Gallery, London, 1923 (17);
French Art, Royal Academy, London, 1932
(376); Tate Gallery, 1948 (20); Orangerie, Paris,
1955 (17); *Daumier: Paintings and Drawings*, Arts
Council at Tate Gallery, 1961 (97); Courtauld
Centenary, 1976 (15); Japan and Canberra, 1984
(19); United States, 1987–8 (4).

LITERATURE   Jamot-Turner, no. 3; Home House
Catalogue, no. 2; R. Fry, 'French Art of the
Nineteenth Century', *Burlington Magazine*, June
1922, pp. 277–8; E. Klossowski, *Honoré Daumier*,
Munich, 1923, no. 51; E. Fuchs, *Der Maler
Daumier*, Munich, 1927, no. 165; J. Lassaigne,
Daumier, Paris, 1938, pl. 155; H. Shipp, 'The
Courtauld Collection', *Apollo*, September 1947,
p. 58; Cooper, 1954, no. 20; Maison, 1968, I,
no. 227 and pl. 168; C. Gordon, in *100
Masterpieces from the Courtauld Collections*, ed. D.
Farr, London, 1987, p. 74.

16   DEGAS, EDGAR   1834–1917
      Woman at a Window   c.1871–2
      Femme à la fenêtre
      Oil (peinture à l'essence) on paper,
         mounted on linen, 61.3 × 45.9
      Signed, bottom right: 'Degas'; stamped in
         red, bottom right: 'Degas'
      Courtauld Institute Galleries (The Samuel
         Courtauld Trust)

The picture is clearly not formally finished, but by very abbreviated means it succeeds in capturing the effect of a figure against a brightly lit window. The play of light on the sitter's left hand is suggested with some delicacy, and the contour of her profile drawn with some care; but the background light is only very broadly blocked in, and the forms of the chair on the left and the seat on which she sits are simply drawn in with fluent black lines of paint, applied with the brush. The figure, seen *contre-jour*, is primarily laid in with black in contrast to the slabs of light beyond, while the brown-toned underlying paper is left bare across much of the rest of the picture. The paper has more recently been affixed to canvas, which has greatly affected its surface, and the picture's tonality has been darkened by varnishing.

Degas was fascinated by the ways in which such effects of light altered the appearance of figures and seemingly dematerialised them (compare the effect of the footlights in cat. no. 17); this is related to his interest in viewing figures from unexpected angles (see cat. no. 18). He was concerned with exploring the ways in which the visible world was actually seen in everyday life, in marked contrast to the conventions of pictorial representation which placed figures in a good light so as to show off their features (as Renoir did in *La Loge*, cat. no. 39).

Although not fully finished, the picture appeared on the market during Degas's lifetime, though we do not know when it left his hands, and whether as a gift or a sale (the majority of his less finished works were still in his studio at his death, e.g., cat. nos 18 and 76). The English painter Sickert bought the painting from Durand-Ruel around 1901–2 for Ellen Cobden (his former wife with whom he remained on friendly terms); he wrote to his patron Sir William Eden to announce his purchase: 'I have just bought Degas's finest work, had my eye on it for 12 years or so!, for £400! for Mrs Sickert, and sold the one I bought for £74 or so to an American for £3000.' The painting he sold was *Rehearsal of a Ballet on the Stage* (the oil version of the subject now in the Metropolitan Museum of Art, New York, which was bought from him by H.O. Havemeyer). When he asked Durand-Ruel why he was able to buy the present picture for a lower price than a pastel, he was told it was 'because the amateur of Degas always wanted ballet girls'.

Sickert recorded that Degas told him the work was painted 'during or soon after' the siege of Paris. An annotation on Sickert's own copy of Jamot's book on Degas records that the artist said that the sitter was a *cocotte* and that during the siege he had bought her a piece of raw meat 'which she fell upon, so hungry was she, & devoured whole'. According to the title the picture bore when Courtauld bought it, the background represents a view over the Tuileries Gardens, though the picture itself gives little clue to the location.

Infra-red photographs demonstrate more clearly Degas's exploitation of oil painting 'à l'essence'. When some of the oil medium is soaked from the paint and then thinned with a diluent, it can be used, as here, in a manner similar to watercolour and brush drawing; in the photograph the tone of the paper is rendered light showing the application of extensive thin washes and astonishingly lucid and fluent line drawing. This use of white to delineate the forms and to point highlights has reduced covering power, and even where vigorously applied retains no trace of impasto. An adjustment to the sitter's right arm can be seen through the white, and the slightly smudged marks on the sitter's face and right hand suggest the dabbing and wiping of the wet paint as a watercolourist might employ a small sponge to soften or thin a tonal wash.

PROVENANCE   Read [i.e., Alexander Reid], Glasgow; Read [Reid] Sale (Vente de M.A. . . .), Paris, 10 June 1898 (lot 26; 2,900 francs); Durand-Ruel, Paris; Mrs Walter Sickert, London; Mrs Cobden-Sanderson, London; Miss M.F.C. Knox, London, 1917; Mrs Cobden-Sanderson, 1917; Miss Stella Cobden-Sanderson, London, 1926; Leicester Galleries, London; bought by Courtauld, March 1927, £1,500. Courtauld Gift 1932.

EXHIBITED   International Society, The New Gallery, London, 1908 (86, wrongly described as 'watercolour'); Goupil Gallery Salon, London, 1923 (72); *Degas*, Musée de l'Orangerie, Paris, 1937 (not catalogued); Tate Gallery, 1948 (22); *Degas*, Edinburgh and London, 1952 (13); Orangerie, Paris, 1955 (19); Courtauld Centenary, 1976 (16); Japan and Canberra, 1984 (22); United States, 1987–8 (7).

LITERATURE   Home House Catalogue, no. 14; P. Jamot, *Degas*, Paris, 1924, pp. 56, 140; P.A. Lemoisne, *Degas et son oeuvre*, Paris, 1946, II, no. 385; W. Sickert, 'Monthly Chronicle: Degas', *Burlington Magazine*, December 1923, p. 308; Jamot-Turner, no. 12; Cooper, 1954, no. 22; D. Sutton, *Walter Sickert: A Biography*, 1976, pp. 111–12; R. Bruce-Gardner, G. Hedley and C. Villers, 'Impressions of Change', in United States, 1987–8, p. 23.

17 DEGAS, EDGAR 1839–1917
Two Dancers on the Stage 1874
Deux danseuses en scène
Oil on canvas, 61.5 × 46
Signed, bottom left: 'Degas'
Courtauld Institute Galleries (The Samuel
    Courtauld Trust)

This composition is closely related to a group of three compositions with many figures which show dancers rehearsing on a clearly defined stage, with other waiting dancers and the ballet-master (two in Metropolitan Museum of Art, New York, one in Musée d'Orsay, Paris). Here, though, Degas concentrated on the two figures, with stage-flats beyond them that seem to suggest foliage, but gave no indication of whether we are watching a performance or a rehearsal. Our attention is focused on their poses, as seen from the unexpected angle of a box virtually above the edge of the stage.

The figures are in standard ballet positions, one *sur les pointes*, the other in fourth position with her arms in *demi-seconde*, and their gestures clearly suggest some sort of interchange. But we are given no clue to the drama or narrative being enacted. The viewer's attempt to see this as a coherent, framed grouping is also undermined by the appearance of the edge of a third dancer, her figure cut by the frame, at the far left, set back on the stage; the presence of this dancer challenges any attempt to understand the gestures of the other two, but this is all we are told.

There is also a paradoxical relationship between the style and elegance of their poses and their facial features – snub-nosed and slightly simian. According to contemporary notions of physiognomy, in which Degas was much interested, there was a correlation between facial appearance and personality; physiognomies such as these were associated with a lower order of human development, and with the lower classes. Degas regularly gave such features to the dancers in his paintings, as if to signpost the contrast between the humble working-class girls (the *rats*) who made up the *corps de ballet*, and the finesse that the discipline of classical ballet imposed on them.

On occasion, Degas painted actual ballet performances, but more often he showed the dancers rehearsing, or left ambiguous exactly what they were doing, as he did here. The ballet, with its precision of movements, fascinated him, but he always presented it in ways that revealed its artificiality, by including other extraneous elements – figures who do not watch the dancers, waiting dancers scratching themselves or dancers who play no part in the main action, like the figure on the left here. His interest in this theme is also part of his attempt in the 1870s to study the visible world from many angles that had not been sanctioned in previous art, but that seemed to him characteristic of the ways in which everyday life appeared in the modern city.

This canvas is unusually highly finished for Degas and was put on exhibition and sold soon after its completion; contemporary reviews show that it was exhibited in London in November 1874 in the Ninth Exhibition of the Society of French Artists, organised by the Parisian dealer Durand-Ruel, and it was bought at this show by the pioneering Degas collector, Captain Henry Hill of Brighton; it was the first painting by Degas that he bought.

Degas had exhibited the similarly treated, multi-figure composition in which this pairing of figures appears (now Musée d'Orsay, Paris) at the first Impressionist group exhibition, and this painting, with the present canvas, makes an interesting contrast to the techniques with which the group is usually associated. The stage-flats in *Two Dancers on the Stage* are treated in free dabs of colour, but the figures are modelled with comparative delicacy. The overall colour scheme is quite subdued, with vivid points of pink, yellow and green on the figures' shoes, flowers, bodices and head-dresses. The generally simple paint surfaces and muted tonality are in marked contrast to the broken touch and vivid colour characteristic of the landscapists in the group (see cat. no. 31); this shows how difficult it is to use the first group exhibition, at which the group was named the 'Impressionists', as the means of defining the nature of their art (see also Renoir's *La Loge*, cat. no. 39).

The canvas is the product of extensive preparatory work, both in the form of the other paintings that show much the same grouping, and in separate drawings; moreover, Degas made a number of alterations to the composition during its execution: the dancer cut off at the left was originally a little larger and about half an inch further to the right; and there are changes in the placing of the feet and legs of the two main dancers.

PROVENANCE Captain Henry Hill, Brighton (by 1874); Hill Sale, Christie's, 25 May 1889 (lot 31, £64 1s 0d), bought Goupil (i.e., Theo van Gogh); Victor Desfossés; sold by Desfossés, 4 November 1889, to Goupil-Boussod & Valadon successeurs (5,000 francs); Goupil-Boussod & Valadon successeurs, sold 13 November 1899 (6,000 francs) to Paul Gallimard, Paris; Alex. Reid, Glasgow; Sir James Murray, Aberdeen, sold Christie's, 29 April 1927 (lot 41, £7,200); Knoedler, London; bought by Courtauld, June 1927, £8,560. Courtauld Gift 1932.

EXHIBITED Ninth Exhibition of Society of French Artists, Paul Durand-Ruel, London, 1874 (9) as 'Scène de Ballet'; Galerie 'Les Arts', Paris, 1912 (16); *French Impressionists*, Lefèvre Gallery, London, 1920 (8); Opening Exhibition, Modern Foreign Gallery, Tate Gallery, London, 1926; *Degas*, Musée de l'Orangerie, Paris, 1937 (26); Tate Gallery, 1948 (24); *Degas*, Edinburgh and London, 1952 (16); Orangerie, Paris, 1955 (21); *Impressionism*, Royal Academy, London, 1974 (56); Courtauld Centenary, 1976 (17); Japan and Canberra, 1984 (23); United States, 1987–8 (8).

LITERATURE Home House Catalogue, no. 25; Jamot-Turner, no. 11; Lemoisne, 1946, II, p. 234, no. 425; L. Browse, *Degas Dancers*, London, 1949, pp. 56, 355, and pl. 50; Cooper, 1954, no. 24, as 'c.1877'; R. Pickvance, 'Degas's Dancers: 1872–6', *Burlington Magazine*, June 1963, pp. 263–6; J. Rewald, 'Theo Van Gogh, Goupil and the Impressionists, II', *Gazette des Beaux-Arts*, February 1973, p. 90.

*After the Bath, Woman Drying
    Herself* (?)*c*.1895
Apres le bain, femme s'essuyant
Bound pastel on paper, 67.7 × 57.8
Stamped bottom left with mark of Degas's
    studio sale
Courtauld Institute Galleries (The Samuel
    Courtauld Trust)

The subject of women bathing in tubs or drying themselves first appeared in Degas's monotypes of about 1880 and was to become one of the artist's recurring themes in the late drawings.

At the eighth Impressionist group exhibition in 1886, Degas showed a set of pastels under the collective title *Sequence of Nudes of Women Bathing, Washing, Drying, Wiping Themselves, Combing their Hair or Having it Combed. After the Bath, Woman Wiping Herself* was probably executed some years later than this series, although it awaits a more precise dating. It has been assigned by Lemoisne to *c*.1889–90(?). Four variants of this composition, also in pastel (Lemoisne 1340–3), are, however, dated by him to 1899: of these, two (1340 and 1341) may be reassigned to *c*.1895. Degas also examined the present model's pose in a wax sculpture of about 1897–8 (Mellon Collection, Upperville, Va.).

Closely related, these works are a further nine drawings in charcoal(?) and one counterproof, included in the sale of Degas's atelier (first sale, 6–8 May 1918, lot 314; second sale, 11–13 December 1918, lots 266, 269, 293, 309, 311; third sale, 7–9 April 1919, lots 186, 292, 309; fourth sale, 2–4 July 1919, the counterproof, lot 365). The Courtauld drawing's place in this complex sequence of evolving images is as yet unclear. The series, however, vividly illustrates Degas's dictum: 'Make a drawing, begin it again, trace it; begin it again and trace again.'

Degas began to draw *After the Bath, Woman Drying Herself* on the higher of the two sheets of thin, smooth, machine-made paper that make up the composition's support. The sheets may have been lightly oiled to increase their transparency, enabling Degas to trace more easily the figure of the bather from one of the designs mentioned above: the upper sheet has now discoloured to a pale yellow-buff. After a bold initial drawing in black chalk, Degas appears to have blocked in substantial areas of the sheet with broad, open strokes of pink-red pastel. This colour is visible in the curtain, right, and underlies the wall, the model's neck, the interior of the bathtub and the carpet. At an early stage in the drawing campaign, the composition was extended at the bottom by adding a second strip of paper: this is inaccurately abutted with the higher sheet, overlapping it at the left and leaving a slight gap at the right. At this point, too, the top, and apparently all other edges of the composition, were trimmed, and the sheets were laid down on a secondary support of thin card: and in laying the drawing down, Degas also ensured that the tear at the upper right, in the area of the tub, no longer posed a problem. It is significant that, as well as enlarging drawings by adding paper, Degas was here also using the reverse process of trimming to achieve a more satisfactory composition. Sometime after completion, the drawing and card support were mounted on stout millboard.

The texture of the pastel in virtually all areas of this drawing indicates that it has been bound. The pale yellow towel on the chair has a dense, paste-like surface, suggesting that the pastel may in part have been applied with the brush. Its surface is furrowed by zigzag striations associated with strokes of yellow: it is possible that these were drawn with a stick of bound pastel that had since dried and hardened. A similarly hardened black pastel or crayon seems to have been used for lines defining the model's spine and ribcage, which equally have been incised into the sheet. In other areas, pastel or chalk has been applied either moist, or in a liquid state. The spattered appearance of the black shadow on the chair to the right of the towel indicates that it has been brushed or wiped on, while the blacks, yellows and touches of red in the hair have been dabbed in with a rag, or perhaps, for the smaller touches, with the fingertips. Stippling in the bather's wrist and raised left hand, and on the rim of the bath at the right, is applied with the moist point of the pastel, as are the delicately stroked diagonals that model the interior of the tub. In other parts of the composition, for example, the edges of the towel with which the bather dries herself, her neck, raised arm, and back, the pastel is heavily impacted – indeed, almost encrusted – on the paper's surface in dense parallel- or cross-hatchings, or in screens of vigorous zigzags. Such energetic and texturally varied handling is closely comparable with that seen in Degas's monotypes.

The figure is modelled by meshed veils of 'V'-shaped hatching in blacks, white, Indian red and a tender pink contrasted with pale olive; widely spaced yellow strokes at the base of the spine record the reflection of the bathtowel draped over the chair. For the most part, the hatching follows the planes of the torso; however, in the right shoulder – an area Degas extensively revised – sharp raking lines affirming the new form also cut across it, denying its three-dimensionality. The inside of the tub, defined by veils of strokes comparable to those creating the bather, is treated with a palette of pinks, purples, white and grey-blues. The cool, nuanced tones of flesh, bath and towels are surrounded by the intense, hot colours of wall, carpets and chair.

Despite the informality of the model's pose, the composition is carefully organised both spatially and as a linear framework. The bather's left upper arm and thighs are aligned with the diagonals of bathtub, skirting-board and carpet, while the left forearm, linked with the top left of the sheet, is echoed at the upper right by the form of the curtain: the curves of bathtowel, chairback and tub resonate with the rounded form of her back.

That this composition coalesced only after a period of deep contemplation, precise observation and imaginative experiment is evident in the number of daring alterations: indeed, there is almost no area of the figure that has not been revised. Two deeply impressed lines in the hair indicate earlier and lower positions for the head, while the *pentimento* of vibrant orange on the wall – a colour otherwise sparingly used only in the chair – masks a higher placing of this form; the left arm has been raised considerably – its earlier position now subsumed in the rim of the bathtub – while being extended towards the left. Brusque notations in black chalk indicate late ideas for the placing of the model's nose and for a possible reworking of the right hip, while the left hand is accented by drawing with the (moist?) point of a dark, crayon-like material. This unidentified medium, which deposits on the paper a compact track of glistering particles of equal size, is also visible in underdrawing of the model and the towel with which she dries herself. At a number of points the modelling of the figure remains unresolved, notably in the knees and in the curious invention of the right arm, which appears to incorporate residual breast imagery; and as with nearly all of Degas's later drawings, this work was abandoned in a provisional state.

In the mid-1880s Degas told George Moore that his aims in his pictures of bathing women were to show 'a human creature preoccupied with herself – a cat who licks herself: hitherto, the nude has always been represented in poses which presuppose an audience, but these women of mine are honest and simple folk, unconcerned by any other interests than those involved in their physical condition . . . It is as if you looked through a key-hole.' Images such as these have at times been seen as misogynic, by critics from J.K. Huysmans onwards, but they show the same studied detachment of viewpoint as his treatment of many other themes (compare cat. nos 17 and 76). There is no hint of savagery in the way that his models are presented.

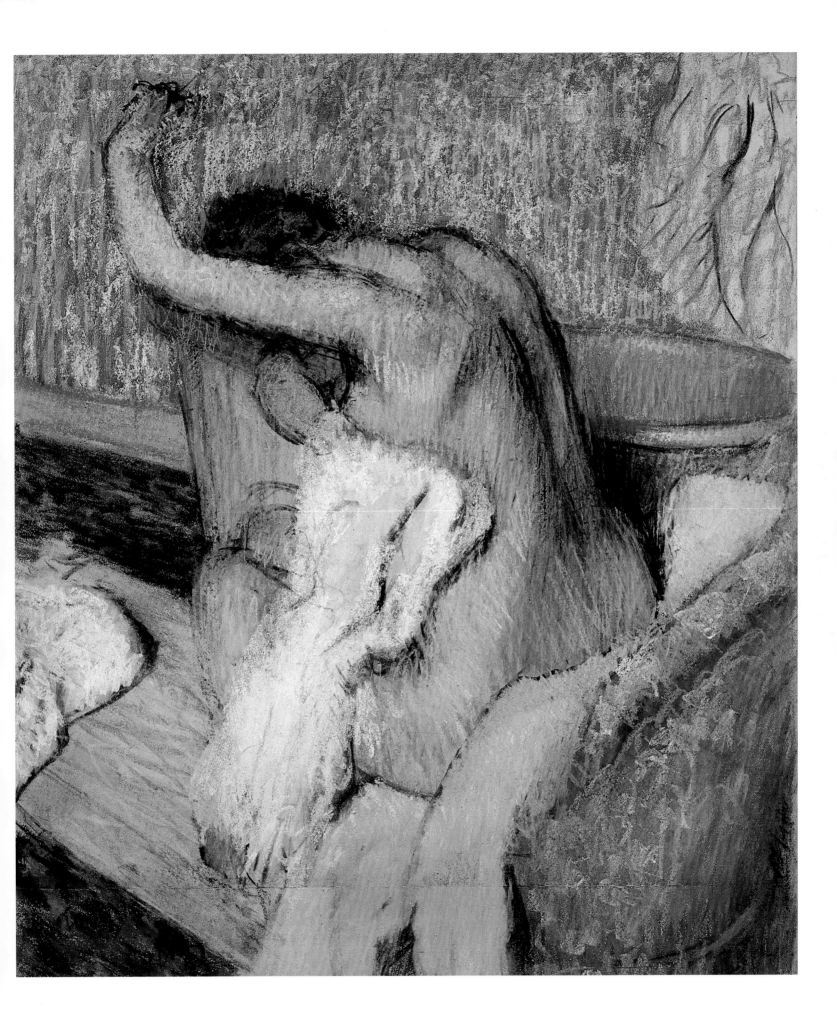

(Cat. no. 18 continued)

PROVENANCE   First Degas Sale, Paris, 6 May 1918 (lot 281, 25,000 francs); Trotti, Paris; Winkel and Magnussen, Copenhagen; Galerie Barbazanges, Paris; Percy Moore Turner; Lord Ivor Spencer-Churchill, London; Percy Moore Turner; Samuel Courtauld by 1929 (price unknown). Courtauld Gift 1932.

EXHIBITED   *Degas Utställning*, Nationalmuseum, Stockholm, 1920 (30); *Degas Udstilling*, Ny Carlsberg Glyptothek, Copenhagen, 1920 (30); Tate Gallery, 1948 (93); Courtauld Centenary, 1976 (18); Japan and Canberra, 1984 (24); United States, 1987–8 (10); C.I.G., 1988 (17).

LITERATURE   Jamot-Turner, no. 14; Home House Catalogue, 1935, no. 26; Lemoisne, 1946, III, p. 558, no. 1011; Cooper, 1954, no. 27; Russoli and Minervino, 1970, no. 949; R. Thomson, *Degas: The Nudes*, London, 1988, p. 183, pl. 180; C.F. Stuckey *et al.*, *Degas: Form and Space*, Paris, and New York, 1984, fig. 119; E. Camesasca, *Trésors du Musée de São Paulo: De Manet à Picasso*, Martigny (Fondation Pierre Gianadda), 1988, p. 74.

19   GAUGUIN, PAUL   1848–1903
The Haystacks   1889
Les Meules
Oil on canvas, 92 × 73.3
Signed, bottom right: 'P. Gauguin '89'
Courtauld Institute Galleries (The Samuel Courtauld Trust)

This is one of two haymaking scenes that Gauguin painted at Pont-Aven in Brittany in July 1889. Gauguin had first visited Pont-Aven in 1886, partly to get away from Paris and partly to find a cheaper place to live (the Pension Gloanec where he stayed was noted for giving credit to artists). Brittany was by then becoming an attractive tourist centre and was gaining in agricultural prosperity, but it retained an image as a place where primitive peasant types and folkloric customs could still readily be found. Paintings of picturesque Breton costumes and customs were common at the annual Salon exhibitions in Paris. Pont-Aven was one of the main artists' colonies in Brittany; Gauguin avoided the main groups of painters there, but a group of younger artists formed around him, including Emile Bernard, Paul Sérusier and Meyer de Haan, all of whom, like Gauguin, were committed to rejecting naturalistic depiction in favour of an art that expressed the stereotypical notion of the primitive essence of Breton life.

Gauguin had worked with Pissarro in the late 1870s and early 1880s, and painted at times in a style very close to his (similar to cat. no. 37); in the mid-1880s, though, he began to simplify his forms and to subordinate naturalistic representation to a clearer, more stylised surface pattern. This was an explicit rejection of the variegated textures and rich surface effects of Impressionism. He described his aims in letters to Emile Schuffenecker in 1888: 'A word of advice, do not copy nature too closely. Art is an abstraction; derive it from nature while dreaming in front of it and think more of the creation which will result.' 'This year I have sacrificed everything – execution and colour – in favour of style.'

The Haystacks bears witness to these experiments. Its brushwork is quite thin and crisp, lacking the density of paint and flexibility of Pissarro's, and its colour is simplified, with a clear dominant colour in each area, rather than complex harmonies of related hues. Gauguin had painted with Cézanne in 1881 and owned several of his works, and in some ways his handling here still reflects Cézanne's example – in the sequences of parallel strokes and in the way in which certain zones in the picture (like the trees and the bush) have a clear, distinct shape (compare the foliage in Cézanne cat. no. 6). However, Gauguin's brushwork is thinner and streakier than Cézanne's, his

drawing far more schematic, and there is little hint of the nuances of atmospheric colour so prominent in Cézanne's canvas. Moreover, Gauguin presented the space in his picture in a way that cannot readily be understood; the forms seem to be stacked one on the other up the canvas, and the position of the bush on the left is particularly ambiguous. Above the necks of the oxen, the fine diagonal strokes wholly ignore the spatial recession that is suggested below and to the right of the bush.

In his chosen subject, Gauguin avoided any possible narrative reading or any direct appeal to the viewer. The simplified forms of the oxen at the front, and the rhyming, rhythmic poses of the women in their Breton costumes, their forms indicated with a deliberate simplicity and *naïveté*, evoke a sense of timeless rural labour, while the handling of the picture further distances it from immediately perceived reality, presenting the activities as if they were a sort of secular ritual.

PROVENANCE   Ambroise Vollard; Dr Frizeau, Bordeaux; Jos. Hessel, Paris; bought by Courtauld, January 1923, £1,500 (price including Gauguin, *Baigneuses, Tahiti*). Courtauld Gift 1932.

EXHIBITED   *Gauguin*, Leicester Galleries, London, 1924 (61); Tate Gallery, 1948 (27); Orangerie, Paris, 1955 (29); *Gauguin*, Tate Gallery, London, and Royal Scottish Academy, Edinburgh, 1955 (28); *Gauguin and the Pont-Aven Group*, Arts Council at Tate Gallery, 1966 (20); Japan and Canberra, 1984 (30); United States, 1987–8 (39).

LITERATURE   Jamot-Turner, no. 36; Home House Catalogue, no. 10; Cooper, 1954, no. 29; J. Rewald, *Post-Impressionism: From Van Gogh to Gauguin*, New York, 1956, p. 248; G. Wildenstein, *Gauguin*, I, Paris, 1964, no. 352; R. Bruce-Gardner, G. Hedley and C. Villers, 'Impressions of Change', in United States, 1987–8, pp. 21–2, 32–3.

20 GAUGUIN, PAUL 1848–1903
   Nevermore 1897
   Oil on canvas, 60.5 × 116
   Signed, top left: 'NEVERMORE/P. Gauguin
     97/O. TAÏTI'
   Courtauld Institute Galleries (The Samuel
     Courtauld Trust)

Gauguin painted *Nevermore* in February 1897, during his second visit to Tahiti. He described the painting in a letter to Daniel de Monfreid, the fellow painter who was acting as his agent in Paris:

> I wished to suggest by means of a simple nude a certain long-lost barbarian luxury. The whole is drowned in colours which are deliberately sombre and sad; it is neither silk, nor velvet, nor batiste, nor gold that creates luxury here but simply matter that has been enriched by the hand of the artist. No nonsense . . . Man's imagination alone has enriched the dwelling with his fantasy. As a title, Nevermore; not the raven of Edgar Poe, but the bird of the devil that is keeping watch. It is badly painted (I'm so nervy and can only work in bouts) but no matter, I think it's a good canvas.

Nevermore belongs to a long tradition of reclining female nudes. The pose, with the exaggerated curve of the figure's hip, perhaps echoes the sensuous exoticism of Ingres's *Odalisque with a Slave*, but whereas the luxury in Ingres's picture is presented as tranquil and undisturbed, Gauguin reworked the tradition so as to produce an image as complex and challenging as that other pioneering avant-garde odalisque of the previous generation, Manet's *Olympia* (Musée d'Orsay, Paris). But, whereas Manet's picture (of which Gauguin had a photograph in his hut in Tahiti) confronts the subject of public sexuality and prostitution in the modern city, *Nevermore* explores in a more allusive way more private realms of sensual experience.

The painting sets up a triangular relationship between the nude figure, the bird, seemingly watching, and the clothed figures in the background, turned away and talking. The turn of the nude's eyes suggests that she is aware of the bird or the other figures, but beyond this nothing is clear. The contrast of unclothed with clothed, of reverie with conversation, may evoke the loss of innocence; indeed, in his vast canvas *Where do we come from? What are we? Where are we going to?* of 1898 (Museum of Fine Arts, Boston), two very similar clothed figures, who have eaten of the Tree of Knowledge and 'dare to talk of their own destiny', are contrasted with the simple people amid virgin nature in the foreground. His reference in the letter about *Nevermore* to 'a certain long-lost

barbarian luxury' suggests that the image should be understood not just as the awakening of a particular woman, but rather in the context of the corruption of 'primitive' cultures – Oceanic Gardens of Eden – by the influx of western values. Gauguin's own experiences on Tahiti bore eloquent testimony to this corruption, since colonialism and Christian missionary activity had virtually erased the remnants of the Polynesian culture which he had gone there to explore.

The bird's role, too, is ambiguous. Although in his letter Gauguin played down its relationship to Poe's *The Raven*, the bird, in conjunction with the title, would inevitably have evoked Poe's poem for the painting's original viewers; Poe's work was widely known in artistic circles in Paris in the late nineteenth century, and Mallarmé's translation of *The Raven*, illustrated by Manet, had appeared in 1875. Gauguin may well have sought to minimise this association in order to avoid too explicitly literary a reference, but the bird's presence here is as ominous as in the poem, in which it stands above the poet's door, croaking 'Nevermore'; in the picture, it contributes, with the conversing figures, to the sense of threat that invades the luxury of the nude's surroundings.

The elements in the interior, as Gauguin's letter insists, are imagined, their luxury the product of the painter's imagination. Amid the swinging curves of the plant forms, the stylised gourds on the bed-head and beneath the bird hint at sexual penetration, bringing the décor into a more active relationship with the figures, but without any explicit meaning. Allusive elements like these were integral to Gauguin's idea of Symbolism; he wrote in 1899, quoting Mallarmé, of one of his paintings as a 'musical poem without a libretto', insisting that it could not be read allegorically.

It is in this way that *Nevermore* operates, enriched by its lavish pictorial surface and colour. The sharp yellow of the nude's pillow and the red by her feet heighten her strangeness and further separate her from her surroundings, but cannot be interpreted literally. The iconic quality of the whole picture is enhanced by its smooth, dense surface (in marked contrast to cat. no. 21), but this arose for practical reasons: the present picture was painted over another quite different subject, which Gauguin largely obliterated with a further layer of white priming before starting work on *Nevermore*. X-rays suggest that this may have contained trees. However, the final effect makes positive use of the density of these underlying layers; clearly Gauguin found that their presence allowed him to give the picture a distinctive physical quality.

The English composer Frederick Delius was

the first owner of the painting. Gauguin wrote to de Monfreid in 1899 to express his pleasure that Delius had bought it, 'given that it is not a speculative purchase for re-sale, but for enjoyment'. The Tate Gallery considered purchasing the canvas on several occasions before Courtauld acquired it in 1927 (see above, p. 12).

PROVENANCE   Bought from Daniel de Monfreid by Frederick Delius, 1898 (500 francs); Alfred Wolff, Munich; Alex. Reid, Glasgow; Agnew, London and Manchester; Herbert C. Coleman, Manchester; bought by Courtauld, after February 1927, price unknown. Courtauld Gift 1932.

EXHIBITED   Salon d'Automne, Paris, 1906 (216); Sonderbund Ausstellung, Cologne, 1912 (168); *Masterpieces of French Art of the 19th Century*, Agnew, Manchester, 1923 (17); *Gauguin*, Leicester Galleries, London, 1924 (52); Tate Gallery, 1948 (28); *Gauguin, Exposition du centenaire*, Musée de l'Orangerie, Paris, 1949 (48); Orangerie, Paris, 1955 (25); *Gauguin*, Tate Gallery, London, and Royal Scottish Academy, Edinburgh, 1955 (55); Courtauld Centenary, 1976 (21); National Gallery, London, 1983 (no catalogue); Japan and Canberra, 1984 (31); United States, 1987–8 (40); *The Art of Paul Gauguin*, Washington, D.C., Chicago, Paris, 1988 (222).

LITERATURE   Jamot-Turner, no. 37; Home House Catalogue, no. 4; *Lettres de Paul Gauguin à Daniel de Monfreid*, ed. Mme Joly-Ségalen, Paris, 1950, pp. 101, 135, 190, 210–11; Cooper, 1954, no. 30; Wildenstein, 1964, no. 558; R. Bruce-Gardner, G. Hedley and C. Villers, 'Impressions of Change', in United States, 1987–8, pp. 33–4.

21 GAUGUIN, PAUL 1848–1903
The Dream 1897
Te Rerioa
Oil on canvas, 95.1 × 130.2
Signed, bottom left centre: 'TE RERIOA/
  P.Gauguin 97/TAÏTI'
Courtauld Institute Galleries (The Samuel
  Courtauld Trust)

Te Rerioa was painted in Tahiti in March 1897, about three weeks after *Nevermore*. Some of the forms shown on the walls of the room bear a relationship to Gauguin's surviving wood carvings, but it is probable that the decorations were largely imaginary, created as appropriate décor for the picture (compare *Nevermore*, cat. no. 20, and Gauguin's letter about the decoration there); the leftmost animal in the decoration may well be the only kangaroo in Post-Impressionist painting. However, the carvings on the cradle head have recently been shown to relate to a carved bowl by the Maori carver Patoromu Tamatea, probably made in the 1860s; Gauguin would have seen it in the Auckland Museum during the ten days he spent in Auckland on his second journey to Tahiti in August 1895; he used the bowl more directly as the source for a still life in 1901.

Gauguin described the painting in a letter when he despatched it to Daniel de Monfreid in France:

Te Rereioa (the Dream), that is the title. Everything is dream in this canvas; is it the child? is it the mother? is it the horseman on the path? or even is it the dream of the painter!!! All that is incidental to painting, some will say. Who knows. Maybe it isn't.

The spelling of the Tahitian title in this letter is correct; it is wrongly spelt on the canvas. The word in fact means nightmare, but, as he wrote, Gauguin was using it more generally to mean dream.

The uncertainties that Gauguin spelt out in this playful fashion are integral to the painting, since no figures communicate with each other, and none has a clearly legible expression. The image is made up from a set of contrasts: sleeping child and daydreaming women; sleeping child and the seemingly active, carved figure on the cradle; the women seated still and the figures making love in the wall decoration; the principal figures seated passively and the active man, riding on the path and placed precisely between the heads of the two women; live animal on the floor beside carved animals on the wall decoration.

A recent interpretation of the picture has suggested a more specific set of meanings. The figures in the decorations have been associated with particular figures in Tahitian mythology, and Gauguin himself has been identified as the 'dreamer'; his dream 'reflects upon the cultural origins of the Tahitians and their lost heritage'. However, this degree of precision seems inappropriate both to the tone of Gauguin's letter and to the evident open-endedness of the formal relationships in the picture itself.

Gauguin's letter reminds us that none of the elements in the picture is 'real', for all are the creation (and, in this sense only, the dream) of the painter who has conjured up this series of puzzles and possibilities; this is emphasised by the physical appearance of the painting itself – thinly and broadly painted over coarse sacking, so that its flatness and the physical presence of the paint and the sacking are constantly apparent.

In its ambiguities, and also in the qualities of its surface, this canvas, perhaps more than any other by Gauguin, answers the requirements of the poet Stéphane Mallarmé for a true 'symbol'. In an interview in 1891, Mallarmé stated:

I think that there should only be allusion. The contemplation of objects, the image emanating from the dreams they excite, this is poetry . . . To name an object is to suppress three-quarters of the enjoyment of the poem, which is created by the pleasure of gradually apprehending it. To suggest, that is the dream. That is the perfect use of mystery that constitutes symbol.

Mallarmé also saw literature as absolutely self-conscious about its means – about the words that make it up – as opposed to reportage, which was primarily concerned to give a sense of reality; this, too, parallels Gauguin's emphasis of the physical quality of the painting itself, as an artefact, rather than as a window on another, actual world beyond the frame.

A painting such as *Te Rerioa* was intended for a European audience, presenting an archetype of 'primitive' reverie in unspoilt surroundings, and a fusion of eroticism and innocence. As we know from historical evidence, this vision bore no relation to the state of society in Tahiti in the 1890s (see cat. no. 20), but the picture was a contribution to a long European tradition of images of the 'noble savage'; particularly relevant to *Te Rerioa* was perhaps Delacroix's *Women of Algiers* (1834; Musée du Louvre, Paris), in which sensuous reverie was sited in a North African Orientalist context. These visions owe their origins not to the 'primitive' worlds they show, but to the reactions of European artists against the complexities of modern urban society; the idylls they create from the 'otherness' of their material belong firmly in the west, as projections of dissatisfaction with the values of western society.

PROVENANCE Bought from Daniel de Monfreid by Gustave Fayet, Igny (1,100 francs); Paul Rosenberg, Paris (November 1928); bought by Courtauld, July 1929, £13,600. Courtauld Gift 1932.

EXHIBITED Musée de Béziers, 1901; Salon d'Automne, Paris, 1906 (4), as 'Intérieur de case à Tahiti', lent by Fayet; *French Art*, Royal Academy, London, 1932 (520); Tate Gallery, 1948 (29); *Gauguin*, Exposition du centenaire, Musée de l'Orangerie, Paris, 1949 (49); *Gauguin*, Tate Gallery, London, and Scottish Royal Academy, Edinburgh, 1955 (56); Orangerie, Paris, 1955 (26); Courtauld Centenary, 1976 (22); Japan and Canberra 1984 (32); United States, 1987–8 (41); *The Art of Paul Gauguin*, Washington, D.C., Chicago, Paris, 1988 (223).

LITERATURE Jamot-Turner, no. 35; Home House Catalogue, no. 5; *Lettres de Paul Gauguin à Daniel de Monfreid*, pp. 102, 237, 239–40; Cooper, 1954, no. 31; C. Gray, *The Sculptures and Ceramics of Paul Gauguin*, Baltimore, 1963, pp. 75, 266–7, 276; Wildenstein, 1964, no. 557; B. Daniellson, 'Gauguin's Tahitian Titles', *Burlington Magazine*, April 1967, p. 233; J. Teilhet-Fisk, *Paradise Reviewed: An Interpretation of Gauguin's Polynesian Symbolism*, Ann Arbor, 1983, pp. 119–22; R. Bruce-Gardner, G. Hedley and C. Villers, 'Impressions of Change', in United States, 1987–8, pp. 22–3, 33–4; B. Nicholson, 'Gauguin: a Maori source', *Burlington Magazine*, September 1992, pp. 595–7.

22 GOGH, VINCENT VAN 1853–90
Self-Portrait with a Bandaged Ear 1889
Portrait de l'artiste à l'oreille coupée
Oil on canvas, 60 × 49
Unsigned
Courtauld Institute Galleries (The Samuel
Courtauld Trust)

On 24 December 1888, van Gogh mutilated his
own ear after a violent quarrel with Paul
Gauguin, who had spent the previous two
months staying with van Gogh in Arles. This
event and Gauguin's departure marked the end
of van Gogh's dreams of setting up a 'studio of
the South', where like-minded artists could
share ideas and resources. This and another self-
portrait (Private Collection, U.S.A.) seem to
have been two of the first pictures van Gogh
painted after his release from hospital around
6 January 1889.

Besides personal incompatability, van Gogh's
disagreements with Gauguin were grounded on
a fundamental aesthetic issue – whether the true
painter should work from nature or from the
imagination. For Gauguin, subservience to
external appearances marked a lack of creative
power, while van Gogh, through both his
intellectual upbringing and his artistic
experience, found rich layers of meaning in the
complexities of the natural world. During
Gauguin's stay, he painted a few canvases from
the imagination, but, looking back on this
tragic episode a year later, he wrote to the
painter Emile Bernard, 'Once or twice, while
Gauguin was in Arles, I gave myself free rein
with abstractions . . . and at that time
abstraction seemed to me a charming path. But
it is enchanted ground, and one soon finds
oneself up against a stone wall.'

Self-Portrait with a Bandaged Ear marks his
reversion to an aesthetic grounded in nature.
The painter is standing in clear daylight and
translates his own appearance into highly varied
and improvisatory rhythms of touch and
colour, in marked contrast to the simplified,
schematic surfaces that Gauguin advocated (see
cat. no. 19). The paint-handling distinguishes
markedly between the textures of the different
elements in the figure: a swathe of white
pigment suggests the bandage, while the flesh of
the face is indicated in a complex network of
nuanced coloured touches and crowned by the
ebullient crisp strokes of the brim of the cap.
The face includes a remarkable diversity of
colour, with the colours on the cheek alone
ranging from mauve and pink to orange,
yellow and green. The intense green of the eyes
is set against the startling red that marks out the
eyelids.

The imagery of the portrait is evidently
related to the recent disruption of his life. The
bandaged ear is given great prominence, and on
each side of the painter's head we see a highly
loaded image: to the left, behind him, an easel
with a scarcely worked canvas on it; and to the
right, a Japanese colour print. This has been
identified as a print by Torakiyo that van Gogh
owned; in order to fit it alongside his face, van
Gogh adapted it, moving the figures over to its
right edge. The print is a very typical image of
the mid-nineteenth century, showing in almost
stereotyped form an idyllic view of Japan as a
land of beautiful women and landscape.

But how are we to read these juxtapositions?
Should we see the print as standing for his
renewed inspiration from nature and from
Japan, the land that, in his view, stood for an
art inspired by nature, with the canvas on the
left waiting ready for him to resume his
recently interrupted career? Or should we
rather read it more pessimistically, as a poignant
contrast between the idyll in the print and the
painter's own sad circumstances, with the blank
canvas beside the bandaged ear standing for his
loss of artistic power?

The painting gives us no final answer to these
questions. Rather, in posing the various
possibilities and leaving the viewer to explore
them, it uses a pictorial language closer to a
Mallarméan type of Symbolism; ironically, it
was Gauguin, in paintings like *Te Rerioa* and
Nevermore (cat. nos 20 and 21), who was to
make such suggestiveness the core of his
aesthetic.

PROVENANCE Père Tanguy, Paris; Comte A. de
la Rochefoucauld, Paris; Paul Rosenberg, Paris;
bought by Courtauld, October 1928, £10,000.
Courtauld Bequest 1948.

EXHIBITED *Van Gogh*, Bernheim-Jeune, Paris,
1901 (2); Van Gogh retrospective,
Indépendants, Paris, 1905 (6); *Dutch Art, 1450–
1900*, Royal Academy, London, 1929 (453);
Vincent Van Gogh en zijn Tijdgenooten, Stedelijk
Museum, Amsterdam, 1930 (66); *Van Gogh*,
Arts Council at Tate Gallery, Birmingham,
Glasgow, 1947–8 (64); Tate Gallery, 1948 (32).

LITERATURE Jamot-Turner, no. 26; J.-B. de la
Faille, *L'Oeuvre de Vincent Van Gogh*, Paris and
Brussels, 1928, no. 527; J.-B. de la Faille,
L'Oeuvre de Vincent Van Gogh, rev. edn,
London, Paris and Toronto, 1939, no. 547;
Cooper, 1954, no. 85; *The Complete Letters of
Vincent van Gogh*, III, London, 1958, p. 118;
J.-B. de la Faille (rev. edn by A.M. Hammacher
and others), *The Works of Vincent Van Gogh:
His Paintings and Drawings*, Amsterdam, 1970,
no. F.527 (H.547); D. Cooper, 'Two Japanese
Prints from the Collection of Vincent van
Gogh', *Burlington Magazine*, June 1957, pp. 203–
4; F. Orton, 'Vincent's Interest in Japanese
Prints', *Vincent*, I, no. 3, autumn 1971, p. 12;
J. Hulsker, *The Complete Van Gogh*, New York,
1980, no. 1657 and pp. 382–3; R. Pickvance, *Van
Gogh in Arles*, New York (Metropolitan
Museum of Art), 1984, pp. 245–6; R. Bruce-
Gardner, G. Hedley and C. Villers, 'Impressions
of Change', in United States, 1987–8, p. 23.

23 GOGH, VINCENT VAN 1853–90
The Crau at Arles: Peach Trees in
Flower 1889
La Crau d'Arles: Pêchers en fleurs
Oil on canvas, 65 × 81
Unsigned
Courtauld Institute Galleries (The Samuel
Courtauld Trust)

Painted in Arles in March–April 1889, this canvas shows a view of the Crau, the wide plain that lies to the north-east of Arles, between the River Rhône and the Alpilles – the range of hills across the background of the picture. Van Gogh enclosed a rough pen sketch of the composition in a letter to Paul Signac, and described the picture:

I have just come back with two studies of orchards. Here is a crude sketch of them – the big one is a poor landscape with little cottages, blue skyline of the Alpille foothills, sky white and blue. The foreground, patches of land surrounded by cane hedges, where small peach trees are in bloom – everything is small there, the gardens, the fields, the orchards and the trees, even the mountains, as in certain Japanese landscapes, which is the reason why the subject attracted me.

The idea of the south of France as a western equivalent of Japan had been one of van Gogh's main reasons for travelling to Arles the previous year; here, the seemingly snowcapped peak in the right background may be an echo of Mount Fuji-Yama.

The Crau at Arles: Peach Trees in Flower was painted after Gauguin's visit to Arles, during which he had advised van Gogh to work from his imagination (see cat. nos 19 and 22), and marks van Gogh's renewed commitment to painting from nature. Here he returned to the approximate subject of one of his major works of the previous summer, *The Blue Cart* (Rijksmuseum Vincent van Gogh, Amsterdam). In contrast to Gauguin's schematic paint surfaces, van Gogh conveys the complex textures and patterns of the chosen scene with a great variety of brushmarks, some broad and incisive, but others of extreme finesse. The laden dabs of paint in the blossom reflect his study of Impressionist painting during his stay in Paris (see Monet cat. nos 31 and 33), but elsewhere the forms are far crisper and more clearly drawn, particularly in the web of very fine, dark red strokes added in many parts of the picture very late in its execution in order to emphasise the forms of the elements shown – in the houses, the trees and the foreground verge. Added very late, too, was the sequence of blue strokes on the road at the bottom, together with blue accents elsewhere in the landscape and sky; these serve to knit the main elements of the scene together into an atmospheric unity, whose keynote is the vivid blues of the far mountains and the lower band of the sky.

In its translation of this display of blossom into a rich coloured harmony, the picture is clearly indebted to Impressionism; yet its subject also reflects van Gogh's Dutch heritage. He often likened the wide spaces of the Crau with the panoramas of Dutch seventeenth-century landscape painting. When he began *The Blue Cart* in June 1888, showing a very similar scene, he wrote to his brother: 'I am working on a new subject, fields green and yellow as far as the eye can reach . . . It is exactly like a Salomon Koninck, you know, the pupil of Rembrandt who painted vast level plains.' A month later he commented: 'Here, except for an intenser colouring, it reminds one of Holland: everything is flat, only one thinks rather of the Holland of Ruysdael or Hobbema or Ostade than of Holland as it is.' In the inclusion of the working figure on the left of *The Crau at Arles: Peach Trees in Flower*, along with the prominent small houses, van Gogh emphasised that this was a social, agricultural landscape, its forms the result of man's intervention. Of the Impressionists, Pissarro was always concerned to emphasise the human context of his chosen landscape subjects, whereas Monet (see cat. no. 34) was by the later 1880s concentrating primarily on effects of light and atmosphere.

When van Gogh sent the picture to his brother Theo in Paris in the summer of 1889, its dense paint layers were not yet fully dry. He removed his canvases from their stretchers before despatching them, and packed them with one canvas directly on top of another; the imprint of the canvas texture of the back of the picture placed on top of this painting can be seen in the thickest paint, most visibly on the hat of the working figure.

PROVENANCE Bernheim-Jeune, Paris; Percy Moore Turner, London; bought by Courtauld, June 1927, £9,000. Courtauld Gift 1932.

EXHIBITED *Van Gogh*, Marcel Bernheim, Paris, 1925 (32); *Ingres to Cézanne*, Independent Gallery, London, 1925 (26); *Dutch Art, 1450–1900*, Royal Academy, London, 1929 (454); Tate Gallery, 1948 (32); Orangerie, Paris, 1955 (66); Courtauld Centenary, 1976 (60); National Gallery, London, 1983 (no catalogue); Japan and Canberra, 1984 (98); United States, 1987–8 (38).

LITERATURE Jamot-Turner, no. 28; Home House Catalogue, no. 12; de la Faille, 1928, no. 514; de la Faille, 1939, no. 531; Cooper, 1954, no. 86; *The Complete Letters of Vincent van Gogh*, III, London, 1958, pp. 149–51; de la Faille, 1970, no. F.514 (H.531); J. Hulsker, *The Complete Van Gogh*, New York, 1980, no. 1681 and p. 388; R. Bruce-Gardner, G. Hedley and C. Villers, 'Impressions of Change', in United States, 1987–8, p. 23.

24 MANET, ÉDOUARD 1832–83
Le Déjeuner sur l'herbe *c*.1863?
Oil on canvas, 89.5 × 116.5
Signed, bottom left: 'Manet'
Courtauld Institute Galleries (The Samuel
    Courtauld Trust)

This is a smaller version of the famous *Déjeuner sur l'herbe* (Musée d'Orsay, Paris), which was rejected by the Salon jury in 1863 and exhibited with the title *Le Bain* at the Salon des Refusés in 1863. The models in the large picture have been identified as Victorine Meurent (a professional model), either Gustave or Eugène Manet (brothers of the painter) and Ferdinand Leenhoff, a Dutch sculptor, whose sister Manet married in 1863. The picture caused much controversy when it was exhibited at the Salon des Refusés, and critics and historians still dispute the artist's intentions. Antonin Proust records Manet's ambition to rework the theme of the Titian/Giorgione *Concert champêtre* in the Louvre in a more luminous, outdoor ambience; but the final painting was undoubtedly executed in the studio, apparently based on studies made on the Ile Saint-Ouen, on the Seine on the northern outskirts of Paris. There are other links with Renaissance painting besides the *Concert champêtre*; the poses of the three main figures are directly based on a group of nymphs and river-gods from the right side of an engraving by Marcantonio Raimondi after Raphael's lost *Judgement of Paris*. Manet was also aware of the *fêtes galantes* of French eighteenth-century painters such as Watteau, and of recent popular romantic prints by artists such as Devéria and Morlon, which, in a more 'popular' medium, lent a more overtly erotic content to Watteau-like themes.

The large painting puzzled contemporary critics for several reasons. The juxtaposition of a naked woman with men in modern dress was regarded as indecent; the woman's body was seen as ugly – not conforming to academic canons of beauty – and the men's clothing, particularly the smoking-cap of the figure on the right, led critics to identify them as students; the handling of the picture did not give the figures their due status, but treated them and the background alike, in broad, vigorous touches of paint. Moreover, it was unclear what type of subject it was: its very large scale (about 7 by 9 feet) led them to expect a picture with a significant subject; its naked figure led them to expect nymphs and naiads; and the picnic scene recalled the *fête galante*. However, the painting itself conformed to none of these types, but rather deliberately flouted the conventions of each; in a sense, it was a parody of the tenets of contemporary academic 'high' art, enshrining a scene from contemporary bohemian life in the rhetoric, and on the scale, of history painting.

Moreover, the gaze of the naked woman, looking away from her companions and directly at the viewer, made it impossible to conceive of the scene taking place in some sylvan glade of the imagination.

The exact status of the Courtauld version has been the subject of much debate, some seeing it as a preparatory sketch, and some as a replica made after the large version, from which it differs in a number of details (the exact placing of the figures and their relationship to the figure in the stream, the colour of the naked woman's hair, and perhaps the model used). X-ray examination of both canvases has clarified the issues. The Courtauld picture shows no significant changes during its execution; the figure group and the background were immediately laid-in on the canvas very simply and directly. By contrast, the large version was very extensively changed, and originally included an open vista with small trees in its left background, instead of the trunk and foliage that now frame it. It thus seems virtually certain that the Courtauld version is a replica, made after the big one was completed, and refining its arrangement in minor ways. The early history of the painting makes this very plausible, since its first owner was Manet's friend the Commandant Lejosne; it seems likely that Lejosne, unable to house the big painting, asked the artist to make a reduced version. We cannot be sure when this was done; indeed, the breadth and simplicity of handling in the Courtauld picture makes it possible that it was executed a few years after the large version.

PROVENANCE   Given by the artist to Commandant Lejosne, Paris; Lejosne family, Maisons-Lafitte (until 1924); Galerie Druet, Paris; Percy Moore Turner, London; bought by Courtauld, June 1928, £10,000. Courtauld Gift 1932.

EXHIBITED   Tate Gallery, 1948 (36); Orangerie, Paris, 1955 (27); Courtauld Centenary, 1976 (23); *Manet at Work: An Exhibition to mark the Centenary of the Death of Edouard Manet 1832–1883*, National Gallery, London, 1983 (10); Japan and Canberra, 1984 (48); *The Hidden Face of Manet*, Courtauld Institute Galleries, 1986 (24); United States, 1987–8 (1).

LITERATURE   P. Jamot and G. Wildenstein, *Manet: Catalogue critique*, Paris, 1932, I, no.78; A. Tabarant, *Manet: Histoire catalographique*, Paris, 1931, no.63; A. Tabarant, *Manet et ses oeuvres*, Paris, 1947, no.65 and pp.73–4; Jamot-Turner, no.7; Home House Catalogue, no.6; Cooper, 1954, no.32; D. Rouart and D. Wildenstein, *Edouard Manet: catalogue raisonné*, I, Paris, 1975, pp.74–5, no.66; A. Bowness, 'A Note on Manet's Compositional Difficulties', *Burlington Magazine*, June 1961, p.277, n.9; J. Wilson Bareau, 'The Hidden Face of Manet', *Burlington Magazine*, April 1986, pp.39, 92; R. Bruce-Gardner, G. Hedley and C. Villers, 'Impressions of Change', in United States, 1987–8, p.21.

25 MANET, ÉDOUARD 1832–83
Banks of the Seine at Argenteuil 1874
Bords de la Seine à Argenteuil
Oil on canvas, 62.3 × 103
Signed, bottom left: 'Manet '74'
Private Collection, on extended loan to the
Courtauld Institute Galleries

Banks of the Seine at Argenteuil was painted while Manet was visiting Monet at Argenteuil in the summer of 1874; the models were very probably Monet's wife, Camille, and his seven-year-old son, Jean. Manet had refused to participate in the Impressionists' first group exhibition earlier that year, preferring to continue showing at the Salon, but he was on close personal terms with Monet and gave him much financial help in difficult times.

The picture marks Manet's closest approach to the open-air Impressionism by which the movement is best known, with its broken brushwork and vivid, variegated colour; indeed, it was very probably (in part at least) painted out of doors. But comparison with Monet's *Autumn Effect at Argenteuil* (cat.no.31), painted the previous year, reveals important differences. Manet still used clear black paint for certain salient points in the composition – most notably for the ribbons on the back of the woman's hat, and also on the hulls of the boats. Moreover, he did not record the reflections in the water with any close attention to their actual appearance: the patterns of masts and rigging seen in the water bear little relationship to the forms they reflect, whereas Monet's reflections were always closely observed, spreading vertically downwards directly below the objects reflected. Nor did Manet systematically indicate shadows by the use of colour; we are left with little idea of how the light is falling on the figures.

Strict attention to such notions of naturalism held little value for Manet. Whereas Monet was at this date using the close study of natural effects as the means for rethinking the basic conventions of landscape painting, Manet was primarily concerned with figure subjects, with finding ways of suggesting the unexpected groupings that modern people presented in their surroundings. Though the vivid blue of the water in *Banks of the Seine at Argenteuil* evokes bright summer light, the main focus of the picture is the figures and the boats: the sailing-boats in the river, and the wash-boats along the far bank, and the figures standing inexpressively in front of the view. The factory chimneys seen over the trees echo the lines of the masts and stress the diversity of the scene.

However, there is always a tension in Manet's later work between the formal organisation and pattern of his canvases and their evocation of modernity. Certainly, the broken rhythms and staccato focuses of a picture like the present one can be seen as standing for the nature of experience in the modern world. But, at the same time, the rhythms of the forms – of the masts and boats here, and the play of highlights in the water – can also be read as showing a preoccupation with formal qualities, detached from any representational purpose. It was by focusing on this – on the primacy of the *tache* of colour in Manet's art – that many critics in his lifetime diverted attention from the problematic aspects of his subject matter.

Whereas Monet exhibited many river scenes of this size, Manet did not show this canvas; as a result of his stay at Argenteuil, he painted two larger, more elaborate scenes of figures by the river which he did submit to the Salon (including *Boating*, Metropolitan Museum of Art, New York). However, he did regard it as a fully complete work and sold it to the wealthy collector Ernest May.

PROVENANCE Ernest May, Paris; Auguste Pellerin, Paris; Durand-Ruel, Paris; Theodor Behrens, Hamburg; Galerie Barbazanges, Paris; Knoedler, London; bought by Courtauld, August 1923, price unknown; Lady Aberconway, 1948; private collection.

EXHIBITED *Centennale de l'art français*, Exposition Universelle, Paris, 1889 (490); Exposition Universelle, Paris, 1900 (445); *35 Manet de la Collection Pellerin*, Bernheim-Jeune, Paris, 1910 (6), and at Moderne Galerie, Munich, 1910 (6); *Exposition Centennale de l'art français*, St Petersburg, 1912 (403); *19th Century French Painters*, Knoedler, London, 1923 (28); *Masterpieces of French Art of the 19th Century*, Agnew, Manchester, 1923 (22); Centenary Exhibition, Norwich, 1925 (45); *French Art*, Royal Academy, London, 1932 (420); Tate Gallery, 1948 (38); *Landscape in French Art*, Royal Academy, London, 1949–50 (247); Courtauld Centenary, 1976 (24); *Manet at Work: An Exhibition to mark the Centenary of the Death of Edouard Manet 1832–1883*, National Gallery, London, 1983 (20); United States, 1987–8 (2).

LITERATURE Jamot and Wildenstein, 1932, I, no.242; Tabarant, 1931, no.216; Tabarant, 1947, no.227; Jamot-Turner, no.9; Cooper, 1954, no.33; Rouart and Wildenstein, 1975, I, pp.184–5, no.220; A.C. Hanson, *Manet and the Modern Tradition*, New Haven and London, 1977, pp.68, 77, 173; T.J. Clark, *The Painting of Modern Life*, London, 1985, p.165.

The Road-Pavers, Rue Mosnier 1878
Les Paveurs, rue Mosnier
Oil on canvas, 64 × 80
Signed, bottom left: 'Manet'
Private Collection, on loan to the
Kunsthaus, Zurich

The scene depicted is the view from Manet's studio in the rue de Saint-Pétersbourg, looking on to the newly built rue Mosnier (renamed rue de Berne in 1884), in the Batignolles quarter of inner north-western Paris. This seems to be the first of Manet's three oil paintings of the scene; the other two (Bührle Collection, Zürich; J. Paul Getty Museum, Malibu) include a parade of *tricolor* flags, celebrating the *fête nationale* of 30 June 1878, and the spring-like foliage colours in the present painting suggest a date slightly earlier in the year.

At first sight, it looks like an archetypally Impressionist street scene, with a vivid sketch-like technique rapidly notating the comings and goings in a sunlit city street; indeed, the luminous sunlight and soft clear blue shadows make this, in technical terms, one of Manet's closest approaches to Impressionism (compare Renoir cat. no. 41).

However, both the picture's subject matter and its technique become more complex as it is explored further. The presence of the pavers records the completion of the street, just in time for the *fête nationale*; but the street already has a complex social life. Some idea of the nuances of this part of the new Paris can be gained from the description of the same street in Zola's *Nana*, written shortly after Manet painted the scene: 'a new, silent street . . ., without a single shop, whose fine houses, with tiny narrow apartments, are inhabited by *dames*'.

But we cannot see this, any more than Manet's painting, as documentary evidence for the life of the place. Zola's knowledge of the scene probably came from Manet, and from visiting him there; and both, in their very different media, were exploring broader questions about the nuances of social life in modern Paris (see cat. no. 27). Within this context, the image of a new back-street in one of the less respectable parts of the city has to be seen as generic rather than specific — as a figure for the uncertain relationship between respectability and immorality in modern Paris (compare critics' responses to Renoir's *La Loge*, cat. no. 39). Whereas Zola, with his insistence on seemingly documentary detail, precisely identified the inhabitants in his description of rue Mosnier, Manet characterised it far more allusively and inexplicitly. The scenario of newness is clear, with the pavers, the unbuilt plot of land at far left, and the implications of the removals van on the right of the street in

the middle distance; but it is we, the viewers, who deduce that the smart carriage in the right foreground is waiting for the fashionable client of a *dame*.

The studied ambivalence of the subject is complemented by the technique. Despite the generally luminous atmosphere, the image is punctuated by darker tones, of coaches, carts and figures; the accents by the fence at far left are particularly crisp, but also very inexplicit: do they suggest a couple of figures, a man and a woman? The whole is framed by two brown zones, the narrow entryway on the right, and the frontal advertising hoarding at top left, which seems to counteract the perspective of the rest. Likewise, the highlights do not sit comfortably within the atmospheric space; the white accents in the distance, at the far end of the street on the left, are the lightest points in the whole image.

The brushwork, too, complicates our perception of the picture. The road-pavers in the foreground are particularly loosely and vaguely indicated, though they were nearest to Manet's viewpoint and are also the feature signposted by the title of the picture. Other elements float in and out of focus as we look at the image. The poster on the wall seems to advertise made-to-measure children's clothing; and the traffic on the street seems carefully differentiated — a humble horse and cart on the left, the smart carriage with coachman on the right, and the small removals van beyond. But we cannot read clearly the delightful single red accent on one of the balconies on the right: do we see it as a pot of geraniums, or perhaps as a female figure?

It was by his technique, combined with his imagery, that Manet, in his later work, turned decisively away from the pseudo-scientific 'naturalism' propagated by writers such as Zola. Using the studied imprecision of the Impressionists' sketch-like technique, he found a means to create an imagery of the modern city that conveyed the sense of illegibility that many commentators felt to be the most distinctive characteristic of modernity.

PROVENANCE Bought from Manet by Roger de Portalis, 1879 (1000 francs); Victor Chocquet, Paris; Chocquet Sale, Paris, 1–4 July 1899 (lot 70); Durand-Ruel, Paris; Bernheim-Jeune, Paris; Paul Rosenberg, Paris; Paul Cassirer, Berlin; Georges Hoentschel, Paris; Georges Bernheim and Galerie Barbazanges, Paris (jointly); Bignou, Paris; Alex. Reid, Glasgow; bought by Courtauld, December 1924, £6,000; Mrs R.A. Butler; private collection; Christie's, 1 December 1986 (lot 52); private collection.

EXHIBITED *Exposition Manet*, Salon d'Automne, Paris, 1905 (21); *Chefs d'oeuvre de l'école française*, Galerie Georges Petit, Paris, 1910 (121); *French Art*, Royal Academy, London, 1932 (416); Tate Gallery, 1948 (37); *Landscape in French Art*, Royal Academy, London, 1949–50 (248); Orangerie, Paris, 1955 (28); *Impressionism*, Royal Academy, London, 1974 (64); Courtauld Centenary, 1976 (25); *Manet*, Grand Palais, Paris, and Metropolitan Museum of Art, New York, 1983 (158).

LITERATURE E. Moreau-Nélaton, *Manet raconté par lui-même*, Paris, 1926, II, pp. 46, 57; M. Dormoy, 'La Collection Courtauld', *L'Amour de l'art*, 1929, pp. 49–50; Jamot and Wildenstein, 1932, I, no. 291; Tabarant, 1931, no. 227; Tabarant, 1947, no. 290; Jamot-Turner, p. 5; Cooper, 1954, no. 33; Rouart and Wildenstein, 1975, I, no. 272; J. Rewald, 'Chocquet and Cézanne', in *Studies in Impressionism*, London, 1985, pp. 161–2; K. Adler, *Manet*, Oxford, 1986, p. 180; D. Farr, 'Edouard Manet's *La Rue Mosnier aux drapeaux*', in J. Wilmerding (ed.), *Essays in Honor of Paul Mellon*, Washington, D.C., 1986, pp. 97–109.

27 MANET, ÉDOUARD 1832–83
    A Bar at the Folies-Bergère 1881–2
    Un Bar aux Folies-Bergère
    Oil on canvas, 96 × 130
    Signed on bottom label, bottom left:
        'Manet/1882'
    Courtauld Institute Galleries (The Samuel
        Courtauld Trust)

A Bar at the Folies-Bergère was Manet's last major completed painting, exhibited in 1882, a year before his death. It is the only painting in the Courtauld Collection that was exhibited at the Salon, which remained the most important outlet for contemporary art until the last years of the nineteenth century.

It shows the interior of one of the most fashionable *cafés-concerts* in Paris, and Manet made rapid sketches in the Folies-Bergère itself; however, the final painting (and also, it seems, the oil sketch for it) was executed in Manet's studio, using as a model one of the barmaids who worked in the Folies-Bergère. Georges Jeanniot described Manet at work on the canvas in his studio, with the model posed behind a table laden with bottles and foodstuffs: 'Although he worked from the model, he did not copy nature at all closely; I noted his masterly simplifications . . . Everything was abbreviated; the tones were made lighter, the colours brighter; the values were more closely related to each other, the tones more contrasting.' Manet insisted that 'concision in art was a necessity'.

In the preliminary oil sketch (Stedelijk Museum, Amsterdam), the barmaid's head is half turned towards the right, with her reflection in the mirror behind the bar in a readily intelligible position, just to the right of the figure, while the reflection of her customer appears near the right edge of the composition, at a lower level; he wears a bowler hat and carries a cane. In the final version, the maid looks out at (or rather, past) the spectator from the centre of the picture with a detached expression, while her reflection has been displaced much further to the right, and her top-hatted customer appears in reflection in the extreme top right of the canvas.

In their final form, these reflections cannot be logically understood. The figure of the barmaid is separated far too far from her reflection; in the reflection, the customer is shown close to the barmaid, whereas the spectator is placed at some distance from the image that looks out of the picture; and the placing of the bottles in the reflection does not correspond to their position on the bar in the foreground – they are near the 'wrong' edge of the bar. X-ray photographs of the final painting show that initially its forms were close to those in the sketch, and thus were logically coherent. Substantial changes were made during the execution of the picture, most notably the moving of the reflection of the barmaid to the right (this took place in two stages), and the replacement of the customer with the bowler hat and cane (as in the sketch) by the man in the top right. Thus the discrepancies between the principal image and the reflections in the final version were introduced absolutely deliberately and evolved as Manet worked up the picture. The result is that the barmaid is presented to the viewer very directly, as an iconic centre of the composition; but a disturbing dislocation is created, between her apparent close encounter with the man seen in the mirror and her seeming distance and abstractedness as she faces the viewer.

Much has been written about the possible reasons for these distortions of perceived reality, which would have seemed more unexpected to nineteenth-century viewers, not habituated to the radical anti-naturalism of much twentieth-century painting. Throughout his career, Manet had avoided compositions that showed easily legible relationships between figures and presented clear-cut narratives, in favour of subjects where the status of the figures remained unclear and groupings that defied the viewer's attempts to interpret them (see the grouping in *Le Déjeuner sur l'herbe*, cat.no.24). This can be seen in part as a rejection of the conventions of the fashionable genre painting of the day, but also as an attempt to convey a more vivid sense of actuality, in which relationships between people are rarely so clear-cut and unambiguous as they had traditionally been depicted in painting.

The subject of *A Bar at the Folies-Bergère* enshrined particularly clearly the uncertainties that many contemporary commentators felt about the social and moral status of the most characteristic types in modern urban society. The Folies-Bergère was a popular place of entertainment for fashionable figures in Parisian society and for the *demi-monde*, and prostitutes apparently plied their trade overtly in its foyers and galleries. The status of the barmaids was ambivalent: they were primarily there to serve drinks, but they themselves were also potentially available to their clients; they might themselves become commodities, like the bottles on the bar. Manet's picture, with its wilful distortion of perceived experience, seems designed to enshrine this uncertainty.

This is enhanced by the way in which it is painted, for the bottles and fruit-bowl on the bar are treated with great richness and finesse, while the figure of the barmaid is more broadly and simply treated. Critics had often criticised Manet for failing to distinguish the salient points of his compositions by treating them in more detail (see cat.no.24), but here this serves the very positive purpose of highlighting the barmaid's merchandise, the primary reason for her presence behind the bar, and thus of bringing out the ambivalence of her own status in the transactions she enacts.

Writing about Manet, and about modern art in general, during the twentieth century has, until recently, favoured formalist explanations of the structure of Manet's paintings and has argued that he was, at base, concerned with aesthetic questions, about the relationships of forms and colours, and that the oddities in the paintings were mere by-products of these formal concerns. However, in relation to the context in which they were originally displayed, at the Paris Salon, it is clear that they systematically broke with then-current conventions of representation and undermined the coherence of the world that these conventions created; Manet's pictorial world was a challenge to social as well as artistic values.

PROVENANCE Inventory prepared after Manet's death 1883, no.9; Manet Studio Sale, Drouot, Paris, 4–5 February 1884 (lot 7; 5,850 francs), bought Chabrier; Emmanuel Chabrier; Chabrier Sale, Drouot, Paris, 26 March 1896 (lot 8; bought in, 23,000 francs); Durand-Ruel, Paris, 1897; Auguste Pellerin, Paris; Bernheim-Jeune, Paris, and Paul Cassirer, Berlin; Eduard Arnhold, Berlin; Baron Ferenc Hatvany, Budapest, by 1919; Justin K. Thannhauser, Munich; Eric Goeritz, Berlin; Thannhauser, Lucerne; through Percy Moore Turner, London; bought by Courtauld, March 1926, approx. £22,600 plus £1,500 commission. Courtauld Gift 1934.

EXHIBITED Salon, Paris, 1882 (1753); Salon, Antwerp, 1882 (903); *Exposition posthume Manet*, Ecole des Beaux-Arts, Paris, 1884 (112); *Exposition Manet*, Durand-Ruel, Paris, 1894 (59); *Manet*, Durand-Ruel, New York, 1895 (3); Exposition Universelle, Paris, 1900 (448); Grafton Galleries, London, 1905 (93), exhibition organised by Durand-Ruel; *Manet and the Post-Impressionists*, Grafton Galleries, London, 1910–11 (7); *Exposition centennale de l'art français*, St Petersburg, 1912; exhibitions in Frankfurt-am-Main, Vienna, Dresden and Copenhagen 1912–14; Galerie Thannhauser, Lucerne, 1926; Tate Gallery, London, 1926; *French Art*, Royal Academy, London, 1932 (405); *Manet*, Musée de l'Orangerie, Paris, 1932 (82); Tate Gallery, 1948 (40); Orangerie, Paris, 1955 (30); Courtauld Centenary, 1976 (26); National Gallery, London, 1983 (no catalogue); *Manet*, Grand Palais, Paris, and Metropolitan Museum of Art, New York, 1983 (211); Japan and Canberra, 1984 (49); *The Hidden Face of Manet*, Courtauld Institute Galleries, 1986 (62); United States, 1987–8 (3).

(Cat. no. 27 continued)

LITERATURE   Jamot and Wildenstein, 1932, I,
no. 467; Tabarant, 1931, no. 369; Tabarant,
1947, no. 396; Jamot-Turner, no. 10; Home
House Catalogue, no. 77; Cooper, 1954, no. 36;
Rouart and Wildenstein, 1975, I, pp. 286–7,
no. 388; G. Mauner, *Manet, Peintre-Philosophe*,
Pennsylvania, 1975, pp. 161–2; A.C. Hanson,
Manet and the Modern Tradition, New Haven
and London, 1977, pp. 68, 130, 204–5; T.J.
Clark, *The Painting of Modern Life*, London,
1985, pp. 205–58; J. Wilson Bareau, 'The
Hidden Face of Manet', *Burlington Magazine*,
April 1986, pp. 76–83, 96; J. House, 'Manet's
Naïveté', *Burlington Magazine*, April 1986, pp. 8,
13, 16; R. Bruce-Gardner, G. Hedley and C.
Villers, 'Impressions of Change', in United
States, 1987–8, pp. 23, 30–2.

28   MARCHAND, JEAN HIPPOLYTE   1883–1941
      Saint-Paul   1921
      Oil on canvas, 61.5 × 74.5
      Signed, bottom right: 'J. Marchand'
      Courtauld Institute Galleries (The Samuel
      Courtauld Trust)

Saint-Paul was one of the first two canvases
bought by Samuel Courtauld, acquired with
Renoir's *Woman at her Toilet* (cat. no. 43) in
September 1922 (see also p. 22). At this date,
Cézanne and the late work of Renoir were
regarded as the prime examples for young
artists involved in what Cocteau later called the
'recall to order' after the First World War, and
Marchand was perhaps the best known and
most influential of the younger Cézannists.

The subject and structure of *Saint-Paul* are
immediately reminiscent of Cézanne's views of
Gardanne of the mid-1880s (e.g., in the Barnes
Foundation, Merion, Pa.). But, in place of
Cézanne's richly modulated colour and
complex relationships of line and plane (see
especially cat. nos 6–8), Marchand has adopted a
simpler, less vibrant palette and a clean, crisp
modelling for the forms of the buildings. The
Impressionist legacy in Cézanne's work, so
central to his use of colour and his ideas about
modelling, is abandoned, in favour of a notion
of Cézanne as a classicist, creator of simplified,
monumental compositions. The light of the
Mediterranean coast is here translated into
clean, clear contrasts, rather than vibrant colour.

In the simplification of forms in *Saint-Paul*,
there are echoes also of much earlier
prototypes – the landscape backgrounds of mid-
fifteenth-century Florentine paintings. Both the
cube-like buildings and the rather schematic
clouds echo images such as the background of
Fra Angelico's *Descent from the Cross* in San
Marco, Florence. The combination of this
example with Marchand's particular exploration
of Cézanne's art marks a deliberate return to
aesthetic basics, in reaction against both the
atmospheric, colouristic concerns of
Impressionism and the hermetic complexities of
pre-war Cubism.

In the detailed execution of the picture, blues
are no longer used to evoke atmosphere or the
modelling of forms in sunlight. The sunlit walls
are depicted in clear, simple light tones, mostly
with the brush, but on occasion with the palette
knife. The effect of intense southern light is
conveyed by setting these light tones against
areas of sombre shadow, both in the buildings
of the town and across the base of the picture,
on the foreground terrace, which, down the left
side, acts as an unexpected *repoussoir* to the
whole composition. The surface planes of the
buildings are clearly legible as representing
three-dimensional forms, except perhaps for the
intense light-toned plane at bottom left of the
town, just to the right of the foreground wall,
which seems to float very flatly on the picture
surface. Read in one way, this can be viewed as
a deliberate device to challenge the illusionism
of the overall effect of the scene and to reinstate
the primacy of the pictorial surface, in a way
comparable to the early Cubist landscapes of
1908, such as Braque's views of L'Estaque; but
it can be seen equally as a failure of perspective.

PROVENANCE   Galerie Barbazanges, Paris; Percy
Moore Turner; bought by Courtauld,
September 1922, £1,750 (price including
Renoir cat. no. 43). Courtauld Gift 1932.

EXHIBITED   *Jean Marchand*, Galerie Barbazanges,
Paris, 1921 (12) Independent Gallery, London,
1922; Opening Exhibition, Modern Foreign
Gallery, Tate Gallery, London, 1926; Tate
Gallery, 1948 (41).

LITERATURE   Jamot-Turner, no. 52; Home
House Catalogue, no. 54; Cooper, 1954, no. 37.

29 MODIGLIANI, AMEDEO 1884–1920
Nude c.1916
Nu
Oil on canvas, 92.4 × 59.8
Signed, top left: 'Modigliani'
Courtauld Institute Galleries (Home House
Trustees)

Modigliani's nudes are a combination of poses that often relate to the main traditions of western art (to Manet, Ingres and other earlier artists) with a type of drawing and execution that in its radical simplifications challenged the whole European figurative tradition. In *Nude*, the face is elongated, its features boldly simplified, in ways that testify to Modigliani's knowledge of Egyptian, African and Oceanic sculpture, though in generalised terms; yet the angle of the model's head recalls the very conventional imagery of the sleeping model, a favourite theme at the Salon exhibitions. Likewise, the contours and modelling of the body are treated in simplified arabesques, but elements such as the breasts and especially the pubic hair are described more attentively.

Modigliani's brushwork is highly individual: characteristic scallop-shaped strokes can be seen in X-rays, the paint being applied with a short stabbing action. The paint has been manipulated while still wet, ploughed through with a stiff brush in the background left and around the outline of the head, and scratched into with the end of the brush in the hair.

When a group of Modigliani's nudes were put on show at Berthe Weill's gallery in Paris in December 1917, the police first ordered the removal of the painting in the gallery window, and then the closure of the whole exhibition; apparently the prime cause of outrage was his explicit rendering of pubic hair, a taboo in the often very naturalistic depictions of the nude that hung every year at the Salon without any protests. This painting, with its combination of traditional and avant-garde elements, was one of the very few paintings in Samuel Courtauld's collection by a member of one of the avant-garde groups that emerged after 1900 (see cat. nos 28 and 61); Cubism and even Fauvism were outside the parameters of his taste.

PROVENANCE Léopold Zborowski, Paris; C. Zamaron, Paris; Zborowski, Paris; bought by Courtauld, by 1931, price unknown. Courtauld Gift 1932.

EXHIBITED *Modigliani*, Palais des Beaux-Arts, Brussels, 1933 (22); *Modigliani*, Kunsthalle, Basel, 1934 (14); Tate Gallery, 1948 (42); Orangerie, Paris, 1955 (31); Courtauld Centenary, 1976 (27); *Modigliani*, Musée Saint-Georges, Liège, 1980 (7); Japan and Canberra, 1984 (63); United States, 1987–8 (48).

LITERATURE Jamot-Turner, no. 54; Home House Catalogue, no. 21; Cooper, 1954, no. 38; A. Ceroni, *Modigliani peintre, suivi des 'souvenirs' de Lunia Czechowska*, Milan, 1958, no. 29; J. Lanthemann, *Modigliani 1884–1920: catalogue raisonné, sa vie, son oeuvre pein,t son art*, Barcelona, 1970, no. 160; A. Ceroni and F. Cachin, *Tout l'oeuvre peint de Modigliani*, Paris, 1972, no. 127; D. Hall, *Modigliani*, Oxford, 1984, pl. 26; R. Bruce-Gardner, G. Hedley and C. Villers, 'Impressions of Change', in United States, 1987–8, p. 21.

30 MONET, CLAUDE 1840–1926
Argenteuil, the Bridge under Repair 1872
Argenteuil, le pont en réparation
Oil on canvas, 60 × 80.5
Signed, bottom right: 'Claude Monet'
Private Collection, on loan to the
Fitzwilliam Museum, Cambridge

When Monet went to live around the end of
1871 at Argenteuil, a town on the Seine about
eight miles north-west of Paris, the place was
still recovering from the very visible scars left
by the Franco-Prussian War. Most notably, the
town's two bridges, for road and rail, had been
demolished, thus severing its most direct links
to the capital. But rebuilding work was quickly
undertaken, and, by the time that Monet
painted *Argenteuil, the Bridge under Repair*,
probably in early spring 1872, the structure of
the road bridge seems to have been largely
complete, amid the complex network of wood
scaffolding.

The overall effect of the picture is very
subdued. It is a still, grey day, with a leaden
sky, and the glassy surface of the water seems
undisturbed even by the passing steam tug.
There seem to be leaves on the trees, but little
sense of their colour penetrates through the
heavy atmosphere. What colour there is comes
from the soft contrasts that run throughout the
picture, between warm beiges and browns and
cool grey-blues. The simplicity and directness
of the paint application makes a fascinating
contrast to *Autumn Effect at Argenteuil*
(cat. no. 31), painted only eighteen months later,
on the same stretch of the River Seine.

In terms of the conventional expectations of
landscape painting, such a scene is wholly
lacking in picturesque potential; yet Monet
found in the scaffolding a motif with a very
distinctive visual interest; with firm direct
strokes of the brush he was able to suggest a
spatial effect of great complexity, as the eye
tracks the elaborately woven grid of the
wooden struts into space, both in the principal
image and its reflection in the water. Alongside
this, a different type of visual animation is
suggested by the traffic on the bridge and the
dark accent of the tug, belching smoke.

But how should we interpret such an image?
The picture has recently been seen as essentially
optimistic and celebratory, evoking France's
rapid renewal after the war; and certainly the
illustrated magazines of the period included
images of the post-war rebuilding programmes,
animated by busy working figures, that
signalled just such a recovery. But in Monet's
picture little seems to be made of the
implications of the subject; any sense of
buoyancy and energy is neutralised by the
sombre effect and the all-pervading stillness. As
in many Impressionist paintings of the 1870s

(compare cat. no. 32 and Sisley cat. no. 58), there
seems to be a disjunction between the scene
depicted and the way in which it is treated,
which prevents any ready assumption that the
essential meaning of the picture is equivalent to
the significance of its material subject. Here, the
stillness and inactivity seem to question, rather
than reinforce, the imagery of France's renewal,
and to create an ironic distance between image
and subject.

PROVENANCE Freret; Durand-Ruel; Frank
Thomson, Philadelphia; Miss Anne Thomson,
Philadelphia; Comtesse de la Motte, Paris;
Robert Lebel, Paris; Adolf Wuster, Paris;
Rosenberg & Helft, London; bought by
Courtauld, July 1937, £1,800 (price including
Seurat cat. no. 45); Mrs R.A. Butler; private
collection.

EXHIBITED *Monet*, Lotos Club, New York,
1901 (8); *Ingres to Picasso*, Rosenberg and Helft,
London, 1937 (21); Tate Gallery, 1948 (45);
Monet, Edinburgh and London, 1957 (34).

LITERATURE Cooper, 1954, no. 41; D.
Wildenstein, *Claude Monet: biographie et
catalogue raisonné, I: 1840–1881*, Lausanne and
Paris, 1974, no. 194; P. Tucker, *Monet at
Argenteuil*, New Haven and London, 1982,
pp. 58–62.

31 MONET, CLAUDE 1840–1926
Autumn Effect at Argenteuil 1873
Effet d'automne à Argenteuil
Oil on canvas, 55 × 74.5
Signed, bottom right: 'Claude Monet/73'
Courtauld Institute Galleries (The Samuel
Courtauld Trust)

The town of Argenteuil is in the background, seen looking upstream along a side branch of the River Seine, with the Ile Marante on the left; the bold blue stripe running across the centre of the canvas below the buildings represents the main channel of the river, flowing from right to left. At this period Argenteuil was rapidly expanding, both as an industrial town and as a centre for recreational sailing (see Manet cat. no. 25). Often Monet presented the contemporary facets of the place (see cat. no. 30); in some views from the same branch of the river, modern houses can be seen on the riverbank to the right. But here it appears as if timeless, a few houses presided over by a church spire, framed by the splendour of the sunlit trees.

The picture corresponds closely to Frederick Wedmore's description of a canvas shown at Dowdeswell's Gallery in London in 1883: '. . . palpitating light and golden hue. The whole of one side of the canvas is filled with flame-coloured autumn trees which throw their bright reflection of a rosier flame-colour upon a broad river-water otherwise turquoise and coral.'

Of all Monet's paintings of the early 1870s, this is the one in which he most completely abandoned traditional methods of chiaroscuro modelling, by gradations from dark to light tones, in favour of a composition based on clear colours, which are used to model form and evoke space. The picture is dominated by the bold contrast between orange and blue, but the glowing bank of autumnal trees is built up from constantly varied warm hues – pinks and yellows as well as oranges. On the right, soft clear blues indicate the shadows in the trees, and the blues on the far buildings, together with the diminishing scale of the brushstrokes in the water, suggest recession into atmospheric space.

The brushstrokes in the picture are extremely varied, ranging from the broad, firm strokes in the foreground reflections, which anchor the whole composition, to the little dabs and hooks of colour in the shaded side of the tree on the right. The touch in the sky – conveying scattered, broken clouds – is particularly freely improvised. In parts, the paint surface is densely worked – almost as if encrusted, on the trees on the left. Late in the execution of the picture, Monet scraped away some of this paint in long crisp strokes, probably made with the handle of a brush; these are most visible on the right tree,

where the strokes removed the whole depth of the paint layer, revealing the very light grey priming; but they also appear throughout the foliage on the left. Presumably, they are the result of Monet's dissatisfaction with the density of the paint layers, but such scraping is extremely unusual in his work.

As often in his landscapes, Monet avoided a direct perspectival lead into the pictorial space, in favour of an open-fronted view across water. The viewer is invited to contemplate the spectacle rather than enter into the space in the imagination. By placing the horizon half-way up the picture (in direct contravention of academic precept) Monet gave a startling symmetry to image and reflections; but, at a very late stage in the execution of the picture, he seems to have felt the need to temper this extreme frontality, and added the small area of more muted blue tones around the horizon line at the far right; this suggests the shadow of a low bush, but also helps to hold in the margin of the picture.

PROVENANCE Durand-Ruel, Paris; Erwin Davis, New York, 1886; Durand-Ruel, Paris, 1901; G. Hoentschel, Paris, 1904; Comte de Rasti, Paris; Alexandre Rosenberg, Paris; Hodebert; Bernheim-Jeune, Paris, 1924; bought by Courtauld, May 1924, £2,500. Courtauld Gift 1932.

EXHIBITED (?) *La Société des impressionnistes*, Dowdeswell and Dowdeswell's (exhibition organised by Durand-Ruel), London, 1883 (16), as 'Le petit bras à Argenteuil'; *The Impressionists of Paris*, American Art Galleries, New York, and National Academy of Design, New York, 1886 (282); *Monet*, Union League Club, New York, 1891 (68); Tate Gallery, 1948 (44); *Impressionism*, Royal Academy, London, 1974 (71); Courtauld Centenary, 1976 (28); Japan and Canberra, 1984 (64); United States, 1987–8 (11).

LITERATURE (?)F. Wedmore, 'The Impressionists', *Fortnightly Review*, January 1883, p. 82; 'The Impressionists' Exhibition', *The Academy*, 28 April 1883, p. 300; Reuterswärd, 1948, p. 283; Cooper, 1954, no. 40; Wildenstein, I, 1974, no. 290, for full literature; J. House, *Monet: Nature into Art*, New Haven and London, 1986, pp. 18, 53, 79, 115, 180, and 242, n. 3 (Ch. 11); R. Bruce-Gardner, G. Hedley and C. Villers, 'Impressions of Change', in United States, 1987–8, pp. 23–4.

32 MONET, CLAUDE 1840–1926
The Gare Saint-Lazare 1877
La Gare Saint-Lazare
Oil on canvas, 53.3 × 72.5
Signed, bottom right: 'Claude Monet'
The Trustees of the National Gallery,
London

This is one of the less highly finished of the twelve views of the Gare Saint-Lazare that Monet painted early in 1877. He included seven of them in the third Impressionist group exhibition in May 1877. He did exhibit some of the sketchiest of the Gare Saint-Lazare paintings, alongside the most highly finished ones, but we do not know whether this canvas was among them. During these years, Monet was signing and selling many paintings that he left in quite a roughly finished state. These he characterised as *esquisses*, in contrast to his more elaborately worked *tableaux*; much of the criticism of his work in these years, for instance by Zola in 1880, focused on his willingness to sell such informal works in order to raise small sums of money in difficult times.

Railway trains had appeared in a number of Monet's paintings from 1870 onwards, but the Gare Saint-Lazare paintings are by far his most sustained exploration of the theme – one of the iconic images of modernity in the literature and visual imagery of the period. Trains were generally given a grand and almost heroic status when they were included in visual images. In Turner's *Rain, Steam and Speed* (which Monet saw in the National Gallery, London, in 1870–1), the engine becomes a sort of elemental force. Writing in 1867, the painter Thomas Couture encouraged painters to treat the subject of the railway engine as a sort of modern Vulcan: '. . . this strange mysterious power, which contains a vulcan in its sides, this monster of bronze, with mouth of fire, devouring space, and crushing all that resists it . . .'. Even in Pissarro's resolutely suburban *Lordship Lane Station, Dulwich* (cat. no. 36), the train and its smoke play a pivotal role.

In Monet's Gare Saint-Lazare paintings, too, the comings and goings of the trains, under the sheds of the station and on the tracks outside, play a central part. But the treatment of the subject, and particularly the paint-handling, serve to undermine this centrality. In his brushwork in the early 1870s (e.g., cat. no. 30), Monet had developed a crisp shorthand which clearly differentiated the various elements in the scene. However, as he became more preoccupied with atmospheric effects (see cat. no. 31), he began to subordinate the separate elements to an overall harmony of light and colour; this is expressed by broken touches of paint that challenge the separateness of the

objects, in favour of a carefully co-ordinated play of coloured textures.

In *The Gare Saint-Lazare*, the silhouettes of the two engines, framed by the station roof, give the whole image a clear, taut structure; but the forms of the engines are dissolved into fluent accents of paint that give them no special status. Likewise, the figures on the platform are so summarily indicated that one cannot be distinguished from another, apart from the delightfully economical notation of one man's trousers at the front right of the figure group.

Within the framework of the shed, the principal focus is on the play of light through the smoke and steam from the trains. The brushwork is boldly improvised, with softer sweeps of paint and some more distinct, cursive strokes, but deliberately refusing to create broader rhythms and patterns across the surface. But, for all this apparent spontaneity, the arrangement of the patches of smoke was integral to Monet's initial plan for the canvas. When laying in the form of the shed roof, he left a substantial area unpainted above the right engine, to allow the principal area of smoke here to exploit the light tones of the canvas priming. By contrast, where smaller areas of smoke overlie the dark tones of the roof, they appear darker and less airy.

The weather effect is an overcast, grey day, and the overall effect of the picture is quite subdued in colour. But the colours used are never neutral. Soft, variegated blues run throughout the smoke and steam, and the picture is enlivened by a sequence of reddish accents, on the figures and the buffers of the right train, which are picked up by some reddish tones in the station roofs and some delicate warmer, mauver hues amid the blues of the smoke and on the roof struts at the top of the picture.

Pigment analysis has shown that even the darkest zones of the canvas – the roof and the engines – are executed in a colour made up of mixtures of virtually all the pigments on his palette, with only a very small admixture of black to darken the tone slightly. The elaborate colour mixtures reveal the complexity and deliberation involved in Impressionist colour procedures, even if the final results were reached in a very informal way as Monet worked up the painting; the presence of a little ivory black shows that the stock watchcry that black should be banished from the Impressionist palette was not a literal prescription but rather a rhetorical device, to signal their insistence that the effects of light should be conveyed not by tonal chiaroscuro, but by the play of colour.

PROVENANCE Lazare Weiller, Paris; Weiller Sale, Paris, 29 November 1901 (lot 31); Oscar Schmitz, Dresden; Wildenstein, London; bought by Courtauld, November 1936, £2,000; Lady Aberconway; private collection; National Gallery, London.

EXHIBITED *Monet*, Thannhauser, Berlin, 1928 (25); *Sammlung Oscar Schmitz*, Kunsthaus, Zürich, 1932 (36); *Oscar Schmitz Collection*, Wildenstein, Paris, 1936 (42); Tate Gallery, 1948 (46); *Monet*, Marlborough, London, 1954 (10); *Monet*, Edinburgh and London, 1957 (50); *Monet*, New York and Los Angeles, 1960 (17); *Impressionism*, Royal Academy, London, 1974 (73); *Art in the Making: Impressionism*, National Gallery, London, 1990–1 (10).

LITERATURE P. Fechter, 'Die Sammlung Oscar Schmitz', *Kunst und Künstler*, 1910, no. 1, p. 20; K. Scheffler, 'Die Sammlung O. Schmitz in Dresden', *Kunst und Künstler*, 1920–1, p. 186; M. Dormoy, 'La Collection Schmitz à Dresde', *L'Amour de l'art*, 1926, p. 342; Cooper, 1954, no. 42; Wildenstein, I, 1974, no. 441; A. Roy, 'The Palettes of Three Impressionist Paintings', *National Gallery Technical Bulletin*, 1985, pp. 13–15; *National Gallery Report*, 1985, p. 20.

33 MONET, CLAUDE 1840–1926
    Vase of Flowers c.1881–2
    Vase de fleurs
    Oil on canvas, 100.4 × 81.8
    Signed, bottom right: 'Claude Monet'
    Courtauld Institute Galleries (The Samuel
      Courtauld Trust)

Between 1878 and 1882, for the only time in his career, Monet concentrated extensively on still lifes, alongside his painting of landscapes. In these years, he was beginning to find a more regular market for his paintings, and he was able to sell still lifes more readily and for higher sums than landscapes; when the dealer Durand-Ruel began to buy his landscapes regularly from 1881 onwards, he soon virtually gave up still-life painting. *Vase of Flowers*, a picture of a lavish display of wild mallow, very probably belongs to the last group of still lifes that he undertook in this phase, a group of particularly large flower paintings, which, his letters show, caused him great trouble.

The final state of *Vase of Flowers* testifies to his difficulties. Although it is densely and elaborately worked, Monet did not complete it for sale at the time of its execution. It was one of many paintings from earlier years which he signed and sold in the last years of his life; indeed, this canvas can be seen hanging on the wall in photographs of his house at Giverny taken around 1920; shortly after this he sold it to the dealers Bernheim-Jeune.

In contrast to the paintings that he completed for sale in the 1880s (such as cat. no. 34 and *Chrysanthemums* (in the Metropolitan Museum of Art, New York), another of the same group of still lifes), the forms of leaves and flowers in *Vase of Flowers* are less crisply handled, treated in rapid dabs and dashes of colour which, though complex, do not always define the forms clearly. In his still lifes of these years, he was seeking to show lavish displays of flowers and fruit that broke out of the more rigid, structured conventions of still-life painting in the Chardin tradition, but on this occasion, he did not succeed in finding a fully resolved pictorial form for this mass of blooms and greenery. Its vigorous, but slightly crude and even disorderly touch is more akin to twentieth-century tastes than it would have been to those of the buyers of Monet's paintings in the 1880s.

PROVENANCE Bernheim-Jeune, Paris; Alex. Reid, Glasgow; bought by Courtauld, May 1923, £2,500. Courtauld Gift 1932.

EXHIBITED *French Art*, City Museum and Art Gallery, Birmingham, 1947 (no catalogue); Tate Gallery, 1948 (49); *Monet*, Edinburgh and London 1957 (59); Courtauld Centenary, 1976 (31); Japan and Canberra, 1984 (65); United States, 1987–8 (12).

LITERATURE Jamot-Turner, no. 17; Home House Catalogue, no. 24; Reuterswärd, 1948, p. 280; Cooper, 1954, no. 43; Wildenstein, I, 1974, no. 626.

34 MONET, CLAUDE 1840–1926
Antibes 1888
Oil on canvas, 65.5 × 92.4
Signed, bottom left: 'Claude Monet 88'
Courtauld Institute Galleries (The Samuel
    Courtauld Trust)

Monet worked at Antibes from February until
May 1888, and on his return exhibited ten
paintings of the surroundings of Antibes at the
subsidiary branch of the dealers Boussod &
Valadon, run by Theo van Gogh, brother of
the painter. The present picture was very
probably one of these. It shows the view south-
west from the Cap d'Antibes across the Golfe
Juan, with the Montagnes de l'Estérel in the
background. The city of Cannes is just out of
sight on the right side of the bay.

In his two spells of painting the
Mediterranean in 1884 and 1888, Monet was
faced with the problem of capturing the
intensity of southern light and colour. He wrote
to Berthe Morisot from Antibes about his
experiments: 'It's so difficult, so tender and so
delicate, while I am so inclined to brutality.' In
a letter to Alice Hoschedé, he commented:
'What I bring back from here will be sweetness
itself, white, pink and blue, all enveloped in this
magical air.' In his southern paintings, Monet
evoked the effect of the light in part by
heightening his colours, but also by co-
ordinating the colour relationships throughout
the picture into clear sequences of contrasts.
Here, greens and blues are set against sharp
accents of pink, red and orange, with related
colours recurring all over the canvas. In 1888,
an English interviewer described how Monet
used colour to unify his paintings:

   One of his great points is to use the same
   colours on every part of the canvas. Thus the
   sky would be slashed with strokes of blue,
   lake, green and yellow, with a preponderance
   of blue; a green field would be worked with
   the same colours with a preponderance of
   green . . . By working in this way, the same
   colour appearing all over the canvas, the
   subtle harmony of nature . . . is successfully
   obtained without the loss of colour.

It was by combining this weave of colours with
emphatic oppositions of complementary
contrasts that Monet sought to evoke in paint
the effects of the southern sun. Late in the
execution of the painting, he stressed the warm
end of its colour range, by adding little hooks
and dashes of red and orange across the far
mountains and the foliage of the tree, and by
adding his signature in a bold red-orange.

Although it ostensibly conveys a passing
effect of outdoor light, the painting is
elaborately executed and was clearly extensively
reworked. Local preparatory underpainting is

visible in the sky and sea. This paint was dry
before the upper layers were applied. X-ray
examination shows that the sea was originally
executed far more boldly, and perhaps
originally showed an effect of strong wind,
whereas the crisp yet delicate final strokes that
enrich the water surface suggest a far calmer
effect. During the execution of the picture, he
also moved the position of the tree-trunk a little
to the left; the rich blues on the upper area of
the sky were added over a layer of paler colour,
and many of the crisp touches that define the
outer margins of the foliage were added at a
later stage, after the initial painting of the sky
had had time to dry. Many of these adjustments
may have been made at Antibes, where Monet
was plagued by changing conditions of wind
and weather, but by this date he had come to
feel that the final touches on a picture, which
gave it its coherence and harmony, needed to
be added in the controlled surroundings of his
studio. The apparent immediacy and vivacity of
his finished paint surfaces was the product of
elaborate processes by which he sought to give
his canvases an air of spontaneity.

The composition of *Antibes*, with its
silhouetted tree and open sides, reflects in
general terms Monet's interest in Japanese
prints, of which he was an avid collector. In the
1880s, he travelled widely, exploring subjects
that showed nature at its most lavish and
extreme, and his knowledge of Japanese art
helped him to find ways of formulating these
dramatic effects in pictorial terms. This sort of
spectacular subject and treatment is very
different from the less obviously picturesque
subjects he favoured near home in the Seine
valley. In the 1880s, these vivid scenes – often,
like Antibes, of places that were becoming
favoured tourist sites – began to win him buyers;
but after 1890, he began to concentrate on
nuances of atmosphere in the Seine valley,
when he started to paint in long series of
canvases showing single subjects under different
conditions of light.

Vincent van Gogh was not in Paris when his
brother exhibited Monet's Antibes paintings,
but his friend the Australian painter J.P. Russell
reported on the exhibition to him. Vincent
relayed Russell's reactions back to his brother
from Arles, mentioning a painting that is very
probably the present canvas:

   [Russell] criticises the Monets very ably,
   begins by liking them very much, the attack
   on the problem, the enfolding tinted air, the
   colour. After that he shows what there is to
   find fault with – the total lack of construction,
   for instance one of his trees will have far too
   much foliage for the thickness of the trunk,
   and so always and everywhere from the
   standpoint of the reality of things, from the

standpoint of natural laws, he is exasperating
enough. He ends by saying that this quality
of attacking the difficulties is what everyone
ought to have.

PROVENANCE   (?) bought from the artist by
Boussod & Valadon, June 1888; (?) with
Georges Petit, 1888; Mme Vve Barbedienne,
Paris, 1894; sold Hôtel Drouot, Paris, 24
February 1894 (lot 39), bought Durand-Ruel;
Decap, Paris, 1894; Bernheim-Jeune, Paris,
1907; Baron Caccamisi, Paris, 1907; Mrs
Blanche Marchesi, London, c.1910; Paul
Rosenberg, Paris; Knoedler, London; bought by
Courtauld, August 1923, price unknown. To
Sir John Atkins, London (with a life interest),
thence to Home House Society Trustees, a year
before Sir John's death, in 1962.

EXHIBITED   (?)*Monet*, Boussod Valadon et Cie.,
Paris, 1888; *Monet et Rodin*, Georges Petit, Paris,
1889 (103); *Tableaux par Besnard, Cazin, etc.*,
Georges Petit, Paris, 1899 (51); International
Society of Sculptors, Painters and Gravers,
Grafton Galleries, London, 1910 (133); *19th
Century French Painters*, Knoedler, London, July
1923 (35); Tate Gallery, 1948 (47);
Impressionism, Royal Academy, London, 1974
(77); Courtauld Centenary, 1976 (32); Japan and
Canberra, 1984 (66); United States, 1987–8 (13).

LITERATURE   (?)G. Geffroy, 'Dix tableaux de Cl.
Monet', *La Justice*, 17 June 1888, p. 1; (?)A. de
Calonne, 'L'Art contre nature', *Le Soleil*, 23
June 1889, p. 1; A. Alexandre, *Claude Monet*,
Paris, 1921, pp. 87–8; Jamot-Turner, no. 18; L.
Venturi, *Les Archives de l'Impressionnisme*, I,
Paris, 1939, p. 236; Cooper, 1954, no. 44; J.
Rewald, 'Theo Van Gogh, Goupil, and the
Impressionists', Parts I and II, *Gazette des Beaux-
Arts*, January–February 1973, p. 25, Appendix I,
(?) pp. 92–3 and 99; Cleveland Museum of Art,
*Japonisme: Japanese Influence on French Art 1854–
1910*, 1975, p. 130 and fig. 42; Wildenstein, III,
1979, no. 1192, as 'Montagnes de l'Estérel'; J.
House, *Monet: Nature into Art*, New Haven and
London, 1986, pp. 168–70, 173, 187, 189; R.
Bruce-Gardner, G. Hedley and C. Villers,
'Impressions of Change', in United States,
1987–8, p. 27–8.

35 PICASSO, PABLO 1881–1973
Child with a Pigeon 1901
L'Enfant au pigeon
Oil on canvas, 73 × 54
Signed, centre left: 'Picasso'
Private Collection, on loan to the National
Gallery, London, © DACS 1994

Painted in the latter half of 1901, *Child with a Pigeon* marks the beginning of what has come to be known as Picasso's 'blue period'. Abandoning the vigorous brushwork, indebted to Impressionism and especially to van Gogh, that had characterised his recent work, he simplified both his palette and his paint-handling, to produce this image of great simplicity and immediate impact.

The schematic, almost crude outlining of the figure and the largely flat colour planes are an evident tribute to Gauguin, whose art Picasso would have known through the dealer Ambroise Vollard. At the same time, there is a deliberate childlikeness in the painting, in the outlining of the figure, in the deliberately naïve treatment of the bird's tail-feathers and the child's eyelashes, and in the presentation of the whole image. This may be intended to evoke the vision of the child who is the picture's subject. The theme of children with birds had been a stock-in-trade of sentimental genre painting throughout the later nineteenth century. In *Child with a Pigeon*, the gaze of the child's eyes and the tilt of his or her head, together with the gesture of holding the bird, make a comparable appeal to the viewer's feelings, despite the evident avant-gardism of the technique.

This picture, set in a wholly undefined space with no indication of topographical or social context, marks a shift away from Picasso's recent explicitly Parisian subject matter; very generalised settings such as this, often combined with figures who seem rootless and outcast, were to become central to his imagery during the 'blue period' of 1901–4.

The present image is executed over a densely impasted paint layer which covers the whole surface of the canvas in broad, roughly horizontal sweeps; this was dry when the present picture was executed. Traces of the painted surface of this underlayer can be seen, particularly on either side of the dark outline of the right edge of the child's skirt. X-ray examination has shown that this opaque layer covers a wholly different composition, a seated half-length figure of a female nude, closely comparable to another surviving canvas of the same date (Daix and Boudaille, VI.18). Thus the primary purpose of the dense underpainting of the present image was to allow Picasso to reuse a discarded canvas; but its rough, textured surface also adds a degree of crudeness and

'primitiveness' which Picasso may have felt appropriate to the effect he was seeking in *Child with a Pigeon*.

PROVENANCE   Paul Rosenberg, Paris; Alex. Reid, Glasgow; Mrs R.A. Workman, London; Reid and Lefèvre, London; bought by Courtauld, October 1928, £1,400; Lady Aberconway; private collection.

EXHIBITED   *French Painters of Today*, Alex. Reid Gallery, Glasgow, and Lefèvre Gallery, London, 1924 (24); Opening Exhibition, Modern Foreign Gallery, Tate Gallery, London, 1926; *A Century of French Painting*, Knoedler, New York, 1928 (47); *The School of Paris*, Reid and Lefèvre, London, 1945 (33); Tate Gallery, 1948 (50); Orangerie, Paris, 1955 (36); *Picasso*, Tate Gallery, London, 1960 (14); *Picasso and Man*, Toronto and Montréal, 1964 (12); *Hommage à Pablo Picasso*, Grand Palais, Paris, 1966–7 (9); Courtauld Centenary, 1976 (33); *Pablo Picasso: A Retrospective*, Museum of Modern Art, New York, 1980, p.42; Japan and Canberra, 1984 (70).

LITERATURE   Jamot-Turner, no.50; C. Zervos, *Pablo Picasso*, I, Paris, 1932, no.83; P. Daix and G. Boudaille, *Picasso 1900–1906*, Paris, 1966, no. VI.14.

36 PISSARRO, CAMILLE 1830–1903
Lordship Lane Station, Dulwich 1871
Oil on canvas, 44.5 × 72.5
Signed, bottom right: 'C. Pissarro 1871'
Courtauld Institute Galleries (The Samuel Courtauld Trust)

Pissarro painted this picture while living in London as a refugee from the Franco-Prussian War in 1870–1. Formerly known as Penge Station, Upper Norwood, its correct location has recently been identified as Lordship Lane Station (now demolished) on the old Crystal Palace (High Level) Railway, seen from the footbridge across the cutting to the south of the station. The line was opened in 1865 to cater for the crowds coming to the Crystal Palace, very popular as a recreation and exhibition centre since its reconstruction in this South London suburb in 1852–4. Thus the scene shows a modern landscape in the making, with the rows of new houses on either side of the station punctuated by still-undeveloped open land. Many of Pissarro's canvases painted while he was living in nearby Norwood focus on the burgeoning suburban developments around the Crystal Palace, and some show the palace itself.

Here the chosen subject is deliberately anti-picturesque, with the rough slopes and drab fences framing the central motif of tracks and train; the wedge of scrubby terrain on the right takes up almost a quarter of the whole picture. X-ray and infra-red photographs show that there was originally a figure, perhaps holding a scythe, on the bank to the right of the tracks, above the point where the grass meets the ballast of the track at the bottom edge of the picture. The position of the arms was altered before the figure was painted out altogether, thus removing the only feature of any obvious pictorial interest in this whole zone of the canvas.

Several of the Impressionist group painted railway trains, including Manet and Monet (see cat. no. 32), but this canvas seems to be the first occasion on which one of them made a train into his central motif. It may echo Turner's famous *Rain, Steam and Speed*, which Pissarro saw in the National Gallery in London, but, in place of Turner's lavish atmospherics, Pissarro adopted a far more detached view, closer in its treatment to contemporary topographical prints of the new railway landscape. The signal, silhouetted against the sky in the exact centre of the picture, can be seen as an utterly secularised equivalent of a crucifix – an overt rejection of traditional elevated subject matter, in the search for the truly contemporary.

The picture is quite subdued in colour; the effect of an overcast day is evoked by varied greens and soft red-browns, with the white of the smoke and the clear black of the engine as a central focus. This comparatively tonal treatment, with nuances of a restricted range of colour, is in marked contrast to the lavish colour that, soon afterwards, Monet began to adopt in sunlit scenes (see cat. no. 31), and to the multicoloured interplay of touches that Pissarro himself later adopted (see cat. no. 37). The brushwork is softly variegated to suggest the different textures in the scene; there is no dominant rhythm to the touch, which stresses the diversity of the elements that went to make up this characteristically modern landscape. By contrast, twelve years later at Rouen, Pissarro subordinated the elements in an industrial scene such as cat. no. 37 to an overall play of coloured touches. This change, from a concentration on the distinctive elements in a subject to a preoccupation with overall unifying effects of light, is fundamental in the development of Impressionism in these years.

PROVENANCE Alexandre Rosenberg, Paris; Lazare Weiller, Paris; Weiller Sale, Paris, 29 November 1901 (lot 34; 1,750 francs); Tavernier, Paris; Pearson, Paris; Pearson Sale, Berlin, 18 October 1927 (lot 53); Anonymous Sale, Paris, 23 June 1928 (lot 82; 51,000 francs); Schoeller, Paris; Morot, Paris; Durand-Ruel, Paris; Arthur Tooth & Sons, London; bought by Courtauld, June 1936, £850. Courtauld Bequest 1948.

EXHIBITED *Flèche d'Or*, Tooth's Gallery, London, 1936 (20); Tate Gallery, 1948 (51); *The Impressionists in London*, Hayward Gallery, London, 1973 (32); Courtauld Centenary, 1976 (34); *Pissarro*, Hayward Gallery, London, Grand Palais, Paris, and Museum of Fine Arts, Boston, 1980–1 (16); Japan and Canberra, 1984 (72); United States, 1987–8 (5).

LITERATURE L.-R. Pissarro and L. Venturi, *Camille Pissarro: Catalogue de son oeuvre*, Paris, 1939, no. 111; Cooper, 1954, no. 47; J. Gage, *Turner: Rain, Steam and Speed*, Harmondsworth, 1972, pp. 67–8; M. Reid, 'Camille Pissarro: three paintings of London. What do they represent?', *Burlington Magazine*, April 1977, pp. 251–61; N. Reed, *Camille Pissarro at Crystal Palace*, London, 1993, pp. 36–9.

37 PISSARRO, CAMILLE 1830–1903
The Quays at Rouen 1883
Les Quais à Rouen
Oil on canvas, 46.3 × 55.7
Signed, bottom left: 'C. Pissarro, 1883'
Courtauld Institute Galleries (The Samuel
    Courtauld Trust)

Pissarro spent three months at Rouen in the autumn of 1883 in a hotel run by Eugène Murer, a professional pastry-cook who had met the Impressionist painters through his childhood friend Armand Guillaumin and made an extensive collection of their work. While in Rouen, Pissarro concentrated on scenes of the banks of the Seine, generally focusing on industrial scenes with boats and docks. In this picture, the view is to the east from the Ile Lacroix, with factories at the base of the Côte Sainte-Catharine across the river, and, silhouetted against the sky, the church of Notre-Dame de Bonsecours, an elaborate Neo-Gothic structure of 1840–2, celebrated as a pilgrimage centre.

The raised viewpoint, above and somehow distanced from the scene, is characteristic of Pissarro's treatment of subjects of this type. By contrast, in his contemporary scenes of peasants in the countryside of the Ile de France, he adopted a closer viewpoint, integrating the figures more fully with their surroundings. This different treatment of different themes is clearly significant, and perhaps expresses the contrasts that he saw between city and country life, in line with the sympathies with anarchist political beliefs that he was evolving in these years: the countryside appears as the repository of a harmonious, coherent way of life, while the activities of the city are more distanced from each other – life is detached from labour. However, there is nothing in this painting, either in the subject or in the way it is treated, that makes any overt social criticism or judgement. The viewpoint is in line with a long tradition of urban topographical prints, to which Monet, too, looked in his urban scenes, and all the elements in the subject are integrated into a densely wrought overall harmony; church and factories, boats, carts and figures are all given equal weight and significance in the ensemble.

The handling of the picture is particularly unified, with virtually every area built up from successions of small dabs and dashes of colour which give it a constantly mobile surface, allowing Pissarro to introduce variations of colour throughout it, so as to evoke the play of coloured light and atmosphere. Though each area has a dominant colour, small touches of other colours recur, which relate to other areas of the picture, linking lit and shadowed areas, foreground and distance; across the whole, too, small, very light-toned accents create flecks of light which enliven every part of the picture. With these calculated devices, Pissarro suggested the effect of the unifying hazy sunlight.

The paintwork is broader where the surface is more thinly painted, showing that Pissarro began with a simpler, flatter lay-in before elaborating the surface (as Cézanne did in the same period, see cat. no. 6); over this, the final touches refine the effect and give the surface a distinctive rhythm, which is comparable to, though less rigid than, the structures of parallel strokes that Cézanne applied to his more highly finished paintings at this date (seen in parts of cat. no. 6). In Pissarro's Rouen paintings, this refinement of the surface took place, in part at least, after he had taken the paintings back home to his studio; he wrote on his return from Rouen: 'Result of my trip: I return with pleasure to my studio, and look over my studies with greater indulgence, with a better idea of what needs to be done to them.'

In 1898, fifteen years after painting this canvas, Pissarro depicted it hanging on the wall of his studio in *Bouquet of Flowers* (Fine Arts Museums of San Francisco), which suggests that it was a canvas to which he still attached a real significance.

PROVENANCE Private collection, Berlin; Paul Cassirer, Berlin; bought by Courtauld, 1926, price unknown. Courtauld Gift 1932.

EXHIBITED British Institute of Adult Education, Silver End, Essex, 1935; Tate Gallery, 1948 (52); Orangerie, Paris, 1955 (38); Courtauld Centenary, 1976 (35); Japan and Canberra, 1984 (43); United States, 1987–8 (6).

LITERATURE Jamot-Turner, no. 6; Home House Catalogue, no. 18; Pissarro and Venturi, 1939, no. 601; C. Pissarro (ed. J. Rewald), *Lettres à son fils Lucien*, Paris, 1950, pp. 59–70 (English edn, London and New York, 1943, pp. 40–8), especially letter of 1 December 1883; Cooper, 1954, no. 48; J. Bailly-Herzberg (ed.), *Correspondance de Camille Pissarro, I: 1865–1885*, Paris, 1980, p. 257.

Spring (Chatou)   c.1873
Le Printemps (Chatou)
Oil on canvas, 59.6 × 73.7
Signed, bottom right: 'Renoir'
Private Collection

Although the picture has always been known as *Spring (Chatou)*, there is nothing in this view of an open meadow with a glimpse of a river on the left to link it to a particular site. However, the indication of Chatou marks it out as a landscape of the outer fringes of Paris and associates the image with the world of suburban recreation (see cat.no.41), though nothing of this is conveyed by the picture itself.

The subject is utterly mundane, with no distinctive feature and no clear spatial structure. The eye finds its way past the saplings and the pools of soft shadow to the pivotal figure, thigh-deep in the grasses, but the bank of trees beyond allows only a glimpse of the river, with a sharp white accent above it which is so inexplicit in form that it cannot be identified in representational terms. However, the arrangement of even this very informal image was carefully thought through: the tiny tree just to the left of the figure, which plays a vital role in suggesting the space, was added at a very late stage in the execution of the picture.

Among the landscapists of the previous generation, it was Corot, in particular, who had made unassuming subjects such as this acceptable in landscape painting. The saplings, flowers and foliage in *Spring (Chatou)* evoke Corot's example particularly clearly. In 1893, Camille Pissarro wrote:

> One can make such beautiful things with so little. Motifs that are too beautiful end up by seeming theatrical – think of Switzerland. What lovely little things old Corot did at Gisors: two willows, a bit of water, a bridge . . . What a masterpiece! Happy are those who see beautiful things in modest places where others see nothing. Everything is beautiful, what matters is to know how to interpret it.

Some aspects of the technique here are also reminiscent of Corot – the soft brushing of the background trees, the flickering highlights on the tree-trunks and the colour-contrasts set up by the warm accents of the deep red flowers in the foreground. However, the brushwork is far more active and variegated than Corot's, and the colour richer and more varied. The plants and grasses across the foreground are conveyed in an astonishing display of free-floating dabs and dashes of paint which manage to suggest the complex textures of the natural subject quite without any illusionistic detail. The patches of shadow are treated comparatively traditionally, in darker, duller tones, though even the darkest accents are not without colour. It is the range of coloured nuances in the sunlit areas that mark Renoir's move towards the high-key Impressionist palette of the mid- to late 1870s.

PROVENANCE   Durand-Ruel, Paris; Paul Cassirer, Berlin; Galerie Barbazanges, Paris; Percy Moore Turner; bought by Courtauld, June 1927, £5,500; Lady Aberconway; private collection.

EXHIBITED   *Renoir*, Durand-Ruel, Paris, 1883 (43); *French School of the Last Hundred Years*, Burlington Fine Arts Club, London, 1922 (37); *Ingres to Cézanne*, Independent Gallery, London, 1925 (15); Centenary Exhibition, Norwich, 1925 (60); *French Art*, Royal Academy, London, 1932 (545); Tate Gallery, 1948 (58); *Landscape in French Art*, Royal Academy, London, 1949–50 (266); *Impressionism*, Royal Academy, London, 1974 (97); *Renoir*, Hayward Gallery, London, 1985–6 (24).

LITERATURE   Jamot-Turner, no. 32; Cooper, 1954, no. 53.

39 RENOIR, PIERRE-AUGUSTE 1841–1919
   La Loge 1874
   Oil on canvas, 80 × 63.5
   Signed, bottom left: 'A. Renoir 74'
   Courtauld Institute Galleries (The Samuel
      Courtauld Trust)

The artist's brother Edmond and a model, Nini (otherwise known as Gueule-de-Raie or 'fish-face'), from Montmartre posed for this painting, which was one of Renoir's prime exhibits at the first group exhibition of the Impressionists in Paris in 1874. The dealer Durand-Ruel then exhibited it in London but did not buy it, and Renoir sold it in 1875 to another, less ambitious dealer, *père* Martin, for 425 francs–money that Renoir badly needed in order to pay the rent.

It was at the first group exhibition in Paris in 1874 that the comments of critics about Monet's *Impression, Sunrise* (Musée Marmottan, Paris) led to the group's being named 'Impressionists'. However, Renoir's *La Loge* is very different from Monet's rapid sketch and far more elaborated than some of Renoir's other exhibits at this show; he continued throughout his career to paint comparatively elaborate, highly finished canvases like this, alongside his more informal canvases.

Yet the technique of *La Loge* is very varied and fluent: forms are delicately and softly brushed without crisp contours, and the execution of the model's bodice and the flowers on it is a particularly virtuoso display. Her face, though, is executed more minutely, its modelling more fully suggested; the viewer's eye fluctuates between bodice and face in search for the principal focus of the composition. The model's gown, with its bold stripes, gives the composition a strong black-and-white underpinning; actual black paint is used here, though often mixed with blue to suggest the play of light and shade across it. Around its strong pattern, richly varied nuances of blue, green and yellow recur in the white materials, set against the soft warm hues of her flesh and the pinks and reds in the flowers on her bodice and hair.

The subject of the theatre box was a favoured one among painters of modern Parisian life during the 1870s. In *La Loge*, Renoir makes a play on the contrast between the poses of the two figures: the woman looks out with a half smile on her face and her opera glasses beside her, in her hand, as if to receive the gaze of other members of the audience, while her male companion looks through his opera glasses out from the box and upwards, and thus implicitly at another box, not down at the stage. The caricaturist Gavarni had already explored the same idea in a well-known drawing titled *A Lioness in Her Box*, but with the added satirical point that his woman, seated in the confident expectation of the admiration of her onlookers, is clearly ageing and past her prime, while her male companion peers through his binoculars with evident excitement. Renoir defused this, by presenting his model as young and pretty, seated to receive the gaze of her (male) viewers, while her companion is relegated to the half shadow behind her. The implied position of the viewer within the theatre is uncertain: we seem to be quite close to the figures, and yet we are clearly outside the front edge of the balcony, which we see at bottom left. By creating this 'impossible' viewpoint, seemingly floating above the stalls, Renoir set up a further obstacle to the spectator reading the picture in narrative terms.

In his treatment of his model, Renoir left her exact social and sexual status ambiguous; one of the reviewers of the first group exhibition (where the canvas was well received) described her as a typical *cocotte* and humorously used her as a warning to young girls of what they might become if they were waylaid by fashion and vanity, while another saw her as 'a figure from the world of elegance'. Such an elision of the signs of difference was very characteristic of Renoir; unlike Manet (see cat. no. 27), he never painted images that suggested any social uncertainty or division, but, in his paintings of modern Parisian life of the 1870s, he presented all aspects of it as if they were equally harmonious and untroubled.

After the early 1880s, he ceased to paint modern Paris altogether (see cat. no. 43), and at the same time adopted a more classical treatment of form and modelling.

PROVENANCE Bought from the artist by Martin, Paris 1875 (425 francs); M. Fleurnois, Paris, sold by him to Durand-Ruel, 9 February 1899 (8,500 francs); Durand-Ruel, Paris; through Percy Moore Turner; bought by Courtauld, May 1925, approx. £22,600 plus commission £1,600. Courtauld Bequest 1948.

EXHIBITED *Première exposition*, Société anonyme . . . , Paris, 1874 (142); *Ninth Exhibition of the Society of French Artists*, London, November 1874 (12); Exposition des Beaux-Arts, Nantes, 1886 (893); *Renoir*, Galerie Durand-Ruel, Paris, 1892 (63); *Renoir*, Galerie Durand-Ruel, Paris, 1899 (74); Exposition Internationale Universelle, Grand Palais, Paris 1900 (562); La Libre Esthétique, Brussels, 1904 (128); Grafton Galleries, London, 1905 (251); *French Art*, Royal Academy, London, 1932 (415); *Renoir*, Musée de l'Orangerie, Paris, 1933 (17); Tate Gallery, 1948 (56); *Renoir*, Tate Gallery, London, 1953 (6); Orangerie, Paris, 1955 (39); Courtauld Centenary, 1976 (36); National Gallery, London, 1983 (no catalogue); Japan and Canberra, 1984 (75); *Renoir*, Hayward Gallery, London, Grand Palais, Paris, and Museum of Fine Arts, Boston, 1985–6 (26, with bibliography); United States, 1987–8 (14).

LITERATURE Jamot-Turner, no. 29; Cooper, 1954, no. 51; F. Daulte, *Auguste Renoir. Catalogue raisonné de l'oeuvre peint*, I Lausanne, 1971, pp. 26, 29, 37–8; no. 116; J. Rewald, *The History of Impressionism*, New York and London, 4th edn, 1973, pp. 316–34; R. Bruce-Gardner, G. Hedley and C. Villers, 'Impressions of Change', in United States, 1987–8, pp. 23, 28–30.

40 RENOIR, PIERRE-AUGUSTE 1841–1919
Place Clichy c.1879–80
Oil on canvas, 64.5 × 54.5
Signed, bottom left: 'A. Renoir'
The Syndics of the Fitzwilliam Museum,
Cambridge

Renoir's brother Edmond wrote an account of
Renoir's art in 1879 in which he described his
work as 'a faithful picture of modern life . . . it
is our very existence that he has registered, in
pages which are certain to remain among the
most living and most harmonious of our age'.
However, Renoir's view of modern life was
very selective. The mood in his pictures is
always carefree, and the scenes and settings
generally belong either to the informal street
and café life of Paris or to the recreation places
on the outer fringes of the city (see cat.no.41).

Although the painting has been known as
Place Clichy at least since its appearance in the
Tavernier sale in 1900, there is nothing obvious
to link it with this particular busy intersection
just to the south of the hill of Montmartre.
However, a title that linked it to this area of
Paris, already well known for public
entertainments and lax morals, would have
given an extra *frisson* of suggestiveness to the
image of the young woman alone in the street,
which itself raised moral issues in an age when
respectable women did not go out without a
companion or a chaperone.

The painting itself deliberately denies any
anecdotal reading. We do not know what the
woman is looking at: is she merely about to
cross the street, as the diagonal of the kerb
might suggest, or is her gaze more purposeful?
Behind, some sort of interchange seems to be
taking place between the top-hatted man and
the woman with the red scarf, but it cannot be
clearly deciphered. It is left to the viewer to
write his or her own narratives.

The composition of the picture is very
distinctive, with the foreground figure in close
focus, cropped by the corner of the canvas and
set against a lightly brushed background
without any clear focal point, in which the
figures are only summarily indicated. The
existence of a number of preparatory studies for
the picture – both of the whole image and of
individual elements in it – shows that the whole
thing was particularly carefully worked out by
Renoir. The cut-off form and sharp jump in
scale and space are immediately reminiscent of
Degas and can be closely compared with
Degas's *Dancing Lesson* of c.1878 (Metropolitan
Museum of Art, New York), then in the
collection of Gustave Caillebotte. On
Caillebotte's death, Renoir chose this as the one
picture he was allowed to choose from
Caillebotte's collection, under the terms of his

will (to Degas's fury, Renoir later exchanged it
for a Corot).

This sort of compositional disjunction was
used by Degas to suggest the distinctive ways in
which figures and forms were experienced in
the city (see cat.no.17). Such devices were
indebted in turn to Japanese colour prints,
though Renoir did not share Degas's enthusiasm
for these. To twentieth-century eyes, the
composition also evokes the art of
photography. Indeed, such a juxtaposition
between foreground focus and background blur
would have been very characteristic of
nineteenth-century photographs, which were
unable, when using brief exposure times, to
maintain a clear focus throughout a deep visual
field. However, there is no evidence that this
sort of effect in photography was seen in
positive aesthetic terms as early as 1880. Indeed,
it seems likely that the aesthetics of
photography are indebted to paintings such as
this.

The picture's technique is integral to the
effect it creates. It is painted on a dense, opaque
white priming, which shows through much of
the thinly brushed colour across the
background. The area of the roadway at
bottom left is particularly little painted – in
sharp contrast to the highly finished figure on
the right, whose face is modelled with delicate,
filigree strokes, themselves so unlike the
ebulliently cursive and almost graphic handling
of the feathers in her hat. Despite these very
different types of execution and degrees of
working, there is no doubt that Renoir saw this
as a fully finished painting; the underlying
white layer and the rapid, summary execution
of the background lend freshness and
luminosity to the whole image.

Bluish tones, evoking a hazy atmospheric
effect, dominate the picture, but these are set
against a few clear yellow zones, notably on the
omnibuses in the background and the
foreground woman's coat, and a sequence of
smaller accents of deep red and purple; a
number of emphatically impasted white
highlights stand out boldly from the underlying
white of the priming.

The technique of *Place Clichy* is fascinatingly
different from *The Skiff* (cat.no.41), although
they are very close in date. At this period,
Renoir was experimenting with very diverse
types of handling as he sought to translate form,
space and atmosphere into colour.

PROVENANCE   Adolphe Tavernier, Paris;
Tavernier Sale, 6 March 1900 (lot 64); Madame
Bénard, Paris; Alexandre Rosenberg, Paris;
Prince de Wagram, Paris; H.J. Laroche, Paris;
Bignou, Paris; Reid & Lefèvre, London; bought
by Courtauld, June 1924, price unknown; Mrs
R.A. Butler; private collection; Fitzwilliam
Museum, Cambridge.

EXHIBITED   *Grands maîtres du 19me siècle*, Paul
Rosenberg, Paris, 1922 (76); *Exposition au profit
des amis du Luxembourg*, Paris, 1924 (147); Tate
Gallery, 1948 (59); *Impressionism*, Royal
Academy, London, 1974 (100); *Renoir*,
Hayward Gallery, London, Grand Palais, Paris,
and Museum of Fine Arts, Boston, 1985–6 (49).

LITERATURE   J. Meier-Graefe, *Auguste Renoir*,
Paris, 1912, p.64; Jamot-Turner, no.31; P.
Jamot, 'Renoir', *Gazette des Beaux-Arts*,
November/December 1923, p.280; M.
Drucker, *Renoir*, Paris, 1944, p.55; Cooper,
1954, no.55; D. Sutton, 'An Unpublished
Sketch by Renoir', *Apollo*, May 1963, pp.392–
4; Daulte, 1971, no.326; A. Callen, *Renoir*,
London, 1978, p.69; J. Isaacson, 'Impressionism
and Journalistic Illustration', *Arts Magazine*,
June 1982, p.107.

41 RENOIR, PIERRE-AUGUSTE 1841–1919
The Skiff c.1880
La Yole
Oil on canvas, 71 × 92
Signed, bottom left: 'Renoir'
The Trustees of the National Gallery,
London

Although the picture was titled *The Seine at Asnières* in the sale of Victor Chocquet's collection in 1899, its site does not seem to correspond to the riverside at Asnières, the setting of Seurat's *Une Baignade, Asnières* (fig. 8). It is more likely to show the river rather further downstream, around Chatou – about ten miles west of central Paris, though the exact site has not been identified. Renoir was painting in the Chatou region during the summer of 1880, primarily working on his *Luncheon of the Boating Party* (Phillips Collection, Washington, D.C.), and the present painting may well have been painted the same summer. *La Yole* (*The Skiff*) was the title given to the painting when Courtauld bought it in 1929.

The picture is an archetypal Impressionist image of recreation on the edges of Paris. The rowing-boat (technically a gig) and the sailboat, the chic villa and the railway bridge, and in the background a train approaching from Paris – all combine to give a serene vision of the leisure and pleasure of the city-dweller. The two women in the boat evoke the stock images current at the time of flirtation and sexual intrigue among the pleasure-seekers by the river (such as Guy de Maupassant's virtually contemporary 'La Femme de Paul'), but Renoir's painting gives no clues to any narrative beyond the moment depicted.

The overall effect is one of shimmering light and colour, but the techniques used are very varied. The white canvas priming is thinly and very irregularly applied, presumably by Renoir himself, which allows the brownish tone of the canvas to show through in many places, particularly around the edges. In marked contrast to the translucent layers over a white priming in cat. no. 40, here the final effect of the picture is achieved by vivid accents of opaque colour. The final surface is dominated by the mesh of delicate and variegated strokes that convey the water surface and the reeds in the foreground, and the softer textures of the bushes and trees across the back.

The composition of the picture is a clear rejection of traditional notions of landscape composition, which demanded a clearly legible recession into space, framed by emphatic *repoussoirs* (see also cat. no. 38 and Monet cat. no. 31). But the virtuoso play of coloured touches is given a strong structural underpinning by the dominant horizontals of riverbank and boat, with the two figures, and especially the dark head-scarf of the left woman, acting as the clear central pivots; and the margins of the picture are held in by the sail of the boat and the emphatic sunlit patch beneath the railway bridge on the right.

In many ways, the colouring of the picture represents the archetypal notion of Impressionism in its purest form (see also Monet cat. no. 31). The colour scheme of the picture is dominated by the bold contrast between the yellow and orange of the boat and the blues in the water; strong red-oranges recur, particularly in the left background, on the hull of the sailboat and in the bushes on the left, where they are played off against the greens of the foliage. But throughout the picture, the colour is varied and modulated, to produce a continuous effect of shimmering light. Technical analysis has shown that Renoir used a very limited range of pigments in the picture, with no black or earth colours. Even the dark head-scarf of the left figure is painted with a mixture of clear colours; elsewhere, the colours are little mixed (contrast Monet cat. no. 32).

PROVENANCE Victor Chocquet, Paris; Chocquet Sale, 1, 3 and 4 July 1899 (lot 93; 11,000 francs), bought Bernheim-Jeune, Paris; Durand-Ruel, Paris; Bernheim-Jeune, Paris; Bignou, Paris; Reid and Lefèvre, London; bought by Courtauld, July 1929, £12,500 plus approx. £1,600 (price of Matisse *Danseuse*); Lady Aberconway; private collection; National Gallery, London.

EXHIBITED Grafton Galleries, London, 1905 (236); *Renoir*, Bernheim-Jeune, Paris, 1913 (16); *Renoir*, Durand-Ruel, Paris, 1920 (61); *Cinquante Renoir*, Bernheim-Jeune, Paris, 1927; *Exposition Impressionniste et Néo-Impressionniste*, Lucerne, 1929 (13); *Ten Masterpieces*, Alex. Reid and Son, Glasgow, 1929 (7); *Ten Masterpieces*, Lefèvre Gallery, London, 1929 (6); *French Art*, Royal Academy, London, 1932 (429); Tate Gallery, 1948 (57); *Landscape in French Art*, Royal Academy, London, 1949–50 (268); *Renoir*, Hayward Gallery, London, Grand Palais, Paris, and Museum of Fine Arts, Boston, 1985–6 (47); *Van Gogh à Paris*, Musée d'Orsay, Paris, 1988 (102); *Art in the Making: Impressionism*, National Gallery, London, 1990–1 (11).

LITERATURE Jamot-Turner, no. 34; Cooper, 1954, no. 53; W. Gaunt, *Renoir*, with notes by K. Adler, Oxford, 1982, no. 33; A. Roy, 'The Palettes of Three Impressionist Paintings', *National Gallery Technical Bulletin*, 1985, pp. 15–16; *National Gallery Report*, 1985, p. 19; R. L. Herbert, *Impressionism: Art, Leisure, and Parisian Society*, New Haven and London, 1988, pp. 252 and 313, n. 49.

42 RENOIR, PIERRE-AUGUSTE 1841–1919
Portrait of Ambroise Vollard 1908
Portrait de M. Ambroise Vollard
Oil on canvas, 81.6 × 65.2
Signed, top left: 'Renoir. 08'
Courtauld Institute Galleries (The Samuel
   Courtauld Trust)

Renoir met the young dealer Vollard around
1895. Born on the island of Réunion, Vollard
began to buy from Renoir, and after 1900
became one of the principal dealers in his work,
though, in retrospect, his main claim to fame is
as the organiser of the first extensive exhibitions
of Cézanne's work, from 1895 onwards.
Vollard was later to write important books on
both Renoir and Cézanne.

Vollard commissioned portraits of himself
from many of the artists whose work he
bought – from Cézanne, Picasso, Bonnard and
others. Of all these, Renoir's is one of the least
acute, either as a record of the dealer's ugly,
bulldog features, or as an evocation of his
cunning, quirky personality. Rather, Renoir
chose to make his picture into an image of an
archetypal connoisseur, appreciatively holding a
statuette, very much in the tradition of such
collector portraits of the Italian Renaissance. At
the same time, though, the painting evokes the
dealer's power over the sensuous image of a
woman that he holds in his hands and in his
gaze; his pudgy fingers are startlingly similar to
the limbs of the statuette.

Vollard is shown holding a statuette by
Aristide Maillol, the *Crouching Woman* of 1900,
apparently in its original plaster form. It was
around this time that Maillol, at Vollard's
request, visited Renoir to execute a portrait bust
of him, and the inclusion of the piece by
Maillol here may refer to this. Moreover, the
simplified, monumental classicism that Maillol
evolved from the late 1890s onwards may well
be relevant to the development of Renoir's art
during these years. In the 1890s, he had looked
in particular to the Rococo painters of the
French eighteenth century, but after 1900, he
deliberately adopted a broader treatment and a
more monumental type of composition and
modelling – a sort of timeless classicism (see
cat. no. 43).

This development appears in *Portrait of
Ambroise Vollard* in the firmly modelled,
rounded treatment of the figure, far more
distinctly separated from its surroundings than
the figures in *La Loge* (cat. no. 39), and also in
his return to grey and black as a means of
modelling. Black had still been used in *La Loge*,
but in the mid-1870s he largely abandoned it,
using it only when a particular commission
demanded it, in favour of modelling suggested
by the play of colour alone. He re-adopted
black in the 1890s, partly as a result of his

studies of the techniques of the old masters, and
thereafter he insisted that it was a colour of
prime importance in his palette. In this portrait,
the comparatively monochrome treatment of
the jacket, enriched by only a few coloured
nuances on the folds, is set off against the
warmth of the flesh modelling and the
background. In marked contrast to his earlier
work, blue is used very sparingly, appearing
only at a few points on the tablecloth and in the
pottery on the table.

PROVENANCE   Given by the artist to the sitter;
bought from Vollard by Courtauld, June 1927,
approx. £6,450. Courtauld Gift 1932.

EXHIBITED   *Portraits par Renoir*, Durand-Ruel,
Paris, June 1912 (48); *Exposition Renoir*, Durand-
Ruel, Paris, November 1920 (21); Tate Gallery,
1948 (48); Orangerie, Paris, 1955 (43);
Courtauld Centenary, 1976 (40); *20th Century
Portraits*, National Gallery, London, 1978 (30);
Japan and Canberra, 1984 (76); *Renoir*,
Hayward Gallery, London, Grand Palais, Paris,
and Museum of Fine Arts, Boston, 1985–6
(107); United States, 1987–8 (15).

LITERATURE   Jamot-Turner, no. 30; Home
House Catalogue, no. 15; A. Vollard, *La Vie et
l'oeuvre de Renoir*, Paris, 1919, p. 217; A.
Vollard, *En écoutant Cézanne, Degas, Renoir*,
Paris, 1938, p. 266; Cooper, 1954, no. 56; J.
Renoir, *Renoir*, Paris, 1962, p. 399; W. Gaunt,
Renoir, with notes by K. Adler, Oxford, 1982,
no. 44; T. Garb, 'Renoir and the Natural
Woman', *Oxford Art Journal*, VIII, no. 2, 1985,
p. 5; R. Bruce-Gardner, G. Hedley and C.
Villers, 'Impressions of Change', in United
States, 1987–8, p. 21.

43 RENOIR, PIERRE-AUGUSTE 1841–1919
Woman at her Toilet c.1918
Femme faisant sa toilette
Oil on canvas, 50.5 × 56.5
Signed, bottom left: 'Renoir'
Courtauld Institute Galleries (The Samuel Courtauld Trust)

One of the first two French paintings bought by Samuel Courtauld, this painting was probably executed in 1918 at Cagnes, near Nice on the Mediterranean coast. Renoir had begun to spend his winters in the south in the 1890s, and from 1903 onwards was based in Cagnes, where he built himself a house in 1907–8.

This move was made in part for reasons of health – Renoir was increasingly troubled by rheumatism and arthritis – but it also coincided with important changes in his art. He had become disillusioned with Impressionism's preoccupation with fleeting effects of light and atmosphere, and with the modern Parisian subjects, of fashionable recreations like *La Loge* (cat. no. 39), that he had favoured in the 1870s. Instead he came to seek more timeless subjects, treated in a way that drew out the form of the figures, rather than absorbing them in their surroundings; and he looked back to the great tradition of western figure painting, to Raphael, and later to Titian and Rubens.

In his last years, the female nude was one of his principal themes, but he also painted many images of women, dressed or half dressed, engaged in their toilette, playing music, or just seated still. These figures, monumentalised, inexpressive and inactive, express a view of women's role in society to which Renoir clung with increasing insistence – seeing women as creatures of nature, practical, physical and simple, in contrast to man, whose rightful province was the world of intellect and 'culture'.

In his last paintings, he evolved a technique that emphasised this surface physicality of woman's world. In *Woman at her Toilet* the simple bulk of the figure dominates the composition, with bold ribbons of paint modelling her petticoat, and fine threads of varied colour enriching the treatment of her flesh. Her surroundings are handled in vigorous swirls of colour – the cushions and clothing beyond her and the cushion beneath her feet – which emphasise the lavish physicality of this vision of womankind. The details are deliberately unspecific: the figure is not a modern, fashionable woman, but presented rather as a simple country woman – a creature of 'nature'.

In *Vision and Design* (1920), Roger Fry vividly characterised Renoir's late technique:

Whatever Cézanne may have meant by his celebrated saying about cones and cylinders, Renoir seems to have thought the sphere and cylinder sufficient for his purpose. The figure presents itself to his eye as an arrangement of more or less hemispherical bosses and cylinders, and he appears generally to arrange the light so that the most prominent part of each boss receives the highest light. From this the planes recede by insensible gradations towards the contour, which generally remains the vaguest, least ascertained part of the modelling.

The colour here is very rich, dominated by the reds and oranges that Renoir used to evoke the idea of the south as a warm, health-giving region where, Renoir said, 'it seems as if misfortune cannot befall one'. The soft blue wall-covering sets off all this warmth below it, but Renoir was no longer using blue to model shadows; for these, he had returned to blacks and greys, used to anchor the parade of warm colour around them.

PROVENANCE   Atelier Renoir, Cagnes; Galerie Barbazanges, Paris; Percy Moore Turner, London; bought by Courtauld, September 1922, £1,750 (price including Marchand, cat. no. 28). Courtauld Gift 1932.

EXHIBITED   Galerie Barbazanges, Paris, June 1922; Independent Gallery, London, 1922; Tate Gallery, 1948 (61); Orangerie, Paris, 1955 (44); Courtauld Centenary, 1976 (39); Japan and Canberra, 1984 (77); United States, 1987–8 (16).

LITERATURE   Jamot-Turner, no. 33; Home House Catalogue, no. 13; Cooper, 1954, no. 57.

44 ROUSSEAU, HENRI ('LE DOUANIER')
    1844–1910
    The Toll-Gate   c.1890?
    L'Octroi
    Oil on canvas, 40.6 × 32.75
    Signed, bottom right:'H. Rousseau'
    Courtauld Institute Galleries (The Samuel
    Courtauld Trust)

Rousseau served in the army from 1863–8, then as a low-ranking customs official from 1871–93, manning toll-gates on the outskirts of Paris. He began painting, untaught, around 1880; rejected by the Salon in 1885, he began exhibiting with the jury-free Société des Artistes Indépendants from 1886. He gradually became known in avant-garde circles, meeting Gauguin and the playwright Alfred Jarry in the 1890s, and Picasso and his friends in the last years of his life. Only after the institution of a jury-less exhibition such as the Indépendants could an artist like Rousseau, from wholly outside any of the contemporary institutional frameworks of the art world, find an outlet and an audience for his work.

Rousseau's art has generally been viewed in the context of the avant-garde, but there is clear evidence that his initial models when he decided to become a painter were the academic Neo-Classicists, Jean-Léon Gérôme and Charles Clément; apparently he sought their advice, and he used to claim that they had encouraged him to follow his own temperament. The precise definition of forms and smooth finish of his paintings corresponds to the expectations of masters such as Gérôme and Clément. The few small outdoor studies of his that survive belong to an already well-established tradition of open-air sketching and have no significant relationship to Impressionism, while the finished paintings he made from these studies, and his other completed works, are essentially academic in finish.

The subjects of his large pictures—exotic jungles (which he never visited in reality) and large-scale allegories—are also comparable to favoured themes in academic art. But, in addition, he painted many smaller landscapes like *The Toll-Gate*, which show the everyday surroundings of the Parisian suburbs and often focus particularly on the intrusion of distinctively modern elements into the scene—like the chimneys here, and balloons, and (later) even aeroplanes. These subjects can be closely compared to the suburban landscapes painted by the Neo-Impressionists and other young independent artists in the 1880s and 1890s, such as Seurat's *The Bridge at Courbevoie* (cat.no.51). The scenes that he painted around Paris were mainly the regions where he worked, near the toll-gates that ringed the city; it is one of these gates that is depicted here.

Rousseau knew little or nothing about linear or atmospheric perspective, but rather laid the elements in his scenes across the picture surface and suggested space by successions of planes stacked one on top of the other up the canvas, so that forms on the horizon may be as crisply defined as those nearby. Forms are treated as silhouettes, like the figures here, or, like the tree-trunks, as simple cylindrical tubes. Out of these subjects, though, he created paintings very tautly organised in two-dimensional terms: verticals and horizontals, from clouds to footpaths, mesh into patterns of great coherence and real grandeur. Such picture-making would, of course, have seemed absurd to the academic masters of the nineteenth century, but Rousseau's simplifications and stylisations at once struck a chord with vanguard painters of the generations that rejected naturalistic depiction, first with Gauguin and his circle, then with Picasso and his friends.

PROVENANCE   Wilhelm Uhde, Paris; Dr Hartwich, Berlin; Alfred Flechtheim, Berlin; bought by Courtauld, 1926, price unknown. Courtauld Bequest 1948.

EXHIBITED   Wiedereröffnung der Galerie Flechtheim, Düsseldorf, December 1919; *Henri Rousseau*, Galerie Flechtheim, Berlin, March 1926 (12); Tate Gallery, 1948 (62); *Rousseau*, Venice Biennale, 1950 (4); Orangerie, Paris, 1955 (45); Courtauld Centenary, 1976 (41); Japan and Canberra, 1984 (80); United States, 1987–8 (42).

LITERATURE   W. Uhde, *Henri Rousseau*, Paris, 1911, pl. 20; W. Uhde, *Rousseau*, Berlin, 1914, pl. 19; Jamot-Turner, no. 51; Cooper, 1954, no. 58; D. Vallier, *Tout l'oeuvre peint de Henri Rousseau*, Paris, 1970, no. 39; Y. le Pichon, *The World of Henri Rousseau*, Oxford, 1982, pp.94–5: R. Bruce-Gardner, G. Hedley and C. Villers, 'Impressions of Change', in United States, 1987–8, p.21.

45   SEURAT, GEORGES   1859–91
      Fisherman in a Moored Boat   *c.*1882
      Pêcheur dans un bateau amarré
      Oil on panel, 16.5 × 24.8
      Unsigned
      Private Collection, on extended loan to the
         Courtauld Institute Galleries

Virtually all Seurat's early oil paintings are
small studies on wood panels, broadly and
seemingly rapidly executed, very probably in
front of their outdoor subjects. His favoured
subjects, of the suburban riverside around Paris,
were those that the Impressionists had favoured
(see cat. nos 25,31,58), but by the early 1880s
such open-air sketching was a common
practice, even among artists who, like Seurat,
had gone through a thorough academic training
at the Ecole des Beaux-Arts.

Fisherman in a Moored Boat is dominated by
the crisp, dark forms of the fisherman, the boats
and the railing, set off against the luminous
background – a sharp tonal contrast quite unlike
the interplay of clear light colour that the
Impressionists used to suggest atmospheric
effects. However, deep blues are used to model
the dark forms, and soft blues recur in the
foliage, which suggests that Seurat was also
exploring methods of conveying the
atmosphere. These blues are set against the
warm orange-brown tones that recur
throughout the picture; these (again in a way
quite unlike Impressionist practice) are
primarily obtained, not by coloured paint, but
by the rich colour of the underlying unprimed
wood panel, which is wholly unpainted in
places, and elsewhere shows through thinly
applied paint layers. In other small sketches
(e.g., cat. no. 46), Seurat did adopt the
Impressionist practice of painting on a white or
very light-toned priming.

Unlike cat. no. 47, this panel does not relate
directly to any larger project, but Seurat's many
outdoor studies of the early 1880s must all have
contributed to his first monumental figure
painting, *Une Baignade, Asnières* (National
Gallery, London; fig. 8). The theme of the
riverside fisherman was to appear again in the
preparatory studies for *A Sunday Afternoon on
the Ile de la Grande Jatte* (see cat. no. 50).

PROVENANCE   Emile Seurat, Paris; Félix
Fénéon, Paris; Galerie Barbazanges, Paris;
Georges Bernheim, Paris; Joseph Hessel, Paris;
Gaston Lévy, Paris; Rosenberg & Helft,
London; bought by Courtauld, July 1937,
£1,800 (price including Monet cat. no. 30);
Lady Aberconway, 1948; private collection.

EXHIBITED   *Seurat*, Bernheim-Jeune, Paris,
1908–9 (15); *Seurat*, Bernheim-Jeune, Paris,
1920 (7); *Seurat*, Joseph Brummer, New York,
1924 (12); *Seurat et ses amis*, Galerie des Beaux-
Arts, Paris, 1933–4 (70); *Georges Seurat*, Galerie
Paul Rosenberg, Paris, 1936 (16); *Ingres to
Picasso*, Rosenberg and Helft, London, 1937
(30); Tate Gallery, 1948 (66a); *Landscape in
French Art*, Royal Academy, London, 1949–50
(296); Orangerie, Paris, 1955 (47); Courtauld
Centenary, 1976 (43); United States, 1987–8
(30).

LITERATURE   Inventaire Posthume Seurat,
Panneaux, no. 49; Cooper, 1954, no. 61; H.
Dorra and J. Rewald, *Seurat, l'oeuvre peint,
biographie et catalogue critique*, Paris, 1959, p. 76,
no. 79; C.M. de Hauke, *Seurat et son oeuvre*,
Paris, 1961, no. 64.

46   SEURAT, GEORGES   1859–91
      Man Painting his Boat   *c.*1883
      Homme peignant son bateau
      Oil on panel, 15.9 × 25
      Unsigned
      Courtauld Institute Galleries (The Samuel
          Courtauld Trust)

In contrast to cat. no. 45, this is a richly coloured
painting, whose varied palette and strong blue
shadows clearly testify to the influence of
Impressionism. Its luminosity is enhanced by
the fact that (again unlike cat. no. 45) it was
painted on a white priming, not directly on the
wood panel; though this priming is largely
covered, it appears just below the feet of the
figure.

   Its brushwork, though, owes little to
Impressionism. In cat. no. 47, probably painted
in the same year, Seurat conveyed the diverse
natural textures in the scene with a flexible,
broken touch, but here the brushwork is far
more even, built up of crisp little strokes,
mainly applied with quite a wide brush and
running in various directions; the result is an
opaque paint surface of an even rhythm and
density. Only the vertical fence posts, which
give the panel a clear-cut central axis, are
treated with longer, more separated strokes; the
man and his boat are absorbed into the play of
deft, criss-crossing touches that fill the rest of
the picture.

   Like cat. no. 45, *Man Painting his Boat* does
not relate to any larger painting, though it, too,
treats a theme of outdoor recreation by the
river. The forms it depicts are treated broadly,
without any precise detail, but in its brushwork,
carefully harmonised throughout the picture, it
is one of the more highly finished of Seurat's
small oils. There is no evidence that he ever
exhibited it during his lifetime, but, on
occasion, he did show such small pictures,
alongside fully finished, larger canvases like
cat. no. 51.

PROVENANCE   Mme Seurat, the artist's mother,
Paris; Félix Fénéon, Paris; Percy Moore Turner,
London; Lord Ivor Spencer-Churchill, London;
Lord Berners, London; Percy Moore Turner,
London; bought by Courtauld, November
1928, £700. Courtauld Bequest 1948 (on loan
to Lord (R.A.) Butler until 1983).

EXHIBITED   *Seurat*, Bernheim-Jeune, Paris, 1909
(14); *Seurat*, Bernheim-Jeune, Paris, 1920 (9);
Ingres to Cézanne, Independent Gallery,
London, 1925 (20); *19th and 20th Century French
Masters*, Independent Gallery, London, 1928
(31); Tate Gallery, 1948 (64); Orangerie, Paris,
1955 (48); Courtauld Centenary, 1976 (44);
Japan and Canberra, 1984 (81); United States,
1987–8 (31).

LITERATURE   Inventaire Posthume Seurat,
Panneaux, no. 44; Jamot-Turner, no. 43;
Cooper, 1954, no. 62; Dorra and Rewald, 1959,
p. 80, no. 82; de Hauke, 1961, no. 66; R. Fry,
Seurat, with Foreword and Notes by A. Blunt,
London, 1965, p. 78; R. Bruce-Gardner, G.
Hedley and C. Villers, 'Impressions of Change',
in United States, 1987–8, p. 23.

47 SEURAT, GEORGES 1859–91
    White Horse and Black Horse in the
        Water   c.1883
    Cheval blanc et cheval noir dans l'eau
    Oil on panel, 15.2 × 24.8
    Unsigned
    Private Collection, on extended loan to the
        Courtauld Institute Galleries

Seurat made many studies for his first major canvas, *Une Baignade, Asnières* (National Gallery, London; fig. 8), rejected at the 1884 Salon and first shown at the Salon des Indépendants in May 1884. These take two forms – small oil sketches on panel, like the present one, of the riverbanks at Asnières variously peopled (see also cat. nos 48 and 49), and conté crayon drawings in which Seurat worked out the poses of the figures in more detail. This is one of a small group of studies in which Seurat introduced horses, an idea he discarded in the final picture.

Seurat's methods in working up *Une Baignade, Asnières* bear the stamp of his academic training. The quick oil sketches like *White Horse and Black Horse in the Water* play the role of *esquisses*, as notations of possible compositional formats and colour relationships for the big painting, while the black-and-white drawings, studies of separate elements for the final picture, are *études* in the traditional sense. In oil sketches like this one, though, Seurat revealed another source of inspiration, which may have led to the rejection of the large picture at the 1884 Salon: this is the influence of Impressionism, seen in the luminous atmospheric colour and bold brushwork. In the final painting, the crisp, broken brushwork is rather more tautly ordered than in most Impressionist paintings, but oil sketches like the present one, with their free and varied handling, are the closest of all Seurat's works to the informality of surface of the typical Impressionist landscapes of the 1870s (compare, in particular, Sisley cat. no. 58).

In *Une Baignade, Asnières* and its studies, figures relaxing by the river are set against the backdrop of the factories of Clichy, seen across the river, with the tip of the Ile de la Grande Jatte seen on the extreme right. These scenes of informal relaxation make a marked contrast with the subject of *A Sunday Afternoon on the Ile de la Grande Jatte*, in which the weekend promenaders on the riverbank opposite are presented in stiff, hieratic poses (see cat. no. 50). It was by this formal contrast that Seurat suggested the difference between two types of recreation, which belonged to two different classes: the informality of the working-class types on the Asnières bank, with the factories beyond, set against the self-conscious artifice of the bourgeoisie and the *demi-mondaines* over on the wooded island.

PROVENANCE   Mme Seurat, the artist's mother, Paris; Bernheim-Jeune, Paris; Galerie Barbazanges, Paris; Percy Moore Turner, London; bought by Courtauld, June 1925, £400; Lady Aberconway, 1948; private collection.

EXHIBITED   *Georges Seurat* (organised by *La Revue blanche*, Paris, 1900 (6); *Ingres to Cézanne*, Independent Gallery, London, 1925 (21); Centenary Exhibition, Norwich, 1925 (56); *French Modern Art*, Bristol Museum, 1930 (79); *Masters of French 19th Century Painting*, New Burlington Galleries, London, 1936 (115); Tate Gallery, 1948 (65); *Landscape in French Art*, Royal Academy, London, 1949–50 (316a); Orangerie, Paris, 1955 (46); *Neo-Impressionism*, Guggenheim Museum, New York, 1968 (71); Courtauld Centenary, 1976 (42); *Seurat: Paintings and Drawings*, Artemis (David Carritt), London, 1978 (15); *Post-Impressionism*, Royal Academy, London, 1979–80 (197); United States, 1987–8 (32); *Seurat*, Grand Palais, Paris, and Metropolitan Museum of Art, New York, 1991 (105).

LITERATURE   Jamot-Turner, no. 41; Cooper, 1954, no. 60; Dorra and Rewald, 1959, p. 87, no. 88; de Hauke, 1961, no. 86.

48 SEURAT, GEORGES 1859–91
Boat near the Bank, Asnières c.1883
Bateau près de la berge, Asnières
Oil on panel, 15 × 24
Unsigned
Private Collection

PROVENANCE Mme Seurat, the artist's mother, Paris; Denys Cochin; Bernheim-Jeune, Paris; Léon Marseille, Paris; Princesse de Bassiano, Paris; Percy Moore Turner; bought by Courtauld, December 1927, £700; Mrs R.A. Butler; private collection.

EXHIBITED *1re Exposition au profit de la Société des Amis du Luxembourg*, Paris, 1924 (41); *Ingres to Cézanne*, Independent Gallery, London, 1924 (22); *Vincent Van Gogh en zijn Tijdgenooten*, Stedelijk Museum, Amsterdam, 1930 (275); *French Art*, Bristol, 1932 (89); *Seurat et ses amis*, Wildenstein, Paris, 1933 (66); Tate Gallery, 1948 (63); *Landscape in French Art*, Royal Academy, London, 1949–50 (297); Orangerie, Paris, 1955 (49).

LITERATURE Jamot-Turner, no. 44; Cooper, 1954, no. 63; Dorra and Rewald, 1959, p. 81, no. 83; de Hauke, 1961, no. 76.

49 SEURAT, GEORGES 1859–91
Man in a Boat c.1883
Homme dans une barque
Oil on panel, 15 × 24
Unsigned
Private Collection

PROVENANCE Mme Seurat, the artist's mother, Paris; Camille Pissarro; Pissarro Sale, 3 December 1928, lot 90; Percy Moore Turner; bought by Courtauld July 1929, £800; private collection.

EXHIBITED Tate Gallery, 1948 (67).

LITERATURE Jamot-Turner, no. 42; Cooper, 1954, no. 65; Dorra and Rewald, 1959, p. 79, no. 81; de Hauke, 1961, no. 63.

Both cat. nos 48 and 49 seem to relate to the campaign of work that led to *Une Baignade, Asnières* (fig. 8), but, unlike cat. no. 47, they cannot be seen as studies directly related to the large painting. In both, we are looking back from the river to a bank. In cat. no. 48 the low wall with a gate may well be the wall seen at top left in *Une Baignade*, while the more open background in cat. no. 49 might represent the Ile de la Grande-Jatte, on the opposite bank (see cat. nos 50 and 51).

In both, too, Seurat focused on elements in the scene that were to play their part in the big picture. The figure of the man in the boat in cat. no. 49 and the boat by the bank in cat. no. 48 both relate to the little ferry-boat at back right of *Une Baignade* (this recurs, too, in *A Sunday Afternoon on the Ile de la Grande Jatte*), while the man standing at the water's edge in cat. no. 48 bears some similarity to the figures on the bank.

These studies suggest how Seurat set about conceiving *Une Baignade*. He began by making many sketches like these, of elements in the scene which attracted his notice, seemingly without any idea of their playing a specific function in the large work. Then, as he began to focus on the large project, his studies came to concentrate on the actual bank to be depicted in it, and on potential features (figures, animals and so on) that might animate it; cat. no. 47 belongs to this later stage.

50   SEURAT, GEORGES   *1859–91*
        The Angler   *c.*1884
        Pêcheur à la ligne
        Oil on panel, 24.1 × 15.2
        Unsigned
        Private Collection, on extended loan to the
            Courtauld Institute Galleries

The Angler is one of the many small oil studies
that Seurat made for *A Sunday Afternoon on the
Ile de la Grande Jatte* (Art Institute of Chicago),
as he had for *Une Baignade, Asnières* (see
cat.no.47). However, unlike cat.no.47, *The
Angler* relates only to a small part of the final
composition: a similar male figure, though
without a fishing rod, appears by the water in
the left background of the large painting. The
arrangement of this study, with the figure's
dark silhouette framed by a little sailing-boat in
the top left and the reflection of a white
building in the top right, shows that Seurat was
already studying possible relationships between
forms, but in the event these elements were
subsequently rearranged, though similar forms
were included in the final picture.

In cat.no.47, the study for *Une Baignade*,
Seurat had adopted a loose, Impressionistic
handling, whereas here the grass is treated in
longer, crisper strokes which are closer to the
appearance of the grass in the final version of
Une Baignade and in the initial state of *A Sunday
Afternoon on the Ile de la Grande Jatte* in 1884–5;
this 'chopped straw', or *balayé* technique is
characteristic of Seurat's finished pictures of
1883–5, before he began to evolve the pointillist
execution, in small dots of colour, which is seen
in cat.no.51 and which was added in 1885–6 to
the *Grande Jatte*. Various nuances of green and
yellow are used in the sunlit grass, and clear
blues in the water, but these light hues revolve
around the crisp, dark focus of the figure.
Though it is treated in dull blues and browns,
rather than in neutral dark tones, it stands out
crisply against the lightness and colour around
it, in contrast to the figure in *Man Painting his
Boat* (cat.no.46), which is absorbed into the
colour scheme of the whole picture.

In the final picture of the Grande Jatte,
virtually all of the figures are treated as static,
stylised silhouettes like that in *The Angler*; the
effect of this is to emphasise the artificiality of
the parade of the fashionable bourgeoisie and
demi-monde, in contrast to the more easy-going
attitudes of the lower-class figures shown on the
opposite bank of the same stretch of the River
Seine in *Une Baignade, Asnières* and its studies
(such as cat.no.47).

PROVENANCE   Mme Seurat, the artist's mother,
Paris; Félix Fénéon, Paris; Galerie Barbazanges,
Paris; Knoedler, London; bought by Courtauld,
November 1926, £750; Lady Aberconway,
1948; private collection.

EXHIBITED   *Modern French Painters*, Knoedler,
London, 1926 (18); Tate Gallery, 1948 (68);
Landscape in French Art, Royal Academy,
London, 1949–50 (295); Orangerie, Paris, 1955
(51); Courtauld Centenary, 1976 (47); *Seurat:
Paintings and Drawings*, Artemis (David Carritt),
London, 1978 (20); United States, 1987–8 (33).

LITERATURE   Jamot-Turner, no.39; D.C. Rich,
Seurat and the Evolution of the Grande Jatte,
Chicago, 1935, no.32; Cooper, 1954, no.66;
Dorra and Rewald, 1959, p.142, no.115; de
Hauke, 1961, no.115.

The Bridge at Courbevoie 1886–7
Le Pont de Courbevoie
Oil on canvas, 46.4 × 55.3
Signed, bottom left: 'Seurat'
Courtauld Institute Galleries (The Samuel
  Courtauld Trust)

The Bridge at Courbevoie is one of the clearest pictorial manifestos for the divisionist painting technique evolved by Seurat and his colleagues in 1885–6. The technique was intended as a means of translating into paint the effects of natural light and colour, lending a scientific precision to the more empirical solutions that had been adopted by Monet and Pissarro (see cat. no. 37). The dot, or point, of colour was the means that seemed best able to control precisely the relative quantities of each colour used in any area of the picture. However, the effect of these points has caused confusion. Although Seurat, like many of his contemporaries, stated that they were intended to produce an 'optical mixture' of colour, this is not exactly what takes place, for the dots are not small enough to fuse in the viewer's eye and produce a single resultant colour, when the picture is viewed from a normal viewing distance. Camille Pissarro, at the time that he was closely associated with Seurat, stated that the optimum viewing distance for a picture was three times its diagonal measurement, which in this case would mean seven feet. The effect of the canvas from this distance is that the dots are still clearly visible as dots, and the varied colours included can still be identified separately; far from fusing, they seem to shimmer and vibrate – in a sense, to recreate in the eye of the viewer something of the sense of vibration produced by actual outdoor sunlight, but recreated by the complex artifice of painting technique. Ogden Rood's *Modern Chromatics* (1879; French translation 1881), one of the manuals of colour theory that Seurat studied most carefully, noted this phenomenon, quoting the findings of the German physicist Dove, and it seems certain that Seurat, with his close analytical concern for the optical properties of colour, was deliberately seeking such effects. The absence of varnish, the use of very lean paint and possibly the lack of a ground also combine to produce an intentionally matt surface that enhances the sensation of shimmering.

In *The Bridge at Courbevoie*, Seurat's analysis of the different elements present in a light effect is most evident in the treatment of the riverbank. The dominant colour is green – the 'local' colour of grass – rather lighter and yellower in the sunlight, duller and bluer in shadow; warm, pinker touches further enliven the sunlit grass, and clear blues the shadowed areas. In addition, there is a scatter of mauve touches across most of the shadowed grass, and they reappear in the topmost band of sunlit grass, along the edge of the river. The scientific justification for these is unclear: they may be meant to suggest a complementary colour induced by the dominant green of the grass, or simply to evoke the warmth of the light of the sun; their effect is to enhance the play of warm and cool colours, whose elaborately interwoven relationships give the surface its richness and mobility. The background is treated with softer, paler hues, the same colour repeating in many parts of the picture, in a way closely comparable to the background of Pissarro's *The Quays at Rouen* (cat. no. 37).

The scene represents the Ile de la Grande Jatte, looking south-westwards, upstream along the Seine towards the Courbevoie bridge; the same stretch of riverbank is seen in the opposite direction in *A Sunday Afternoon on the Ile de la Grande Jatte* (see cat. no. 50). In contrast to the elaborate parade of modern society in the *Grande Jatte*, *The Bridge at Courbevoie* is still and silent, with three small figures standing immobile by the river. Its mood seems elusive and difficult to interpret; though it has recently been described as a 'plangent evocation of melancholy and alienation', the picture employs none of the devices then favoured by French painters to invoke these feelings – indeed, Seurat seems to have studiously avoided any clear-cut indication of its mood. However, the picture retains an intriguing strangeness through its very stillness, and through the curious juxtaposition of the foliated trees on the left, and the stark bare branches on the right (traces of overpainted foliage can still be seen to the left of this tree). All the elements in it are presented in an ordered, harmonious co-existence: the vertical of the central factory chimney is closely paralleled by the boats' masts and the fence-posts, establishing with the figures a taut series of pictorial intervals.

There is a further oddity about the picture. The verticals of the chimney, the masts and the house on the far right are all inclined at a slight but perceptible angle to the left. Seurat organised his compositions with such care that this cannot have been accidental, but the reasons for it are unclear; its effect, it seems, is to emphasise the parallel lines within the picture, for the viewer's eye does not immediately relate them to the grid of the picture frame around them.

A number of adjustments and alterations are visible; their presence tends to underline the care that Seurat took over the very precise placing of the compositional elements. For example, the foliage on the tree on the left of the painting has been reduced and the tall mast immediately adjacent partially painted out; a number of illegible brushmarks between the sails of the barge and the mast of the dinghy indicate changes here too. The most interesting alteration from the point of view of working methods is to the tree on the right. X-rays illustrate the clarity of original composition, showing, for example, that Seurat left a 'space' for the tree-trunk in the sky to cover underpainting; and between gaps in the paint it is possible to distinguish the Prussian blue and crimson lake drawing with which the composition was initially laid in. Seurat subsequently moved the tree just one centimetre to the right so that that edge is now painted over the river, whilst the left-hand contour of the tree has been painted out in blue. Over and above the changes made to the tree on the right, the canvas was clearly the result of an elaborate process of reworking, with the small dots of colour added over broader paint layers; it may have been begun out of doors, but its final effect can have been achieved only in the studio. A detailed preparatory drawing exists for the whole composition. Moreover, the play of shadow in the foreground is so specific, and (if it records an actual effect) must have changed so rapidly, that Seurat would have had little opportunity to work on the canvas in front of its subject while the lighting remained unchanged. Later in his career, he came to use his pointillist technique to achieve far more overtly artificial effects (see cat. no. 53), though he also continued to use it for landscape scenes such as cat. no. 55.

PROVENANCE Arsène Alexandre, Paris (1887); Alexandre Sale, Paris, 18 May 1903 (lot 57; 630 francs); Georges Petit, Paris; with L.W. Gutbier, Dresden; Bignou, Paris; Reid and Lefèvre, London; bought by Courtauld, July 1926, £2,850. Courtauld Bequest 1948.

EXHIBITED 3me Exposition de la Société des Artistes Indépendants, Paris, 1887 (442); *Exposition commémorative Seurat*, Société des Artistes Indépendants, Paris, 1892 (1090); *Georges Seurat* (organised by *La Revue blanche*), Paris, 1900 (25); *Seurat*, Bernheim-Jeune, Paris, 1909 (64); *Georges Seurat*, Lefèvre Gallery, London, 1926 (4); *French Art*, Royal Academy, London, 1932 (541); Tate Gallery, 1948 (69); Orangerie, Paris, 1955 (52); Courtauld Centenary, 1976 (48); Japan and Canberra, 1984 (82); United States, 1987–8 (34): *Seurat*, Grand Palais, Paris, and Metropolitan Museum of Art, New York, 1991 (171).

LITERATURE Jamot-Turner, no. 47; Cooper, 1954, no. 67; Dorra and Rewald, 1959, no. 172; de Hauke, 1961, no. 178; Fry and Blunt, 1965, p. 82; R. Thomson, *Seurat*, Oxford, 1985, pp. 134–5.

52 SEURAT, GEORGES 1859–91
Study for The Chahut c.1889
Etude pour Le Chahut
Oil on panel, 21.8 × 15.8
Unsigned
Courtauld Institute Galleries (The Samuel
Courtauld Trust)

This is the first and smaller of two oil studies
for *The Chahut* (Rijksmuseum Kröller-Müller,
Otterlo), which Seurat exhibited at the
Indépendants in Paris in the spring of 1890. The
principal composition remained as it appears
here, but further details were added, which
further emphasise the upward-moving lines that
dominate the composition.

In a letter of 1890 Seurat described the
devices he used in his paintings in order to
evoke a mood of happiness and gaiety: lines
moving upwards from a point and a
dominantly light and warm-coloured tonality.
He seems to have emphasised these qualities in
most parts of *The Chahut* (the final version is
warmer and lighter than the present study), but
it remains uncertain just what effect he intended
these devices to have on the viewer; according
to the theories of his associate Charles Henry,
they had an immediate physical impact, but
Seurat seems to treat them rather more
allusively, more as signs or emblems for
happiness (see also cat.no. 53).

The chosen subject of *The Chahut*
compounds the uncertainties: of all his subjects,
it refers most explicitly to the seamier side of
Parisian entertainments. The dance, also known
as the *quadrille naturaliste*, with its characteristic
high-kick, was popularised in the later 1880s,
particularly by La Goulue, whom Toulouse-
Lautrec often painted; the high-kick was
deliberately suggestive or overtly indecent,
designed to show stockings, flesh and
underwear (or lack of it). Seurat plays down
this suggestiveness in *The Chahut*, by viewing
the high-kick from the side, and by
transforming it into a complex stylised pattern,
but a contemporary audience would readily
have picked up the associations of the subject.

Seurat left no statement of his intentions in
treating this subject, but his friends had no
doubt that he wanted to reveal the ambivalence
of the subject – between its surface gaiety and its
underlying implications. Gustave Kahn noted
the contrast between 'the hieratic structure of
the canvas and its subject, a contemporary
ignominy'. It was by the formal device of
placing the viewer's angle of vision to the side
of the dancers, with the stark silhouette of the
bassist, mainly cool in colour, at the front, that
Seurat distanced the spectator from the central
action: we are able to look in on it from
outside, but are clearly not a part of it.

In the present sketch, the white primed panel
shows through at many points, and the forms
were initially notated very simply in rather
broader strokes of colour, before the surface
was enriched with its skin of multicoloured
points. On the figure of the nearest dancer,
there are traces of pencil drawing on top of the
paint layers of the face and dress, which may
suggest that he planned to elaborate it further.
The border that surrounds it on three sides was
added by the artist; that on the fourth was
probably removed after his death. He began to
add painted borders to his canvases in the later
1880s, using them to focus the viewer's
attention on the picture itself (see cat.nos 53 and
55).

PROVENANCE   Mme Seurat, the artist's mother,
Paris; Félix Fénéon, Paris; Ambroise Vollard,
Paris; bought by Courtauld, March 1929,
£1,000. Courtauld Bequest 1948.

EXHIBITED   *Seurat*, Bernheim-Jeune, Paris, 1920
(29); Tate Gallery, 1948 (70); Orangerie, Paris,
1955 (53); Courtauld Centenary, 1976 (49);
Japan and Canberra, 1984 (83); United States,
1987–8 (35): *Seurat*, Grand Palais, Paris, and
Metropolitan Museum of Art, New York, 1991
(217).

LITERATURE   Jamot-Turner, no. 46; Cooper,
1954, no, 68; Dorra and Rewald, 1959, no. 197;
de Hauke, 1961, no. 197; Fry and Blunt, 1965,
p. 84; R. Thomson, *Seurat*, Oxford, 1985,
pp. 201–2.

53 SEURAT, GEORGES 1859–91
Young Woman Powdering
Herself c.1888–90
Jeune femme se poudrant
Oil on canvas, 95.5 × 79.5
Signed, on painted border, bottom right:
'Seurat'
Courtauld Institute Galleries (The Samuel
Courtauld Trust)

This is the only one of Seurat's paintings that reflects anything about his private existence: it shows his mistress, Madeleine Knobloch, at her toilette. Apparently, Seurat's own face originally appeared in the frame on the wall, but a friend warned him that this might appear laughable and he replaced it with the vase of flowers. Examination of the painting under the microscope and of X-rays clearly shows that the artist did obliterate a previous reflection in the mirror. Vague outlines that do not correspond with any part of the present image can be discerned, but an interpretation of these as the face of Seurat himself is highly subjective.

The painting is composed of a sequence of contrasts between rounded and angular forms: the figure and table are set against the wall with its picture-frame and arrow-shaped patterns; and it plays on a set of visual incongruities – between the massive figure and her impracticably small table (the *poudreuse* by which the picture has sometimes been incorrectly named), and between the curving lines and pseudo-dix-huitième ornament of this table and the imitation bamboo frame above it.

Seurat left no indication of the picture's meaning, but it, like *The Chahut* (see cat. no. 52), contains many instances of his sign for happiness and gaiety: the motif of lines rising from a point, which is used here to decorate the wall. The motif on the wall is echoed by the bow on top of the mirror, the frame top, the plant form at lower left, and even the model's right arm and the curl of hair behind her neck. But Seurat does not seem to have been using these directional lines in a literal way to uplift the spirits of the viewer. They all belong to the woman's personal décor, to her furniture and cosmetics; the weighty model and her impassive expression counteract them, and the spirit that emerges from the painting is ironic.

In this light, the picture is a return to the theme that had characterised the contrast between *Une Baignade, Asnières* and the *Grande Jatte* (see cat. nos 47 and 50) – the contrast between nature and artifice; it explores the art of cosmetics, which, like the model's corsetry, force nature into the mould of style; the spectator, viewing the woman in mid-toilette, catches her in the middle of the process of making her natural self artificial. The satire is not, though, directed against the model herself, but rather against her trappings, which were so characteristic a part of modern urban life; in these terms, the theme belongs with *The Chahut* (cat. no. 52), in exploring the anomalous relationships between public and private in modern Paris. After his death in 1891, some of Seurat's friends attributed radical political views to him, but he left no clear indication of his politics; what emerges from his paintings is a keen and critical sense of the anomalies and ironies of contemporary urban capitalism.

In contrast to *The Bridge at Courbevoie* (cat. no. 51), the brushwork and colours here do not evoke the play of natural light and shade. Rather, they are used to augment the pictorial impact of the canvas. The background wall becomes darker and bluer where it approaches lit contours of the figure, and lighter where it meets its shadowed edges; throughout the picture there is an eddy of interwoven warm and cool touches (pinks and yellows against blues and greens) which create a shimmering effect over the whole surface, but without in any way suggesting closely observed lighting. This effect is augmented by the way in which the painted border changes in colour so as to achieve maximum contrast with the area of the picture next to it; the arched top of this border seems to make the picture itself into a sort of altarpiece or shrine – like the little table and mirror before which the model sits. The modelling of the figure is wilfully anti-naturalistic; it is impossible to sense the form of the model's hips and legs within the sweeping, stylised curves of her skirt. The dots of colour, though comparatively even in size, are often slightly elongated and follow the contours of the forms; it is evident that this final skin of colour was applied over more broadly applied, initial layers of paint, as Seurat worked up the picture to completion.

PROVENANCE Mlle Madeleine Knobloch, Paris; Félix Fénéon, Paris; Dikran Khan Kélékian, Paris; Kélékian Sale, American Art Association, New York, 31 January 1923 (lot 154; $5,200); Eugene O.M. Liston, New York; Percy Moore Turner, London; John Quinn, New York; Paul Rosenberg, Paris; French Gallery, London; bought by Courtauld, 1926, price unknown. Courtauld Gift 1932.

EXHIBITED 6me Exposition de la Société des Artistes Indépendants, Paris, 1890 (727); *Exposition Seurat*, Musée Moderne, Brussels (9me Exposition des XX), 1892 (14); *Exposition commémorative Seurat*, Société des Artistes Indépendants, Paris, 1892 (1085); *Georges Seurat* (organised by *La Revue blanche*), Paris, 1900 (35); exhibitions at Munich, Frankfurt-am-Main, Dresden, Karlsruhe (1906) and at Stuttgart (1907); *Seurat*, Bernheim-Jeune, Paris, 1909 (73); Sezession, Berlin, 1913; Brooklyn Museum, 1921 (not in catalogue); Brummer Gallery, New York, 1924 (18); French Gallery, London, 1926 (41); *French Art*, Royal Academy, London, 1932 (503); Tate Gallery, 1948 (71); Orangerie, Paris, 1955 (54); Courtauld Centenary, 1976 (50); *Post-Impressionism*, Royal Academy, London, 1979–80 (204); National Gallery, London, 1983 (no catalogue); Japan and Canberra, 1984 (84); United States, 1987–8 (36); *Seurat*, Grand Palais, Paris, and Metropolitan Museum of Art, New York, 1991 (213).

LITERATURE Jamot-Turner, no. 45; Home House Catalogue, no. 11; Cooper, 1954, no. 69; Dorra and Rewald, 1959, pp. 247–9, no. 195; de Hauke, 1961, no. 200; Fry and Blunt, 1965, pp. 16, 84; J. House, 'Meaning in Seurat's Figure Paintings', *Art History*, September 1980, pp. 345–56; R. Thomson, *Seurat*, Oxford, 1985, pp. 193–7; R. Bruce-Gardner, G. Hedley and C. Villers, 'Impressions of Change', in United States, 1987–8, p. 21–2.

54 SEURAT, GEORGES 1859–91
At Gravelines 1890
A Gravelines
Oil on panel, 16 × 24.5
Unsigned
Courtauld Institute Galleries (The Samuel
Courtauld Trust)

Seurat spent the summer of 1890 (the last of his
life) at Gravelines, on the Channel coast near
Dunkerque and the Belgian border. He
regularly visited the coast in summer, seeking,
he told Emile Verhaeren, 'to cleanse his eyes of
the days spent in the studio and to translate as
exactly as possible the luminosity of the open
air, with all its nuances'.

Despite this apparent declaration of
Impressionist principles, Seurat made both small
oil sketches and drawings of Gravelines, in
addition to the four finished oil paintings that
resulted from the trip (see cat.no. 55). Some of
the small works relate to these larger works, but
At Gravelines is one that does not. These small
paintings were very probably executed out of
doors, at least in part: particles of sand have
been found in the wet paint layers of the
present painting. The larger oils may have been
begun outside, but (like cat.no. 51) were
undoubtedly much elaborated in Seurat's studio
when he was back in Paris. *At Gravelines* is a
deceptively simple image; though apparently
informal in arrangement, the slightly greater
weight of the shoreline on the left is carefully
balanced by the placing of the boat just right of
the centre. The treatment of the shapes is so
simplified that we do not know whether the far
shoreline at the left represents a distant cliff or a
nearer beach, or even a man-made jetty;
although the little boat is more crisply
indicated, its forms are similarly inexplicit.

The scene was painted on a white primed
mahogany panel; the priming is left visible in
small areas all over the picture, thus heightening
the luminosity of this bright but overcast effect.
The colour range is limited, almost all built up
from contrasts of blues against yellows and
oranges, ranging from the extremely pale tones
in sky and sea, enlivened by certain rather
brighter touches, to the quite strong contrasts in
the foreground, where greens are introduced
alongside the blues. The brushwork is more
informal than in *Young Woman Powdering
Herself* (cat.no. 53) but is fairly evenly weighted
across the whole picture; many of the touches
are slightly elongated, creating a gentle
horizontal movement that complements the
expansiveness of the subject itself, looking out
to sea across the wide sands of the northern
French coast.

PROVENANCE   Mme Seurat, the artist's mother,
Paris; Alfred Tobler, Paris; with Bernheim-
Jeune, Paris; Alphonse Kann, Saint-Germain-
en-Laye; Bignou, Paris; Reid and Lefèvre,
London; bought by Courtauld, July 1928,
£500. Courtauld Bequest 1948.

EXHIBITED   *Seurat*, Bernheim-Jeune, Paris, 1909
(78); *Seurat*, Bernheim-Jeune, Paris, 1920 (31);
12th International Biennale, Venice, 1920 (56);
Van Wisselingh et Cie, Amsterdam, 1928 (59);
Tate Gallery, 1948 (293); Orangerie, Paris, 1955
(55); Courtauld Centenary, 1976 (51); Japan and
Canberra, 1984 (85); United States, 1987–8 (37).

LITERATURE   Jamot-Turner, no. 49; Cooper,
1954, no. 70; Dorra and Rewald, 1959, p. 261,
no. 201; de Hauke, 1961, no. 204; Fry and Blunt,
1965, pp. 84–5.

55 SEURAT, GEORGES 1859–91
*The Channel of Gravelines, Grand Fort
Philippe* 1890
Le Chenal de Gravelines, Grand Fort Philippe
Oil on canvas, 64 × 81
Unsigned
The Berggruen Collection, on loan to the
National Gallery, London

The Channel of Gravelines, Grand Fort Philippe is one of the four finished paintings that resulted from Seurat's last working trip to the Channel coast in the summer of 1890 (see cat. no. 54). Gravelines is a quite nondescript small port on the mouth of the River Aa between Calais and Dunkerque. In these paintings, Seurat did not even focus on the town itself, but rather on the clusters of humble buildings at the entry of the port, with on one side the signal mast (the semaphore) seen here, and on the other the lighthouse.

These are the sparest and least picturesque subjects of all Seurat's seascapes. They have neither the genre-like interest of the port scenes that were so often exhibited at the Paris Salon during the 1880s, nor the dramatic natural features that characterise Monet's coastal scenes of the decade (see cat. no. 34). The motifs depicted are all emphatically artificial, man-made, but conspicuously without obvious points of pictorial interest. The choice of subjects like this was evidently very deliberate and can be linked to the broad theme of the contrast between nature and artifice that was central to his Parisian subjects (see cat. nos 50 and 53). Here, the interest of the paintings lies in the way in which such a humdrum scene can be transformed by delicate nuances of colour and touch, to evoke the play of the soft light of the English Channel coast.

No preparatory studies survive for *The Channel of Gravelines, Grand Fort Philippe*; but, despite its apparent simplicity, the composition is extremely tautly structured. The area of grass at bottom left and the diagonal indentation in the sand lead the eye up to the central band, itself set on a very shallow diagonal upwards to the right. This band holds the principal interest in the picture and is punctuated by a complex set of accents–most obviously, buildings, boat and bollards; but there are also far smaller points alongside these: the shadows of the masts, and perhaps a little figure and a kiosk on the roadway in front of the buildings, and two tiny rowing-boats by the water. To the left of the principal boat, there are signs that another shape has been painted out.

The brushstrokes across the picture are not wholly uniform. The small points of colour vary slightly in size, and in some areas are slightly elongated, giving a gentle, directional movement across the surface, for instance on the beach. The points do not cover the whole surface: in both sky and sand, the underpainting is still visible in many places, laid on in more blended, mainly horizontal strokes, less varied in colour, which lend an overall luminosity to the scene.

The soft contrasts between very pale warm and cool hues in the foreground suggests the light shimmering on the wet sand, while the sharper colour accents on the buildings evoke the play of sunlight across their variously coloured surfaces. Only the whitest parts of the buildings are treated in virtually undifferentiated colour. Across the top half of the picture, Seurat unobtrusively used the device that plays such an important part in *Young Woman Powdering Herself* (cat. no. 53), by making the sky a little darker and bluer where it meets the semaphore mast or a light roof edge, and lighter above the bank of bushes in the centre; but at far right, both sky and sand dissolve into a light, luminous distance. This luminosity is enhanced by the sharper contrasts set up with the painted border that surrounds the image, consistently quite deep in tone, but varying in colour so as to set up the maximum contrast with the adjacent area of the picture.

PROVENANCE   Mme Seurat, the artist's mother, Paris; Léon Appert, Paris; Bignou, Paris; Reid and Lefèvre, London; bought by Courtauld, February 1926, £3,100; Mrs R.A. Butler; private collection; the Berggruen Collection.

EXHIBITED   Les XX, Brussels, 1891 (4); Société des Artistes Indépendants, Paris, 1891 (1103); *Georges Seurat* (organised by *La Revue blanche*), Paris, 1900 (36); *Exposition rétrospective Seurat*, Société des Artistes Indépendants, Paris, 1905 (3); *Seurat*, Bernheim-Jeune, Paris, 1908–9 (79); *Pictures and Drawings of Georges Seurat*, Lefèvre Gallery, London, 1926 (3); *Masters of French 19th Century Painting*, New Burlington Galleries, London, 1936 (122); *Seurat and his Contemporaries*, Wildenstein, London, 1937 (32); Tate Gallery, 1948 (73); *Landscape in French Art*, Royal Academy, London, 1949–50 (298); Orangerie, Paris, 1955 (56); *Post-Impressionism*, Royal Academy, London, 1979–80 (205); Berggruen Collection, Geneva, 1988 (26); *Seurat at Gravelines*, Indianapolis, 1990 (1); *Van Gogh to Picasso: The Berggruen Collection at the National Gallery*, National Gallery, London, 1991 (16); *Seurat*, Grand Palais, Paris, and Metropolitan Museum of Art, New York, 1991 (218).

LITERATURE   Jamot-Turner, no. 48; J. Rewald, *Georges Seurat*, New York, 1943, pp. 73, 114; Dorra and Rewald, 1959, no. 206; de Hauke, 1961, no. 205; J. Russell, *Seurat*, London, 1965, pp. 249, 254, 257, 261.

56 SIGNAC, PAUL 1863–1935
   Saint-Tropez 1893
   Oil on canvas, 19.5 × 28
   Signed, bottom left: 'P. Signac', and on
      reverse: 'P.S. St Tropez'
   Courtauld Institute Galleries (The Samuel
      Courtauld Trust)

Saint-Tropez is a preparatory study for *The Port of Saint-Tropez* (Van der Heydt-Museum, Wuppertal), dated 1893, which shows just the same arrangement, but is presented in a vertical format, including a wider zone of reflections in the water at the base. The finished painting is handled in the rather larger and bolder version of the pointillist brushwork that Signac evolved after Seurat's death.

During the 1890s, Signac began to execute his finished paintings entirely in the studio, working out of doors in front of the subject only on small studies in oil or (particularly after 1900) in watercolour. However, it is not clear that the present picture is one of these open-air studies. It includes extensive underdrawing, fluent in handling, but closely conforming to the final forms of the larger painting; moreover, the paint-handling, very varied and rather schematic, is very unlike the rapid and fully brushed sketches of natural subjects that Signac was producing in these years. It seems more likely that *Saint-Tropez* served as a sort of cartoon for the final painting, notating in summary form both its compositional arrangement and the essentials of its colour composition – the arcs of masts and sails played off against the houses, and the blues of the sky and central sail set against the yellow and orange of the sunlit buildings.

Painted the year after Signac moved to live in Saint-Tropez on the Mediterranean coast, then a remote and little-known fishing village, *Saint-Tropez* explores the intense colour contrasts that Signac evolved during the early to mid-1890s to express the effect of Mediterranean light (compare Monet cat.no.34). The luminosity of the white-primed wood panel enhances the effect.

Signac regularly included oil studies and watercolours in his exhibitions, alongside his finished paintings, showing that he saw his studies as works of art in their own right, and not merely as preparatory material. The bold and improvisatory application of vivid colour in his sketches had a significant influence on the Fauve style evolved by Matisse and Derain in 1905 – Matisse worked with Signac at Saint-Tropez in 1904.

PROVENANCE   Alfred Gold, Berlin; bought by Courtauld, June 1928, approx. £1,260 (price including work sold as by Rubens). Courtauld Bequest 1948.

EXHIBITED   Tate Gallery, 1948 (74); *France 1850–1950*, The Art Gallery, Kettering, 1950 (85); Orangerie, Paris, 1955 (57); Courtauld Centenary, 1976 (53); *Post-Impressionism*, Royal Academy, London, 1979–80 (213); Japan and Canberra, 1984 (87).

LITERATURE   Cooper, 1954, no. 72.

57 SISLEY, ALFRED 1839–99
   Snow at Louveciennes 1874
   Neige à Louveciennes
   Oil on canvas, 46.3 × 55.8
   Signed, bottom right: 'Sisley'
   Courtauld Institute Galleries (The Samuel
      Courtauld Trust)

The village of Louveciennes lies near the River
Seine, about ten miles west of Paris; Sisley
painted many views in and around the place in
the 1870s, and both Monet and Pissarro also
painted there. The subject of the picture is a
simple, everyday scene, of no obvious
picturesque potential: humble houses set along a
road, with a particularly uninviting
foreground – rough verge, open road, tree-
trunks and a stretch of wall. The figures give a
sense of scale, but, treated very summarily and
placed in the middle distance, they do little to
characterise the scene. It is by the delicacy of the
treatment of atmospheric effects – by the
nuances of colour and touch – that Sisley gave
this outwardly unprepossessing scene its
pictorial interest.

   Although the tonality of the painting is
comparatively subdued, and the trees to the
right and left give it a dark-toned frame, the
effect of an overcast winter day is evoked by
soft variations of colour – blues across the distant
hills and houses set against the soft creams and
beiges of the road and nearer buildings. The
paint is quite thin throughout the picture; more
broadly painted areas alternate with zones built
up from successions of varied smaller touches,
like the scatter of broken accents across the
verge at the bottom left. Though the
brushwork has no dominant rhythm, the soft
variegations of touch and colour give the whole
painting a freshness and mobility. The light-
toned priming of the canvas shows through the
paint at many points and heightens the
luminosity of the effect.

   In 1875 Sisley painted a second picture of
precisely the same subject, in summer, but there
is no evidence that he intended the two to be
seen as a pair.

PROVENANCE   Ch. de Hèle, Brussels; de Hèle
Sale, Amsterdam, 13 June 1911 (lot 13; 2,750
florins); Bernheim-Jeune, Paris; Durand-Ruel,
Paris; Paul Rosenberg, Paris; Percy Moore
Turner, London; bought by Courtauld, June
1926, £1,350. Courtauld Gift 1932.

EXHIBITED   *Exposition Sisley*, Durand-Ruel,
Paris, 1902 (6); *Sisley*, Durand-Ruel, Paris, 1922
(9); *Masterpieces of French Art of the 19th Century*,
Agnew, London, 1923 (1); Tate Gallery, 1948
(75); Orangerie, Paris, 1955 (58); Courtauld
Centenary, 1976 (54); Japan and Canberra, 1984
(89); United States, 1987–8 (17).

LITERATURE   Jamot-Turner, no. 5; Home House
Catalogue, no. 17; Cooper, 1954, no. 73;
F. Daulte, *Alfred Sisley: Catalogue raisonné*,
Lausanne, 1959, no. 150; R. Bruce-Gardner,
G. Hedley and C. Villers, 'Impressions of
Change', in United States, 1987–8, p. 21.

58 SISLEY, ALFRED 1839–99
    Boats on the Seine *c*.1877
    Bateaux sur la Seine
    Oil on canvas, laid down on plywood,
        37.2 × 44.3
    Signed, bottom right: 'Sisley'
    Courtauld Institute Galleries (The Samuel
        Courtauld Trust)

This canvas is smaller and more sketchily
treated than most Impressionist paintings of the
1870s, but the fact that it is signed shows that
Sisley regarded it as a complete work in its own
right. Throughout the decade, the landscapists
of the group painted rapid sketches such as this
alongside more elaborated canvases; the sketches
were particularly appreciated by fellow artists
and the most 'artistic' of collectors, whereas
their more highly worked pictures were more
likely to find buyers through the dealer market.

By 1877, Sisley's brushwork had become
more broken and energetic (see cat. no. 57): the
whole scene is animated by hooks, dashes and
streaks of colour which capture with great
vigour the effect of a sunny, breezy day. Little
figures can be distinguished on the near bank,
but there is nothing in the way in which they
are treated to differentiate them from the other
elements around them (compare Monet
cat. no. 32). However, for all the picture's
apparent speed of execution, the light and
weather on a day such as this must have
changed far too quickly for Sisley to capture
them at once, while they lasted; even a picture
such as this must have involved a complex act
of memory and synthesis, in order to evoke so
fresh an effect.

The light-toned canvas priming, seen in
many places, enhances the luminosity, but the
true highlights of the picture are the vigorous
white accents in the clouds and on the barges
and the far houses. Even the darkest tones in the
scene – on the barge and the bank – are coloured,
built up of very deep blues and reds, and the
distance is suggested by gradations of blue set
against the green foliage and the sharp red
accents of the distant roofs. These warm
accents, picked up in the floating logs at bottom
centre and on the near bank, act as an important
contrast to the dominant blues and greens of the
picture, and sharpen the overall colour effect.

The subject, dominated by the unloading of
wood from a river barge, with a passing
passenger-ferry on the river, is explicitly
contemporary, presenting the Seine at
Billancourt (across the river from Sèvres on the
south-western outskirts of Paris) not as a rural
retreat but as a commercial and recreational
waterway.

PROVENANCE (?) Richard Samson, Hamburg;
Matthiesen Gallery, London; bought by
Courtauld, March 1947, £1,575. Courtauld
Bequest 1948.

EXHIBITED Tate Gallery, 1948 (77); Courtauld
Centenary, 1976 (55); Japan and Canberra, 1984
(90); United States, 1987–8 (18).

LITERATURE Cooper, 1954, no. 75; Daulte,
1959, no, 273; R. Bruce-Gardner, G. Hedley
and C. Villers, 'Impressions of Change', in
United States, 1987–8, p. 21.

170

59 TOULOUSE-LAUTREC, HENRI DE 1864–1901
Jane Avril in the Entrance of the Moulin Rouge, Putting on her Gloves 1892
Jane Avril dans l'entrée du Moulin Rouge mettant ses gants
Pastel and oil on millboard, laid on panel, 102 × 55.1
Signed, bottom left, initials in monogram: 'T–Lautrec'
Courtauld Institute Galleries (The Samuel Courtauld Trust)

Jane Avril was a celebrated popular dancer, reportedly the illegitimate daughter of an Italian nobleman and a Parisian *demi-mondaine*, who first appeared at the Moulin Rouge in 1889, and became one of its star performers. She was nicknamed 'La Mélinite'–the name of a recently invented form of explosive. She was one of Lautrec's favourite models and became his close friend and supporter. Often, he depicted her dancing. The English poet Arthur Symons described his first experience of watching her dance in 1892: 'Young and girlish, the more provocative because she played as a prude, with an assumed modesty, *décolletée* nearly to the waist, in the Oriental fashion. She had about her an air of depraved virginity.' But here Lautrec shows her in street clothes, either arriving at or leaving a performance. The thinness of the figure is emphasised by the elongated format–created by the addition of a large extra piece of millboard at the bottom. The apparent immateriality of her figure is wittily set against the looming presence of the male hat and coat seen on the left, apparently hanging on the wall alongside Jane Avril.

The experimental combination of techniques here is comparable to methods pioneered by Degas (see cat. nos 16 and 18). Lautrec laid in broad areas of the picture in oil, while the pastel elaboration allowed him to combine colour and drawing–simultaneously to sharpen the indication of the forms and to enrich the play of colour; this is most conspicuous around the figure's face and hat, where finer strokes of reds, yellows and greens are set off against the bold slashes of blue paint in the right background. These sharp colour relationships, and the pallid yellow that lights the figure's face, heighten the sense of the artificiality of this world of urban entertainments.

PROVENANCE Murat, Paris; Eugène Blot, Paris; Blot Sale, Paris, 9 and 10 May 1900 (lot 161; 1,250 francs, bought in); Blot Sale, Paris, 10 May 1906 (lot 74; 6,600 francs); Mancini, Paris; Prindonoff, Paris; J. Seligmann, New York; Percy Moore Turner, London; bought by Courtauld, December 1929, £10,400. Courtauld Gift 1932.

EXHIBITED Galerie Goupil, Paris, 1893 (18); International Society, London, 1898 (5); *Toulouse-Lautrec*, Goupil Gallery, London, 1898 (18); *Exposition Toulouse-Lautrec*, Durand-Ruel, Paris, 1902 (72); Salon d'Automne, Paris, 1904 (19); *Toulouse-Lautrec*, Musée des Arts Décoratifs, Paris, 1931 (95); *French Art*, Royal Academy, London, 1932 (551); Tate Gallery, 1948 (79); *Toulouse-Lautrec*, Musée de l'Orangerie, Paris, 1951 (37; wrong provenance); Orangerie, Paris, 1955 (60); Courtauld Centenary, 1976 (56); Japan and Canberra, 1984 (91); United States, 1987–8 (43); *Toulouse-Lautrec*, Hayward Gallery, London, and Grand Palais, Paris, 1992 (81).

LITERATURE M. Joyant, *Henri de Toulouse-Lautrec, peintre*, Paris, 1926, pp. 136–40, 274; Jamot-Turner, no. 38; Home House Catalogue, no. 3; Cooper, 1954, no. 79; M.G. Dortu, *Toulouse-Lautrec et son oeuvre*, New York, 1971, p. 417.

60 TOULOUSE-LAUTREC, HENRI DE 1864–1899
In the Private Booth 1899
En cabinet particulier
Oil on canvas, 55.1 × 46
Signed, top right, the initials in
   monogram: 'T–Lautrec'
Courtauld Institute Galleries (The Samuel
   Courtauld Trust)

The picture shows a tête-à-tête supper at the famous Rat Mort, a café and restaurant on the Rue Pigalle, at the foot of the hill of Montmartre. By the late 1890s, it retained a popular café downstairs, with a restaurant upstairs which was noted as a meeting-point for stylish *demi-mondaines*; it is this that Lautrec portrayed here: his sitter was Lucy Jourdain, a celebrated *cocotte* of the day.

In the placing of the figures, and particularly in the disconcerting device of cutting off the man's face with the picture frame, Lautrec has deliberately denied the viewer the possibility of reading a straightforward narrative into their relationship. Degas, in *L'Absinthe* (Musée d'Orsay, Paris), had used a similar arrangement in order to suggest psychological distance and separation, but here the mood is less readily legible. The vivid red slash of the woman's smiling lips is echoed by the ebullient, flowing brushwork of her clothes and the bowl of fruit, creating a sense of vivacity as well as a rather startling analogy between woman and fruit. The effect is enhanced by the use of paint much thinned with diluent and applied fluidly and transparently, exploiting the light tone of the ground; but the seeming lack of focus in the woman's eyes, together with the man's averted gaze and the glass of champagne before her, may suggest that this gaiety is superficial. The artificiality of her position is emphasised by her costume—clearly a fancy stage costume, in contrast to her companion's formal evening dress. These signs would have made it clear to the painting's original viewers that this was a scene of *demi-mondaine* entertainment, but beyond that its mood and meaning are not closely fixed, leaving scope for the viewer's interpretation.

PROVENANCE   G. Séré de Rivières, Paris; with Georges Bernheim, Paris; Caressa, Paris; Percy Moore Turner, London; bought by Courtauld, March 1928, £2,500. Courtauld Bequest 1948.

EXHIBITED   *Exposition Toulouse-Lautrec*, Durand-Ruel, Paris, 1902 (38); *Exposition rétrospective Toulouse-Lautrec*, Galerie Manzi-Joyant, Paris, 1914 (34); *Toulouse-Lautrec*, Galeries Paul Rosenberg, Paris, 1914 (21); *30 Ans d'art indépendant*, Paris 1926 (3252); *French Art*, Royal Academy, London, 1932 (513); Tate Gallery, 1948 (80); Orangerie, Paris, 1955 (61); Courtauld Centenary, 1976 (57); National Gallery, London, 1983 (no catalogue); Japan and Canberra, 1984 (92); United States, 1987–8 (44); *Toulouse-Lautrec*, Hayward Gallery, London, and Grand Palais, Paris, 1992 (163).

LITERATURE   Joyant, 1926, p. 298; Jamot-Turner, no. 40; Cooper, 1954, no. 80; Dortu, 1971, p. 677; R. Thomson, *Toulouse-Lautrec*, London, 1977, p. 103; R. Bruce-Gardner, G. Hedley and C. Villers, 'Impressions of Change', in United States, 1987–8, p. 21.

61 UTRILLO, MAURICE 1883–1955
Road at Sannois *c.*1912
Rue à Sannois
Oil on canvas, 55 × 82
Signed, bottom right: 'Maurice Utrillo'
Courtauld Institute Galleries (The Samuel
Courtauld Trust)

The life and career of Utrillo, alcoholic son of
the painter Suzanne Valadon (arguably herself a
far finer artist), became the stuff of Montmartre
legends between the wars. His lifestyle,
combined with the simple, approachable
imagery of his paintings, satisfied the demands
of artistic bohemianism without challenging the
viewers of his paintings in aesthetic terms. More
recently, his reputation has been in sharp
decline.

Most of his imagery was frankly touristic –
paintings of celebrated Montmartre scenes (see
fig. 18, in the Courtauld Gift), very comparable
to, and often based upon, picture postcards.
Road at Sannois, by contrast, shows a less well-
known site, a street in a village near Argenteuil,
around ten miles north-west of Paris. It is not a
particularly picturesque scene – a winding road
with a house and garden walls on either side;
but it is presented with great immediacy, with
the walls as bold, simple slabs of paint, set off
by the rough, broken textures of the foliage.
The dry, chalky surface of the painting, happily
unvarnished, seems to evoke the materiality of
the stuccoed walls it depicts.

In conventional terms the perspective is
clearly faulty: at no point do the walls and road
come together to suggest a credible recession
into space; but are such naturalistic criteria the
most appropriate ones for judging the picture?
In its simple forms and distinct, clearly
articulated shapes, it might instead suggest
comparisons with the *naïveté* of the *douanier*
Rousseau (see cat.no.44) – himself quite unable
to handle linear perspective. And in the
frontality and immediacy of the light-toned
planes of paint, Utrillo's picture might even
have some relationship to Picasso and Braque,
and in particular to their far more complex
explorations of the ambiguities of space and
surface plane in the early phase of Cubism
around 1908. Much 'modernist' art history has
sought such parallels in order to upgrade the
status of lesser figures in the Paris art world of
the early twentieth century; but in the final
analysis, Utrillo's gaucheness and seeming
unconcern with the subtler nuances of form and
space suggest that any such comparisons are
inappropriate, and that a picture such as *Road at
Sannois* should be taken at face value –
immediate and direct in impact, but coarse in
execution and slight in ambition.

PROVENANCE Libaude, Paris; Reid and Lefèvre,
London; bought by Courtauld, by 1931, price
unknown. Courtauld Gift 1932.

EXHIBITED British Institute of Adult Education,
Silver End, Essex, March 1935; Tate Gallery,
1948 (82); Orangerie, Paris, 1955 (62);
Courtauld Centenary, 1976 (58); Japan and
Canberra, 1984 (97).

LITERATURE A. Tabarant, *Utrillo*, Paris, 1926,
p.94; Jamot-Turner, no.53; Home House
Catalogue, no.51; Cooper, 1954, no.82.

62 VUILLARD, ÉDOUARD 1868–1940
Interior: The Screen c.1909–10
Intérieur: le paravent
Oil (peinture à l'essence) on paper, laid
down on panel, 35.8 × 23.8
Signed, bottom right: 'E. Vuillard'
Courtauld Institute Galleries (The Samuel
Courtauld Trust)

PROVENANCE   Paul Gemetti, London; Leicester
Galleries, London; bought by Courtauld, July
1927, £404 5s. Courtauld Bequest 1948.

EXHIBITED   Tate Gallery, 1948 (83); Orangerie,
Paris, 1955 (69); Courtauld Centenary, 1976
(61); Japan and Canberra, 1984 (100); United
States, 1987–8 (47).

LITERATURE   Jamot-Turner, no. 55; Cooper,
1954, no. 89 (where dated c.1912).

The subject of this picture is a nude model in an
artist's studio (suggested by the huge windows
at top right). The figure is seemingly caught
between poses, in an awkward gesture as she
reaches across a sofa for her clothes. This theme,
of an artist's model depicted off guard, was very
common in Salon painting in France during the
1880s, in works by artists such as Edouard
Dantan. The *frisson* evoked by such paintings
was overtly voyeuristic. The viewer was offered
a glimpse of the naked model at a moment
when her nakedness was not legitimised, or
implicitly defused, by assuming a formal artistic
pose – by becoming a 'nude'.

However, Vuillard, in turn, has undercut the
associations of the subject, by the way in which
the picture, and particularly the figure, is
treated. The whole image is handled in a
particularly summary way: the toned paper is
left unpainted in many places to serve as a mid-
tone. But the figure is particularly little worked;
paradoxically the primary element in the
composition is among the least defined. The
woman's body is almost evoked in negative,
which defuses the eroticism customarily
associated with the theme. The richest colours
occur in the screen, whose green, pink and blue
panels set the figure off, while soft, muted, blue
streaks suggest the modelling of her body, and a
few crisp highlights, along her extended arm
and her left thigh, locate her pose in relation to
the studio window at top right. This window,
with the wall and the screen, set up a grid-like
structure across the whole picture, behind the
curved shapes of figure and sofa. The colour is
quite muted, with true black used for the
cushion or drapery on the sofa and, in a tiny
dab, to suggest the model's pubic hair. The
surface of the painting is very matt, and has
happily never been varnished, thus leaving it in
the state which Vuillard would have wished.

Here Vuillard exploits *peinture à l'essence* in a
technique that contrasts with that of Degas's
Femme à la fenêtre (cat. no. 16). The choice of an
absorbent, fairly coarse, tinted paper, much of it
left exposed, and the essentially opaque pigment
mixtures, such as those in the thinned, flat
marks of the screen behind the figure, suggest
the appearance of gouache. Where the paint has
not been so diluted, the surface retains the
impasto of the brushstrokes, and, in the light of
the window, a trace of the gloss of the reduced
oil medium.

63   BOSSHARD, RODOLPHE-THÉOPHILE   1889–?
     Tulips   *c*.1925
     Tulipes
     Oil on canvas, 51 × 62
     Signed, bottom left: 'R. Th. Bosshard'
     Courtauld Institute Galleries (The Samuel
          Courtauld Trust)

64   FRIESZ, EMILE OTHON   1879–1949
     Anemones   *c*.1922
     Les Anémones
     Oil on canvas, 47 × 38.5
     Signed, bottom left: 'E. Othon Friesz'
     Courtauld Institute Galleries (The Samuel
          Courtauld Trust)

65 ROY, PIERRE 1880–1950
Still Life with Bonnets c.1924
Nature morte aux bonnets
Oil on canvas, 61 × 74
Signed, bottom right: 'P. Roy'
Courtauld Institute Galleries (The Samuel
Courtauld Trust)

66 TCHELITCHEW, PAUL 1898–1957
Pears 1927
Les Poires
Oil on canvas, 46.5 × 55.5
Signed, bottom right: 'P. Tchelitchew, '27'
Courtauld Institute Galleries (The Samuel
Courtauld Trust)

67 GAUGUIN, PAUL 1848–1903
 Portrait of Mette Gauguin 1877
 Portrait de Mette Gauguin
 White marble, height: 34.5
 Signed, on the back of the collar:
 'P. Gauguin' (incised)
 Courtauld Institute Galleries (The Samuel
  Courtauld Trust)

In the spring of 1877 Gauguin and his wife, Mette-Sophie Gad, rented an apartment at 74 rue des Fourneaux, in premises owned by the sculptor Jules-Ernest Bouillot. At this date, Gauguin carved *Portrait of Mette Gauguin*, the first of two marble sculptures in his oeuvre. The second, also datable to 1877, is a portrait of Gauguin's son, Emil (Metropolitan Museum of Art, New York). In 1933, a Danish nephew of Mme Gauguin recalled that on many occasions he had seen at her home (to which she returned after separating from Gauguin in 1882) a bust-length portrait of her modelled in wax by Gauguin; this has not been traced, and its relationship to the marble is unknown. It is probable, however, that such a work, in cheap and malleable material, was a maquette for the present bust. Pissarro's son Ludovic-Rodo remembered that his father also owned a bust of Mette by Gauguin; again, this work is unknown, and its connection with the Courtauld sculpture remains unresolved.

 The style of *Portrait of Mette Gauguin* reflects the conventional academic realism popular at the Salon in the second half of the nineteenth century. The illusionistic device of animating the eyes by hollowing out part of the pupil, thus encouraging the play of light over a shaded area, and the use of the drill to create the lace effect of the ruche at her neck and to suggest by striations the texture of the open collar's folds were standard practices of the professional stonecarver. In a certificate dated September 1925, Emil Gauguin raised doubts about Gauguin's contribution to the New York bust and to this work. While Emil's reliability is questionable (born in 1874, he was three when the portraits were carved), it is probable that Gauguin was assisted in some manner, and certainly by Bouillot. Cooper concluded that this journeyman-sculptor supervised the modelling of the maquette, then carved the marble with the collaboration of Gauguin. The degree of Bouillot's intervention, however, seems difficult to assess, since almost nothing is known of his work. He is recorded as having exhibited at the Salon between 1888 and 1895 statuettes, medals and busts, principally in marble, and doubtlessly, he would have influenced Gauguin's choice of this material and the adroit manner in which it was worked for this portrait.

Gauguin showed the busts of Mette and Emil at the fifth Impressionist group exhibition in 1880, but attracted little critical attention.

PROVENANCE Mette Gauguin, Copenhagen; Pola Gauguin, Copenhagen; Leicester Galleries, London (Ernest Brown & Phillips) by 1924; bought by Courtauld, March 1925, £288 15s. Courtauld Gift 1932.

EXHIBITED Fifth Impressionist exhibition, Paris, 1880 (62); *Den frie Udstilling*, Copenhagen, 1893 (169); Gauguin exhibition, Grossherzoglichen Museum am Karlsplatz, Weimar, 1905 (no catalogue); *Gauguin*, Leicester Galleries, London, 1924 (B); *Gauguin*, Royal Scottish Academy, Edinburgh, and Tate Gallery, London, 1955 (72); *Cent Oeuvres de Gauguin*, Galerie Charpentier, Paris, 1960 (4); *Paul Gauguin*, Haus der Kunst, Munich, 1960 (140); *Paul Gauguin 1848–1903*, Österreichische Galerie im Oberen Belvedere, Vienna, 1960 (132); *Gauguin og van Gogh i København 1893*, Ordrupgaard, Copenhagen, 1984–5 (1).

LITERATURE F. Fénéon, 'Impressionnisme', *L'Art Moderne*, 19 September 1886; J. de Rotonchamp, *Paul Gauguin: 1848–1903*, Paris, 1925, p. 18; P. Gauguin, *My Father, Paul Gauguin*, New York, 1937, p. 45; R. Burnett, *The Life of Paul Gauguin*, New York, 1937, p. 28; M. Malingue, *Gauguin*, Monaco, 1944, p. 20; M. Malingue, *Gauguin, le peintre et son oeuvre*, Paris, 1948, p. 14; P. Gauguin, *Letters to his Wife and Friends*, ed. M. Malingue, trans. H. Stenning, New York, 1949, p. 16; U.F. Marks-Vandenbroucke, 'Gauguin, ses origines et sa formation artistique', in *Gauguin, sa vie, son oeuvre*, ed. G. Wildenstein, Paris, 1958, p. 543; J. Loize, *Amitiés de Monfried*, Paris, 1951, no. 463; Cooper, 1954, no. 227; C. Gray, *Sculpture and Ceramics of Paul Gauguin*, Baltimore, 1963, pp. 1, 2, no. 1; *Gauguin: A Retrospective*, ed. M. Prather and C.F. Stuckey, New York, 1987; *The Art of Paul Gauguin*, Washington, D.C., Chicago, Paris, 1988, fig. 15.

68 DEGAS, EDGAR 1834–1917
 Arabesque over the Right Leg, Left Arm in Line c.1890–5
 Arabesque sur la jambe droite, le bras gauche dans la ligne
 Bronze cast by Hébrard, Paris, 1919–20, height: 28.8
 Signed: 'Degas' (incised)
 Private Collection

69 DEGAS, EDGAR 1834–1917
 Dancer Looking at the Sole of her Right Foot (Fourth Study) c.1895
 Danseuse regardant la plante de son pied droit (4ème étude)
 Bronze cast by Hébrard, Paris, 1919–20, height: 46.2
 Signed: 'Degas' (incised)
 Private Collection

70 RODIN, AUGUSTE 1840–1917
 Hanako 1908
 Bronze cast by Rudier, Paris, 1908, height: 16
 Unsigned
 Private Collection

71 CÉZANNE, PAUL 1839–1906
A Shed *c.*1880
Une Cabane
Pencil and watercolour on paper,
    31.4 × 47.5
Unsigned
Courtauld Institute Galleries (The Samuel
    Courtauld Trust)

The date of *c.*1880, first proposed for this work by Alfred Neumeyer, is supported by later scholars. Interpreting the motif as a cottage, Neumeyer perceived in this comparatively early watercolour (Cézanne took up the medium seriously only in 1885, having experimented with it since 1868) implications of tranquil domesticity: he thus connected it with two watercolour studies of the entrance to a garden, datable to 1878–80 (Metropolitan Museum of Art, New York, and Hohl Collection, Basel), to which relates a third and possibly earlier (1875–8) garden scene, also in New York (Private Collection). In these works, however, Cézanne records details and texture in an almost purely linear manner, which has little in common with the treatment of the present subject. Nor can the motif and style of *A Shed* be allied, as a more recent writer suggests, to a drawing of part of a cottage roof assigned to 1889–92 (Kunstmuseum, Basel).

Rather than a cottage, the building Cézanne represents here appears to be either a shed or an outhouse. The site of the building is unknown but may have been on his father's estate, the Jas de Bouffan (see cat. no. 6). This shed motif, unusually, has not been discovered in any other oil, watercolour or pencil study by Cézanne.

Related to the Courtauld composition's extensive pencilwork, in which forms are projected into relief by sinuous, qualified contours and patches of vigorous diagonal hatching suggesting shadows passing over textured surfaces, is the handling of a distantly related subject, the 1880–3 sketch, *Tree with Foliage* (Purrmann Collection, Starnberg). There, the image of crisply delineated leaves obscuring a tree-trunk also compares closely with that of the clusters of scalloped – almost decorative – foliage that in the Courtauld drawing relieves the line of the shed's roof.

In *A Shed*, Cézanne echoes the shed's rectangular form by the interplay of the door's verticals and the masonry's predominant horizontals. These lines underpin a slender diagonal tree-trunk (right) supporting an extensive foliage canopy whose arching rhythm varies that of the earth's contours. Counterbalancing the tree-trunk is a forked diagonal form at the left – either a lesser trunk, or perhaps an implement for harvesting fruit. In this composition's frontality, in its suggestion of receding foreground and in its forging of linear conjunctions may be seen comparisons with the pictorial structure of the 1880 watercolour showing men in a punt (Hirschl and Adler Galleries, New York). And as in that work, Cézanne here employs a limited palette of local colour – greys, tinted ochres, touches of blue, and emerald green – which, except for the green, has little life of its own unsupported by the armature of drawing. Allied with the pencilwork, its patches and strokes 'carve back' into pictorial space, and in so doing, expose the compositional framework and sharpen contrasts between the edges of contiguous forms.

PROVENANCE Paul Rosenberg, Paris; bought by Courtauld, date unknown. Courtauld Gift 1932.

EXHIBITED City Art Gallery, Leicester, 1936; *Cézanne Watercolours*, Tate Gallery, London, 1946 (3); Tate Gallery, 1948 (84); *Landscape in French Art*, Royal Academy, London, 1949–50 (546); Orangerie, Paris, 1955 (70); *Paul Cézanne*, Österreichische Galerie, Vienna, 1961 (47); *Watercolour and Pencil Drawings by Cézanne*, Laing Art Gallery, Newcastle-on-Tyne, and Hayward Gallery, London, 1973 (42); Courtauld Centenary, 1976 (62); British Museum, 1983 (98); Japan and Canberra, 1984 (16); C.I.G., 1988 (4).

LITERATURE *L'Amour de l'Art*, 1924, p. 36; Home House Catalogue, no. 23; Venturi, 1936, no. 837; Cooper, 1954, no. 109; A. Neumeyer, *Cézanne Drawings*, New York, 1958, p. 27 and no. 67; V. W. Anderson, 'A Cézanne Copy after Couture', *Master Drawings*, I, no. 4, 1963, p. 44; J. Rewald, *Paul Cézanne: The Watercolours*, London, 1983, no. 102.

72 CÉZANNE, PAUL 1839–1906
The Montagne Sainte-Victoire c.1890
La Montagne Sainte-Victoire
Pencil and watercolour on paper,
  32.8 × 50.5
Unsigned
Courtauld Institute Galleries (The Samuel
  Courtauld Trust)

In this drawing, Cézanne observes the Montagne Sainte-Victoire from Bellevue (approximately one-third of a mile south-west of the Jas de Bouffan) looking due west. This vantage point affords the most balanced view of the mountain's peak, and was adopted by Cézanne for compositions in oils in the Courtauld Collection (cat. no. 8) and the Barnes Foundation (Merion, Pa.); in two further watercolours, in the Fogg Art Museum (Harvard University, Cambridge, Mass.) and formerly in the Sadler Collection, in which the mountain is observed from a lesser and greater distance, respectively; and in a pencil drawing on the verso of an unrelated watercolour, also in the Fogg Art Museum. These works are all ascribed to the later half of the 1880s, and writers agree that the present watercolour may be similarly dated to the period 1885–7.

Closest to the present composition is that of the Barnes painting. In both, an unimpeded view of the mountain set against an unmodulated sky is located in the upper half, and slightly to the left, of the pictorial area. The mountain in the Barnes canvas is weighted and stabilised by trees and buildings connecting middleground to a band of vegetation cropped by the painting's bottom edge. Here, by contrast, the motif is arranged more subtly, so that middleground imagery of trees and foothills predominates, while the mountain's peak is balanced by the configuration of foreground forms (bushes, and hedges or boundaries of fields?) parallel with, but distant from, the paper's lower edge.

The drawing with soft pencil, both below and apparently over paint surfaces, is of two types. In the composition's lower two-thirds, free horizontals and curves are complemented – especially at the left – by lozenges of intense diagonal hatching. In Sainte-Victoire's higher slopes, hatching is reduced to two light, open patches, and all other drawing is linear, fixing the contour through a series of free revisions, particularly sweeping and numerous at the summit's top and right.

The vocabulary of pencil marks is complemented and extended by the manner in which watercolour or dilute gouache is applied. Contours are revised or affirmed with strokes from the point of the brush used either singly (contrast the fluid delicacy of stroke indicating the extreme, distant, left of the mountain with the forceful, broken line of the drying brush marking the edge of rockface, right) or repeated, to create thin bands, or broader glides. Oblong patches, which describe broad planes, can sometimes be seen to result from alignments of short, diagonal strokes (visible in the left of the mountain and in the foliage below) analogous to areas of pencil hatching; other patches may have been similarly formed, but the diagonals of fluid watercolour have fused, and the discrete strokes are no longer visible. Comparable groups of directional brushstrokes are seen in all areas of the Barnes composition.

Colours following the sequence of the spectrum are grouped over the Courtauld sheet in three lateral zones. In the lowest, vivid pink moves through orange-ochre to yellow and is opposed by greens ranging from yellow to emerald, blues and a cool grey-violet. Across the composition's centre, greens, blues and violet predominate, while on the mountain's upper slopes, the palette is restricted to blues and grey-violets, opposed to pinks, and, at the summit, to strokes of a startling yellow which echoes the hue in the lowest zone. Variations of colour-clusters thus reverberate up the pictorial area, linking mountain with forms of vegetation, and revealing fore-, middle- and background areas which are unified on the paper's surface and in which atmospheric perspective is suggested. The colouristic indication of distance is complemented by watercolour washes which become increasingly dilute as they progress up the sheet, from fore- to background.

PROVENANCE Bernheim-Jeune, Paris (bought from the artist, 1904); Percy Moore Turner; bought by Courtauld, July 1924, £350. Courtauld Gift 1932.

EXHIBITED *Cézanne*, Leicester Galleries, London, 1925 (4); *French Art*, Royal Academy, London, 1932 (989); City Art Gallery, Leicester, 1936; *Modern French Paintings*, Art Gallery, Melbourne, 1939 (24a); Tate Gallery, 1948 (85); *Landscape in French Art*, Royal Academy, London, 1949–50 (554); *Het Franse Landschap*, Rijksmuseum, Amsterdam, 1951 (151); *French Drawings*, Arts Council, 1952 (15); Orangerie, Paris, 1955 (71); *Paul Cézanne*, Österreichische Galerie, Vienna, 1961 (65); Manchester, 1962 (55); *Cézanne Watercolours*, Columbia University, New York, Benefit Exhibition, Knoedler Galleries, New York, 1963 (27); *Watercolour and Pencil Drawings by Cézanne*, Laing Art Gallery, Newcastle-on-Tyne, and Hayward Gallery, London, 1973 (55); Courtauld Centenary, 1976 (63); British Museum, 1983 (100); Japan and Canberra, 1984 (17); *Impressionist Drawings*, Ashmolean Museum, Oxford, Manchester City Art Gallery, The Burrell Collection, Glasgow, 1986 (34); C.I.G., 1988 (9); *Cézanne and Poussin: The Classical Vision of Landscape*, National Gallery of Scotland, Edinburgh, 1990 (52).

LITERATURE Home House Catalogue, no. 22; Venturi, 1936, no. 1023; E. Loran, *Cézanne's Composition*, Berkeley and Los Angeles, 1946, 1959, 1963 and 1985, p. 101; R. Huyghe, *Le Dessin français au XIX siècle*, Lausanne, 1948, pl. 105; Cooper, 1954, no. 110; L. Gowing, 'The Logic of Organized Sensations', in *Cézanne. The Late Work*, New York, 1977, p. 58; Rewald, 1983, no. 279.

73   CÉZANNE, PAUL   1839–1906
Apples, Bottle and Chairback   c.1900–6
Pommes, bouteille, dossier de chaise
Pencil and gouache on paper, 45.8 × 60.4
Unsigned
Courtauld Institute Galleries (The Samuel
Courtauld Trust)

Cézanne's final conception of still life is most clearly seen in the late watercolours. Between 1900 and 1906, the dates assigned to the present drawing, he composed some twenty-four works in this medium, treating arrangements of fruit, bowls, glasses, bottles and skulls. By contrast, his oil paintings of this period deal almost exclusively with landscape and bathers or other figure subjects.

The background of striped wallpaper shown in this watercolour is included in *The Fruit Dish* (Haegel Collection, Paris), while both wallpaper and glass are seen again in *The Dessert* (formerly Bernheim de Villers Collection, Paris). These two watercolours share the dating of *Apples, Bottle and Chairback*.

In the present still life, vigorous sweeps, loops and horizontals with the pencil suggest initial positions for fruit, bowl, chairback and table's edge; similar strokes allied to patches of vigorous diagonal hatching underlie the composition's darkest areas – the bottle and the mysterious curvilinear form, upper right. A comparable manner and freedom of preliminary drawing are visible in a number of the late still lifes, most notably in *Blue Pot and Bottle of Wine* (Thaw Collection, New York), in which the neck of the wine bottle, as in this work, terminates before the upper edge of the sheet to preserve a harmoniously weighted composition.

In a letter to Emile Bernard of 25 July 1904, Cézanne defined the patch of paper left bare near the centre of motifs in the late watercolours as the 'culmination point' of the form, or that area of the object closest to the eye. In the later watercolours, colour emanates from this point in the logical sequence of the spectrum; and after 1900, a greater concentration on primary colour becomes evident, while hues gain in intensity. From the culminating point of the apples here radiate, in order, red, yellow and blue. Of the secondary colours, orange is sparingly applied, always between red and yellow, while green, usually juxtaposed with blue, is here also introduced to activate the reds and brown of table-top and chairback, and to control the placing of fruit and dish.

The arcs of colour that interlock with the white of the paper to construct the pile of fruit are contained by the curving crosspiece of the chairback: this boldly brushed form has close affinities with *The Rococo Clock* (Kunstmuseum,

Basel), possibly one of Cézanne's last works in pencil. Within the upper chairback's kidney shape, minor arcs palely echo the colours of the bowl of fruit and may perhaps represent its reflection in a mirror on the rear wall.

The watercolour is composed from zones of like brushstrokes: towards the composition's centre, however, all brushwork is transformed to resonate with the concentration of curves in the bowl, fruit and chairback. The irregular, multidirectional patches that overlap at the extreme left and right of the table's surface are consolidated into strokes whose thinness, length and flexibility increase as they advance towards the fruit dish, curving round its base to suggest a reflection in the table-top. Similarly, vertical strokes indicating the lateral edges of the wall become shorter and curved as they approach the chairback. At the centre of the table's edge – which, as in many of Cézanne's still-life watercolours after 1895, is not sharply defined – horizontal strokes are concentrated to support and stabilize the motifs above.

The thickness of the gouache describing fruit and leaves – sufficient to create a ridge at the edge of certain strokes, for example, in the blue contour of the apple to the right of the dish, on the edge of the penultimate apple on the right and in the leaves, far right – complements the intensity of colour and heightens the physical presence of these motifs. In contrast, Cézanne uses throughout the remainder of the sheet paint that is fluid and transparent – properties he exploits to maintain the autonomy of each colour patch and to suggest in all contours, except those in blue, an edge or direction. He achieves this by momentarily resting the brush either at the line's lateral edge, or by tilting the sheet to encourage the flow of paint to specific areas. Such directional contours are particularly visible around the crosspiece of the chairback and in the bottle and glass. The blue contours, less modified in density and hue, simultaneously create space between the apples and unite them into a compositional wedge: the blue is echoed by paler glides of colour at the top and bottom of the composition. The blue curves immediately below the alignment of apples, right, may be interpreted as *pentimenti*. Since there are no pencil indications of an originally lower position for these fruits, however, the arcs may represent reflections in the table-top of the spaces between the apples, thus demonstrating a facet of Cézanne's rich imaginative and interpretative vision.

PROVENANCE   Paul Cézanne *fils*, Paris; Galeries Thannhauser, Berlin and Lucerne; Wildenstein & Co. Ltd, New York and London; bought by Courtauld, September 1937, £3,500. Courtauld Bequest 1948.

EXHIBITED   *Eighth Exhibition of Watercolours and Pastels*, Cleveland Museum of Art, 1930 (no catalogue) ; *Works of Cézanne*, Philadelphia Museum of Art, 1934 (55); *Homage to Paul Cézanne*, Wildenstein, London, 1939 (73); *Cézanne Watercolours*, Tate Gallery, London, 1946 (56); Tate Gallery, 1948 (86); *Paul Cézanne*, Österreichische Galerie, Vienna, 1961 (81); *Watercolour and Pencil Drawings by Cézanne*, Laing Art Gallery, Newcastle-on-Tyne, and Hayward Gallery, London, 1973 (98); *French Paintings from the Courtauld Collection*, Graves Art Gallery, Sheffield, 1974 (64); Courtauld Centenary, 1976 (64); *Cézanne: The Late Work*, Museum of Modern Art, New York, and Museum of Fine Arts, Houston, 1977–8 (77); *Cézanne Aquarelle*, Kunsthalle, Tübingen, and Kunsthaus, Zürich, 1982 (93, with erroneous provenance); British Museum, 1983 (102); Japan and Canberra, 1984 (18); C.I.G., 1988 (10).

LITERATURE   E. d'Ors, *Paul Cézanne*, Paris, 1930, pl. 20; Venturi, 1936, no. 1155; Cooper, 1954, no. 111; F. Elgar, *Cézanne*, London, 1969, p. 249; T. Reff, 'Paintings and Theory in the Final Decade', p. 36, and J. Rewald, no. 77, in *Cézanne: The Late Work*, New York, 1977; Rewald, 1983, no. 643; W. Bradford, in *100 Masterpieces from the Courtauld Collections*, ed. D. Farr, London, 1987, p. 214.

74 DAUMIER, HONORÉ 1808–1879
  The Defence (?)1860–70
  La Défense
  Pencil, pen and ink, and wash on paper,
    23.7 × 31.5
  Signed lower right: 'h.D.'
  Courtauld Institute Galleries (The Samuel
    Courtauld Trust)

The possiblility of establishing a chronology
based on stylistic analysis of Daumier's
drawings is remote, since no known works on
paper are dated by him. The problem is
complicated by Daumier's prodigious facility as
a draughtsman, which was such – as an
examination of datable lithographs executed for
newspaper publication confirms – that he was
able to draw with equal ease in a variety of
manners as the occasion demanded.

In *The Defence* a lawyer plays upon the
emotions of a bewildered, lowly defendant by
gesticulating theatrically towards Pierre-Paul
Prud'hon's (1758–1823) allegorical Salon
painting *Justice and Divine Vengeance Pursuing
Crime*, which hangs behind the judges'
bench. The painting, commissioned by the
French Supreme Court of Appeal in 1808, hung
in its chambers until 1826, when it entered the
Louvre.

A similar scene to that shown in the
Courtauld drawing is the subject of the oil
painting *The Pardon* (Boymans-van Beuningen
Museum, Rotterdam) and of two cognate
drawings (Roger-Marx Collection, and Private
Collection, Paris), in which the lawyer now
points towards a painting of the Crucifixion.

The present composition, however, is not a
study for a painting, yet is repeated in a smaller,
unsigned sheet (Private Collection, Germany).
In that work, the forms of table and lawyer are
rendered more substantial by strokes of a darker
carbon black ink wash, while the agitation of
the lawyer's pointing hand is heightened by
additional *pentimenti*. No satisfactory
explanation can be advanced for Daumier's
repetition, in the same medium, of this subject:
that one version was executed from a tracing of
the other is denied by the spontaneous vitality
of line in both drawings.

PROVENANCE   Georges Lecomte; Percy Moore
Turner; bought by Courtauld, October 1928,
£450. Courtauld Bequest 1948.

EXHIBITED   *Daumier*, Ecole des Beaux-Arts,
Paris, 1901 (217); *Daumier–Gavarni*, Maison
Victor Hugo, Paris 1923, (80); *Daumier*, Galerie
Dru, Paris, 1927 (4); *French Art*, Royal
Academy, London, 1932 (949); Tate Gallery,
1948 (89); *Honoré Daumier*, Tate Gallery,
London, 1961 (220); Manchester 1962 (57);
Courtauld Centenary, 1976 (65); Arts Council,
1977–9 (6); British Museum, 1983 (104); Japan
and Canberra, 1984 (20); C.I.G., 1988 (11).

LITERATURE   E. Klossowski, *Honoré Daumier*,
Munich, 1908 and 1923, no.152; L. Marotte and
C. Martine, *Dessins de maîtres français*, IV:
Honoré Daumier, Paris, 1924, no.31; E. Fuchs,
Der Maler Daumier, Munich, 1927, no.184a;
Cooper, 1954, no.112; Maison, 1968, II, no.657.

75 DAUMIER, HONORÉ   1808–1879
The Hypochondriac   (?)1860–70
Le Malade imaginaire
Black chalk and watercolour on paper,
   20.7 × 27.1
Signed, lower left: 'h', and below:
   'h.Daumier'
Courtauld Institute Galleries (The Samuel
   Courtauld Trust)

The Hypochondriac relates to a group of works
inspired by Molière's satire *Le Malade
imaginaire*, among which are two paintings, *The
Hypochondriac* (Philadelphia Museum of Art)
and *Dr Diafoirus* (Bakwin Collection, New
York), which have been dated to 1860–3 and
1870, respectively. It has been suggested that
many of the drawings in watercolour or wash
also treating the subject of doctor and patient
may have been executed during this same
period, when Daumier's contract with the
newspaper *Le Charivari* had been broken.

   While thematically related to the
Philadelphia painting (in which interest is
focused mainly on the figure of Argan, who
wears a nightcap tied with a foppish bow
similar to that shown here), the Courtauld
drawing is compositionally more closely allied
to a charcoal-and-crayon study, *The Sick Man
and Death* (Private Collection, Paris), a work
whose sombre theme places it outside the
Malade imaginaire group proper. In that
drawing, the patient, whose pinched features
are a terror-stricken variant of Argan's in *The
Hypochondriac*, lies in profile facing right,
powerless against the contesting wills of the
doctor, right, and Death at the left.

   The comic doctors in the Courtauld
composition are variants of those who feel the
dying man's pulse in the otherwise bitter
drawing in Yale University Art Gallery, and
also relate to the charlatan seen in the highly
wrought watercolour of *The Hypochondriac* and
its preliminary study, both of which are now
lost (reproduced in Maison, 1968, II, nos 473,
476). Similar figures of doctors, one of whom is
armed with a monstrous syringe of the type
visible here, appear in force in a lithograph
captioned: 'Yesterday the breech-loading gun,
tomorrow these fellows . . .', published in the
newspaper *Actualités* of 28 May 1867. Perhaps
the earliest motif of such a syringe-wielding
doctor is to be seen, appropriately, in the guise
of Aesculapius, in Daumier's caricature also
published by *Actualités* on 16 March 1859.

PROVENANCE   Lemaire, Paris; Bignou, Paris;
L'Art Moderne S.A., Lucerne; bought by
Courtauld, March 1929, £1,800. Courtauld
Gift 1934.

EXHIBITED   *Works by Corot, Daumier*, Museum
of Modern Art, New York, 1930 (98); *French
Art*, Royal Academy, London, 1932 (904);
British Institute of Adult Education, Silver End,
Essex, 1935 (13); Tate Gallery, 1948 (90);
Daumier, le peintre, Bibliothèque Nationale,
Paris, 1958 (211); *Daumier: Paintings and
Drawings*, Arts Council at Tate Gallery,
London, 1961 (165); *Daumier*, Ingelheim-am-
Rhein, 1971 (38); Courtauld Centenary, 1976
(66); Arts Council, 1977–9 (5); *Daumier et ses
amis républicains*, Musée Cantini, Marseille, 1979
(65); British Museum, 1983 (103); Japan and
Canberra, 1984 (21); C.I.G., 1988 (12).

LITERATURE   'Cahiers d'Art', III, 1928, p. 49; E.
Fuchs, *Der Maler Daumier*, Munich, 1927,
no. 337; Home House Catalogue, no. 76;
Cooper, 1954, no. 113; *Revue Municipale*, no. 29,
Marseilles, 1956, p. 39; K.E. Maison, *Daumier
Drawings*, New York, 1960, no. 98; Maison,
1968, II, no. 486; W. Bradford, in *100
Masterpieces from the Courtauld Collections*, ed. D.
Farr, London, 1987, p. 202.

76 DEGAS, EDGAR 1834–1917
Seated Woman Adjusting her Hair (?)c.1884
Femme assise se coiffant
   Charcoal, chalk and pastel on paper,
      63 × 59.9
   Stamped bottom right with mark of
      Degas's studio sale
   Courtauld Institute Galleries (The Samuel
      Courtauld Trust)

Originally dated by Lemoisne to 1884, this pastel bears a complex relationship to an apparently unresolved painting of horizontal format, *Woman Doing her Hair* (formerly Viau Collection, Paris). The pose of the model in this canvas relates to that of the woman seen in a drawing included in the fourth sale of Degas's atelier (2–4 July 1919, lot 140); and, elaborated and reversed, it is also taken up in the painting *At the Milliners* of 1882–5 (Lathrop–Brown Collection, New York).

Many changes are visible in the pose of the model here; of these, the most fundamental are the redrawing of the left hip, the elongation of the line of the back and the repositioning of arms and head higher in the composition. To accommodate this lengthened figure, a strip of paper was abutted with the top of the original sheet. The woman's initial pose is now difficult to decipher, due to extensive effacing and redrawing. However, an earlier position of the head, cropped by the top of the lower sheet and turned more to the right, is indicated by vestiges of charcoal and black chalk to the right of what is now the collar, while the original torso, described by comfortably rounded contours, shows the model's bodice fastened at the back by a row of large buttons. A faint ruled line underlying the knees marks the initial extent of the skirt. In this state, the pastel closely corresponds to the composition of the Viau canvas, for which it may have been a preparatory study.

Degas probably began to revise *Seated Woman Adjusting her Hair* after completing the painting, and may have reworked it over several campaigns of drawing. A broader dating than that suggested by Lemoisne should therefore be ascribed to it.

The pastel shows marked differences of execution between its parts. Degas summarily restated head, arms and torso with heavy, continuous contours, which also indicate alternative positions for a dressing-table, upper right. Similarly vigorous strokes model more fully the woman's bodice at the right, and the front of the skirt. Contrasted with these are the precise hatchings describing the dramatically illuminated folds of olive material at the back of the skirt. Such handling, unusually crisp for Degas's work at this time, recalls that of Holbein, Cranach and Dürer, whose drawings

he had closely copied between 1859 and 1864. This elaborate draughtsmanship is set off against the vibrant pinkish-red verticals of the wall (indicated in an early stage of the drawing, and later strengthened), and the solid, warm brown of the woman's seat. This detailing seems to have been added late in the execution of the pastel and suggests that Degas was beginning a more complex reformulation of the subject.

The present work's combination of disparate manners of drawing, in which colour is allied with widely varying textural effects, has affinities with the aesthetic of Degas's *Little Dancer (Clothed)* of 1878–81 (Mellon Collection, Upperville, Va.), a wax sculpture that incorporates satin, ribbed silk and mesh gauze of different colours. The final appearance of *Woman Adjusting her Hair* confirms that for Degas the work of art – and in particular, the drawing – could become an arena for sustained, overt experimentation, in which the working out of ideas of composition and facture remained eminently visible.

The drawing was purchased by Samuel Courtauld in the frame in which it is displayed here. Its shallow, convex section, regularly grooved, is of the type designed by Degas for exhibiting his own works and may be the artist's own frame. Should its authenticity be proven, it would confirm the status accorded by Degas to this frank working drawing as an independent work of art.

The subject of *Seated Woman Adjusting her Hair* relates to the theme of the milliners' shops which Degas began to explore in about 1880. This interest in the world of fashion was perhaps encouraged by his friend Manet, who, with the poet Stéphane Mallarmé (1842–98), had been visiting fashionable dress shops since 1874. It represents part of Degas's wider fascination with the most artificial elements of modern urban life, seen also in his treatment of subjects from the theatre and *café-concert*.

PROVENANCE   Second Degas Sale, Paris, 11 December 1918 (lot 94); Nunès et Fiquet, Paris; Leicester Galleries, London by 1922; bought by Courtauld 1923, price unknown. Courtauld Bequest 1948.

EXHIBITED   *Degas Exhibition*, Leicester Galleries, London, 1922 (42); Tate Gallery, 1948 (92); Orangerie, Paris, 1955 (75); Manchester, 1962 (58); *Degas: Pastels and Drawings*, Nottingham University, 1969 (20); Courtauld Centenary, 1976 (19); British Museum, 1983 (105); Japan and Canberra, 1984 (25); United States, 1987–8 (9); C.I.G., 1988 (12).

LITERATURE   Lemoisne, 1946, III, no. 781; D. Cooper 'The Courtauld Collection', *Burlington Magazine*, CX, June 1948, p. 170; Jamot-Turner, no. 13; Cooper, 1954, no. 115; F. Russoli and F. Minervino, *L'Opera completa di Degas*, Milan, 1970, no. 620.

77 DUFY, RAOUL 1879–1953
The Sailing-Boat 1907–8
Le Bateau à voile
Pencil and watercolour on paper,
17.1 × 23.3
Signed, bottom right: 'R dufy'
Courtauld Institute Galleries (The Samuel
Courtauld Trust)

In 1905 Dufy – who until this date had had a
modest success with paintings in the
Impressionist idiom indebted mainly to
Boudin – saw Matisse's *Luxe, calme et volupté*
exhibited at the Salon d'Automne. The
profound impact of this revolutionary painting
significantly altered the course of his early
career, and he began to experiment with
compositions in which simplified forms were
indicated by a bolder palette. In November of
that year, he began to exhibit with the Fauves
at Berthe Weill's gallery in Paris.

By 1907, Dufy's style had become
increasingly spare and synthetic, influenced
perhaps by Gauguin, whose paintings he saw in
the retrospective exhibition at the 1906 Salon
d'Automne. In the autumn, the artist visited the
small fishing port of les Martigues, situated at
the mouth of the Eau de Berre, some fifteen
miles west of Marseilles. Of seven identified
paintings of Martigues, six (in the Gumowitz
Collection, New York; sold from the Gaffié
Collection at Sotheby's, London, 26 March
1895 (lot 18a); sold from Bernheim-Jeune at
Christie's, London, 27 June 1978 (lot 46); in the
Hamon Collection, France; in the Cummings
Collection; and exhibited in Bordeaux, 1970)
show the port, with forms of fishing vessels
arranged in tiered perspective and contained at
the top of the canvas by the strong curve of the
harbour wall, above which are summary
indications of buildings. The Cummings
painting incorporates off-centre at the top the
prominent motif of a chimney or tower.

The topography shown in the Courtauld
watercolour confirms that it is a Martigues
scene, and it shares with the works mentioned
above many formal characteristics, now
simplified. The orange-red, green and blue
visible here in the architecture summarise the
colour oppositions of the most intensely
worked harbour views, while the line-and-
block treatment of buildings and landscape
elements corresponds with that seen in the
Bordeaux picture. Closely comparable in its
general disposition and type of imagery with
The Sailing-Boat is the painting *Man Fishing at
Martigues* in the Hamon Collection. That work,
however, shows an uncertainty in both drawing
and placement of the foreground angler, who is
seen in profile to the left. The motif of the
angler, usually with stout, yellow rod, was first

explored by Dufy in paintings made at Sainte-
Adresse in the summer of 1907.

The recapitulatory nature of the Courtauld
watercolour suggests that it be placed towards
the end of the sequence of Martigues subjects,
and it may thus be studio work created in Paris.
As such, it may be dated to the end of 1907, or
at the latest, to the beginning of 1908. In the
early months of this year, Dufy's interests
shifted decisively towards a firm, constructional
manner of representation, already heralded by
the Martigues paintings.

PROVENANCE ?; Samuel Courtauld (price
unknown). Courtauld Gift 1932.

EXHIBITED On loan to the City Art Gallery,
Wakefield, 1946–7; Tate Gallery, 1948 (94);
France 1850–1950, The Art Gallery, Kettering,
1950 (16); *Centenary Exhibition*, The Royal
Scottish Society of Painters in Water-Colours,
Royal Scottish Academy, Edinburgh, 1979–80
(no catalogue).

LITERATURE Home House Catalogue, no. 66;
Cooper, 1954, no. 117.

78 FORAIN, JEAN-LOUIS 1852–1931
Scene at the Court of Assizes *c.*1909
Scène de cour d'assises
Chalk, watercolour and gouache on paper,
37.9 × 51.5
Signed, lower right: 'forain'
Courtauld Institute Galleries (The Samuel
Courtauld Trust)

The dating of Forain's works on paper is
problematical. Few published watercolours are
dated by him, and to assign to these the dates
on oils in which comparable motifs appear is
hazardous: for, adopting drawing methods
derived from Degas which were rooted in
academic practices, Forain habitually reused the
same motif–which was frequently traced and
could thus be reversed, refined and combined
with other images as occasion demanded–in
paintings, watercolours and prints executed
over decades.

By about 1890, Forain had begun to limit his
palette to blacks, browns and white. Some five
years later, he introduced into his work subjects
that were to occupy him for the next twenty-
five years–religious and political themes, and
scenes from domestic life and the lawcourts.
Inspired by Daumier's drawings and lithographs
of lawcourt subjects, such scenes predominate in
Forain's paintings of 1900–10 but continue to
appear in lithographs drawn as late as 1915.

The foreground barrister in the present
watercolour appears in the oil *The Unmarried
Mother*, dated 1909 (City of Bristol Museum
and Art Gallery), in a close variant (National
Gallery of Art, Washington, D.C.), and in a
related painting sold at the Galerie G. Petit,
Paris, 22–4 June 1927 (lot 12). Variants of the
attentive defendant and the standing and seated
barristers are seen in the lithograph *Legal Justice*
dated 1915. The pose of the bored lawyer,
slumped at his desk with head in hand,
indifferent to the events unfolding behind him,
is indebted to that assumed by Edmond
Duranty in Edgar Degas's two portraits of 1879.

PROVENANCE   Arthur Tooth & Sons Ltd,
London, by 1925 (bought from the artist, date
unknown); bought by Courtauld, February
1925 (with Forain, *Painter and Model*) £140.
Courtauld Gift 1932.

EXHIBITED   *Drawings by Forain*, Arthur Tooth
& Sons Ltd, London, 1925 (18); British Institute
of Adult Education, Silver End, Essex, 1935;
Fighting French Exhibition, London, 1943; Tate
Gallery, 1948 (95); Orangerie, Paris, 1955 (77);
Forain, Roland Browse and Delbanco, London,
1964 (29); Japan and Canberra, 1984 (28);
C.I.G., 1988 (19).

LITERATURE   Home House Catalogue, 1935,
no. 71; Cooper, 1954, no. 120.

79 FORAIN, JEAN-LOUIS 1852–1931
Dancer in the Wings *c.*1920–3
Danseuse dans les coulisses
Watercolour on paper, 45.2 × 29
Signed, lower right: 'forain'
Courtauld Institute Galleries (The Samuel
Courtauld Trust)

Forain frequently treated the behind-the-scenes subject of dancer and elderly protector or patron of the ballet from his artistic début in the late 1870s until the later 1890s, and returned to it some twenty years later. The present composition is a reworking of that seen in the watercolour *The Dancer and the Subscribers to the Ballet*, datable to 1890 (Private Collection, Paris), in which, however, the artist employed a subdued, tonal palette, and detached the figures from the background with sharp, continuous pen contours.

Except for the white, all colours of the Courtauld drawing have been stained with a brown cast, from over-exposure to light. The original clarity of the high-key palette – greys and blues contrasted with violet-pinks, orange and rich browns – is visible at the edges of the sheet, which were protected by a passe-partout mount. Paint is freely and fluidly applied to all areas of the composition, either by the point or flat of the brush or by staining, and the forms of figures fuse at intervals with their surroundings. This nuanced and suggestive paint-handling is juxtaposed with selective drawing which varies the type of incisive penwork seen in the 1890 watercolour. A comparable variation of drawing between the composition's parts, and similarly painterly brushwork and vibrant colour, are visible in the watercolours *Dancer in a Tutu*, dated to 1920 (Chagnaud-Forain Collection, Paris), and *In the Wings* of *c.*1923 (Boston Public Library, Mass.); and the present sheet may be ascribed to a similar date in the first half of the 1920s.

PROVENANCE Arthur Tooth & Sons Ltd, London, by 1925 (bought from the artist, date unknown); bought by Courtauld, March 1925, £160. Courtauld Gift 1935.

EXHIBITED *Drawings by Forain*, Arthur Tooth & Sons Ltd, London, 1925 (2); Tate Gallery, 1948 (98); Orangerie, Paris, 1955 (76); Japan and Canberra, 1984 (29); C.I.G., 1988 (19).

80 GOGH, VINCENT VAN 1853–90
A Tile Factory 1888
Une Tuilerie
Pencil, pen and ink on paper, 25.6 × 34.8
Unsigned
Courtauld Institute Galleries (The Samuel
   Courtauld Trust)

A Tile Factory has been assigned to March 1888, on the basis of the date inscribed by van Gogh on a drawing of comparable size, technique and subject matter, the *Path through a Field with Pollarded Willows* (Rijksmuseum Vincent van Gogh, Amsterdam). Two further drawings, *Landscape with Two Trees, Plowman and Houses*, and *Field with Houses under Sky with Sun Disk* (Mellon Collection, Upperville, Va., and Rijksmuseum Vincent van Gogh, Amsterdam, respectively) are related by technique and format to the present composition and may also be similarly dated.

Confirmation that the Courtauld sheet dates from mid- or late March is found in van Gogh's letters to his brother, Theo. At the beginning of the month, the district around Arles was covered by freezing snow, which, by the 10th, had melted. Van Gogh now ventured out of doors, but was prevented from sustained work by the force of the mistral. By the middle of March the almond-trees had begun to blossom, and the artist reported having made three drawings from nature with the aid of a perspective frame.

This portable wooden frame, bisected vertically, horizontally and diagonally by wires, could be pinned at either side, and at the required height, into posts that the artist sank into the ground in front of the motif he had selected to draw. The frame, derived from that illustrated in Dürer's treatise on perspective, was constructed in the summer of 1882 and was a refinement of an earlier device van Gogh had used, probably at Nuenen. An initial ruled pencil drawing of the frame, with free-hand reductions of scale to accord with the format of the sheet, underlies both Courtauld and Amsterdam compositions. In the former, its bisecting vertical lies to the right of the pictorial area's centre, its horizontal aligning with the tops of the palings.

The present image seems to have evolved in two stages. The first – the preliminary drawing – was made from nature with a broad pencil, perhaps one of the carpenter's pencils the artist had favoured since 1882; at this point, major contours may also have been fixed with reed pen and iron-gall ink. The second stage, the selective and decorative drawing of detail with reeds of varying nib thicknesses, was probably executed in the studio. The use of the reed pen indicates debts both to the Rembrandtesque tradition of draughtsmanship and to the

handling of Japanese drawings and woodcuts, a collection of which van Gogh had formed with his brother by 1887. In *A Tile Factory*, directional penstrokes of similar type are organised over the paper's surface in lateral bands: within each band, the strokes diminish in scale as they advance up the sheet, indicating spatial recession. This is reinforced by ink lines radiating from the horizon, which coincide with pencil notations of the perspective frame's diagonal wires. Such ink strokes were probably a late addition, since they in part override the delicate delineation of undulating earth near the road.

Both subject and composition of *A Tile Factory* look back to drawings of the Paris period, such as *Factories at Asnières* (St Louis Art Museum, Miss.) or *Street with People Walking and a Horsecar near the Ramparts* (Rijksmuseum Vincent van Gogh, Amsterdam). Ultimately, these works are indebted to Signac's depictions of factories in the capital's semi-rural environs.

By 1 May 1888, van Gogh had sent to Theo a dozen small pen drawings: among these may have been the Courtauld sheet, whose first recorded owner was Joanna van Gogh-Bonger, the artist's sister-in-law.

PROVENANCE Mevr. J. van Gogh-Bonger, Amsterdam; V.W. van Gogh, Laren; Leicester Galleries, London (Ernest Brown & Phillips) by 1923; bought by Courtauld, December 1926, £178 10s. Courtauld Bequest 1948.

EXHIBITED *Van Gogh*, Stedelijk Museum, Amsterdam, 1905 (408); *Vincent van Gogh Teekeningen uit de verzameling mevr. J. van Gogh-Bonger en V.W. van Gogh*, Stedelijk Museum, Amsterdam, 1914–15 (169); *Vincent van Gogh Teekeningen collectie van mevr. J.van Gogh-Bonger*, Vereiniging Voor de Kunst, Utrecht, and Kunstkring, Rotterdam, 1923 (48); *Vincent van Gogh*, Leicester Galleries, London, 1923 (37); Tate Gallery, 1948 (100); Orangerie, Paris, 1955 (92); Manchester, 1962 (21); Courtauld Centenary, 1976 (80); Arts Council, 1977–9 (77); British Museum, 1983 (108); Japan and Canberra, 1984 (99); C.I.G., 1988 (23).

LITERATURE *Lettres de Vincent van Gogh à Émile Bernard*, ed. A. Vollard, Paris, 1911, pl. LXVIII; de la Faille, 1970, no. 1500; F. Novotny, 'Reflections on a Drawing by Van Gogh', *Art Bulletin*, XXXV, March 1953, pp. 35–43, pl. 1; Cooper, 1954, no. 155; Hulsker, 1980, no. 1373.

81 GUYS, CONSTANTIN 1802–92
Two Women with Muffs *c.*1864
Deux Femmes aux manchons
Pencil, pen and brush with ink and
watercolour on paper, 34.6 × 23.6
Unsigned
Courtauld Institute Galleries (The Samuel
Courtauld Trust)

The few facts known about the life of
Constantin Guys, an obsessively private
personality who, in his early years, had been
drawing-master to the grandchildren of the
British Romantic watercolourist Thomas Girtin,
had been a draughtsman for the *Illustrated
London News*, and had documented the Crimean
War, are summarised in an article of 1956 by A.
M. and P.-A. Lemoisne.

Guys's principal interest was in contemporary
female fashion. During the 1860s, his
independent artistic production increased, and
towards the end of the decade his preoccupation
with 'high-life' fashion began to shift to the
dress favoured by the *demi-monde*. During this
period, he seems to have faithfully recorded
changes of style, although later, he began to
recall the 'low-life' fashions of his early adult
life and depicted them in monochrome wash, or
in small, vigorously scratchy pencil drawings.

The present drawing records two fashionable
ladies from the upper strata of Parisian society.
The type of mid-calf crinolines they wear and
the height of their hairstyle – for hairstyles rose
to become quite high by the end of the 1860s –
indicate a date during the first half of the
decade. A comparable fashion is documented by
Charles Vernier (1831–87) in the engraving
entitled *Charmant! délicieux . . .*, dated 1864, and
a similar date may be assigned to the Courtauld
drawing.

In 1859–60, Charles Baudelaire wrote the
essay *The Painter of Modern Life*, of which
Guys – to whom the poet referred with utmost
discretion – is the hero. Baudelaire's observations
of Guys's technical methods are entirely
consistent with those seen in *Two Women with
Muffs*. Having marked out the images of the
this design in pencil on a sheet prepared with a
ground of dilute carbon black ink wash, the
artist boldly revised the principal contours with
pen and iron-gall ink, applying immediately
thereafter a second grey wash (which has mixed
with, and in certain areas almost effaced, the
brown ink lines) to establish a harmony of
values. Details of dress and tone having been
fixed, a dilute orange-pink flesh tint was
introduced into the composition, and towards
the end of the working process, blue
watercolour was added to the bonnets, and
yellow to mark the fur trimmings of the muffs,
and of the collar, cuffs and hem on the jacket of
the woman at the left. A final restatement of
the face of the woman at the left, and of her
companion's boots, was made with a fine brush
in black ink.

Baudelaire also records that Guys would
complete the preliminary painting campaign of
as many as twenty compositions
simultaneously; from these, at some later date,
he would select certain designs whose lights and
shadows would be intensified. This explains the
frequent repetition or close variation of motifs
in his oeuvre: and indeed, two similarly dressed
women, treated with a comparable
monumentality to those seen in *Two Women
with Muffs*, are visible in the drawings *In the
Street* (Cabinet des Dessins, Louvre) and *The
Conversation* (reproduced in Geffroy, 1926, opp.
p. 108).

PROVENANCE ?; Paul Rosenberg, Paris; bought
by Courtauld, November 1928 (as 'Lorettes',
35,000 francs) £282. Courtauld Gift 1938.

EXHIBITED Orangerie, Paris, 1955 (80); Arts
Council, 1977–9 (22); Japan and Canberra, 1984
(43); C.I.G., 1988 (24).

LITERATURE G. Geffroy, *Constantin Guys*, Paris,
1926, opp. p. 38; Cooper, 1954, no. 126; L.
Jamar-Rolin, 'La Vie de Guys et la Chronologie
de son Oeuvre', *Gazette des Beaux-Arts*, XLVIII,
July–August 1956, p. 97, fig. 23.

82 MANET, ÉDOUARD 1832–83
The Toilette 1860–1
La Toilette
Red chalk on paper, 29 × 20.8
Unsigned
Courtauld Institute Galleries (The Samuel
  Courtauld Trust)

Datable to about 1860–1, this drawing is preparatory to the etching *Woman at her Toilet*, published in 1862. The motif's principal contours are pressed through with a stylus in order to transfer them to the copper plate, which, when printed, produces a reversed image. Manet used the stylus with sufficient pressure to pierce the upper portion of the sheet.

The bather seen here represents the culmination of a series of five drawings of nudes, together with a related incised tracing on mica, heightened with black chalk. These date from the period 1858–60. The earliest, Rembrandtesque ink-and-wash drawings (Boymans-van Beuningen Museum, Rotterdam, and Private Collection, London), reverse the pose of the bathing female seen in the painting *The Nymph Surprised* (a fragment cut from a larger canvas: Museo Nacional de Bellas Artes, Buenos Aires), and in its cognate oil sketch in Oslo (Nasjonalgalleriet). A red-chalk drawing, corrected and squared up in pencil, in which the nude is seen with arms raised (Bibliothèque Nationale, Paris), may relate to a lost or abandoned intermediate composition. In that drawing, Manet transforms the earlier poses which convey alarm – probably derived from a Bathsheba etched by J. Corneille le Jeune after Giulio Romano – into one indicating composure, echoing those of the tranquil nudes in paintings by Titian and the Venetian masters. The red-chalk study in Chicago (Art Institute), from which the Louvre's tracing on mica was taken, is the first in which the bather, now with Titianesque maid and a second, partly effaced figure, is located in an interior.

Manet's spare line and zones of diagonally hatched, uniform shadow, which map out the form of the Courtauld nude's head, torso and thighs, owe much to the crisp, abbreviated draughtsmanship of Thomas Couture (1815–79), in whose atelier the young artist had studied during 1850–6. Of the group of bather subjects, the present study is drawn with the most reductive of contours, which share with the traced lines on the mica sheet comparable hermetic properties. And in *The Toilette*, the bather's equally unrevised form, together with the silhouetting of her right hand (similarly rendered as a blank form in the first state of the etching), also suggest the recapitulation of a well-rehearsed image. Indeed, vestiges of faint, uninflected contours of a decidedly orange-hued red chalk, visible in the hair at the top and left of the head and over the right shoulder, in the right hand, in the left shoulder, elbow and fore-arm, and above the left knee, signal the possible presence of a tracing or counterproof underlying the figure.

In contrast to the laconic draughtsmanship that describes the bather, the rapid lines indicating the maid are both loose and exploratory. Manet's search to establish the exact scale, placing and pose of this figure (which finally combines the pose of the two servants in the Chicago study) is seen in the many faint indications of the head at the extreme left of the sheet. A similarly free drawing suggests possible positions for the basin at the bather's feet.

The sparse indications of background visible in the Courtauld drawing are, in the 1862 etching, worked up into an elaborate interior scene. This, together with the handling of the present bather, reinforces the suggestion that Manet was working from a more complete image. A recent writer has noted that almost all Manet's early etchings were copies after his own paintings, and that the etching made from *The Toilette*, published under the title *La Toilette*, may reproduce a painted study of the same title, recorded by Manet's friend, Antonin Proust. This picture is unknown today, and may have been destroyed or overpainted. The framing lines that in this drawing run through the bather's knees and image of the maid are late additions and may indicate Manet's experiment to discover a more satisfying format for either the painted or etched image.

PROVENANCE Marcel Guiot, Paris; Leicester Galleries, London (Ernest Brown & Phillips); bought by Courtauld, August 1928, £225 (with etching *La Toilette*). Courtauld Bequest 1948.

EXHIBITED *French Art*, Royal Academy, London, 1932 (999); Tate Gallery, 1948 (112); *De Fouquet à Cezanne*, Brussels, Boymans-van Beuningen Museum, Rotterdam, and Orangerie, Paris, 1949–50 (183); *Manet and his Circle*, Tate Gallery, London, 1954 (18); Orangerie, Paris, 1955 (83); Nottingham University, 1969 (no catalogue); *The Nude*, Morley Gallery, London, 1975 (51); *Manet: L'Oeuvre gravé*, Ingelheim-am-Rhein, 1977 (Z.7); Arts Council, 1977–9 (34); *Manet: dessins aquarelles, eaux-fortes, lithographies, correspondance*, Galerie Huguette Berès, Paris, 1978 (4); British Museum, 1983 (109); Japan and Canberra, 1984 (51); *The Hidden Face of Manet*, Courtauld Institute Galleries, 1986 (13); *Impressionist Drawings*, Ashmolean Museum, Oxford, Manchester City Art Gallery, The Burrell Collection, Glasgow, 1986 (34); C.I.G., 1988 (26).

LITERATURE J. Meier-Graefe, *Edouard Manet*, Munich, 1912, fig. 19; Vasari Society, 2nd Series, 1930, no. XI, p. 15, pl. 15; M. Guérin, *L'Oeuvre gravé de Manet*, Paris, 1944, p. 26; R. Huyghe, *Le Dessin français au XIXe Siècle*, Lausanne, 1948, pl. 87; Cooper, 1954, no. 140; J. Mathey, *Graphisme de Manet*, I, Paris, 1961, no. 53; A. Mongan, *Great Drawings of All Time*, New York, 1962, no. 107; M. Sérullaz, *Drawings by the French Masters: French Impressionists*, 1963, pp. 21, 69; A. de Leiris, *The Drawings of Edouard Manet*, Berkeley and Los Angeles, 1969, no. 185; J. Leymarie, *Impressionist Drawings from Manet to Renoir*, Geneva, 1969, pp. 30, 31; J. C. Harris, *Edouard Manet, Graphic Works: A Definitive Catologue Raisonné*, New York, 1970, fig. 50, no. 78; J. Wilson Bareau, 'The Hidden Face of Manet', *Burlington Magazine*, CXXVIII, April 1986, p. 34, no. 38.

83 SEURAT, GEORGES 1859–1891
Nude 1881–2
Nu
Pencil and Conté crayon on paper,
   63.2 × 48.2
Unsigned
Courtauld Institute Galleries (The Samuel
   Courtauld Trust)

The authorship of this drawing, doubted by certain critics when it entered the Courtauld Institute, was upheld by Robert L. Herbert in his pioneering study of Seurat's draughtsmanship, published in 1965. The sheet unmistakably displays Seurat's handling, while the inscription on the verso by the artist's friend and champion, the critic Félix Fénéon (1861–1944), and its inclusion in exhibitions organised by Fénéon in 1920 and 1926 provide additional support for its authenticity. Indeed, by 1926, the drawing may have been in Fénéon's possession.

A line study of the female nude (location unknown) which establishes the model's pose shown here, was dated by Herbert to 1879, and a similar date was tentatively ascribed to the Courtauld drawing. The early dating connects these works to the preliminary and finished studies of full-length nudes (*académies*) which Seurat drew from life as a student at the École des Beaux-Arts from about 1875 to 1878. The present drawing, however, shows the webs of curving crayon lines, the massing of shadows from networks of rectilinear strokes, and the subtle gradations of tone indicating diminishing light at the extremities of forms – visible particularly over the legs – which are characteristics of Seurat's independent draughtsmanship of about 1881–2. And it is to this later date, at the culmination of some three years' of rigorous, logical development of Seurat's drawing methods, that the Courtauld sheet should be assigned.

Despite the idealising treatment of the nude here – and comparison with the preliminary sketch reveals that Seurat has eliminated some of the hair, repositioned the limbs and adjusted contours to create a continuously curving form in which the line of breast, arms and right leg echo each other – the model is readily identifiable as that in the line study. Since that sketch doubtless immediately preceded the Courtauld drawing, it, too, should be redated to 1881–2.

This drawing poses problems of interpretation when placed among other studies of Seurat's early maturity, since its subject and handling initially appear to relate to different moments in his career. It seems, however, that the artist returned to the subject of the nude as a touchstone against which to test the capabilities of his newly established personal draughtsmanship; and in both rivalling, and

referring to, the subject and practices familiar from the Beaux-Arts, he presented a critique of his earlier *académies*. The size of this sheet approximates to that used for the Beaux-Arts nudes (which is, on average, 63.5 × 48.5 cm., and larger than those used early in Seurat's independent career), yet the present subject, the nude female, was rarely treated by Beaux-Arts students. Moreover, it is possible that Seurat lit the model by lamplight, an unacademic practice that both he, and his friend Ernest Laurent (1859–1929) employed in the early 1880s. The standard academic drawing implement of stump impregnated with graphite, used in the *académies* to create sharply defined shadows of even tone across pallid figures, is here employed at the left of the model to evoke the tender luminosity of flesh in half light. Its silvery tone becomes a colouristic adjunct to the richly chromatic Conté crayon, while its leanness and evenness of application contrast with Seurat's idiosyncratic handling of variably accented lines of fatty chalk.

The interpretation of this study as both extension and critique of academic life-drawing should not obscure Seurat's dependence upon his contemporaries for this work. In particular, it is to the lithographs of Henri Fantin-Latour (1836–1904), an artist at the height of his popularity in the late 1870s, that the sensuous, intense physicality of the model's form and its mysterious emergence from shadow are indebted in this unique drawing.

PROVENANCE Collection 'X' (?Mme Seurat *mère*; Félix Fénéon); Percy Moore Turner; bought by Courtauld, July 1928, £750. Courtauld Bequest 1948.

EXHIBITED *Georges Seurat*, Galerie Bernheim-Jeune, Paris, 1920 (40); *Les Dessins de Georges Seurat*, Galerie Bernheim-Jeune, Paris, 1926 (78); *The Nude*, Morley Gallery, London, 1975 (76); Courtauld Centenary, 1976 (78); Arts Council, 1977–9 (62); *Drawing Technique and Purpose*, Victoria & Albert Museum, London, 1981 (100); Japan and Canberra, 1984 (86); *Impressionist Drawings*, Ashmolean Museum, Oxford, Manchester City Art Gallery, The Burrell Collection, Glasgow, 1986 (73); C.I.G., 1988 (32).

LITERATURE G. Kahn, *Les Dessins de Seurat*, 2 vols, Paris, 1928, pl. 62; R. L. Herbert, *Seurat's Drawings*, New York, 1962, pp. 25, 26, no. 23; R. Thomson, *Seurat*, Oxford, 1985, p. 27, pl. 20; W. Bradford, in *100 Masterpieces from the Courtauld*, ed. D. Farr, London, 1987, p. 208.

84 SIGNAC, PAUL 1863–1935
  Still Life with Watermelon 1918
  Nature morte avec pastèque
  Pencil and watercolour on paper, 34.4 × 39
  Signed, bottom left: 'P. Signac 1918'
  Courtauld Institute Galleries (The Samuel
    Courtauld Trust)

Still-life subjects are few in Signac's work when
compared with land- or seascapes. The present
example, dated 1918, was probably painted at
Antibes, where the artist had lived since 1913.
At the right of the sheet, a watermelon and its
segment are arranged on a shallow circular dish
with curved handle; at the left, a carafe echoes
and counters the arcs of dish and fruit. Oblong
strokes of colour follow the contours of
watermelon, dish, carafe's spout and raffia
container, while dashes and rectangles aligned
with the composition's upper left edge suggest
the plane of a background wall. The table-top
in the foreground is described by concentrations
of thin diagonals, clearly influenced by
Cézanne's constructive brushstroke, while the
blue outline below the melon and above its
segment indicates a debt to the blue space-
creating contours also visible in this artist's later
paintings. Signac's brushwork here,
characterised by simplified borrowings used in
conjunction with a variety of other less
systematic strokes, suggests something of the
eclecticism of Matisse's early handling of paint.
Indeed, Signac had a brief and uneasy friendship
with the younger artist during the summer of
1904.

The brushwork is complemented by
decorative colour, in which the Neo-
Impressionist system of pairing opposed hues is
relaxed. Other than the dominant red/green
contrast of the melon (which may initially have
dictated the artist's choice of this motif) and
touches of orange-ochre relieving the violet-
blue of the table, Signac's palette describes
intensified but accidental juxtapositions of local
colour.

An almost identical composition, but placed
higher on the sheet, and tentatively painted
over laborious pencil drawing, is in the Preston
Harrison Collection, U.S.A.; this work
probably predates the Courtauld version. Both
watercolours form the basis of the oil *Still Life
with Watermelon* (Private Collection, France), a
work that has recently been assigned to 1914,
but whose close relationship with a further
drawing, *Still Life with a Jug*, dated 1919, in
New York (Metropolitan Museum of Art),
confirms a similarly later dating.

Signac continued to use the motifs of flat
dish, carafe and watermelon, in combination
with other brightly coloured fruits and
vegetables, in a group of drawings and
watercolours that explore increasingly complex

and intricate compositions. These culminate in
the ambitious watercolour dated 14 July 1926 in
the Butler Collection, New York.

PROVENANCE Percy Moore Turner, by 1920;
bought by Courtauld, December 1924, £26 5s.
Courtauld Gift 1932.

EXHIBITED *Modern French Paintings and
Drawings*, Independent Gallery, London, 1920
(84); on loan to City Art Gallery, Wakefield,
1946–7; Tate Gallery, 1948 (120); *France 1850–
1950*, The Art Gallery, Kettering, 1950 (84);
Orangerie, Paris, 1955 (90); Nottingham
University, 1969 (no catalogue); *Centenary
Exhibition*, The Royal Scottish Society of
Painters in Water-Colours, Royal Scottish
Academy, Edinburgh, 1979–80 (no catalogue);
Japan and Canberra, 1984 (88); C.I.G., 1988
(33).

LITERATURE Home House Catalogue, 1935,
no. 69; Cooper, 1954, no. 152.

P. Segnac 1918

85 TOULOUSE-LAUTREC, HENRI DE 1864–1901
In Bed c.1896
Au lit
Pencil and chalk on paper, 30.3 × 48
Signed, lower left: 'H T-Lautrec' (the
 initials in monogram)
Courtauld Institute Galleries (The Samuel
 Courtauld Trust)

The model for this drawing is the prostitute Pauline Baron, known as Mlle Popo, whose mother managed a luxurious brothel at 26 rue des Moulins, in which Toulouse-Lautrec lodged intermittently during 1895 and 1896. Mlle Popo is also the focus of attention in four plates of the suite of ten colour lithographs of brothel subjects entitled *Elles*, published by Gustave Pellet in April 1896. She is seen again in the thematically related print, *Reclining Woman – Laziness*, of the same period.

In Bed cannot be included among the twelve designs catalogued by Dortu for figures or entire compositions preparatory to *Elles*, yet its subject and handling connect with certain plates of the series. It shares with these a mood of mundane domesticity observed with sly wit, but also with a sympathy bordering on tenderness which is not normally present in Lautrec's work. Without a more precise date for the drawing, its relationship with the lithographs remains speculative: it may have been an exploratory study executed before the compositions for *Elles* were fully realised, but may equally be a recapitulatory work.

The form of Mlle Popo is positioned diagonally across the paper. She lies on a double bed beneath a carelessly arranged cover which slides to the floor at the left and exposes her (stockinged?) calves and feet. The head is subtly and precisely modelled with short diagonal strokes of a sharp pencil, which indicate shadows around the eyes, cheekbones, nose and lips. A touch of dilute carbon ink or watercolour wash suggests the luminous mid-tone of flesh to the left of the nose. The waves of hair are rendered with appropriately freer, cursive strokes, which run into, and are echoed by, the more coarsely drawn folds of the bedclothes. These fan out in a series of 'S' curves forming a triangular configuration which both stabilises and draws attention to the head. The head's position on the page is ultimately secured by the sinuous creases in the cover, which descend from the corner of Mlle Popo's mouth to the bottom of the composition. Towards the centre of the sheet, the drapery's folds become larger, and are drawn with dislocated and frequently revised strokes. Lightly indicated lines in this area imply the form of the model's crossed legs beneath the cover, but otherwise the artist's concern here is to establish the plunging perspective of the bedclothes' silhouette.

Counterbalancing the tonal weight of the head, and contrasting with its minutely accurate draughtsmanship, are the legs and feet which thrust dramatically from under the cover. The approximate location of the heels is hurriedly noted at the extreme right of the sheet, while legs and feet are continually redefined by rapid, sweeping contours. The size of the feet (approximately two and a half times that of the head), allied to their handling with loose, open contours, suggests the exaggerated prominence of blurred foreground forms visible in early photographs. Such perspectival distortions were by the 1890s accepted as part of the formal language of many French avant-garde artists; and Lautrec's interest in, and use of photography, was second only to that of Edgar Degas. Indeed, an undated photograph of Lautrec reclining in a garden chair on his mother's estate at Malromé includes the unfocused image of the magnified soles of the artist's boots, the form of which is closely comparable with that of Mlle Popo's feet in this drawing.

PROVENANCE Gustave Pellet (?bought direct from the artist); (?)Claude Sayle; Leicester Galleries, London (Ernest Brown & Phillips); bought by Courtauld, February 1922 (price unknown). Courtauld Bequest 1948.

EXHIBITED *French Art*, Royal Academy, London, 1932 (976); Tate Gallery, 1948 (121); *De Fouquet à Cézanne*, Brussels, Boymans-van Beuningen Museum, Rotterdam, and Orangerie, Paris, 1949–50 (215); *French Drawings*, Arts Council, 1952 (156); Orangerie, Paris, 1955 (91); *Documenta III*, Kassel, 1964 (part II: *Handzeichnungen Toulouse-Lautrecs*, 1); *Henri de Toulouse-Lautrec 1864–1901*, Österreichisches Museum für Angewandte Kunst, Vienna, 1966 (56); *Toulouse-Lautrec*, Nationalmuseum, Stockholm, 1967–8 (109A); *Henri de Toulouse-Lautrec*, Ingelheim-am-Rhein, 1968 (24); Nottingham University, 1969 (no cat.); *Henri de Toulouse-Lautrec*, Musée d'Ixelles, Brussels, 1973 (37); Courtauld Centenary, 1976 (79); Arts Council, 1977–9 (69); British Museum, 1983 (112); Japan and Canberra, 1984 (93); C.I.G., 1988 (33); *Toulouse-Lautrec*, Hayward Gallery, London, 1992 (148).

LITERATURE R. Huyghe *Le Dessin français au XIXe Siècle*, Lausanne, 1948, pl. 134; G. Reynolds, *19th Century Drawings, 1850–1900*, London, 1949, pl. 31; J. Boudrot-Saupique, 'De Fouquet à Cézanne: les Maîtres du dessin français', *Art et Style*, no. 14, 1950, unpaginated but p. 48; E. Julien, *Lautrec: Dessins*, Paris, 1951, pl. 13; *Illustrated London News*, Christmas 1953, pl. 13; Cooper, 1954, no. 154; Anon., *Toulouse-Lautrec*, Génie et Realités Séries, Paris, 1962, p. 138; Dortu, 1971, VI, D4.264.

The following is a checklist of the other modern French drawings from Samuel Courtauld's collection. All are now in the Courtauld Institute Galleries.

86 BLANCHARD, MARIA 1881–1932
Girl at an Open Window c.1924
Jeune fille à la fenêtre ouverte
Pastel on paper, 91.7 × 65.5
Signed, bottom left: 'M. BLANCHARD'

87 DERAIN, ANDRÉ 1880–1954
Head of a Woman c.1922
Tête de femme
Pencil and pastel on paper, 59 × 45.5
Signed, lower right: 'a derain'

88 DUFY, RAOUL 1879–1953
Nude with a Shell c.1927
Nu au coquillage
Watercolour on paper, 55.3 × 70.9
Signed, lower right: 'Raoul Dufy'

89 FORAIN, JEAN-LOUIS 1852–1931
On Stage c.1920?
En scène
Pencil and watercolour on paper,
    53.2 × 37.1
Signed, lower right: 'forain'

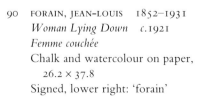

90 FORAIN, JEAN-LOUIS 1852–1931
Woman Lying Down c.1921
Femme couchée
Chalk and watercolour on paper,
    26.2 × 37.8
Signed, lower right: 'forain'

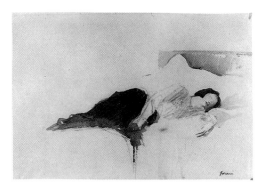

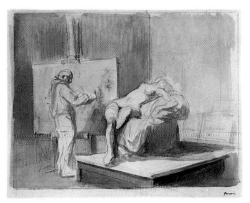

91 FORAIN, JEAN-LOUIS 1852–1931
Painter and Model c.1923
Peintre et modèle
Pencil, watercolour and bodycolour on
    paper, 40.5 × 55.8
Signed, lower left: 'forain'

92 GUYS, CONSTANTIN 1802–92
Two Grisettes and Two Soldiers c.1855
Deux grisettes et deux soldats
Pen and ink, and watercolour on paper,
    24.9 × 32.5
Unsigned

93 GUYS, CONSTANTIN 1802–92
A Woman of Easy Virtue (formerly
    entitled A Woman of
    Fashion) c.1867–70
Une Lorette (formerly entitled Une
    Élégante)
Ink wash on paper, 33.8 × 22.8
Unsigned

93

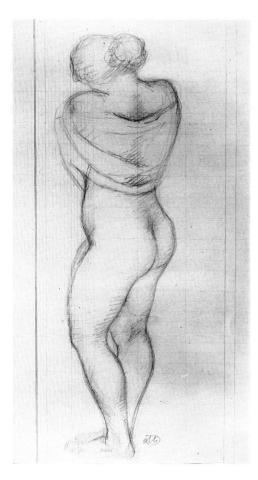

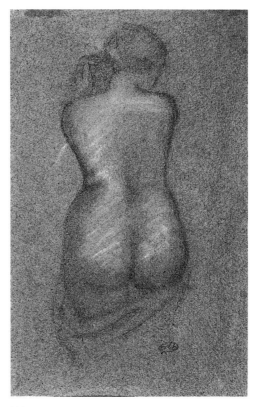

100

102 MARCHAND, JEAN HIPPOLYTE 1883–1941
Standing Woman c.1924
Femme debout
Chalk on paper, 55.7 × 40
Signed, lower right: 'J H Marchand' (the
initials in monogram)

99 MAILLOL, ARISTIDE 1861–1944
Woman Undressing c.1920
Femme se déshabillant
Pencil on mechanically squared paper,
34.9 × 22.1
Signed, lower right of centre: 'M'
(encircled)

100 MAILLOL, ARISTIDE 1861–1944
Nude Seen from the Back c.1922
Nu, vue de dos
Pencil on paper, 34 × 23
Signed, lower right: 'M' (encircled)

101 MAILLOL, ARISTIDE 1861–1944
Kneeling Nude c.1924
Nu agenouillé
Pencil on paper, 30.5 × 21.6
Signed, lower left: 'M'.

103 MATISSE, HENRI 1869–1954
Seated Woman 1919
Femme assise
Pencil on paper, 35.1 × 25.2
Signed, top right: 'Henri–Matisse'

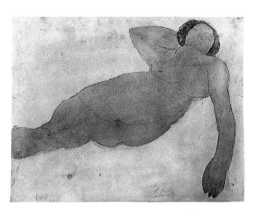

108   RODIN, AUGUSTE   1840–1917, forgery
          after
       Study of a Female Nude   (?)*c.*1896
       Étude de femme nue
       pencil and watercolour on paper
       27.5 × 36.3
       Inscribed lower right: '<u>A Rodin</u>'

104   MATISSE, HENRI   1869–1954
       Woman Leaning with Elbows on a
          Table   1923
       Femme accoudée sur une table
       Chalk and stump on paper, 40.7 × 25.8
       Signed, lower right: 'Henri–Matisse'

106   PICASSO, PABLO   1881–1973
       Seated Woman   1923
       Femme assise © DACS 1994
       Pen and ink on paper, 35 × 26.1
       Signed, bottom right: '<u>Picasso</u>'

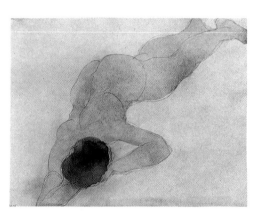

107   RODIN, AUGUSTE   1840–1917, forgery
          after
       Study of a Female Nude   (?)*c.*1896
       Étude de femme nue
       Pencil and watercolour on paper,
          24.5 × 32
       Uninscribed

109   RODIN, AUGUSTE   1840–1917, forgery
          after
       Seated Female Nude   after 1900
       Femme nue assise
       Pencil on paper, 34 × 27.4
       Inscribed lower right: 'Aug <u>Rodin</u>'

105   MOREAU, LUC–ALBERT   1882–1948
       Head of a Woman   1921
       Tête de femme
       Pencil on paper, 33.9 × 26.5
       Signed, lower right: 'luc–albert
          moreau–921'

110   SEGONZAC, ANDRÉ DUNOYER DE
         1884–1974
Landscape with a Bridge   *c.*1924
Paysage avec un pont
Pen and ink and watercolour on paper,
    63 × 48.1
Signed, lower left: 'A. Dunoyer de
    Segonzac'

111   TCHELITCHEW, PAVEL   1898–1957
Nude Boy   *c.*1927
Garçon nu
Pencil and watercolour on paper,
    50.2 × 32.5
Signed, upper right: 'P. Tchelitchew'

CHECKLIST OF PRINTS

The following prints were formerly in Samuel
Courtauld's collection and are now in the
Courtauld Institute Galleries. Dimensions are of
platemarks, unless otherwise stated.

112   CÉZANNE, PAUL   1839–1906
Self-Portrait   *c.*1898
Portrait de Cézanne
Transfer lithograph, 35.5 × 26.4

113   FORAIN, JEAN-LOUIS   1852–1931
End of the Hearing   *c.*1910
Sortie de l'Audience
Etching, 33.8 × 29.1
Signed below the plate, right: 'forain'

114   GAUGUIN, PAUL   1848–1903
Album of ten woodcuts   1893–4, 1899
Printed by Pola Gauguin, Copenhagen,
1921

   1   *Te Po*
        Woodcut and wood engraving,
            20.4 × 35.9
        Signed on the block, upper left:
            'PGo'

   2   *Noa Noa*
        Woodcut and wood engraving,
            35.6 × 20.6
        Signed on the block, upper centre:
            'PGo'

   3   *Manao Tupapau*
        Woodcut with white-line engraving,
            20.4 × 35.6
        Signed on the block, lower left:
            'PGo'

   4   *Maruru*
        Woodcut with white-line engraving,
            20.5 × 35.6
        Signed on the block, bottom right:
            'PGo'

   5   *The Universe is Created*
        L'Univers est crée
        Woodcut with white-line engraving,
            20.4 × 35.4
        Signed on the block, lower right:
            'PGo'

   6   *Nave Nave Fenua*
        Woodcut with white-line engraving,
            33.4 × 20.4
        Signed on the block, lower left:
            'P/G/o'

   7   *Mahna no Varua ino*
        Woodcut with white-line engraving,
            20.2 × 35.4
        Signed on the block, lower left:
            'PGo'

   8   *Auti te Pape*
        Woodcut with white-line engraving,
            20.5 × 35.5
        Signed on the block, bottom left of
            centre: 'PGo'

   9   *Mahana Atua*
        Woodcut with white-line engraving,
            18.2 × 20.3
        Signed on the block, lower left:
            'PGo'

  10   Title for *Le Sourire*, November 1899
        Woodcut with white-line engraving,
            10.1 × 18.3
        Signed on the block, lower left: 'P
            Gauguin'

115   MAILLOL, ARISTIDE   1861–1944
Seated Woman   *c.*1925
Femme assise de profil
Etching, 22.6 × 24
Signed below the plate, right:
    'M'(encircled)

116   MAILLOL, ARISTIDE   1861–1944
Kneeling Nude   *c.*1925
Nu agenouillé
Etching, 21.2 × 27.2
Signed below the plate, right:
    'M' (encircled)

117   MAILLOL, ARISTIDE   1861–1944
Crouching Woman   *c.*1925
Femme accroupie
Etching, 23.8 × 16.8
Signed below the plate, right:
    'M' (encircled)

118   MAILLOL, ARISTIDE   1861–1944
Woman from the Back   *c.*1920
Femme de dos
Transfer lithograph, 28.4 × 18.6
Signed below the stone, right:
    'M' (encircled)

119   MAILLOL, ARISTIDE   1861–1944
Nude Woman with Raised Arm   *c.*1920
Femme nue, bras levé
Transfer lithograph, 31 × 15.8
Signed below the stone, right:
    'M'(encircled)

120   MANET, ÉDOUARD   1832–83
The Toilette   1862
La Toilette
Etching, 28.6 × 22.3
Signed on the plate, bottom right: 'M'

121 MANET, ÉDOUARD 1832–83
Album of thirty etchings
Receuil de trente eaux-fortes
Trial proofs printed by Dumont, Paris,
1894; numbered, mounted and encased
by Strölin and published with his
edition, Paris, 1905

1 *Hat and Guitar.* Frontispiece for an
album of etchings 1862–74
Chapeau et guitare. Frontispice pour
un cahier d'eaux-fortes
23.1 × 21.9
Unsigned

2 *Spanish singer* 1861–2
Le Chanteur espagnol
30.1 × 24.7
Signed on the plate, upper right:
'éd. Manet'

3 *The Urchin* 1862
Le Gamin
20.8 × 14.8
Signed on the plate, upper left:
'éd. Manet'

4 *The Gypsies* c.1862
Les Gitanes
31.6 × 23.7
Signed on the plate, bottom right:
'éd. Manet'

5 *Lola de Valence* 1862
26.6 × 18.5
Signed on the plate, lower left:
'éd. Manet'

6 *The Little Girl* 1861–2
La Petite Fille
20.9 × 11.8
Signed on the plate, upper left:
'éd. Manet'

7 *The Toilette* 1862
La Toilette
28.6 × 22.3
Signed on the plate, bottom right:
'M'

8 *The Dead Toreador* c.1868
Le Torero mort
15.6 × 22.4
Signed on the plate, bottom left:
'Manet'

9 *The Little Cavaliers* 1862–7
Les Petits Cavaliers
25 × 39
Unsigned

10 *Silentium* 1860
21 × 15.8
Signed on plate, lower left: 'M'

11 *The Dancer (Mariano
Camprubi)* 1862
Le Baïlarin (Mariano Camprubi)
30.2 × 20
Signed on the plate, lower left:
'Manet'

12 *The Water-Drinker or the
Drink* (?)1865–6
Le Buveur d'eau ou la régalade
23.9 × 16
Signed on the plate, lower left:
'Manet'

13 *Boy and Dog* 1861
Le Garçon et le chien
20.3 × 14.2
Unsigned

14 *The Smoker* (II) 1866 or 1867
Le Fumeur (II)
17.6 × 15.9
Signed on the plate, upper left:
'Manet'

15 *The Smoker* (I) 1866
Le Fumeur (I)
24 × 15.5
Unsigned

16 *The Infanta Margarita (after
Velázquez)* (?)1862
*L'Infante Marguerite (d'après
Velasquez)*
23 × 19
Unsigned

17 *Seascape* 1866
Marine
14.2 × 20.2
Unsigned

18 *Théodore de Banville, Turned to the
Left* 1874
Théodore de Banville, tourné à gauche
24 × 16
Unsigned

19 *The Philosopher* 1865–6
Le Philosophe
32 × 23.9
Unsigned

20 *Baudelaire in Profile, in a
Top-hat* (I) 1862–9
Baudelaire de profil, en chapeau (I)
13 × 7.4
Signed on the plate, upper left: 'E M'
(in monogram)

21 *Edgar Poe* 1860
19.3 × 15.2
Unsigned

22 *Olympia (Large Plate)* 1867
Olympia (grande planche)
13.1 × 18.3
Unsigned

23 *Olympia (Small Plate)* 1865
Olympia (petite planche)
8.8 × 17.7
Unsigned

24 *Child with Soap Bubbles* 1867–8
L'Enfant aux bulles de savon
25.4 × 21.5
Unsigned

25 *The Tragic Actor–Rouvière in the Role
of Hamlet* 1865–6
*L'Acteur tragique–Rouvière dans le rôle
d'Hamlet*
36.8 × 22
Unsigned

26 *Berthe Morisot* 1872
11.9 × 7.9
Unsigned

27 *Eva Gonzalès–Profile Turned to the
Left* 1870
Eva Gonzalès–profil tourné à gauche
24.2 × 16.2
Unsigned

28 *The Cats* 1868–9
Les Chats
18 × 22.3
Unsigned

29 *The Queue in Front of the Butchers
Shop* 1870–1
La Queue devant la boucherie
23.9 × 16
Unsigned

30 *Jeanne–Spring* 1882
Jeanne–Le Printemps
24.9 × 18.4
Signed on the plate, lower left:
'Manet'

122 MATISSE, HENRI 1869–1954
Nude Squatting in an Armchair 1906
Nu accroupi dans un fauteuil
Transfer lithograph, sheet: 44.5 × 27.7
Signed on the stone, lower right: 'H M'
(in monogram)

123 MATISSE, HENRI 1869–1954
Standing Figure 1913
Figure debout
Transfer lithograph, sheet: 50.3 × 33
Signed on the stone, bottom left: 'H M'

124   MATISSE, HENRI   1869–1954
The Day   1922
Le Jour
Transfer lithograph, 25.8 × 40.9
Signed lower left: 'Henri-Matisse 43/50',
    and on the stone, lower right: 'H M'

125   MATISSE, HENRI   1869–1954
Figure and Vase of Flowers, Palm-Tree in
    Background   1923
Figure et vase de fleurs, palmier au fond
Lithograph, sheet: 43.7 × 28.3
Signed below the pictorial area, right:
    'Henri–Matisse'

126   MATISSE, HENRI   1869–1954
Seated Nude with Tulle Blouse   1925
Nu assis, chemise de tulle
Lithograph, 40.3 × 31.3
Signed lower right: 'Henri–Matisse 33/50'

127   MATISSE, HENRI   1869–1954
Reclining Nude with Bowl of Fruit   1926
Nu allongé à la coupe de fruits
Transfer lithograph, 43.5 × 54
Signed lower left: '47/50 Henri–Matisse'

128   PICASSO, PABLO   1881–1973
The Nude Model   1927
Le Modèle nu
Etching, 27.9 × 19.3
Signed below the plate, left: '37/40
    Picasso'

129   TOULOUSE-LAUTREC, HENRI DE   1864–1901
Yvette Guilbert   1893
Lithograph, 25.3 × 22.3
Signed on the stone, lower right: 'H T-L'
    (in monogram, encircled)

130   TOULOUSE-LAUTREC, HENRI DE   1864–1901
Mademoiselle Lender and Baron   1893
Mademoiselle Lender et Baron
Lithograph, 32 × 23.5
Signed twice on the stone, lower left:
    'H T-L' (in monogram, encircled)

131   TOULOUSE-LAUTREC, HENRI DE   1864–1901
At the Renaissance: Sarah Bernhardt in
    Phèdre   1893
A la Renaissance: Sarah Bernhardt dans
    Phèdre
Lithograph, 35.5 × 23.5
Signed on the stone, lower left: 'H T-L'
    (in monogram, encircled)

132   TOULOUSE-LAUTREC, HENRI DE   1864–1901
Adolphe– The Sad Young Man   1894
Adolphe– le jeune homme triste
Lithograph, 26 × 18.3
Signed on the stone, lower right: 'H T-L'
    (in monogram, encircled)

133   TOULOUSE-LAUTREC, HENRI DE   1864–1901
Miss Ida Heath, English Dancer   1894
Miss Ida Heath, danseuse anglaise
Lithograph, 36 × 26.3
Signed on the stone, upper left: 'H T-L'
    (in monogram, encircled)

134   TOULOUSE-LAUTREC, HENRI DE   1864–1901
Bust of Mademoiselle Marcelle Lender   1895
Mademoiselle Marcelle Lender, en buste
Lithograph (colour), 32.9 × 24.4
Signed on the stone, lower left: 'H T-L'
    (in monogram, encircled)

135   TOULOUSE-LAUTREC, HENRI DE   1864–1901
Lender from the Front, in Chilpéric   1895
Lender de face, dans Chilpéric
Lithograph, 37.2 × 26.5
Signed on the stone, lower left: 'H T-L'
    (in monogram, encircled)

136   TOULOUSE-LAUTREC, HENRI DE   1864–1901
Leaving the Theatre   1896
Sortie de théâtre
Lithograph, 32 × 26.5
Signed on the stone, lower right: 'H T-L'
    (in monogram, encircled)

137   TOULOUSE-LAUTREC, HENRI DE   1864–1901
Sleeping Woman– Awakening   1896
Femme couchée– réveil
Lithograph, 40.5 × 52.5
Signed on the stone, lower right: 'H T-L'
    (in monogram, encircled)

138   TOULOUSE-LAUTREC, HENRI DE   1864–1901
Yvette Guilbert– English Series   1898
Yvette Guilbert– série anglaise
Drawn by H. de Toulouse-Lautrec;
    described by Arthur Byl, translated
    into English by Alexander Te[i]xeira de
    Mattos
An album of nine lithographs with
    lithographic cover, published by Bliss,
    Sands & Co., London, 1898

    1   Cover: *Yvette Guilbert*
       Sheet: 55.5 × 38.2
       Signed on the stone by Yvette
         Guilbert, lower right

    2   Frontispiece for *Yvette Guilbert*
       Frontispice pour *Yvette Guilbert*
       Sheet: 55.5 × 38.2
       Signed on the stone, lower right:
         'H T-Lautrec' (the initials in
         monogram, encircled), and by
         Yvette Guilbert, upper left

    3   *On Stage*
       Sur la scène
       29.8 × 24.2
       Signed on the stone, upper left:
         'H T-L' (in monogram, encircled)

    4   *In the Trap*
       Dans la glu
       29.3 × 24.1
       Signed on the stone, upper left:
         'H T-L' (in monogram, encircled)

    5   *Pessima*
       27.7 × 23.8
       Signed on the stone, lower left:
         'H T-L' (in monogram, encircled)

    6   *To Ménilmontant, from Bruant*
       A Ménilmontant, de Bruant
       29.4 × 24
       Signed on the stone, upper left:
         'H T-L' (in monogram, encircled)

    7   *Old Song*
       Chanson ancienne
       29.3 × 24.3
       Signed on the stone, lower right:
         'H T-L' (in monogram, encircled)

    8   *Drunkard*
       Soularde
       28.9 × 21
       Signed on the stone, upper right:
         'H T-L' (in monogram, encircled)

    9   '*Linger, Longer, Loo*'
       29.7 × 24.2
       Signed on the stone, lower right:
         'H T-L' (in monogram, encircled)

    10   *Taking a Curtain Call*
       Saluant le public
       29.7 × 24.2
       Signed on the stone, lower right:
         'H T-L' (in monogram, encircled)

139   TOULOUSE-LAUTREC, HENRI DE   1864–1901
In Bed   1898
Au lit
Lithograph, 31.1 × 25.7
Signed on the stone, bottom left: 'H T-L'
    (in monogram, encircled)

140   TOULOUSE-LAUTREC, HENRI DE   1864–1901
The Jockey   1899
Le Jockey
Lithograph (monochrome state),
    51.6 × 36.3
Signed on the stone, bottom right:
    'H T-L/1899' (the initials in
    monogram, encircled)

CHECKLIST OF SAMUEL COURTAULD'S
ACQUISITIONS OF MODERN FRENCH PAINTINGS

Elizabeth Prettejohn

The following checklist includes all paintings by modern foreign artists in Samuel Courtauld's private collection and in the Courtauld Gift, including paintings subsequently sold from the collections. The paintings appear in a single chronological sequence, with titles as they appeared at the time of purchase, sources, purchase prices, and details of subsequent sale where applicable. Information has been drawn, wherever possible, from original documents in the Tate Gallery Archives and the Courtauld Institute Galleries Archives. Current locations and titles (where significantly different from the title at the time of purchase) appear in square brackets at the end of each entry, with catalogue numbers or figure numbers referring to illustrations in the text.

1922

September, for private collection
Marchand, *St. Paul*
from Independent Gallery (Percy Moore Turner), £1,750 (price including Renoir, *Femme se chaussant*)
[Courtauld Institute Galleries; cat. no. 28]

September, for private collection
Renoir, *Femme se chaussant*
from Independent Gallery (Percy Moore Turner), £1,750 (price including Marchand, *St. Paul*
[Courtauld Institute Galleries: *Woman at her Toilet*; cat. no. 43]

1923

January, for private collection
Gauguin, *Les Meules*

from Jos Hessel, Paris, £1,500 (price including Gauguin, *Baigneuses: Tahiti*)
[Courtauld Institute Galleries; cat. no. 19]

January, for private collection
Gauguin, *Baigneuses: Tahiti*
from Jos Hessel, Paris, £1,500 (price including Gauguin, *Les Meules*); sold *c.*1930 to/ through Alfred Gold, Berlin, price unknown
[Barber Institute, Birmingham; fig. 25]

May, for private collection
Cézanne, *Le Plâtre*
from Alex. Reid, Glasgow, £2,850
[Courtauld Institute Galleries: *Still Life with Plaster Cupid*; cat. no. 12]

May, for private collection
Daumier, *Don Quichotte et Sancho Panza*
from L.H. Lefèvre & Son, £1,350
[Courtauld Institute Galleries; cat. no. 15]

May, for private collection
Monet, *Fleurs*
from Alex. Reid, Glasgow, £2,500
[Courtauld Institute Galleries: *Vase of Flowers*; cat. no. 33]

May, for private collection
Seurat, *Nu*
from Galerie Barbazanges, Paris, £150
[Courtauld Institute Galleries; not now attributed to Seurat]

July, for private collection
Cézanne, *Le Bois des Soeurs*
from Thos. Agnew & Sons, £2,400
[Courtauld Institute Galleries: *The Etang des Soeurs, Osny*; cat. no. 4]

August, for Courtauld Gift

Manet, *La Servante de Bocks*
from M. Knoedler & Co., £10,000
[National Gallery, no. 3858: *The Waitress (La Servante de Bocks)*; fig. 9]

August, for Courtauld Gift
Renoir, *La Première Sortie*
from M. Knoedler & Co., £7,500
[National Gallery, no. 3859: *The Café-Concert (La Première Sortie)*; fig. 10]

August, for private collection
Manet, *Bords de la Seine à Argenteuil*
from M. Knoedler & Co., price unknown
[private collection; cat. no. 25]

August, for private collection
Monet, *Antibes*
from M. Knoedler & Co., price unknown
[Courtauld Institute Galleries; cat. no. 34]

October, for Courtauld Gift
Van Gogh, *Landscape with Cypress Trees*
from Independent Gallery (Percy Moore Turner), £3,300
[National Gallery, no. 3861: *A Cornfield, with Cypresses*; fig. 11]

1924

January, for Courtauld Gift
Degas, *Jeunes Spartiates s'exerçant a la lutte*
from Goupil Gallery, £1,200
[National Gallery, no. 3860: *Young Spartans (Petites Filles Spartiates provoquant des Garçons)*; fig. 12]

January, for private collection
Degas, *Pastel: 'Deux Danseuses'*
from Paul Rosenberg, Paris, £700; sold to Wildenstein, date and price unknown
[present whereabouts unknown; fig. 27]

February, for Courtauld Gift
Van Gogh, *Sunflowers*
from Mme J. van Gogh-Bonger, £1,304
[National Gallery, no. 3863; fig. 7]

February, for Courtauld Gift
Van Gogh, *The Yellow Chair*
from Mme J. van Gogh-Bonger, £696
[National Gallery, no. 3862: *The Chair and the Pipe*; fig. 6]

March, for Courtauld Gift
Seurat, *La Baignade*
from Félix Fénéon, 300,000 francs plus 30,000 francs Luxe Tax (£3,560 16s 7d plus 10% tax)
[National Gallery, no. 3908: *Bathers at Asnières (Une Baignade, Asnières)*; fig. 8]

May, for private collection
Cézanne, *Trees*
from Paul Rosenberg, Paris, £4,500
[Courtauld Institute Galleries: *Tall Trees at the Jas de Bouffan*; cat. no. 6]

May, for private collection
Monet, *La Rivière en Automne*
from Bernheim-Jeune & Cie., Paris, £2,500
[Courtauld Institute Galleries: *Autumn Effect at Argenteuil*; cat. no. 31]

June, for private collection
Renoir, *Place Clichy*
from L.H. Lefèvre & Son (one quarter owned by each of Lefèvre, London; Alex. Reid, Glasgow; Bignou, Paris; Hodebert, Paris), £5,500
[Fitzwilliam Museum, Cambridge; cat. no. 40]

July, for Courtauld Gift
Monet, *La Plage de Trouville*
from L.H. Lefèvre & Son, £650
[National Gallery, no. 3951: *The Beach at Trouville*; fig. 14]

December, for private collection
Friesz, *Les Anémones*
from L.H. Lefèvre & Son, £125
[Courtauld Institute Galleries; cat. no. 64]

December, for private collection
Manet, *Les Paveurs de la Rue de Berne*
from Alex. Reid, Glasgow, £6,000
[private collection: *The Road-Pavers, Rue Mosnier*; cat. no. 26]

1925

April, for private collection
Cézanne, *La Montagne Victoire*
from Bernheim Jeune, Paris, price unknown
[Courtauld Institute Galleries: *The Montagne Sainte-Victoire*; cat. no. 8]

May, for private collection
Renoir, *La Loge*

from Durand-Ruel, through Independent Gallery (Percy Moore Turner), $110,000 (approx. £22,600 plus Turner's commission, probably £1,600)
[Courtauld Institute Galleries; cat. no. 39]

June, for private collection
Seurat, *Study for La Baignade*
from Independent Gallery (Percy Moore Turner), £400
[private collection: *White Horse and Black Horse in the Water*; cat. no. 47]

October, for Courtauld Gift
Degas, *Miss Lola at the Cirque Fernando*
from French Gallery (Wallis & Son), £3,350
[National Gallery, no. 4121: *La La at the Cirque Fernando, Paris*; fig. 22]

October, for Courtauld Gift
Sisley, *Moret in Sunshine*
from L.H. Lefèvre & Son, £1,200; sold March 1927 to Alex. Reid & Lefèvre Ltd, £1,200
[present whereabouts unknown; not in Daulte]

November, for Courtauld Gift
Pissarro, *Boulevard des Italiens–Effet de Nuit*
from French Gallery (Wallis & Son), £1,575
[National Gallery, no. 4119: *Paris, the Boulevard Montmartre at Night*; fig. 16]

December, for Courtauld Gift
Bonnard, *La Table*, from Independent Gallery (Percy Moore Turner), £750
[Tate Gallery, no. 4134; fig. 20]

December, for Courtauld Gift
Cézanne, *Portrait of Cézanne chauve*
from Independent Gallery (Percy Moore Turner), £6,840
[National Gallery, no. 4135: *Self Portrait*; fig. 21]

December, for Courtauld Gift
Renoir, *Nu dans l'eau*
from Independent Gallery (Percy Moore Turner), £5,160; sold through Arthur Tooth & Sons to Baroness Maria Hatvani, London, October 1944
[present whereabouts unknown; fig. 32]

December, for Courtauld Gift
Sisley, *L'Abreuvoir*
from Independent Gallery (Percy Moore Turner), £1,150
[National Gallery, no. 4138: *The Watering Place at Marly*; fig. 13]

December, for Courtauld Gift
Utrillo, *La rue du Tertre*
from L.H. Lefèvre & Son, £350 plus Utrillo, *St. Etienne du Mont*
[Tate Gallery, no. 4139: *La Place du Tertre*; fig. 18]

1926

month unknown, for private collection
Pissarro, *Les Quais de Rouen*
from Paul Cassirer, Berlin, price unknown
[Courtauld Institute Galleries; cat. no. 37]

month unknown, for private collection
Rousseau, *L'Octroi*
from Alfred Flechtheim, Berlin, price unknown
[Courtauld Institute Galleries; cat. no. 44]

month unknown, for private collection
Seurat, *Jeune femme se poudrant*
from French Gallery (Wallis & Son), price unknown
[Courtauld Institute Galleries; cat. no. 53]

January, for Courtauld Gift
Cézanne, *Aix, paysage Rocheux*
from Leicester Galleries (Ernest Brown & Phillips Ltd.), £4,500
[National Gallery, no. 4138: *Mountains in Provence*; fig. 5]

January, for private collection
Cézanne, *Le lac bleu*
from Independent Gallery (Percy Moore Turner), £8,000
[Courtauld Institute Galleries: *The Lac d'Annecy*; cat. no. 13]

January, for private collection
Cézanne, *Mme Cézanne en bleu*
from Paul Rosenberg, Paris, £4,500; either this or another portrait of Mme Cézanne sold July 1929 to Paul Rosenberg, £8,000
[either Henry P. McIlhenny Collection, Philadelphia Museum of Art: *Mme Cézanne aux cheveux dénoués*, fig. 30; or Museum of Fine Arts, Boston: *Mme Cézanne dans un fauteuil rouge*, fig. 31]

February, for private collection
Seurat, *Le Petit Fort Philippe*
from L.H. Lefèvre & Son, £3,100
[Berggruen Collection: *The Channel of Gravelines, Grand Fort Philippe*; cat. no. 55]

March, for Courtauld Gift
Degas, *Femme assise*
from French Gallery (Wallis & Son), £3,700
[National Gallery, no. 4167: *Elena Carafa*; fig. 23]

March, for private collection
Manet, *Un Bar aux Folies Bergère*
from Thannhauser Gallery, Lucerne, through Independent Gallery (Percy Moore Turner), $110,000 (approx. £22,600, plus Turner's commission of £1,500)
[Courtauld Institute Galleries; cat. no. 27]

May, for Courtauld Gift
Toulouse-Lautrec, *Femme assise*

from Alex. Reid & Lefèvre Ltd., £650
[National Gallery, no. 4186: *Woman Seated in a Garden*]

May, for Courtauld Gift
Van Gogh, *Arles 1889*
from Wallis & Son, £2,100
[National Gallery, no. 4169: *Long Grass with Butterflies*; fig. 17]

June, for Courtauld Gift
Degas, *Les Danseuses*
from Independent Gallery (Percy Moore Turner), £700
[National Gallery, no. 4168: *Ballet Dancers*; fig. 24]

June, for private collection
Sisley, *Louveciennes – Snow*
from Independent Gallery (Percy Moore Turner), £1,350
[Courtauld Institute Galleries: *Snow at Louveciennes*; cat. no. 57]

July, for private collection
Boudin, *A Beach-scene – Trouville*
from M. Knoedler & Co., £50
[Courtauld Institute Galleries: *The Beach at Trouville*; cat. no. 2]

July, for private collection
Seurat, *Pont de Courbevoie*
from Alex. Reid & Lefèvre, £2,850
[Courtauld Institute Galleries; cat. no. 51]

November, for private collection
Seurat, *Pêcheur à la Ligne*
from M. Knoedler & Co., £750
[private collection; cat. no. 50]

1927
after February, for private collection
Gauguin, *Nevermore*
presumably from H.C. Coleman, price unknown
[Courtauld Institute Galleries; cat. no. 20]

March, for Courtauld Gift
Monet, *Le Bassin aux Nymphéas*
from Alex. Reid & Lefèvre Ltd., £2,200
[National Gallery, no. 4240: *The Water-Lily Pond*; fig. 15]

March, for private collection
Degas, *Portrait of a lady seated before a window overlooking the Tuileries Gardens*
from Leicester Galleries (Ernest Brown & Phillips), £1,500
[Courtauld Institute Galleries: *Woman at a Window*; cat. no. 16]

June, for private collection
Degas, *Les deux danseuses*
from M. Knoedler & Co., £8,560
[Courtauld Institute Galleries: *Two Dancers on the Stage*; cat. no. 17]

June, for private collection
Renoir, *Portrait de M. Ambroise Vollard*
from Ambroise Vollard, Paris, 800,000 francs (approx. £6,450)
[Courtauld Institute Galleries; cat. no. 42]

June, for private collection
Renoir, *Le printemps*
from Independent Gallery (Percy Moore Turner), £5,500
[private collection: *Spring (Chatou)*; cat. no. 38]

June, for private collection
Van Gogh, *La Haie*
from Independent Gallery (Percy Moore Turner), £9,000
[Courtauld Institute Galleries: *The Crau at Arles: Peach Trees in Flower*; cat. no. 23]

July, for private collection
Vuillard, *Femme nue*
from Leicester Galleries (Ernest Brown & Phillips), £404 5s
[Courtauld Institute Galleries: *Interior: The Screen*; cat. no. 62]

October, for private collection
Cézanne, *Homme à la pipe*
from Alex. Reid & Lefèvre Ltd., £7,500
[Courtauld Institute Galleries; cat. no. 11]

December, for private collection
Degas, *Après le Bain*
from Independent Gallery (Percy Moore Turner), £1,800
[Courtauld Institute Galleries: *After the Bath, Woman Drying Herself*; cat. no. 18]

December, for private collection
Seurat, *Bords de Seine*
from Independent Gallery (Percy Moore Turner), £700
[private collection: *Boat near the Bank, Asnières*; cat. no. 48]

1928
month unknown, for private collection
Bonnard, *Le Balcon bleu*
from Independent Gallery (Percy Moore Turner), price unknown
[Courtauld Institute Galleries; cat. no. 1]

January, for private collection
Cézanne, *Le Pot de fleurs*
from Alex. Reid & Lefèvre Ltd., £5,000
[Courtauld Institute Galleries: *Pot of Flowers and Pears*; cat. no. 9]

March, for private collection
Toulouse-Lautrec, *Au Rat Mort*
from Independent Gallery (Percy Moore Turner), £2,500
[Courtauld Institute Galleries: *In the Private Booth*; cat. no. 60]

June, for private collection
Manet, *Le Déjeuner sur l'herbe*
from Independent Gallery (Percy Moore Turner), £10,000
[Courtauld Institute Galleries; cat. no. 24]

June, for private collection
Matisse, *Danseuse*
from Alex. Reid & Lefèvre Ltd., £1,600; sold July 1929 to Alex. Reid & Lefèvre Ltd as part of price for Renoir *La Yole* (see below)
[present whereabouts unknown; fig. 28]

June, for private collection
Signac, *St. Tropez*
from Alfred Gold, Berlin, 25,680 marks (approx. £1,260; price including a work by Rubens)
[Courtauld Institute Galleries; cat. no. 56]

July, for private collection
Seurat, *Marine à Gravelines*
from Alex. Reid & Lefèvre Ltd, £500
[Courtauld Institute Galleries: *At Gravelines*; cat. no. 54]

July, for private collection
Tchelitchew, *Painting No. 1*
from Claridge Gallery, £15 15s
[either this or the following picture: Courtauld Institute Galleries: *Pears*; cat. no. 66]

July, for private collection
Tchelitchew, *Painting No. 26*
from Claridge Gallery, £21
[either this or the preceding picture: Courtauld Institute Galleries: *Pears*; cat. no. 66]

October, for private collection
Gauguin, *Paysage Exotique*
from Alex. Reid & Lefèvre Ltd., £3,000; sold before 1932 when it was owned by Evan Charteris, price unknown
[National Museum of Scotland, Edinburgh: *Martinique Landscape*; fig. 26]

October, for private collection
Picasso, *L'Enfant à la Colombe*
from Alex. Reid & Lefèvre, £1,400
[private collection: *Child with a Pigeon*; cat. no. 35]

October, for private collection
Van Gogh, *Portrait*
from Paul Rosenberg, Paris, £10,000
[Courtauld Institute Galleries: *Self-Portrait with a Bandaged Ear*; cat. no. 22]

November, for private collection
Seurat, *L'homme peignant son bateau*
from Independent Gallery (Percy Moore Turner), £700
[Courtauld Institute Galleries; cat. no. 46]

1929

by 1929, for private collection
Cézanne, *Mme Cézanne*, source and price
  unknown; either this or the *Mme Cézanne
  en bleu* (purchased January 1926) sold July
  1929 to Paul Rosenberg, £8,000
[either Museum of Fine Arts, Boston: *Mme
  Cézanne dans un fauteuil rouge*, fig. 31; or
  Henry P. McIlhenny Collection,
  Philadelphia Museum of Art: *Mme Cézanne
  aux cheveux dénoués*, fig. 30]

March, for private collection
Cézanne, *Cardplayers*
from Alfred Gold, Berlin, £12,500
[Courtauld Institute Galleries; cat. no. 10]

March, for private collection
Seurat, *Le Chahut*
from Ambroise Vollard, Paris, £1,000
[Courtauld Institute Galleries: *Study for The
  Chahut*; cat. no. 52]

July, for private collection
Gauguin, *La Case*
from Paul Rosenberg, Paris, £13,600
[Courtauld Institute Galleries: *Te Rerioa*;
  cat. no. 21]

July, for private collection
Renoir, *La Yole*
from Alex. Reid & Lefèvre Ltd, £12,500 plus
  Matisse *Danseuse* purchased June 1928
[National Gallery, no. 6478: *The Skiff*;
  cat. no. 41]

July, for private collection
Seurat, *Homme dans une barque*
from Independent Gallery (Percy Moore
  Turner), £800
[private collection; cat. no. 49]

November, for private collection
Daumier, *Sauvetage*
from Bernheim Jeune, Paris, through
  Independent Gallery (Percy Moore Turner),
  £3,200 plus Turner's commission of £320
[private collection; cat. no. 14]

December, for private collection
Toulouse-Lautrec, *Jeanne Avril*
from Independent Gallery (Percy Moore
  Turner), £10,400
[Courtauld Institute Galleries: *Jane Avril in the
  Entrance of the Moulin Rouge, Putting on Her
  Gloves*; cat. no. 59]

by 1931

for private collection
Modigliani, *Nu*
from Zborowski, Paris, price unknown
[Courtauld Institute Galleries; cat. no. 29]

for private collection
Utrillo, *Rue à Sannois*

from Libaude, Paris, through Alex. Reid &
  Lefèvre Ltd, price unknown
[Courtauld Institute Galleries; cat. no. 61]

1932

partly bought from Courtauld Gift
Pissarro, *The Louvre under Snow*
from Lucien Pissarro
[National Gallery, no. 4671]

1933

June, for private collection
Tissot, *Officer and Ladies on board H.M.S.
  Calcutta*
from Leicester Galleries (Ernest Brown &
  Phillips Ltd), £150; presented to Tate
  Gallery, 1936
[Tate Gallery, no. 4847: *The Gallery of HMS
  Calcutta (Portsmouth)*; fig. 29]

1936

June, for private collection
Pissarro, *Penge Station, Upper Norwood*
from Arthur Tooth & Sons Ltd, £850
[Courtauld Institute Galleries: *Lordship Lane
  Station, Dulwich*; cat. no. 36]

July, for private collection
Boudin, *Plage à Deauville*
from Wildenstein & Co. Ltd, £600
[Courtauld Institute Galleries: *Deauville*;
  cat. no. 3]

November, for private collection
Cézanne, *L'Estaque*
from Wildenstein & Co. Ltd, £8,000
[private collection: *View over L'Estaque*;
  cat. no. 7]

November, for private collection
Monet, *Gare St. Lazare*
from Wildenstein & Co. Ltd, £2,000
[National Gallery, no. 6479; cat. no. 32]

1937

June, for private collection
Cézanne, *Ferme Normande, La Cour Plantée*
from Alex. Reid & Lefèvre Ltd, £2,500
[private collection: *Farm in Normandy: The
  Enclosure*; cat. no. 5]

July, for private collection
Monet, *Le Pont d'Argenteuil*
from Rosenberg & Helft Ltd., £1,800 (price
  including Seurat *Pêcheur sur Bateau Amarré*)
[private collection: *Argenteuil, the Bridge under
  Repair*; cat. no. 30]

July, for private collection
Seurat, *Pêcheur sur Bateau Amarré*
from Rosenberg & Helft Ltd., £1,800 (price
  including Monet, *Pont d'Argenteuil*)
[private collection; cat. no. 45]

1947

March, for private collection
Sisley, *Seine Landscape*
from Matthiesen Ltd, £1,575
[Courtauld Institute Galleries: *Boats on the
  Seine*; cat. no. 58]

Dates and details of purchase unknown
for private collection
Bosshard, *Tulips*
[Courtauld Institute Galleries; cat. no. 63]

for private collection
Roy, *Still Life with Bonnets*
[Courtauld Institute Galleries; cat. no. 65]

MODERN FOREIGN PAINTINGS
AND THE NATIONAL ART COLLECTIONS:
ANTHOLOGY OF BRITISH TEXTS, 1905–1932

Elizabeth Prettejohn

THE FOLLOWING TEXTS HAVE BEEN CHOSEN to demonstrate a range of public reponses to the entry of modern foreign paintings into the British national collections. The texts trace the debate chronologically from 1905, when Frank Rutter launched his largely unsuccessful attempt to present Impressionist pictures to the nation (texts nos 1–2), to 1932, when responses to the Royal Academy's Exhibition of French Art confirmed the status of modern French painting as worthy of representation in the national collections (texts nos 32–5).

During the 1920s, the National and Tate galleries accepted the notion that modern foreign painting required representation, but debate continued over the issues of public versus private funding, and of which painters and works merited inclusion (see above, pp. 10–19, 38–9). Samuel Courtauld's gift to the nation provided one crucial focus for these debates; a section of the anthology is therefore devoted to responses to the announcement of the Courtauld Fund and to the first exhibitions of its purchases (texts nos 19–20, 25–9). Three articles are included to show contemporary views of Courtauld's activities as a private collector (texts nos 24, 30–1). Additional texts have been selected to demonstrate the development of discussion on the entry of modern foreign painting into the national collections, centring on key events: the exhibition of Sir Hugh Lane's collection at the National Gallery (texts nos 3–7); Sir Joseph Duveen's funding of a gallery building for modern foreign art (text no. 8); the Tate Gallery's refusal of the loan of two pictures by Cézanne in 1921 (texts nos 9–14); the Burlington Fine Arts Club exhibition of French art in 1922 (texts nos 15–18); and the Contemporary Art Society's establishment in 1924 of a fund to purchase contemporary foreign art for public collections (texts nos 21–3). For discussion of the issues raised in connection with these key events, see above, pp. 10–19.

The texts have been chosen from the specialist art periodicals and from general newspapers and periodicals ranging across the political spectrum from the *Morning Post* on the right to the *New Statesman* on the left. However, almost all of the writers were experienced professionals in the art world rather than polemicists: the major art critics of this period tended also to hold important posts in art institutions, so that the writers represented here include two keepers of the Wallace Collection (see texts nos 5, 14) and two directors of the National Portrait Gallery (see texts nos 4, 6), as well as the directors of the National and Tate galleries (see texts nos 4, 10). Their contributions to the debates over the national art collections were usually expressed in the moderate terms appropriate to their professional roles in the art world. It was left to writers who were not professional critics to express the most extreme views (texts nos 3, 35).

For surveys of the earlier controversies in the British press, when debates about modern French art itself were at their most impassioned, see Kate Flint (ed.), *Impressionists in England: The Critical Reception*, London, 1984; and J.B. Bullen (ed.), *Post-Impressionists in England: The Critical Reception*, London, 1988.

All articles are reprinted in full, except for sections on issues unrelated to modern foreign painting. Excisions of such sections are indicated with the symbol [...].

1 Frank Rutter, 'Round the Galleries', *Sunday Times*, 22 January 1905, p. 4

Rutter's proposal for a French Impressionist Fund to purchase paintings for the nation; for the fortunes of this initiative, see above, p. 10.

Frank Rutter (1876–1937) was a consistent supporter of Impressionist painting in his art criticism for the *Sunday Times* (from 1903). He was active in a number of ventures in the art world, including the Allied Artists Association (founded 1908) and its journal, the *Art News* (founded 1909; Editor until 1912). He was Curator of the Leeds Art Gallery (1912–17), Editor of *Art and Letters* (1917–20), and European

Editor of *International Studio* (1928–31). His many books included *Revolution in Art* (1910), *Evolution in Modern Art* (1926), and *Art in My Time* (1933), as well as studies of individual artists ranging from Rossetti (1909) and Whistler (1910) to El Greco (1930).

Thanks to the munificence of the late Mr. Ionides, the nation possesses at South Kensington a Degas, and a very characteristic example of Degas. But with this solitary exception there is not in any of our public galleries a single work by a member of that great group of painters known as the French Impressionists. Even those who are still hostile to the theory and practice of impressionist painting must admit that the absence of any work by Manet or Monet leaves a serious gap in our records of the history of painting. Moreover, many who are yet unable to perceive the beauty of the results obtained by the Impressionists are bound to admit the novelty and originality of their methods, and also the indisputable fact that their discoveries in the field of light and colour have had an incalculable influence on contemporary painting. On historic and scientific grounds, then, as well as on purely artistic, I venture to appeal to the generosity of art-patrons of all shades of opinion to give such assistance as they can towards securing for the nation at least one work by Manet and Monet, and, I hope, by Sisley and Camille Pissarro. It is, of course, perfectly open to the Chantrey Trustees to purchase works by Monet, or Pissarro, or Sisley; for all three worked in England, and Sisley, if born in France, was of British parentage. But despite the recent inquiry there is, I fear, but a small chance that even a portion of this 'Academy prize fund' will be devoted to the purchase of a painting by an 'outsider,' however distinguished. Under the circumstances, if we are to take advantage of the presence in London of an unprecedented collection of Impressionist paintings, it seems clear that the initiative must come from some private person. I cannot hope that the proceeds of my lecture will form more than the nucleus towards the establishment of a fund for the purchase of a single work. The days are gone when one could secure a masterpiece of impressionist art for a few francs. At the present moment quite a small work by Monet will fetch anything from four hundred guineas upwards. I am well aware also that among the unrivalled series of works now on view at the Grafton Galleries are not a few paintings which M. Durand Ruel could never be tempted to let pass out of his possession. But, on the other hand, there are several fine works which could be purchased; and I have reason to believe that their price would be not only reasonable but even moderate if it was certain that they were being bought for one of our permanent art collections. Among my readers too, I know, are many who have purchased and are still able to purchase such masterpieces for their own private collections. To these especially I now look with confidence for that generous support which can alone make my own humble efforts effective.

At the present juncture I shall not say very much about the exhibition at the Grafton Galleries, an exhibition larger and, I think, more fully representative of the Impressionist masters than any that has yet been held. All who know and appreciate their work will need no urging to pay a visit without delay. But to those who know little of their work, and have heard little of these painters save abuse, I offer the following advice. Do not believe that Impressionism, as practised by its masters, is an easy way out of the difficulties of painting. Pay no heed to those who tell you that Manet and Monet 'couldn't draw.' Go to the Grafton Galleries and judge for yourself. Stand before that wonderful painting of 'Pheasants' (133) by Monet, and as you look at the incomparably rendered plumage of the birds' necks and the exquisite play of light and shade on the white tablecloth, ask yourself if you ever saw better drawing and better painting in your life. And then take your stand

before Manet's 'Afternoon Music – Tuileries Gardens, 1860' (87), and note with what scrupulous care each detail is worked out with a minuteness that rivals Meissonnier or one of the early Dutch *genre* painters. And if after this you can possibly have the slightest doubt as to the painter's mastery of draughtsmanship, look at his astounding study of 'Still Life' (90). These works I cite not necessarily as the greatest or most characteristic works of these two painters, but, apart from their intrinsic beauty, as *tours de force* which give the lie direct to ignorant detractors. In the face of these marvellous technical performances should we not do well to pause before lightly accusing either painter of want of knowledge or craftmanship? Very possibly among their examples we shall find some later works that puzzle us, that are less easy to understand. But has the painter really failed to express himself, or is it we ourselves who are not yet sufficiently acquainted with the language to be able to read the message? Who could take in and fully realise the beauties of Turner's 'Approach to Venice' at the first glance? Boudin – the link between the Impressionists and the Barbizon group – is now appreciated by all, for we have grown accustomed to the vision of 1830, and there will be few, I imagine, to deny that his 'Leaving Port – Havre' (3) is worthy of a place with the Claudes and Turners in the National Gallery. But let us remember that the men of Barbizon were for many years despised and rejected by dealers and public art officials. Shall we be quicker to appreciate the beauties of their true successors? 'Ah!' sighed Manet, 'I'm before my time. A hundred years hence people will be happier, for their sight will be clearer than ours to-day.' When that time comes, what will posterity think of us if we neglect to secure for them a single example of the great-hearted, chivalrous Impressionist leader?

2 Frank Rutter, 'Round the Galleries', *Sunday Times*, 29 January 1905, p. 4

See text no. 1.

Thirty thousand pounds was the price paid by the nation to secure the portrait by Titian now hanging in the National Gallery. Far be it from me to say that this work was not worth the expenditure of this colossal sum, for it is difficult to estimate the value of a masterpiece in terms of pounds, shillings, and pence. But what I would say is this: If England could afford to spend £30,000 in adding one other example, however excellent, to the several admirable examples of Titian's work which the nation already possessed, then should she certainly be both able and willing to spend a sixth part of that sum on the purchase of works by modern masters at present unrepresented in any of our national art collections. I do not expect to raise anything like £5,000 by the sale of five-shilling tickets for the lecture I am giving in the Grafton Galleries next Sunday evening. The proceeds of this lecture is but my mite towards the fund, and while heartily thanking those readers who have been so kind as to apply for tickets, I must, at the risk of appearing importunate, make further demands on their generosity. Here let me express my gratitude to the readers who have already promised their support, and also to Mr. Claude Phillips, Keeper of the Wallace Collection, and Mr. D.S. MacColl, Slade Professor of Art at University College, who have kindly consented to co-operate with me in selecting the work or works to be purchased out of this fund on behalf of the nation. In making this selection we must, of course, be guided by the amount subscribed, but whether that amount be large or small, the names of the two gentlemen co-operating with me are a sufficient guarantee that subscribers will get the best possible artistic value for their money. Naturally, I hope the amount will be large, and if all my readers who appreciate the beauties of the work of Boudin, of Manet, of Monet – to mention but three – will send their shillings, their guineas, their hundreds – in short, as little or much as they can – I see no reason why we should not be able to raise sufficient to purchase for the nation representative works by the leaders of the French Impressionist movement. Remember this opportunity may not occur again. Five thousand pounds spent now will purchase works which in a hundred years' time £50,000 will not buy. Trust us, you that hesitate, scared by the abuse still showered by the foolish on these brilliant explorers of colour. Rembrandt was abused, Gainsborough was abused, Constable was abused, Turner was abused. Whistler was abused – but at what price will you *now* secure an example of their work? Believe me, this is no passing whim of fashion. The French Impressionists, I know, had their failures as well as their successes: but they have taken a permanent place in the history of painting. We may turn our backs on the sun again, we may mix our colours instead of laying them on pure, but we can no longer paint shadows in the blacks, greys, and browns of a discredited convention. And the light they lit has dimly illumined even the dark recesses of the Chantrey collection. Would either Mr. Clausen or Mr. Adrian Stokes paint quite as they do had Monet never lived? The nation, then, is not entirely devoid of works by the disciples of this luminiferous movement. Shall she have no examples of the masters, of the men who taught us that the light was the principal person in a painting, who made us realise, perhaps more than any other painters have done, that beauty is not absolute, but relative, that for their beauty objects depend not always on themselves, but on the aspects under which they appear? That these things may be known unto all men I ask all who are on my side to give practical proofs of their sympathy.

3   Memorandum from Lord Redesdale, Trustee of the National Gallery, to the National Gallery Board of Trustees, February 1914, on the proposed loan of Sir Hugh Lane's collection of modern continental pictures to the National Gallery (see above, pp. 10–11)

Algernon Bertram Freeman-Mitford, Baron Redesdale of Redesdale (1837–1916) wrote this intemperate response to Sir Hugh Lane's collection late in a colourful life. A cousin of the poet Swinburne and a close friend of Whistler in the 1870s, he chartered a boat to visit Garibaldi on Caprera in 1873. His early career in the Foreign Office included postings in the Far East that resulted in several books, such as *Tales of Old Japan* (1871). From 1874, he held a post at the Office of Works, where he was responsible for the restorations to the Tower of London. After his resignation to take up a large inheritance in 1886, he devoted himself to writing, also serving as Conservative MP for Stratford-on-Avon (1892–5) and in the House of Lords after his elevation to the Peerage in 1902. His *Memories* were published in 1915.

The letter of Sir Hugh Lane to Mr. Hawes Turner, dated February 12th, is hardly courteous.

So far as I have any knowledge of what has taken place Sir Hugh Lane's statement is misleading. But I was out of London when the meeting of the 5th of August was held – and was out of the Country when the question was discussed and the pictures viewed by the Trustees at a later date.

I accept without reserve, so far as I am concerned, Sir Hugh Lane's stricture that I have no expert knowledge of the class of paintings concerned. Neither have I any expert knowledge of the work of the pavement artist, the only school with which some of his paintings can be compared – notably the picture of the woman hunting in the hair of a young girl upon what is presumably intended to be a sand-heap by the sea-shore – the picture of gentlemen with hat-boxes and portmanteaux – the caricature of St. John and some others.

The transaction, as I understand it, is – so far as it has gone – as follows:–

On the 5th of August, 1913, at a thinly attended meeting of the Trustees, the Director submitted for consideration the offer of Sir Hugh Lane [...] The Trustees present, unfortunately as I think, accepted the principle, and on the 13th of January (the paintings having been hung in a room exclusively given up to them) the Trustees viewed them, and accepted as a loan 15 out of the 39 pictures. They do not, however, appear to have been very sure of their decision, for they agreed to call in the advice of two outside experts, and the gentlemen chosen were Mr. Sargent, R.A., and Mr. D.S. MacColl, the keeper of the Wallace Collection.

It is always wise, if possible, to pack a jury. I was abroad at the time, but had I been present I should have pointed out that, independently of the new departure of shifting responsibility, with which I shall deal hereafter, the verdict of these gentlemen was a foregone conclusion. Who suggested the names I know not, but it looks like a clever piece of manipulation in favour of Sir Hugh Lane's proposal.

Mr. Sargent is a painter of recognized genius and brilliant achievement. But his methods are not those of the old Classical School. With almost demonic cleverness he makes a splash or two of paint do duty for a hand, an ear, a fan or what not, sparing himself the tedium of detail. Of late he seems rather to have abandoned portraiture, in which he has been so triumphant, for landscape, and he has produced pictures which, seen at a little distance, are miracles. Look into them and the pictures disappear and are broken up into dabs of paint which under his master hand have been made to serve as trees, mountains, monasteries, &c.

If these paintings are right – without reference to their cleverness – then all the great painters whom we have been taught to revere – Hobbema, Cuyp, Turner, Rembrandt, and Holbein – the whole Italian, French, English, and Spanish schools, &c., are wrong. Yet Rembrandt's 'Mill' fetches £100,000, and Raphael's 'Madonna' £140,000, if report be true.

Himself somewhat of a rebel, Mr. Sargent encourages rebellion in others less gifted, in whom the magician's craft is wanting. So M. Rodin sees in a block of marble a face, a form of divine beauty; he hews away the masking rock and the loveliness is revealed. Unfortunately others try the same trick. Like M. Rodin, Mr. Sargent is unwittingly a danger – a danger as an example and still more so as a critic when he is called upon to express an opinion on such paintings as those offered as a loan by Sir Hugh Lane.

Mr. MacColl is a gentleman of the highest culture and of great learning, but he has been a consistent admirer of the so-called Post-impressionist School, between which and the cubists there is but a step, and that a short one. I may add that as chairman of the Wallace Collection I have had many opportunities of gauging Mr. MacColl's views on Art.

The verdict of these gentlemen was a certainty.

I hope that I shall not be considered wanting in courtesy to my co-trustees if I say that, in calling in outside opinion, I venture to think that the Trustees who were present at the January meeting assumed a responsibility and created a precedent upon which the whole body of Trustees ought to have had an opportunity of expressing an opinion. That opinion should have been obtained by calling a special meeting to consider the principle, and any Trustee not able to be present should have had the opportunity of expressing his opinion in writing. The Trustees of the National Gallery are a body of men, all of whom, if not experts or painters themselves, have been appointed on account of knowledge of and interest in Art. They ought not to delegate their authority or, at any rate, cramp their power by calling in outside help. Their doing so implies two things – timidity in themselves and want of confidence in the Director. Perhaps the Trustees suspected that they were making a mistake and called in prophets to bless them in their wrong doing.

Among the 15 pictures of which the Trustees have accepted the loan, there are a few pleasing examples – three small Corots, a pretty painting by Alfred Stevens, and one or two more; but in my judgment not even one of these could stand the test of being shown with the old masterpieces. It was not for such as these that the National Gallery was originally built, nor for such as these that continual extension has been applied for.

[...]

The National Gallery is – and should remain – a great Temple of Art. It should open its doors only to what is highest and best: never to the productions of a degraded craze, which, it may be hoped, will be shortlived. I should as soon expect to hear of a Mormon service being conducted in St. Paul's Cathedral as to see an exhibition of the works of the modern French Art-rebels in the sacred precincts of Trafalgar Square.

Putting Sir Hugh Lane's motives upon the highest plane conceivable, they are based upon the desire to create a taste for this new departure. Is that the proper function of the National Gallery? If the great National Collection has one duty more incumbent upon it than any other, it is that of educating and elevating the taste of the public. The exhibition of such works as those which I have mentioned at the beginning of this memorandum is not, as I conceive, calculated to effect that object.

If the aim be to encourage this so-called French Art with a view to purchase, the question becomes still more serious. A time when we are told that English Art is languishing for want of proper support is not the moment for advocating the expenditure of public money on the encouragement of the fads of an exaggerated and fantastic (to put it no worse) school of foreign art, which I for one hope may before long be dead and only laughed at as one of the follies of the past.

[...]

4   C.J. Holmes, 'New Exhibits at the National Gallery', *Burlington Magazine*, xxx, February 1917, pp. 80–1

Review of the Lane collection, exhibited at the National Gallery in 1917.

Charles John Holmes (1868–1936) wrote this review as Director of the National Gallery, a post he held from 1916–28, after acting as co-editor of the *Burlington Magazine* (1903–9), Slade Professor at Oxford (1904–10), and Director of the National Portrait Gallery (1909–16); he was knighted in 1921. Holmes was also a landscape painter, exhibiting at the New English Art Club from 1900 (member 1904), and the author of books on the National Gallery collections and other topics in art, including the popular *A Grammar of the Arts* (1931). His reminiscences, *Self and Partners – Mostly Self*, were published in 1936.

War risk and war conditions have made it desirable to place some pictures in discreet asylums and to remove others from houses devoted for the time being to official use. In consequence, by the kindness of the Duke of Buccleuch and the Duke of Westminster, the Trustees are able to show a certain number of pictures from Montague House and Grosvenor House; while changes in the hanging of one of the French Rooms permit the greater part of Sir Hugh Lane's much debated bequest to be placed on view.

[...]

Without trenching upon current controversies, it may anyhow be termed unfortunate if Sir Hugh Lane's collection of modern foreign pictures should have to leave London at the very moment when the provision of a gallery especially designed for them, of which he had dreamed so often, has become an accomplished fact. Meanwhile, the exhibition of the pictures in London enables us to see what we may be in danger of losing.

Hitherto as a nation we have been curiously insular in our attitude to modern continental art, and the rebuffs which Sir Hugh Lane experienced both in London and in Dublin were only the natural outcome of what was undoubtedly a few years ago the popular attitude towards the artists whom he championed. It is to be hoped that the war, which has widened immeasurably our outlook upon the peoples and the politics of the continent, will have something of the same effect upon our attitude towards continental art. To a few in England Sir Hugh Lane's pictures will appear to be ultra-modern, whereas to the artistic public abroad they have long been classics. It is only our national ignorance and indifference to all that goes on outside us that permits the average Englishman still to think of Daumier and Degas, Manet and Puvis de Chavannes as modern artists at all. For France they already form part of the great succession of French masters, and among French masters have indeed almost the highest place, because through them France attained during the latter half of the 19th century the artistic leadership of the world. The exhibition of their works at the National Gallery ought to be of special interest to artists in this country because it enables us to compare them easily with the great artists of the past, and to settle once for all, so far as such things ever can be settled, by how far the art of these men, who may almost be termed our contemporaries, stands the test of juxtaposition with the old masters.

The large unfinished decoration by Puvis de Chavannes, representing the Beheading of S. John the Baptist, obviously challenges comparison with the work of the great Italians of the cinque-cento. Let us suppose for a moment that it could be moved to the Umbrian Room, and that the slight chilliness of the surface were tempered with a glass. I think we should see at once that Luca Signorelli is practically the only master who would not look tame in the presence of so much vehemence, and petty in the presence of such monumental grandeur. The gallery in which it is at present shown is really too small for it, and even the finest of Sir Hugh Lane's other pictures are dwarfed by its largeness of spacing, its austere yet powerful colouration.

Invaluable as this picture would be to the many students of decorative painting in this country, the lessons that painters of easel pictures might learn from some other masters here are no less precious. We have assimilated and perhaps improved upon the realism which once made Courbet's name a by-word. But as a nation we have much still to learn from Manet and Claude Monet. Manet's famous *Concert* in the Gardens of the Tuileries, although time has perhaps somewhat dimmed its first brightness, retains its singular force; while his portrait of Eva Gonzales, in its freshness as in its vivid sense of decorative pattern, makes many another well known portrait at Trafalgar Square look woolly, greasy, dead and dull. Mature impressionism is represented by Claude Monet's exquisite *Vétheuil*, a snow piece as vivid and delicate as such things can well be, and a little picture by Berthe Morisot, rather slight perhaps for such strong company.

But most valuable of all should be the example of Daumier and Degas. The Daumier *Don Quixote*, though not perhaps the finest of his studies of this his favourite subject, illustrates well enough the coming of firm design into modern painting. In virtue of their vivid patterns, this little study and the example of Degas, *La Plage*, arrest the eye and stimulate the attention more than any of the other pictures of moderate size. To this vividness of pattern Degas adds a delicacy of workmanship only less wonderful than the artistic economy with which it is used. A little more 'finish' and all would have been lifeless; a little less and the thing would have been no more than a clever study. The small picture by Forain, as truly Rembrandt-like in its insight as in its tone, shows how the spirit of a great Old Master can be applied with success to a modern subject. Yet comparison with the Degas leaves a disquieting feeling that when the lesson of Daumier and Degas is well learned, and it is no easy lesson, we may never want to paint in Rembrandt's way again. Looking round, we shall notice that Ingres is represented inadequately, Delacroix and Géricault not at all. We badly need these links with the 18th century. But where we are to find them, unless, indeed, we get them from the Louvre, in exchange for some of our superfluous —. But I am on dangerous ground.

5 Sir Claude Phillips, 'National Gallery: II.–Sir Hugh Lane's Pictures', *Daily Telegraph*, 10 February 1917, p.7

Review of the Lane collection, exhibited at the National Gallery in 1917.

Claude Phillips (1846–1924) was appointed regular art critic of the *Daily Telegraph* in 1897, the same year in which he became Keeper of the Wallace Collection. He was knighted on his retirement from the latter post in 1911, but continued to write art criticism for the rest of his life; he left a bequest of money and paintings to the National Gallery. His collection of essays, *Emotion in Art*, was published posthumously in 1925.

Placed in the gallery hitherto devoted to French art, the foreign pictures of the late Sir Hugh Lane form a part of the loan exhibition. There will be great curiosity, no doubt, even on the part of those who are not, in the higher sense, lovers of art, to see these pictures, which have been the cause of so many statements and counter-statements, so many ingenious arguments and counter-arguments, by controversialists of approved skill. An overwhelming effect is made by Puvis de Chavannes's great canvas, '*La Décollation de St Jean Baptiste*,' a composition better known through the smaller version, which has been exhibited more than once in England. This is a great decoration, suffused throughout with the tempered open-air brightness peculiar to the painter. To find a parallel for the monumental grandeur of both conception and rendering, for the intensity of the visual impression that we receive from it, we must go to the French master's own monumental decorations at the Panthéon, at the Sorbonne, and in many museums of provincial France. Certainly no detached canvas of his–not even the '*Trois Ages*,' now in the Dresden Gallery–has this magnificent amplitude, both of style and of dimensions. Everything else disappears for the moment in the full, even light of this astonishingly fine piece; it is only by degrees that one can settle down to a leisurely contemplation of the modern works, French, Flemish, and Italian, with which it has been surrounded. By no means all these canvases are on the same high level of excellence. There are here some things of real artistic and historic value, adequately representing masters whom all Europe now, save only England, delights to honour; but there are others, not more than second-rate, which we have no particular desire to see permanently established at Headquarters.

MANET AND OTHER FRENCHMEN

The full length portrait of Manet's favourite pupil, Eva Gonzalez, makes rather a comic effect as a whole, although the painting of the still-life, the flowers, and accessories is nothing short of magnificent. Manet's legitimate brush-work in this canvas makes Mancini's *tours de force* in two portraits hung next to his look like so much confectionery. And yet the eccentric Italian is a painter of great power, and in the spiritual expression of a human personality goes far beyond anything that the French impressionist ever attempted or desired. The other Manet, '*La Musique aux Tuileries*' (1862)–a picture of considerable reputation–includes passages painted with a Velasquez-like breadth and truth, yet as a whole confuses more than it impresses. The painter lacked vision of the higher truth that soars above the literal. The chief interest is in the faithful representation of Second Empire fashions, and in the portraits

introduced of the painter himself, of Fantin-Latour, Baudelaire, Théophile Gautier, Chaplin, Offenbach, Zacharie Astruc, Aurélien Scholl, and other *sommités* of the time. Less desirable, though it has more vivacity of movement, and is enlivened by a colour-scheme of kaleidoscopic variety, is a large canvas by M. Renoir, a scene of bourgeois open-air rejoicing interrupted by a shower. The best thing in the picture is a group of fully-opened umbrellas. M. Renoir is a realist of the gayer order, a consummate executant, and in many ways an innovator. But this piece of jog-trot vulgarity–ranking less high even than a somewhat similar painting in the Luxemburg–does not adequately represent his late manner. In the same way it is *a* Degas, not *the* Degas, who looks out at us from a rather commonplace seabeach scene with figures. That there are very fine things in the picture goes without saying: for instance, the grouped figures of a woman and a girl lying on the sand in the foreground. It would be a pity, all the same, if this great master of design should be judged from a middling performance such as this is. The nation has long (in the Ionides Collection at South Kensington) possessed an early Degas of high interest, the 'Ballet of the Wicked Nuns in Meyerbeer's "Robert le Diable."'

A BEAUTIFUL MONET

We must mention, just a little out of its right place, a winter-sunlight scene of the most radiant purity and beauty by Claude Monet. That there should have been hesitation in the past to accept such landscape art as this, that it should even now be challenged by some painters over here, seems strange enough. The Courbets will not say much to those who know the great series in the Louvre. There are far better examples, too, at Frankfort and in other German galleries. 'Avignon' a Corot of the earlier time, and unusually full of detail, would be useful here, seeing that all the Salting Corots are of the later time, and have the characteristic *sfumato*. A powerful design by Honoré Daumier, marked by the living force and elasticity of line for which he is famous, is the 'Don Quixote and Sancho Panza.' There have been seen more important variants of this same subject, which was a great favourite with Daumier. Then we have a singularly fine example of the Belgian master, Alfred Stevens, dating from his best time. This is '*La Femme au Tigre*'–a lady in the costume of the Second Empire intently gazing at a grotesque tiger fashioned of gold and encrusted with jewels. Delicate little still-life pieces represent Bonvin and Fantin-Latour; the famous sculptor Barye is responsible for a landscape more or less of the Barbizon type. The greatest novelty, however, is an exquisitely subtle 'still-life' or 'arrangement' by Vuillard, an ultra-modernist, no doubt, but above all things a consummate artist.

There is nothing here by the English-born Sisley, nothing by Cézanne, or Gauguin, or Van Gogh; nothing by Maurice Denis, the successor–with a long interval–of Puvis de Chavannes. Though we have shown that, apart from the masterpiece by this last-named artist, the collection is of varying merit, it is a memorable event that on the walls of the National Gallery–whether temporarily or permanently–such men should find a place as Courbet, Manet, Claude Monet, Degas, and Renoir. To the august Puvis entrance could never have been denied had he presented himself as majestically as he does here. And take note, that the gates of the temple being thus set open, and the barriers of prejudice swept away, these gates can never again be closed, these barriers can never be re-erected.

6   Lionel Cust, 'Manet at the National Gallery', *Burlington Magazine*, xxx, March 1917, pp. 110–15

Review of the Lane collection, exhibited at the National Gallery in 1917.

Sir Lionel Henry Cust (1859–1929) worked in the Department of Prints and Drawings at the British Museum from 1884. Later he became Director of the National Portrait Gallery (1895–1909), Surveyor of the King's Pictures (1901–27), and joint editor with Roger Fry of the *Burlington Magazine* (1909–19). His many publications included works on Dürer, Van Dyck, and the Royal Collections.

Amateurs and Students of the Fine Arts, whose age permits them to cherish personal recollections of the great art-movements of the nineteenth century, must feel some satisfaction that in practically every case of an individual artist, who has been for a time the *cheval de bataille* of his profession, or the butt of critics, professional, literary, or merely *dilettante*, time has tested their sterling worth and brought, where due, reward to the artist's fame, even if this were denied to the artist during his life-time. The second and third decades of the 19th century were periods of portentous gestation in the history of Painting. D.G. Rossetti was born in 1828, Manet in 1832, Whistler and Degas in 1834. Each of these artists was a pioneer on a mighty scale, who cleared the way for new light and new tracks in art, and, as pioneers cannot expect to be popular in the deserts or jungles through which they have to hack their way, it is not surprising that they encountered opposition and difficulties of obstruction, though seldom has the conflict been so bitter and so stubborn as in the case of these four painters. It must be noted that it was among painters themselves that the controversy raged most acutely, and the pen of no art critic, no matter how venomous the ink in which it might be dipped, could be so cruel or so vindictive towards a struggling artist than that of a royal academician or a *membre de l'Institut* some forty or fifty years ago. Time, however, has its revenge, and while the trenches of the past are clogged with the corpses of perished reputations, those painters, who have survived the contest, stand out in much stronger eminence with all the badges of success. This survival is to a great extent due to the influence of writers on art, especially in France. Whistler, more gifted with the art of self-advertisement than his brother-artists, succeeded in making himself felt and known and even adopted as a master before his race was run; he never however forced his way within the austere portals of the National Gallery, and even at this day has only secured a grudged admission to the shrine of Sir Henry Tate. Rossetti faltered in his stride and came to an untimely end, but with our national perversity we have granted to Rossetti and even to Madox Brown the honour of being hung on the walls of the National Gallery. Now it is Manet, who with a kind of trumpet-call from the past has stepped clanking into this august temple and taken his seat among the immortals. The strange thing is that Manet seems to be at home there, while Rossetti does not, and even the brilliant *plein-air* study *La Plage* by Degas seems a bit *dépaysé* and to be longing for a more congenial neighbourhood. Among the modern paintings bequeathed to the nation by Sir Hugh Lane, only the *Beheading of S. John the Baptist* by Puvis de Chavannes, besides the two by Manet, seems to establish a claim to its position. The large painting by Renoir, *Les Parapluies*, strikes a note which does injustice to itself, and makes what is really a remarkable work of art look vulgar and a bit *canaille*. The landscape by Monet has luckily not lost its colour, and is therefore representative, while that by Courbet is rather dark and too subtle for the ordinary spectator; the brilliant study by Berthe Morisot seems hardly strong enough to sustain itself in such an environment. These and other paintings clamour for a gallery devoted to their own period, and we hope to publish some further notes upon them by Mr. Roger Fry in an ensuing number. Manet on the other hand dominates the gallery with his portrait of *Madame Eva Gonzales*, which makes some of the portraits of the English school look cheap and laboured. Moreover Manet in his *Concert aux Tuileries* provides not merely a dexterous and instructive piece of painting, but a valuable document of the Second Empire. It is sufficient to note that in this motley group, yet so uniform in its costume and atmosphere, portraits will be found of Manet and his brother, Baudelaire, Théophile Gautier, Fantin-Latour, Offenbach and his wife, Chaplin the painter, Zacharie Astruc, and other notable persons, now identified with the social history of the Second Empire. This early work by Manet has been too often described to need any further notice here, but in itself it goes far to establish the claim of Manet to his place in the National Gallery.

Time is the only true valuer of the Fine Arts. Contemporaries, amateur or professional, frequently over-estimate a fine artist, and as frequently deride him. The wealthy amateur may be in reality a deadly foe as well as the salesman, who sucks the life-blood of an artist in one case, and casts another on the dust-heap of dishonour. It takes some thirty to fifty years, a generation or two, to decide among the works of art which have survived, those which have any claim to the consideration of posterity. Works of sterling worth need have no fear for the result. The flimsy, fashionable work, or that executed with careless or reckless inattention to pigments or material, will perish before the time for judgment shall arise. Manet, Whistler, Degas and others may have to wait for recognition, even past the term of their own lives. They will meet elsewhere Rembrandt, Watteau and other brother-artists, who have had the same record. Manet, in his turn, was an artist who saw painting differently from his teachers and acted accordingly. Time has shown that he was right, even when he stumbled over difficulties or failed to achieve the actual goal of his ambition.

7   Roger Fry, 'The Sir Hugh Lane Pictures at the National Gallery', *Burlington Magazine*, xxx, April 1917, pp. 147–53

Review of the Lane collection, exhibited at the National Gallery in 1917.

Roger Fry (1866–1934) considered painting his first career, but was best known as a writer, charismatic lecturer, and public figure in the art world. He was art critic of the *Athenaeum* from 1901, and a frequent contributor to the *New Statesman* and other periodicals. He acted as Curator of Paintings, then adviser, at the Metropolitan Museum in New York (1906–10), and was joint editor with Lionel Cust of the *Burlington Magazine* (1909–19). His championship of modern foreign painting began when he encountered the work of Cézanne in 1906; with the two celebrated exhibitions of 1910–11 and 1912 at the Grafton Galleries, he coined the term 'Post-Impressionism' as well as introducing Post-Impressionist painting to Britain. He remained a fervent supporter of modern foreign art, publishing collections of his critical and theoretical articles, *Vision and Design* (1920) and *Transformations* (1926), and works on Cézanne (1927) and Matisse (1930).

All the great revolutionary painters of the 19th century were devoted admirers of the old masters; perhaps they were the only intelligent and discriminating ones. It is they and they alone that take rank naturally in the great sequence of tradition, so that the Hugh Lane room at the National Gallery produces far less sense of incongruity than let us say the portrait of Lord Kitchener. It is true that the collection is oddly miscellaneous and that a good many of the painters here represented have already had their brief moment of fame and are not likely to retain their hold on our interest. Mancini for instance is obviously only on sufferance among serious painters. The pretence of a rather wild and extravagant quality which made a momentary flutter among the less perceptive critics is here shown to be a mere mannerism imposed on the vulgarest photographic vision. His early work which figures in this collection is just the ordinary realistic pot-boiler rather below than above Royal Academy standard.

Alfred Stevens, another master of a peculiar pictorial cuisine, is certainly less blatant, and the sauce with which he dishes up a very commonplace motive is in its way exquisite, but it is clear that there is nothing here but a purely external sensibility, that his technique is not the outcome of a passionately felt vision, but merely a sensual delight in particular kinds of *matière*. In short his painting is merely adornment, not expression.

But there is no need to linger over the lapses of Sir Hugh Lane's rather eclectic and haphazard taste; our gratitude to him is not diminished, since it is much more important that good work should be bought than that bad should be discouraged.

And among the good things there are a few of such supreme merit that without prejudging the much debated question of their final allocation, one may say that their exhibition at Trafalgar Square is of national importance.

What might not happen to the future art of England if all young painters could come and study again and again Renoir's masterpiece *Les Parapluies*! Here are all the hard-won victories, over struggles from which British art has consistently turned aside. It is a work which cost even Renoir immense effort and years of work, and its freshness and gaiety, its brilliance and directness, are not the result of clever improvisation, but of that passionate intensity of feeling which broods upon a theme until it yields up its last particle of material; until all is informed with a single idea; until every touch takes its place inevitably in the whole. It is this discovery of form which is such an intolerable effort even to the most gifted of men that nearly all artists shy from it sometimes, and most artists all the time. Taking refuge in a formula either of their own creation or of another's, they accept some mould into which the material of life can be run, rather than make afresh out of the material itself its own appropriate design.

It is this positive creative effort that marks the classical work of art, and if ever a picture had the quality of a classic, this is one. Here nothing is for effect, no heightening of emotion, no underlining of the impressive or the delightful or the surprising qualities of things, but an even, impartial, contemplative realization of what is essential – of the meaning which lies quite apart from the associated ideas and the use and wont of the things of life. It is from this refusal to take sides about things, this sympathy which probes everything alike and that yet remains aloof from all the instincts and desires of actual life that marks the greatest class of artists.

Renoir rarely, I think, attained to the severe beauty and architectural perfection of this design. His lyrical feeling for whatever is gracious and delicate in life generally urged him in the direction of a vaguer, more elusive design. In this work he comes nearer than elsewhere to his great contemporary Cézanne – indeed this picture might be taken as the complete realization of what Cézanne indicated as his aim – to make of the Impressionist vision something that should have the architectural completeness of early art.

Renoir, like all of his generation, was intensely preoccupied by the exploration of the new aspects of phenomena which Impressionism accepted for the first time. These phenomena of the incidence and reflection of diverse coloured light on differently inclined planes had been completely classified by Leonardo da Vinci, who rejected them for pictorial purposes as interfering too much with the representation of plastic form by means of graduated light and shade of a more or less uniform colour. On the whole we may admit that Leonardo's criticism was justified – certainly the mass of Impressionist painting has not been remarkable for its plastic definition of form – at the same time the most

plastic painter of the 19th century, Cézanne, came out of the Impressionist movement, though his research for plasticity did precisely lead him away from his companions. Renoir was often enough an Impressionist in the ordinary acceptance of the term, dissolving form almost as completely as Monet into a shifting veil of atmospheric colour. Nevertheless with him the passion for design and the research for definitely ascertained formal relations was never absent – he belonged fully to the great French tradition as it was formulated in the 17th century. He never forgot Poussin. In *Les Parapluies* certainly it is design that predominates. Atmospheric colour is used throughout instead of the monochromes of the studio illumination, but atmospheric colour is used always as subordinate to form, as a means of illustrating and defining the sequence of planes in terms of colour. One may even doubt whether the laws of atmospheric colour are followed with anything like scientific rigour – whether the cold grey cloud-light which breaks into such exquisite toned violets and blues on the black umbrellas would not have shown more chill and leaden on the flesh of his women and children or would have allowed of the exquisite pearliness of the ground. One thinks rather that, having got his hint of a new kind of colour scheme based on grey blues and grey violets, he allowed the necessities of pure colour design to influence his observation. Renoir was never a literalist – his observation was never coldly curious, but always impassioned and contemplative.

Renoir did not often attempt such elaborate compositions. This, the *Charpentier Family* in the Metropolitan Museum at New York, and M. Durand Paul's [*sic*] *Lunch on the River* are among the most important. They are not perhaps greater than this or that single figure which one recalls as showing Renoir in his full force, but they show more clearly than his other works the great mental powers, the co-ordinating and constructive ability, that one could scarcely have hoped for in so spontaneous and so lyrical a temperament. After having seen *Les Parapluies* at Trafalgar Square I find it hard to keep an open mind about Dublin's claims to its possession.

We reproduced last month the large Puvis de Chavannes of the *Beheading of John the Baptist*. I need therefore add nothing more on the subject, especially as I find myself completely out of sympathy with the whole aim and tendency of the work. I find Puvis however as a real though quite minor personality in the little composition here reproduced. Whatever a singularly quick and subtle appreciation of great style in drawing could do by itself and without the aid of more direct inspiration Puvis could accomplish at his best. One thinks of Cézanne's dictum: 'Puvis – ah oui – il imite bien'. It is very good and very personal imitation of the style of the great Italians. The distortions and simplifications of the forms are exquisitely chosen with the fullest consciousness of their effect. If art were a matter of works and not of grace, how high a place Puvis would deserve.

Our other reproduction is of the Ingres, where also good works are evident in all truth; what complete consciousness, what critical perception – only the Italians he criticised were of a generation later than Puvis's models – what certainty and deliberation, and yet – and this is the eternal fascination of Ingres – grace, overlaid, oppressed under the weight of learning, neglected and despised, still persists.

The small portrait in the Lane Collection is one of two versions of the Duc d'Orleans for whom Ingres painted his *Stratonice*. The other picture is a three-quarter length portrait in uniform. It is still in the possession of the family. Judging from the photograph of the larger picture, I should say that Sir Hugh Lane's head was the earlier work done from the sitter and used by Ingres in elaborating the larger and more pretentious work. The military cloak in the small head does not figure in the three-quarter length. There is certainly no question here of a copy, the small head is intensely personal and characteristic work of the master. In quality it has the peculiar dead waxy smoothness of handling which he sometimes affected in contrast to the hard almost enamelled brightness of other works. One may admit that it is not an attractive quality in itself or one which allows of any direct beauty of expressiveness in the touch – everything in fact seems reduced to an almost mechanical deadness and precision. Every plane is sand-papered and smoothed over, and yet so intense and passionate is the apprehension of form that Ingres's vehement and sensual nature comes through all the discipline and repression imposed on it. It is not one of those works in which Ingres shocks one with the strange unexpectedness of his discoveries in design, but it is none the less a picture which holds one increasingly every time one revisits it.

8 'English and Foreign Art: A National Modern Gallery', *The Times*, 23 July 1918, p.9

Announcement of Joseph Duveen's gift of a gallery building for modern foreign art.

The news that Mr. Joseph Duveen has generously offered the money to build a national gallery of modern foreign art, and that his offer has been accepted, is good; but it should make us ashamed of ourselves. Such a gallery ought to have been built and stocked long ago, and out of public funds. It is more needed in this country, perhaps, even than a National Gallery of ancient art, certainly more than one of modern English art.

This is not said out of contempt for modern English art, but because many people, including even painters, who know English art well are strangely ignorant of foreign. France is the home of all the most important movements in modern painting; and most Englishmen, even Englishmen of taste, are aware of nothing later than the Barbizon school. Impressionists are to them still dangerously novel; and, if they see an Impressionist picture in the Academy, they wonder what the Academy is coming to. In France Impressionism is of yesterday; and every one who cares for pictures on the Continent, and even in America, is familiar with it. With us it is a sign of enlightenment, and even of rashness, to like Corot. When a few years ago pictures by Cézanne, Gauguin, and Van Gogh were first shown in London they were taken for bad jokes, although they had been well known and esteemed in Paris for years, while the Germans were busily engaged in producing parodies of them.

We sometimes flatter ourselves that by our ignorance we are escaping foreign poison; we remain safe in our island, while other nations are contaminated. The fact is that we take the poison, if poison it be, a generation late; and when we take it it is no longer poison to us. Also, by reason of our lateness, we always buy the masterpieces of French painting, if we buy them at all, at a very high price. If now we can get someone to buy for this new gallery with courage and discretion, we shall get our masterpieces cheap. They will no doubt shock the public at first, but it will quickly grow used to them. Even the French public was shocked once by Manet's 'Olympia'; and now it is in the Louvre, where, if it has a fault, it is that it looks a little academic by the work of Ingres and Poussin.

But above all this new gallery, if it is what it should be, will be of value in the education of our painters. They need not imitate Continental work, but they should at least have the chance of seeing it. To know what is being done all over the world can do a painter no harm and may do him good. In all great ages of art there has always been an eager curiosity about contemporary movements; for the great artist knows that he can learn from anywhere without losing his originality. But in England now there is, as we have said, a strange ignorance of what is being done, even in Paris, and even among painters. We keep ourselves to ourselves, as the saying is; and, as a result of our lack of curiosity about

the art of the rest of the world, the rest of the world has very little curiosity about our art. It is not, as a matter of fact, uninfluenced by foreign art; but the influence comes from the day before yesterday. It is as if our ladies were still copying the fashions of the Second Empire. And where there is imitation of modern French painting, it is often blind and stupid, because the best examples of that painting are not seen. The public is taken in with counterfeits because it does not know the originals.

Nothing, then, is needed to complete Mr. Duveen's generous gift but a brave and judicious buying, and the means for it.

9 Hugh Blaker, 'Cézanne and the Nation', letter to the editor, *Observer*, 3 April 1921, p.17

For the Tate Gallery's rejection of the proposed loan of two pictures by Cézanne from the collection of Gwendoline Davies, see above, p.12.

Hugh Blaker (1873–1936) acted from 1908 as adviser and agent to Gwendoline and Margaret Davies; their collection of French painting is now in the National Museum of Wales. Blaker had trained as a painter in Antwerp and Paris, and exhibited with the International Society (1912–15) and the Allied Artists Association (1917, 1920); he was Curator of the Holbourne of Menstrie Museum, Bath from 1905–13, later devoting himself principally to connoisseurship. He made repeated attempts to introduce modern pictures into the national collections, offering pictures by Modigliani, Vlaminck, Gore, and Gilman from his own collection, as either loans or gifts; all were initially refused. Extracts from Blaker's diary describing these transactions are reprinted in *Apollo*, LXXVIII, October 1963, pp.293–8.

Sir, – It will come as a surprise to students of modern painting that the National Gallery of British Art, Millbank, have recently refused the loan of two representative pictures by Cézanne. I was privileged to offer these (on behalf of a public-spirited collector) for an indefinite period. As your readers are aware, there is a gallery devoted to modern foreign art. The reason given for the rejection by the trustees was 'want of space.' This objection is hardly justifiable when we consider the inclusion of pictures of comparatively minor interest. Even so, the demands of foreign art in our national collections are sufficiently compelling to warrant a second gallery. When so much room is devoted to the preposterous illustrations which comprise the bulk of the Chantrey Bequest pictures, and when space is willingly given to the works of such painters as Augustus Egg and Sidney Cooper, and a whole gallery given to the display of sentimental creations of G.F. Watts, it is surprising that space cannot be found for two small pictures by such a great master as Cézanne.

Artists, at any rate, will be interested to know that I have recently offered to give two fine works by the late Spencer Gore; also a characteristic still-life painting by Gilman, all of which were rejected. And yet works without a tithe of the significance of the painters are apparently accepted with enthusiasm.

To-day our galleries are the only important ones in Europe where Cézanne, the father of the modernists, is excluded. Without the generosity of Hugh Lane and the late Sir Joseph Duveen the works of Manet, Monet, Daumier, Gauguin, Renoir, Degas, and others would be strangers to those students who are not conversant with the Continental galleries.

It is almost inconceivable that so recently as 1914 pictures by Manet and Daumier, offered by Hugh Lane, were rejected by the National Gallery trustees, and only accepted later on the recommendation of a special committee.

Again, are we to be left behind in regard to the works of our great foreign contemporaries, such as Vlaminck, Modigliani, Derain, and

Matisse? I—and others—would willingly lend works of these great painters, but we are deterred from even offering them from the knowledge that such offers would be rejected. Are we always to remain a generation or two behind our Continental brethren?

10 Charles Aitken, 'Cézanne and the Nation', letter to the editor, *Observer*, 10 April 1921, p.15

Response to text no.9.

Charles Aitken (1869–1936) was Director of the Whitechapel Art Gallery (1900–11) before his appointment, in succession to D.S. MacColl (see text no.14), as Keeper (1911), then first Director, of the National Gallery, Millbank (the Tate Gallery; until 1930).

Sir,—In regard to the letter from Mr. Hugh Blaker, which appeared in THE OBSERVER on April 3, I would point out that the new Modern Foreign Gallery has not yet been built, owing to unavoidable difficulties as to labour and materials. Until the new Gallery is open it is impossible for the Trustees to show a large number of Modern French Pictures. By the kind consent of Sir Joseph Duveen one gallery in the Turner wing has been temporarily hung with some of the most important foreign pictures by Manet, Monet, Chavannes, Forain, Degas, Alfred Stevens, Gauguin, etc., but it is not possible to displace these works belonging to the permanent collection, in order to exhibit pictures which are only lent to the gallery, quite apart from any consideration of the quality of the pictures offered. The Trustees have, I feel sure, every desire that Cézanne should be adequately represented in their permanent collection.

For sufficient reasons it is not, except in special circumstances, considered by the Trustees desirable to accept loans from private owners for the National Collection, apart from cases where the option of purchase at a specified price has been agreed upon, or where there is reasonable prospect of ultimate gift or bequest. Generally, in regard to the acceptance of both gifts and loans, the question of space necessitates very careful consideration, as the National Collections at Millbank already contain twice as many pictures as can be exhibited, and the cost of maintenance now works out at not less than £3 per annum per foot of hanging space.

The Board is keenly alive to the desirability of securing representative examples of the work of the younger living or recently deceased painters, and it has recently accepted or purchased works by such artists as John, Innes, Lamb, Grant, Guevara, Gill, Mestrovic, and Spencer Gore. In the case of the last named artist the Trustees have had the offer of several works during the last few years, and after careful consideration accepted 'Window in Cambrian Road, Richmond,' from a body of subscribers in 1920. They have also had several works by Gilman under consideration, and the work of that artist may shortly be represented in the collection by a painting which represents him characteristically.

I would point out that only half of the National Gallery, Millbank, is open as yet, and until the whole of the Gallery is re-opened it is scarcely possible to judge how far efforts to represent recent developments in contemporary art are being made by the Trustees. The second half of this Gallery will, it is hoped, be re-opened within a few weeks.

The power to increase the collections is considerably restricted by the absence of any Government Grant for the purchase of pictures, but the Trustees are most anxious to make the collections of Modern British and Foreign Art at Millbank fully representative, and to give grateful recognition to the generosity of those willing to assist them in this endeavour. It is, however, incumbent on them for the above reasons to weigh carefully the quality of pictures offered as gifts and the conditions of proposed loans.

11 'Editorial: Cézanne and the Nation', *Burlington Magazine*, XXXVIII, May 1921, p.209

Response to texts nos 9 and 10.

Robert R. Tatlock (1889–1954) was Editor of the *Burlington Magazine* from 1920 to 1933. In 1924, he became also art critic of the *Daily Telegraph*, succeeding Sir Claude Phillips (see text no.5); he contributed articles on art and archaeology to other leading periodicals.

We reproduce on another page two Cézannes which have been the subject of a controversy in the columns of the 'Observer.' Mr. Hugh Blaker wrote a wise and indignant letter in which he stated that the pictures, which he had offered on loan to the new foreign section at the National Gallery of British Art, had been rejected. Mr. Aitken, the director, replied in a conciliatory vein, pointing out that there is no room for more than a few foreign pictures until the new wing is built. He adds that 'for sufficient reasons' and 'except in special circumstances' offers of pictures on loan will be refused, and that the whole gallery already contains twice as many pictures as can be shown. The absence of any Government grant is also spoken of; and the letter ends with the assertion that, for the reasons stated, the trustees must 'weigh carefully the quality of pictures offered as gifts and the conditions of proposed loans.'

The position then would appear to be that the two Cézannes were rejected either (i) because of their quality, (ii) because there is no room for them, or (iii) because the conditions of loan were impossible. The concluding sentence of Mr. Aitken's letter seems to imply that the quality of the Cézannes is not up to the Tate standard. The fact that one of them, the landscape, has already been reproduced in THE BURLINGTON MAGAZINE is a sufficient comment on our opinion regarding it, and it will be apparent that the still life is an equally characteristic and important example of Cézanne. As for there being no room for them,—which is the reason formally given—in a large collection like that at Millbank, room can be found for any two small pictures if they are really wanted. And as regards the conditions of loan; the pictures are stated to have been offered simply 'for an indefinite period.' Moreover, they are the property, we are permitted to say, of Miss G. Davies, whose disinterestedness and generosity are, of course, beyond dispute. Mr. Aitken seems almost to say 'I don't think we can take loans because we must reserve our space for purchases. But we cannot make purchases because we have no money.' He certainly implies that, with an occasional exception, none but the unconditional gift—always a *rara avis*—can be accepted.

Experience, however, has shown that the surest way of encouraging gifts is to welcome suitable loans. But besides the Cézannes, many other modern French pictures, some offered on loan and some as gifts, have been from time to time refused, and the fact that most of the largest collectors—among whom a strong feeling undoubtedly exists—are known to be willing to lend examples, makes the policy of refusing loans hard to defend. One of the best collections to be found anywhere could, it is felt, be rapidly formed free of cost. What these collectors and others ask is that modern French art should be shown alongside the other pictures at Millbank, then if after continued examination they come to be condemned, they can at worst be returned to their owners. Now that it is decided that there is to be a foreign section it would surely be well to welcome really heartily the aid of the collectors, who at any rate have for many years studied this section of painting with the faith and passion through which alone, successful collecting, private or public, becomes possible. Although, of course, the opinion of such enthusiasts varies greatly regarding the relative merit of the painters of modern France, all have come to an agreement about Cézanne, who was born as long ago as 1839, is universally recognised as the father of the whole movement, and is now given a place in great public collections throughout the world. A Gallery of Modern Foreign Art without Cézanne is like a gallery of Florentine art without Giotto.

---

12 C.J. Holmes, 'Cézanne and the Nation', letter to the editor, *Burlington Magazine*, XXXVIII, June 1921, pp. 313–14

Response to text no. 11.
For Holmes, see text no. 4.

Sir, – Since Mr. Aitken's name figures rather largely in your article on the lending of pictures by Cézanne to the Tate Gallery, it is only fair to him to point out that the decision about them was taken by the Board as a whole. So far, indeed, as Mr. Aitken's personal record can be guessed in connection with the acceptance of loans by the Tate Gallery, I think it will be found to be one of consistent generosity and of conspicuous success. If the Board on this or any other occasion may seem to depart from that policy, its character and constitution are now surely guarantees that a departure is not made without good reason: and those who have followed the history of the National Gallery with any attention will know that trustees have cause to scrutinize with caution all offers of loans, even when the offers are made by private owners of repute and independence.

To descend from generalities, I much regret that as a member of the Board, I am precluded from commenting on the paintings themselves, but I must compliment your photographer on the tactful flattery with which he has handled the less fortunate of his two subjects.

[We gladly publish the above. We used Mr. Aitken's name only when quoting from his letter to the press which was the immediate occasion of our comment. But we never for a moment thought or suggested that he or any other individual was wholly or chiefly responsible for what we believe to have been a mistake. – EDITOR.]

---

13 Hugh Blaker, 'Cézanne and the Nation', letter to the editor, *Burlington Magazine*, XXXIX, July 1921, p. 50

Response to text no. 12.
For Blaker, see text no. 9.

Sir, – Sir C.J. Holmes is right when he points out that Mr. C. Aitken should be exonerated from the responsibility of rejecting the Cézannes offered on loan to the Tate Gallery by Miss G. Davies. As a former curator I understand.

Sir Charles does not betray any great enthusiasm for Cézanne, and suggests that the photographer is responsible for the merit of one of your illustrations in the BURLINGTON. I know, Sir, that this is not your view or that of anyone else who has seen the pictures. These two examples would have filled an almost inexplicable gap in our national collection.

Mr. Aitken stated in his letter to the *Observer* that it would be necessary to remove work from the foreign gallery in order to hang the Cézannes. In the opinion of myself and others they could have been adequately hung without the removal of a single exhibit.

History is repeating itself. The National Gallery set its face against the Barbizon school as revolutionary, and the 1870 impressionists were considered impossible. When these pictures were established in world opinion it was too late. Fortunately George Salting and Hugh Lane came to the rescue. To-day Gauguin has been forced in, but Van Gogh languishes. Cézanne is spurned. A similar tale will be told with regard to the moderns, both English and French. Prospective donors of French pictures are eagerly waiting for a glimmer of light. Representative works by Spencer Gore and Gilman have been refused.

The nation is indebted to the BURLINGTON for its splendid advocacy of the moderns, and this must surely bear fruit.

---

14 From D.S. MacColl, 'The Nonsense about Cézanne', *Saturday Review*, 19 November 1921, pp. 579–80

Article on Cézanne's influence on contemporary painters, with reference to the appropriateness of his inclusion in the national art collections.

Dugald Sutherland MacColl (1859–1948) had been one of the most enthusiastic supporters of French Impressionism since the beginning of his career as art critic, first for the *Spectator* (1890–6), then for the *Saturday Review* (1896–1906, 1921–30); he also championed the Impressionists as organizer of a section of the Glasgow Exhibition of 1900, and in the resulting book, *Nineteenth Century Art* (1902). In the 1890s, he was active as a watercolour painter, exhibiting at the Goupil Gallery and the New English Art Club (member 1896). Subsequently, he became Editor of *Architectural Review* (1901–5), Keeper of the Tate Gallery (1906–11, succeeded by Aitken; see text no. 10), and Keeper of the Wallace Collection (1911–24, following Phillips; see text no. 5). MacColl was an indefatigable activist on the issue of the national art collections, publishing an indictment of *The Administration of the Chantrey Bequest* (1904); he was involved in the foundation of both the National Art-Collections Fund (1903) and the Contemporary Art Society (see text no. 19).

[. . .] the residuum that needs be considered is Cézanne. So it is high time we tackled him.

I have attempted it more than once before; but discussion with Mr. Fry and Mr. Bell is like talking to the nebular hypothesis. In my isolation therefore I look round for some ally who has the ear of the painters and critics of the *avant garde*, and I find him in Mr. Walter Sickert, included, as he is, in the bundle of their incompatible admirations. Mr. Sickert is not only one of the best painters of his generation, but a sound, as well as brilliant critic, when he is not writing about contemporaries with his tongue in his cheek. I wish I could reprint here the whole of his notice of M. Coquiot's book on Cézanne from the too-cloistered pages of the *Anglo-French Review* for April, 1920: my readers should buy the number, or look it up. After explaining that Cézanne was not a 'Post-Impressionist,' but an Impressionist, by which he means involved in the habit of painting by rapid notation 'direct from nature,' Mr. Sickert reaches the pith of the matter in the following paragraphs:

Cézanne was by nature deplorably, lamentably, tragically, almost incredibly wanting in the two main gifts of a painter: the sense of direction (in the 180° of two right angles), which is the whole and sole basis of drawing, and swiftness, without which nature will leave you hopelessly behind. But he had a sense of colour and a passion, an absorbing, incurable passion for the delicious substance which is a mixture of coloured powders and linseed oil, and for spreading the same in season and out of season on taut and rectangular drums of flax. Any real natural process produces a beauty of its own. The order in which the apples are spilled from a tree has its beauty, and the passion and method of his very incapacity produced a style which was his, the like of which we shall not, it is to be hoped, be asked to look upon again. His service was to reduce to the absurd the habit of painting 'pictures from nature.'

For some fifteen years again and again has the corpse of Cézanne been carried round the capitals of the world as a *convoi d'opposition*. From the Rue Laffitte, from the Prater, from the Fifth Avenue, from the Dultplatz and from Unter den Linden has issued the same stage army of pall-bearers, the Napoleons of the sale-room. And now, even from the West End of London and, I am told, from Whistler's Chelsea, may be seen to emerge a panic-stricken figure or two adjusting its hatband and splitting its funeral gloves in its haste to capture the tail of a *cordon*. The sincere fanaticism of the convinced *critique d'avant-garde* of an earlier day has been succeeded by a frantic and blind toeing of the line. The offices of the critical naturalisation bureaux are besieged by queues of pressmen every one of them tremulous to change his name.

The truth then is that Cézanne was involved in painting by methods which are properly those of sketching, and very imperfectly qualified for that desperate business, because before the subject – living model, landscape, flowers – anything that under conditions of movement, decay, or changing lights required decisive placing, striking of proportions, circumscription of forms, he was nervously impotent. He had to renounce the model altogether, got into a helpless fury over portraiture, abandoned his landscapes in disgust, and had to retreat from flowers, which fade, upon apples and napkins, which are relatively stable but monotonous. His reaction against his brother impressionists arose from a positive quality he possessed and held by, a taste for broad fat patches of colour, as opposed to the broken mosaic of touches adopted by Monet and carried *ad absurdum* by Pissarro with his stipple technique. But over the shaping of those patches he had little control. In a certain number of his pieces his genuine taste for colour and the quality of paint won the battle against his disabilities, and one accepts the arbitrary nature of the demarcations for the sake of the delicious, firmly-struck notes that survive.

Now the Cézannists of *avant-garde* criticism and the imitators reverse this order: they elevate the impotence and the disabilities into virtues, and found an esoteric system upon accidents that the master himself would have gnashed his teeth about. Because his flower-pots tottered and were bashed all flower pots must do the like, and in doing so illustrate the mysteries of 'designing in depth.' Because Cézanne dismissed trees, which are a never-ending problem of rendering, with an angry shorthand gesture, they multiply the defeat *ad nauseam*. Like the followers of Rembrandt, they set up shop upon the failures, and leave out what ensures the survivals, that blond singing colour in succulent pastes. And they attempt to codify the grunts and growls and expletives of Cézanne's conversation into the revelation of a code. Cézanne had as much difficulty with words as with drawing; his conversation, if one may trust M. Vollard, did not go much beyond 'the word of five letters' or of Cambronne, but he muttered something about painting being solid like that in the museums, and over such oracles webs of comment have been spun. Cézanne will have his niche in the museums for the skirmishes in which his gift fought through, and at Millbank, let us hope, among the rest; even the Louvre, at present, has a very mixed lot, and it is useless to show the failures. But the prices are formidable. Thieme and Becker, those close students of history remark dryly, under *Cézanne*,

Nach 1890 kaufte der junge Pariser Kunsthändler Vollard von Cézanne's Sohn 200 Bilder des Meisters fur 80,000 Fr. [*i.e.*, about £16 each], für die er damals nur wenige Liebhaber fand.

We are still under the dispensation, commercial and critical, that filled the places vacated on the market by Manet and Monet, with Cézanne and Renoir. And the like nonsense was talked about Monet, and still is by those who do not use their eyes.

15 A. Clutton-Brock, '"Anarchists" in Painting: French Classics of Last Century: Burlington Fine Arts Club', *The Times*, 23 May 1922, p. 13

Review of the Burlington Fine Arts Club exhibition of 1922.

Arthur Clutton-Brock (1868–1924) was art critic for *The Times* from 1908–24, having begun his journalistic career as literary editor of the *Speaker* (1904–6) and art critic for the *Tribune* and *Morning Post*. He combined critical work with a strong interest in social issues, joining the Fabian Society in 1909; after World War I he wrote increasingly on religion. His *Essays on Art* were published in 1919.

The Summer Exhibition of the Burlington Fine Arts Club, to be seen by invitation only, consists of French art of the last one hundred years. There are fewer than fifty pictures in the main gallery, but most of them are masterpieces, beginning with Corot and ending with Gauguin. Most of them, too, have been thought monstrosities in their time; yet now the general effect is of classic grandeur and simplicity: one sees how the French school has succeeded the Florentine as upholder of the great central tradition of European art. Movements occur which are said to be anarchical at their start; but the more this art changes the more it is the same thing, and Gauguin's 'L'Esprit veille' comes out of Ingres.

In fact, the good critic is he who can discern this tradition at once, and through all its changes; who can detect a real anarchist, which means a fool or a charlatan. There are none of these here. Corot has two lovely and early landscapes, and a beautiful 'girl writing,' painted with the touch of a landscape artist, but with no lack of precision. It proceeds out of Chardin, and equals him. There are two fine Coutures, an artist less known in England than he deserves; one a study for the portrait of Michelet at Versailles, but a study in which all the finished work is implied; the other a nude woman, a noble work in which the modelling flows like music. There are several Manets: a study for the Luxembourg picture, 'On the Balcony,' cool in colour and lucid in design; a portrait of a lady, Victorine Meurard [sic], which reminds one almost of Raphael in its unforced simplification; several still lifes, and an interesting, very early, work, 'Woman at a Door,' in which we see that from the very first he could paint as a bird sings. By Degas is a large portrait, 'Diego Martelli,' brilliant but among the other masterpieces a little superficial, almost farcical in conception, but executed with incongruous seriousness. There is the same brilliant triviality in his 'At the Café.' In other company it would look a masterpiece, but here it seems flimsy.

Renoir is represented by a portrait of a girl, 'L'Ingénue,' which seems to be painted of dew and air; a landscape 'Spring,' which is spring itself rather than any particular place; and a rare and beautiful still life. Courbet, in two examples, looks heavy and laboured compared with the others, but it is strange to remember that he was once called an anarchist in art. Here he is an able but not very living Academic painter. There are several Cézannes, among them one of melancholy interest, the 'Landscape' (40), because it was, we believe, refused as a gift by the Tate Gallery. We are not fanatics for Cézanne – in this very exhibition we find more than enough of his everlasting apples – but this landscape is not only grand in form but flushed with rich and almost heady colour. When we remember some landscapes that have been not accepted, but actually bought for the Tate Gallery, we are bewildered. There is also another fine, if extremely simplified, landscape (44), and yet another, small and with figures (17), in which we see this curious artist at his very best. For here, behind his rough or misty shapes, he seems to give us the very stir and change of life. Gauguin's 'L'Esprit veille' holds its own with everything, and is no more revolutionary than Manet's 'Olympe' or Botticelli's 'Mars and Venus.' Among the sculpture are fine works by Rodin, Barye, and Dalou; and in the room below are some drawings, among them Mr. Heseltine's beautiful Corot, 'A Woman Seated,' and some good Daumiers, Degas, and Manets.

16 Roger Fry, 'The Burlington Fine Arts Club: Cézanne Once More', *New Statesman*, 27 May 1922, pp. 210–11

Review of the Burlington Fine Arts Club exhibition of 1922.
  For Fry, see text no. 7.

I am quite aware how much this caption begins to resemble King Charles's head, but it is not my fault. It is the irrepressible Cézanne's, and perhaps a little the fault of those who make wry faces over the pill that now, for a long time, they have known that they must swallow. For here is Cézanne enthroned in the very sanctum of the Burlington Fine Arts Club, where for many years past he has been the great stone of offence. It has taken eleven years to move him from the Grafton Gallery to Savile Row; how many more will it take, one wonders, to get him to Millbank or, better still, to Trafalgar Square, where he will be more at home? Anyhow, the turn of the tide has come with a vengeance, for no other artist is so fully represented as Cézanne. In spite of the strict limits of space, room has been found for eight of his works. Not all are of the first quality. Except for the tiny picture of apples lent by Mr. Maynard Keynes, none of the still life pieces comes up to the highest level. But the little composition lent by Prince Bibesco, No. 17, and the two landscapes, Nos. 40, 44, lent by Miss Davies, are superb.

No. 40 in particular seems to me one of the greatest of all Cézanne's landscapes, and I dare hardly say how high a place that gives it for me in all known examples of landscape art. It is a typical Provençal landscape. One looks across an expanse of sun-baked slopes carved into ravines and dotted with trees in early summer leafage, to a wide river glimpsed between gaps in the rocks and trees, and beyond that to a distant mass of mountains seen under the vibrating light of an almost colourless sky.

To say that this painting is miraculous may sound like mere rhetoric, but I use the word merely to call attention to the way in which Cézanne has here resolved the antinomies which present themselves inevitably in landscape. Thus, on the one hand, it is necessary to evoke in the spectator's mind the sequences of planes which build up the scene, and the exact recession from the eye of each plane, and on the other it is necessary to do this without destroying in some sense the surface of the canvas. These apparently contradictory claims are resolved in different ways by different artists, generally with a leaning in one direction or the other, one artist inclining to the *trompe l'œil*, another to the decorative panel.

What I call miraculous in this picture is the extent to which both claims seem to be satisfied to their fullest possible extent. One may look at this canvas almost as one would look at some rich Oriental textile, woven out of the rarest and most exquisitely adjusted colours and materials into a pattern of the most complex and yet evident equilibrium; none the less, all the time one is vividly conscious of its plastic relief, of exactly how one plane leads to another, of the rocky structure of the scene, of the recession of the distant mountain and the elusive sky. Such recessions are usually attained by atmospheric perspective, by allowing greater contrasts of tone in the foreground than in the distance, but this implies inevitably some loss of unity of texture. Here there are no marked differences in the scale of tone from the nearest foreground to the furthest distance, and yet every recession is not merely indicated but vividly expressed. Another antinomy:—Are we to give as nearly as possible the full radiance of sunlight by painting in a high key? If we do we go outside the scale in which oil paint produces its finest notes. If not we must transpose the pitch and lose the brilliance and radiance of open-air light.

Renoir in No. 37, and Seurat, No. 25, chose the former. They would have radiance at all costs but they have to pay the price and, for all their astonishing beauty, beside this Cézanne, they look a little fragile. The landscapists of the seventeenth century chose the other alternative; they kept in the scale natural to oil paint and lowered the pitch of nature. But they, too, lose something. How, then, has Cézanne managed as here to make the best of both alternatives. For certainly this is irradiated with light and no less certainly it has the gravity and resonance, the density of colour, which the *pleine-airists* missed and the classic landscapists got at a price.

Again he has conciliated here, even more perhaps than elsewhere, the opposing claims of design and the total vision of Nature. In early art design is effected by some kind of schematisation or another, as for instance, in the Primitives the schematising of the total colour impression into local colours. Impressionism accepted for the first time the resultant total of vision in all its complexity and, to a large extent, had to scrap structural design. Cézanne here seems to have penetrated below appearance to the plastic elements of the scene and to have come back again to clothe it once more in all its complexity and elusiveness. The structural design is as lucid and as absolute as one can possibly demand, and yet at no moment is the unanalysable infinity of Nature lost sight of. Pure and even bright colours are here, but everywhere they are so richly and so minutely modulated that the web of the texture is never interrupted.

It is said that this is one of the pictures that was offered on loan to the Tate Gallery, and refused by the authorities on the ground of want of space; the further reason being given that it was not a good example. Those who have spent their time in abusing Cézanne instead of looking at him might, no doubt, arrive at this conclusion, but I believe everyone who is familiar with his work will agree with me that it is among the master's finest works, and that nothing could be more useful to art students than to have unlimited opportunities to study it.

One aspect, and that a very pleasing one, of Renoir is well represented. One gets no idea here of those great compositions of nude figures which preoccupied him from time to time throughout his career. One sees him here in delightful impromptus, in which all his exquisite sensibility is called into play directly by some fortunate aspect of nature. In the landscape No. 44, it is the dazzle of June sunshine on a meadow of long grass bleached by the intensity of the light. The approach to nature is as direct and spontaneous as in a slight sketch, but Renoir could hold the shock of a first inspiration through the long processes of complete realisation. Nothing of the thrill of lyrical delight is lost in this highly-finished work.

Curiously similar in feeling is the rather unusual still-life of a melon cut in slices, with a vase of flowers. It is a radiantly happy work, in which one is scarcely conscious of anything but a spontaneous and irresistible joy in light and colour. One must almost have wrestled with obstinate pigment oneself to realise how much learning and research must have preceded this apparently instinctive outburst.

If one turns from this to Ingres' *Odalisque* one gets, at first approach, a cold douche of frigid exhortation. It is as though one stepped from a wood full of nightingales to listen to a sermon by a Presbyterian divine—a sermon, too, with a text from the Song of Solomon, in which every voluptuous image is made to serve some dry theological exegesis. All that the imagination can invent to picture to itself the 'gorgeous East' is here piled together, ostensibly for delight, but it is described in an inventory so arid, precise and abstract as to nip the hottest appetite. The delights of the seraglio have precious little to do with what Ingres offers us. There is, indeed, something almost insolent in the contrast between the pretext which promises so much and the performance which refuses all—refuses all, that is to say, except what Ingres gives, namely, his ardent pursuit of a divinely beautiful rhythm. This rhythm is realised completely in the figure of the odalisque, and the accessories which surround her; the figure of the music-making attendant is also a wonderful discovery, but it must be admitted that parts of the background fail to support or continue the dominant theme. They tend to become thin scenic descriptions, with no completely realised relation to the figures. For all that, and in spite of the flat, ungrateful oleographic quality of some of the background, only a very great artist could have disappointed one so magnificently. To realise this, glance for a moment at Courbet's great picture, No. 28, full of splendid generous qualities, but how casual and happy-go-lucky, or his portrait, No. 31, with some great passages of handling and colour in the dress and shawl, but breaking down in rhythm entirely when one comes to the head.

Manet is finely seen in his *Sur le Balcon*, No. 12, a study from the well-known composition in the Luxembourg. It is far better than the finished work; exquisitely distinguished in colour and handling. Corot is but scantily, and in one case, I thought, doubtfully, represented. The little view from the Pincian, No. 3, has passages in the distance where one recognises his intense sensibility to the colour of sun-saturated air, but already in the trees and the fountain the fatal tendency to poetic emphasis is beginning.

I have no room to speak of so difficult a figure as Degas, but it would not be fair to omit altogether the splendid sketch of two women at a café, No. 35. This is Degas almost at his best.

---

17   Frank Rutter, 'A Century of French Art', *Sunday Times*, 28 May 1922, p. 7

Review of the Burlington Fine Arts Club exhibition of 1922.
For Rutter, see text no. 1.

To students of modern painting the exhibition which has recently opened at the Burlington Fine Arts Club is one of the most interesting and one of the most instructive ever held in Savile Row. It consists of pictures, drawings, and sculpture of the French School of the last 100 years, and though it does not pretend to be a complete representation of 'one of the most fertile centuries in the history of French art,' it miraculously fills many gaps that unfortunately still exist in our national collections. This is the supreme value of the exhibition which is now open to the members of the Burlington and their guests.

A hundred years ago or thereabouts the dominant influences in European painting were three French artists—Ingres, Delacroix, and Courbet, who are now recognised by all historians to have been the pillars respectively of Classic, Romantic, and Realist Art. Of this great trio only Delacroix is represented in the Wallace Collection, for the little drawing by Ingres after Raphael cannot be considered an adequate representation. But paintings by all three appear in the Burlington Exhibition. Those by Delacroix are only minor examples; that does not matter, because we always have a fine and characteristic Delacroix in 'The Execution of the Doge Marino Falieri' at the Wallace. What we have not got in our national collections is any painting by Ingres to compare with 'L'Odalisque à l'Esclave' (16), lent by Sir Philip Sassoon to the Burlington. It is a superb example of the great draughtsman who came out of David's studio.

By the youngest of these three giants, Gustave Courbet, we have some small examples in Trafalgar Square and South Kensington, but we have no great figure painting by him like the two in Savile Row. The large 'Woman at a Trellis arranging Flowers' (28), now lent by Mrs. R.A. Workman, was formerly in the collection of Mme. Blanche Marchesi, if I remember correctly, and is a fine example of Courbet's breadth and realism, though in colour it is comparatively dark and it has not the limpid clearness of his superb portrait 'La Dame au parasol' (31), lent by Mr. William Burrell. This charming half-length in its aerial qualities and refined colour is essential Courbet, an epitome of the master who was the forerunner of Manet and the earlier impressionists.

MANET AND RENOIR

The relationship between Courbet and Manet is obvious when we compare this portrait with the latter's 'Victorine Meurard' [*sic*] (42), a superb head lent by M. Alphonse Kann. It is a famous Manet, this, and in its suavity and freshness we recognise the continuation of Courbet's realism. It was only now and again in some of his later paintings, especially in garden and river scenes, that Manet was an impressionist in the sense of rendering the prismatic sparkle of sunlight; this aspect of his art is not represented at the Burlington, but it has some very beautiful examples of his normal practice, an atmospheric realism based on the silver tones of Velasquez. The tiny panel 'Woman at a Door' (29), dated 1858, is exquisitely dainty in colour and handling; the still-life 'Silk Hat, Bottle, Books and Flowers' (24) is a gracious link between Chardin and Fantin, while the small canvas of 'Two Roses' (23), which was in Manet's studio at the time of his death, proves how his brush-work to the end maintained its brilliant bravura. If he were the heir of Velasquez and Courbet, Manet was also the forebear of Sargent and Boldini.

Extraordinarily interesting also are two Renoirs. The landscape 'Spring' (37), painted in 1875, is a transitional work, all delicate greens and yellows, light in key for its period but not painted with the rainbow palette he afterwards adopted. The portrait, 'L'Ingénue' (19), lent by M. Alphonse Kann, is a masterpiece. This little girl with her finger to her mouth is alive and breathing; she is the incarnation of girlish grace, and the execution is of a miraculous lightness. The paint seems not so much laid on as breathed on with a gentle felicity of which only Renoir and Gainsborough appear to have been capable.

DEGAS AND SEURAT

A large, full-length portrait of 'Diego Martelli' (38) is the most important painting here by Degas. It is amazingly original, and I cannot recall a portrait in which the sitter appears so oblivious of the painter. He appears to have been caught unaware amid the litter of his room; he is utterly unconcerned and his surroundings are casual, and yet with all this appearance of accident every accessory has its place and plays its part in the general design. It is a wonderful piece of composition, Japanese in its unexpectedness and happy decorative effect, and it is splendidly drawn and painted. Two smaller works, the painting 'Au Café: Deux Femmes Attablées' (35) and the pastel 'Femme s'essuyant' (63), show other aspects of the art of Degas.

'The Seurat Landscape' (No. 25), lent by Mr. Roger Fry, is a good example of this painter's fine colour-sense and of his complete mastery of the science of divisionism, but it hardly reveals the great powers Georges Seurat also possessed as a designer. No doubt the colour has toned down and was far more brilliant when it was first painted, but though it still contains much beauty it does indicate the inherent weakness in after years of a painting that depends almost entirely on the brilliancy of its colour. The future reputation of Seurat is safe, however, because he has proved in many works that he was great, both as a colourist and as a designer.

CEZANNE

While the works already enumerated are quite enough to make the exhibition memorable, the outstanding feature of the collection has yet to be mentioned. This is the group of paintings by Paul Cézanne, whose work, since his death in 1906, has been the subject of so much controversy, admiration, misunderstanding and enthusiasm. Its appearance in this Mecca of connoisseurship is a sign that educated opinion in England now recognises him as a great master. Unfortunately, this group includes no figure painting, but otherwise it is worthily representative.

The still-life paintings are particularly good and include the superb 'Apples and Tea-cup' (14), from the Alphonse Kann collection, and the fine 'Fruit with a Rug and Tea-pot' (33), lent by Miss G. Davies. Miss Davies also lends a landscape (40) admirably typical of the substantial stateliness with which Cézanne painted the South of France. Recognising in these paintings the essential truth of his vision and the honest vigour of his execution, the visitor may pardonably forget that Cézanne was ever labelled a 'post-impressionist' and may place him justifiably among the great realists of painting.

Of the exotic romanticism of Gauguin, Sir Michael Sadler's 'l'Esprit Veille' (21) is so superb an example that we do not feel the want of any other. This recumbent nude summarises the art of Gauguin and occupies in his *oeuvre* a place analogous to that of the 'Olympie' in the art of Manet.

18 'Burlington Fine Arts Club', *Connoisseur*, LXIII, July 1922, pp. 177–8

Anonymous review of the Burlington Fine Arts Club exhibition of 1922.

Burlington Fine Arts Club

The current exhibition at the Burlington Fine Arts Club (17, Savile Row, W.1) is devoted to examples of French art during the past century. With such a large scope, it was hardly to be expected that the display would prove thoroughly representative, or that it would do more than sample a few of the main styles of painting which obtained in France during the period covered. This assumption proved to be entirely correct, since, as stated in a note to the catalogue, the Committee has neither 'attempted to secure even a single specimen of the work of many of the well-known painters who flourished during those years,' nor has it violated the club's rule which forbids the display of works by living artists. Even allowing for these severe limitations, the record must be considered, on the whole, as one of failure rather than of success. A few masters are, it is true, favourably represented. Corot is happily shown in a delightful gem from the Municipal Gallery of Modern Art, Dublin – *Rome: La Vasque de l'Académie de France* – and in an interesting but uncharacteristic figure study – *Girl Writing* (Mr. John S. Sargent). There is a typically atmospheric Boudin, *Harbour Scene* (Mons. L. Mégret); a fine Daubigny, *The Windmills*, a river scene, grey in tone and lighted up by two or three patches of red (Lt.-Col. Sir W. Hutcheson Poë, Bt.); and a masterly *Study of the Nude*, by Couture (Mr. Ludovic G. Foster). These pictures are all attractive because they appear to be spontaneous expressions of their creators' feelngs; but with the highly laboured *L'Odalisque à l'Esclave* of Ingres (Sir Philip Sassoon, Bt.) one experiences an atmosphere of artificiality. The superb draughtsmanship manifested in the reclining form is neutralised by the excessive general finish, and by the elaboration of unessential detail in the background. More thoroughly satisfying, because less sophisticated and pretentious, are the portrait drawings by Ingres, shown in another room, which, though hard, are wonderfully precise and searching. Degas appears, at first sight, to belong to the opposite pole of art to Ingres, and yet one feels that he, too, suffered through painting according to preconsidered arrangements rather than by giving vent to his natural emotions. His portrait of *Diego Martelli* (Mrs. R.A. Workman) is an attempt, by a master of line and composition, to make an uninteresting figure attractive by sheer force of design. The tumble-down effect imparted by what may be termed the *coup d'œil* perspective is highly uncomfortable, and the figure of the subject vulgar and clumsy. Manet is best seen in some still-life subjects, which command respect by sheer merit of technique. Renoir seems to have sacrificed everything to atmospheric expression in

L'Ingenue (Mons. Alphonse Kann), and has almost completely ignored the claims of form and texture. Seurat's *Landscape* (Mr. Roger Fry) is an effort realistically to express the effect of a broad expanse of herbage seen under ordinary atmospheric conditions, but the result is an impression completely lacking in pictorial interest. The half-dozen works by Cézanne make one wonder how this painter's great reputation has been achieved, since he neither attempted realism nor did he succeed in attaining a decorative effect. A clever, though not a very searching, work is an unknown artist's *Still Life – Oysters* (Mr. P. Wilson Steer); while Daumier's *Head of a Man* (Miss G. Davies) and *L'Avocat Triomphant* (Mr. William Burrell), with Couture's *Portrait of Michelet*, a study for the portrait at Versailles, all display certainly, if somewhat too obviously, the technical abilities of their authors. In *L'Esprit Veille (Manaò Tupaù)*, 1893 (Sir Michael and Lady Sadler), is given an example of Gauguin at his best – a best which is marred by the calculated *naïveté* of the presentation. The colour-scheme is rich and compelling, but the woman, lying face downwards on the couch, is clumsily introduced in the composition, which is singularly lacking in the significance with which a greater man would have invested it.

19 John Maynard Keynes, Comment on the Courtauld Trust, *Nation and Athenaeum*, 18 August 1923, p.633

Published anonymously in the 'Life and Politics' column of the *Nation and Athenaeum*.

John Maynard Keynes (1883–1946), the celebrated economist, was an enthusiastic supporter of art, drama, and ballet. He was instrumental in obtaining Treasury funds for the National Gallery to purchase at the Degas sale of 1918, beginning his own private art collection at the same sale (see above, p. 12). In addition to occasional contributions on the arts to periodicals like the *New Statesman* and the *Nation and Athenaeum*, he was active in many arts organizations, including the Contemporary Art Society, the London Artists' Association, and the Committee for the Encouragement of Music and the Arts (later the Arts Council; Chairman from 1942).

Mr. SAMUEL COURTAULD's munificent gift of £50,000, for the purchase of the works 'of painters centring round the great Frenchmen of the latter half of the nineteenth century' to fill the Modern Foreign Gallery which is being erected as an annexe to the Tate Gallery at the expense of Sir Joseph Duveen, comes just in time to fill a great and notorious gap in our national collections. Within the last ten years the authorities of the National Galleries have refused to purchase works by Cézanne, and more lately even to accept on loan important examples of the master. But time is a mighty one and conquers all things, – even the obstinacy, ignorance and bad taste of the official custodians. Mr Courtauld's assault has been on a big enough scale to overwhelm them, and he deserves the thanks of the nation. It is a little ironical that the Directors of the Galleries in Trafalgar Square and Millbank, who have honestly disliked these pictures for so many years, should be entrusted with the duty of selecting them; and it would be worse than ironical – since the pictures they dislike least are liable to be those least characteristic of the masters – if it were not that their taste is to be corrected and supervised by three genuine lovers of these pictures, Lord Henry Bentinck, Sir Michael Sadler, and Mr. Courtauld himself, who are to be associated with them in the task of selection.

Of course, at this time of day, big prices must be paid for the best examples, – enormous compared with those ruling when Mr. Roger Fry began to educate the British public into an understanding of the great

French masters of the last fifty years, painters as great as any that have ever lived. Nevertheless, heavy absorption into the United States has only lately begun, and it is still just possible to buy at a price the finest specimens of masters, who were by no means prolific, such as Cézanne, Daumier, and Manet, and even, perhaps, of a very rare master such as Seurat, – a thing which may not be possible at all ten years hence. The only regret to be felt is that the works of contemporary Frenchmen are apparently excluded. Would it not be well to secure first-rate specimens of (for example) Derain, Picasso, and Matisse, whilst they can be purchased at a comparatively modest figure, and whilst the living artist is still there to benefit? For, however much individual opinions may differ as to the enjoyment to be got from their art, the position of these original geniuses in the development of European painting is already sufficiently secure to justify their representation in the National Museums. Even if it is inevitable that the official world should move with a slower velocity, and that the voice of Mr. Fry, swiftly voyaging into undiscovered lands amidst new flowers and yet untasted fruits, should seem to come from the wilderness rather than from the Promised Land of the future, one cannot but sigh a little that this should be so.

20 'The Courtauld Gift', *The Times*, 8 February 1924, p. 11

Announcement and commentary on active operation of the Courtauld Trust.

The Director of the National Gallery (Millbank) announces to-day that the Courtauld Trust is now in active operation and that six pictures have been acquired out of the fund. It was during last August that the news of this notable gift was officially made public. The Board of the National Gallery (Millbank), commonly called the Tate Gallery, had accepted the offer of MR. SAMUEL COURTAULD of £50,000 to certain trustees for the purchase of modern foreign pictures of a kind which the nation might not otherwise easily acquire. The purchases were to be confined to the works of a definite list of painters centring round the great Frenchmen of the latter half of the nineteenth century. A great deal lay behind the words: 'Pictures of a kind which the nation might not otherwise easily acquire.' But a few years ago conservative artistic opinion in England was still (to put it very mildly) exceedingly shy of the art of the 'painters centring round the great Frenchmen of the latter half of the nineteenth century.' By the formation and bequest of his own collection, the late SIR HUGH LANE had struck a blow for these dreaded or neglected painters; but it was still realized that before such masters were accepted by the naturally conservative governing bodies, in whose hands lay the fate of our collection of modern art, the last chance of getting examples of their work would long have vanished. And even when changed conditions of trusteeship brought a change of heart to the Tate Gallery, there remained the difficulty, apparently as insurmountable, of so working on the bowels of a harassed and retrenching Treasury as to induce them to make the needed grant for modern art which their peace-time predecessors had stonily withheld. It seemed a desperate case. But now, by his splendid gift and statesmanlike scheme, MR. COURTAULD has accomplished the formation of just such a collection of modern foreign masters as had been despaired of. Already we can feel easier about MANET, RENOIR, DEGAS, and VAN GOGH.

MR. COURTAULD's name will go down to posterity affixed to beautiful things, in the honourable company of those who, prizing beauty, had the patriotism and the vision to contribute to our fund and heritage of art. It may be that MR. COURTAULD's name will be held in esteem distinct from that in which we hold the names of GEORGE BEAUMONT, WYNN ELLIS, TEMPLE-WEST, LAYARD and SALTING; not because their generosity was less than his, but because his way of giving differs from theirs in two ways. It is more practical in detail, in that it includes a list of artists whose works the donor thinks most important to our national collections; and in that it has the great merit of permitting, under certain conditions, the sale of pictures already acquired under the gift. Secondly, it is more clearly directed to a special need. Those others splendidly bequeathed to the nation examples of old art, essential to our national art. MR. COURTAULD, by his immediate gift, has brought within our reach examples of great masters, who, though dead, yet live as standards round which our painters rally and contend. In this his gift ranks with that of HUGH LANE, whom we now salute for having intrepidly prepared the way for an acceptance of MR. COURTAULD's munificence unsullied by scandal and controversy. It comes all the more timely because it falls in the centenary year of our National Gallery.

21 Members of the Contemporary Art Society, 'Modern Art Abroad: Proposed Purchases for the Nation', letter to the editor, *The Times*, 30 May 1924, p. 19

Announcement of the Contemporary Art Society's establishment of a fund for the purchase of contemporary foreign art for the national art collections. See above, p. 19.

Sir. – It has long been a reproach that our national and provincial galleries contain so little representative work by foreign artists of the last half-century. Mr. Samuel Courtauld's recent gift of £50,000 will do something to remedy that defect as regards the deceased masters of the last generation.

The Contemporary Art Society, which works along parallel lines to the National Art-Collections Fund, but confines its activities to modern art, has long felt that it would be very desirable to create a fund for the purchase of contemporary foreign work. Could this be done, it would complement the purchases of the Courtauld fund. An anonymous donor has most generously offered to hand over £1,000 to the Contemporary Art Society for this purpose provided a like amount can be raised by them.

We venture, therefore, to appeal to the art-loving public through your columns in the hope that so favourable an opportunity will not be missed.

The Contemporary Art Society from time to time hands over its purchases to various public galleries not only in London but throughout the provinces. Provincial lovers of art and artists have, as a rule, but little opportunity of becoming acquainted with the more vital work of foreign artists which can be seen from time to time in exhibitions in London. We believe that if by means of such a fund examples of the best foreign work could be shown in the public galleries of the chief centres of artistic training in England it would have a most stimulating effect upon artistic development in this country.

Meanwhile, with a view to starting the fund the committee of the Contemporary Art Society are arranging for an exhibition of work by living foreign masters lent by private collectors in this country. The exhibition will be held at Messrs. Colnaghi's Gallery, New Bond-street. The Prime Minister has kindly consented to open the exhibition on June 20 at 2:30 p.m. Admission to the special private view will be by ticket, which can be obtained at the door. All profits of the exhibition, which will remain open until July 4, will be devoted to the foreign purchases fund. Subscriptions and donations to the fund will be acknowledged by Mr. H.S. Ede, National Gallery, Millbank, London, S.W.1.

We are, Sir, yours &c.,

HOWARD DE WALDEN	CAMPBELL DODGSON
HENRY BENTINCK	ROGER FRY
C. KENDALL-BUTLER	ST. JOHN HUTCHINSON

CHARLES AITKEN   EDWARD MARSH
MUIRHEAD BONE   MICHAEL E. SADLER
S. COURTAULD   PHILIP SASSOON.

22   Roger Fry, Preface to the catalogue of the Contemporary Art Society's *Loan Exhibition of Modern Foreign Painting*, Colnaghi's Galleries, 21 June–4 July 1924

For the circumstances surrounding this exhibition, see text no. 21.
    For Fry, see text no. 7.

It will probably be a surprise to many visitors to find that so large and, on the whole, so representative an exhibition of contemporary foreign painting should have been brought together by a selection from the works in private collections in this country.

To those who believe that each nation should cultivate its own garden and never look over the fence to see how their neighbours do this will be a matter for regret. To those who believe that the interchange of ideas between different nations enriches all it will be a source of satisfaction. To those also whose love of art makes them indifferent to national distinctions in this domain it cannot but be a joy to see how rich and how varied the products of the European tradition have been in the past few decades.

For the real fact is that there is now a European tradition, a common artistic language which is understood throughout the civilised world. And whether we like it or not we have to recognise that the central seat of this European tradition is Paris. Paris itself as regards art is not purely French; it is merely the convenient meeting place and radiating point for the artistic effort of Europe and almost of the whole civilised world. How much that European tradition is affected by these new French elements which it absorbs may be judged by the immense influence on it of a Spanish artist, Pablo Picasso.

This is no new state of things. The artists of the older generaion that are regarded to-day as the leading figures of the British school had the sense to acquire in Paris the European tradition.

Mr. Steer would not have been Steer but for Claude Monet, Sir John Sargent would not have painted Sargents but for Manet, nor would Edward Stott nor Mr. Clausen have painted the pictures they have had they not troubled to learn this traditional speech. They are not the less English artists for speaking in the central language of the art of their day.

Doubtless here and there a genius may express himself in the dialect of some isolated and remote province or even may express himself happily enough in an archaic style, but the great creators always endeavour to comply with the most central tradition of language of their own time.

That European tradition as we see it in the present Exhibition owes much too to non-European influences. Already in Whistler and Van Gogh the art of the Japanese print had made its contribution to the art of Europe; and here, no less, oriental influences may be traced. How much of Persian art may be guessed at behind Matisse's arabesques; there was too a moment when Negro art visibly influenced Picasso and Derain. In the work here seen, however, all these influences have already been assimilated and the European tradition continues unbroken but enriched by the tributary streams which have flowed into it.

That indeed is the history of all vital traditions, and only those who already despair of the art of our own country need fear the contact with foreign ideas which it is the purpose of the present Exhibition to encourage.

23   Raymond Mortimer, 'The French Pictures', *New Statesman*, 28 June 1924, pp. 349–50

Review of Contemporary Art Society's *Loan Exhibition of Modern Foreign Painting* (see texts nos 21–22).
    Raymond Mortimer (1895–1980), a distinguished literary critic, was Literary Editor of the *New Statesman* from 1935–47, moving to the *Sunday Times* in 1947.

A brilliant season. That is to say, that the Kings and Queens of Roumania, Italy and Denmark have visited London, the Regent of Abyssinia is expected, the enclosure at Ascot was crammed, there are innumerable dinners and balls, and the dress-makers have done themselves proud. But artistically the season has hardly existed. After whetting our appetite with superb performances of *Rosenkavalier*, Covent Garden has been content to ring the changes on *Butterfly*, *Tosca*, and the like. In place of Stanislavski showing us how good a private theatre can be, we have been fobbed off with Mademoiselle Cécile Sorel showing us how bad a National Theatre usually is. And the appearance at the Coliseum of Argentina, the greatest Spanish dancer alive, passed comparatively unnoticed by public and Press alike. Till now the only great spectacle to attract attention has been the Rodeo, and magnificently spectacular it is. But at Wembley otherwise the most beautiful object is a locomotive, and the most impressive a gun. Even the so-called renaissance of architecture is merely producing harmless buildings in a genteel tradition, superior to nineteenth century buildings only negatively by their freedom from vulgarity, and in no way likely to be viewed by posterity with passionate admiration or even curiosity. As one walks up Bond Street past the photographs of *débutantes* and the pictures by Messrs. Frank Brangwyn and Tom Mostyn, past the onyx boxes, shagreen writing-pads, and expensively tooled bindings (who are the people I wonder, who buy their books at Asprey's?), past the cool recesses where new automobiles elegantly gleam, it seems that art in the old disinterested sense is dying, that the makers of objects that are merely beautiful are incongruous survivors of another age, and that in the future there will remain only the beauty which comes from perfect adaptation to function, the unintended beauty of the Rodeo, the gun, the factory, and the automobile. But stop your promenade in New Bond Street at No. 144 (Messrs. Colnaghi's) and look at the loan exhibition arranged there by the Contemporary Art Society. In an instant all moroseness and pessimism vanish, for here are pictures, painted all of them by living artists, as good as those that admired Old Masters have produced. Perhaps fine art has a future after all.

The criticism of painting is even more a matter of personal sensibility than the criticism of literature, the practicable arguments are more difficult to find, and the first person singular besets one at every turn. Indeed, once people have been warned not to look in pictures for qualities which the artist has not intended – and education in this respect must by now be pretty general – all the critic can usually do is to indicate his individual reactions in the most unlikely hope that they will interest someone else one-quarter as much as they interested himself. And the only reasons people have to listen to the remarks of a critic of painting are the understanding that he has looked at many works of every sort, and the gradual constatation that their own taste in some respect approximates to his.

Living French painters are on the whole very finely represented at the Contemporary Art Society's Exhibition. But by Picasso, whom I believe to be much the greatest artistic genius alive, there are only four pictures (and one drawing), none of them quite of the first importance. One of these, a poetic study of a girl, belongs to the Blue period (that is to say, it must have been painted some fifteen years ago) and of the three others, all abstract works, only one, Sir Michael Sadler's, can be at all a recent work. (The catalogue unfortunately does not date any of the pictures.) The irrepressible genius of Picasso is always spouting up in new directions, and in my opinion his latest are his most magnificent works. So that the absence of any of them is particularly regrettable. When the Contemporary Art Society has acquired sufficient funds, I hope that its first purchase may be one of these monumental Picassos. There has been no painting like them since Raphael.

Matisse, on the other hand, is superbly represented by a dozen pictures. For my part I would rather have the Braque 'Still Life' than any of them: a perfect example of the master's latest manner, it looms with increasing clearness in my memory as the most exquisite picture in the exhibition. But the Matisses, when one is actually faced with them, are irresistible, and this show is for him a personal triumph. Evidently English collectors find his work especially attractive, perhaps because it represents the gay side of the French character, the Riviera and La Fontaine as opposed to Provence and Pascal. All his pictures sing. The most recent of them, two seascapes, in which he is more occupied with giving a sense of space than he was in his earlier work, seem to me less engagingly painted than the others. The large 'Figure' lent by Mr. Coleman, grows on one the more one looks at it. The delicate pink and jade green in the upper part would seem utterly contradictory of the heavy red and brown in the lower part and of the brutal drawing of the nude figure. Yet the whole picture wonderfully coheres. What other living painter (or, for that matter, what dead one) could have successfully brought off such an effect? But I think the three most lovely Matisses here are Mr. Shearman's 'Lady at Table,' Mr. Hutchinson's 'Promenade des Anglais,' and Mr. Roger Fry's 'Nude.' Between them it would be painful to choose.

There are those who prefer Derain to any living painter. He is just as French as Matisse, but is by nature of the opposing party, austere, classical, deliberate, and, if you like, a Jansenist in paint. The two pictures lent by Mr. Jowitt, a 'Still Life' and a 'Head,' are both admirable examples of his art, and the show also contains two characteristic landscapes. Picasso, Braque, Matisse, Derain – it only needs Bonnard to complete the Big Five of contemporary painting; and here are Bonnards as lovely as anything you can conceive. Belonging spiritually, and, I fancy, actually, to an older generation than the others, he suffers somewhat from being placed among them. Their sensibilities, we feel, are closer to our own, their works make a sharper, more insistent appeal; but Bonnard is not on that account to be thought the lesser man. It is merely that the Shropshire Lad does not look his best when arm in arm with Mr. Prufrock.

Other painters represented include Rouault, Marie Laurencin, Segonzac, Friesz, Marchand, and Utrillo. The two paintings by the last-named are not particularly happy examples of his work, but in any case he is a painter, I consider, whom the more one sees, the less one likes. The Marchands are distinguished by a competence which, though a little unsympathetic and uninspired, makes their presence especially valuable in a country where incompetence in painting is so general. Friesz and Segonzac I prefer when they are not in the society of their betters, and it was particularly interesting to discover this in the case of the latter, because of the enormous claims made for him by some of his admirers, and of the extent to which he is being imitated in France. Marie Laurencin is entirely seductive, a deceptive siren, say some, but I at least cannot resist her. And though the picture lent by Mrs. Stoop is an extremely fine example, the actual paint of the other, and more recent, picture, shows a sure development in her art. Lastly Rouault. The works of this painter are so rarely to be seen even in Paris that the exhibition of six of them in London must interest all admirers of French painting. But for the same reason I can offer no very definite opinion about him. Two things are clear: that he achieves his object with remarkable decision and economy, and that he invests whatever he touches with intense dramatic

interest. From these works and such others as I have seen actually or in photographs I imagine he may be a very important painter.

Here then are to be seen the works of four first-rate painters, of five who are only slightly inferior to these, and of one, Picasso, whom I believe posterity will count among the greatest artists that Europe has produced. Their works are entirely various and individual. Braque's painting has the severe beauty and elegant logic that we admire in an automobile or a gun, while the exquisite texture and iridescent colour of Bonnard's pigment makes it more precious than onyx or shagreen. Matisse lassoes his subject, and Segonzac wrestles with it. No one can venerate the Old Masters more than I do, and at the same time I believe these living Frenchmen can, and will, take their place with the proudest of them. We are under an immense debt to the Contemporary Art Society for organising this exhibition, to the fortunate and perspicacious owners of the pictures for lending them, and to Messrs. Colnaghi for giving them hospitality. By the generosity of Mr. Courtauld the Tate Gallery now possesses one of the greatest masterpieces of nineteenth century painting, Seurat's 'Baignade.' If everyone who cares for such pictures and who can afford two guineas, would give one to the Contemporary Art Society, and if those who can afford a thousand, would give a hundred, the Nation would soon have pictures painted by living men, and worthy to hang by the side of the finest productions of the past as a continual encouragement. For, indeed, to see such pictures as these quite reconciles one to the present age, and, at least while one is in their presence, it is bliss to be alive, and to be young is very heaven.

24 Osbert Sitwell, 'The Courtauld Collection', *Apollo*, II, August 1925, pp.63–9

Article on Samuel Courtauld's private collection.

Sir Osbert Sitwell, fifth baronet (1892–1969), wrote fiction, poetry, and travel books, with an emphasis on art; his five-volume autobiography, *Left Hand, Right Hand*, was published from 1944 to 1950. He was a Trustee of the Tate Gallery from 1951–8.

By the courtesy of Mr. Samuel Courtauld we are in this number enabled to reproduce certain pictures from his magnificent collection of works of the French school. And, fortunately, this collection is sufficiently comprehensive to enable us to review the peculiar virtues of the various artists who compose it. The conclusions to which the painters of this period had already forced us are further strengthened – that the latter half of the French nineteenth century was one of the supreme moments of world-painting, and that the various talents which went to the production of this period were more disconnected from each other than ever before in the history of art. Never was there such an outburst of exuberant fertility, never were there gifts of such immense variety. It is the final triumph of the individual in art. At the same time it is curious to note that this great impulse in painting was totally unaccompanied by any allied impulse in architecture, furniture, or in the applied arts; whereas in earlier periods a movement in one seems always to have indicated a movement in another branch of life.

While England was engaged in an extended period of peace and prosperity, France was given over to wars and revolutions; while England produced at its best Frith and Rossetti, at its worst Alma-Tadema and Burne-Jones, France was indulging in a positive orgy of genius, and of a genius more intensely national than ever before or since. For now French art is Parisian more than French, its music more American than French, its poetry mainly Roumanian or Bowry.

In the collection before us, certain sharp divisions are brought out. It is possible, for example, to imagine Manet or Renoir as the court painters of an artistically-intelligent court, if such there had been. There is in their work an intense and very French feeling for materials, for hair and lace and velvet and pearls and roses and the varying divisions of light; while their expression of the period – and, whatever the faults of its furniture and architecture, the period was a very individual one – was more intense, because so much better, than that of, let us say, Winterhalter or Frith. Manet and Renoir would therefore have reflected as much credit upon the court of the Imperial adventurer as did Velazquez upon that of Philip. The crinoline of the Second Empire would have become as much an object of artistic history as the angular crinolines of the Infantas. But the Empire missed its opportunity, and in so doing condemned modern imperialism. How much more favourable would now be the chances of an imperial revival if the court of the last Emperor could be viewed through the eyes of the great French painters, and the former reign be pointed to as a period of deliberate encouragement of the Fine Arts. Alas! the Emperor was too busy opening railway stations in the South, attempting to found improbable empires in the Americas, and destroying the individuality of the Parisian streets to pay much attention to painting. And, while prosperity is pleasant, it is never more than temporary; the stream engine is never so permanent as the paint brush.

'La Loge' shows us how Renoir in his early and middle periods could have been a court painter, though his latter development would, we fear, have proved a sad disappointment to his Imperial patrons. Here he tackles the problem of prettiness, of pink cheeks, of pearls, velvets and roses; while Manet's magnificent picture of a woman and child watching the boats on the Seine proves that he could have portrayed the royal picnics better than did Winterhalter. That to this court Manet could have added the purely decorative quality, the flower-piece of his that we reproduce is sufficient and final proof. In its delicate array of colour, its feathery divisions of light, it is a decorative painting of the highest order. But with Cézanne, and indeed with Gauguin, the matter was different.

We can never imagine Cézanne confined within the silk-hung tents of the Second Empire. He belonged to a fiercer and more fanatic race. His genius would have put the soft embroideries of the palace to shame. Indeed, Cézanne is the first painter whose work looks better in a public gallery than in a palace, just as the primitives look better in churches than in palaces. In fact, with him the revolution had come. The public gallery had overthrown the palace, as the Renaissance palace had in its turn overthrown the medieval church.

It is perhaps conceivable that Gauguin might have become the court painter of some dusky and exotic prince. Particularly did he revel in places where, to quote Bishop Heber, 'every prospect pleases, and only man is vile'; but the Cézanne landscape which is here reproduced in colour could never have been confined within the suffocating draperies of a palace. It needs for its display, the existence, if not the close neighbourhood, of other pictures. It is the work of a painter untainted by any decorative sense; it is the work of a painter who lived for nothing else in the world but his painting; who would wake in the night to see if the weather of the next morning would be satisfactory to his art, though he would, if necessary, work in the rain, and in the end died by so doing.

Something of the unluxuriousness of the man – of a man who would sleep on a bench in public gardens, first taking off his boots, and using them as a pillow for fear they should be stolen from him in his sleep – creeps into his brush and palette knife; but nothing of his eccentricity. That went into his life, which was to him a waste-product. The hills, the trees, the aqueduct, the solid houses of this landscape are all monumental, yet reasoned through the hand and eye of the artist. The comprehension in his work, even when the conclusions are imperfect, is more extraordinary than in the work of any other painter. Perhaps the most magnificent of his pictures in the Courtauld collection is the study

of trees which we reproduce. Here is poetry again. The poetry of the major poet, the strength, dignity, and wisdom of a Milton. The trees display a truly marvellous combination of strength and lightness; out of strength has once more come sweetness, and after the fluttering leaves and flickering lights of the Impressionist school, this revelation of strength must have shown itself, one would have supposed, like a whirlwind, tearing up the gossamer trees by the roots and laying low the whole of a tradition. As usual, however, the public, in as far as it was interested in art, was still too busy quarrelling over the corpses and dividing the spoils of the last century to pay much attention – except a certain amount of flattering opprobrium – to Cézanne. While the varying qualities of Ingres and Delacroix were being fought over, the Impressionists were neglected, and the Post-Impressionists ignored. Indeed, M. Vollard informs us that the first of Cézanne's patrons was a blind man, who was led round an exhibition feeling the texture of the paintings with his sensitive finger-tips; while one of his later patrons was King Milan of Serbia, who is supposed to have thought that these pictures were obscene, and to have bought them on that account.

In Mr. Courtauld's collection we are fortunately able to compare Cézanne with his predecessors, with the magnificent Manet to which we have referred; a picture in which, it seems to us, can be detected the derivation of a far greater and more original artist, namely Seurat. Of all the painters of this great period he remains the most underrated. Seldom has been more fully exploited a more individual and poetic talent. Anything Seurat touched, even the small picture we reproduce, which is, however, lovely, an unimportant work, becomes invested with an incomparable personality and atmosphere. A mysterious poetry, as of another world, radiates out of his canvases: and here we must pause to congratulate the Tate Gallery on the possession of one of the two finest pictures from his brush. Those who doubt that Seurat was a great master need only take a 'bus to Millbank and go to the Blake Room, where they will behold one of the most beautiful pictures of the age.

Mr. Courtauld also enables us to consider the problem of Renoir, who is well represented in this collection by 'La Loge,' a street-scene, and finally a ballet girl of his late and uncourtly period. It would be interesting to learn to what extent this painter was consciously influenced by the work of the aged Titian. Compare this picture with the late Titian of the Mond Bequest in the National Gallery, and it is easy enough to see that, whether the likeness is conscious or not, such a comparison is possible. In his early pictures Renoir, alone of modern artists, was sufficiently courageous to tackle the problem of prettiness. He could have been commissioned to design a chocolate-box with absolute security to his employers, and perfect comfort to even the most æsthetically-minded of consumers. But in his last period, he has stripped prettiness of every rag. These hot-coloured nudes, these inflated forms, are at first ugly, but gradually out of them emerges that monumental sense of design which could take prettiness captive. These pictures to our mind, though less romantic, less lovely, are infinitely his greatest work. It was once our privilege to see many Renoirs of this period hung together in one of the large rooms of the Salon d'Automne, and the effect of power was overwhelming. Compare again this monumental ballet girl with Degas's two feathery coryphées blown on to the canvas by some chance wind of spring. The Degas is witty in its drawing as a French caricature, full of diamond-dust refractions of colour. Yet, beautiful as this picture is, in the end the Renoir would triumph with an elephantine grace.

There is, too, in the Courtauld collection a magnificent Daumier of Don Quixote riding with his attendant through a rocky gorge. It was Daumier's gift that, beside being a magnificent craftsman, he could convert the most ridiculous episodes into scenes of tragedy. Whereas most satirical draughtsmen bring tragic scenes down to ridicule.

Of the two Gauguins, the Tahitian one is the most important. The other, though painted after his return to Brittany, lacks the inspiration of the South Sea Islands. Certainly in this picture there is a luxury and colour which might offend our æsthetic Puritans. It is often supposed now that pictures should have no literary or romantic interest. But it would be hard to oblige Gauguin to go to the South Seas, and then to return from it bringing back nothing new; and these flat yellow forms wandering through the dusky forests, dripping with ruby and amber lights, were certainly a new and important discovery – the only discovery of æsthetic value which has resulted from the explorations of Christopher Columbus.

25 'Art Purchases for the Nation: The Courtauld Fund: Modern Foreign Paintings', *Morning Post*, 2 January 1926, p. 4

Review of the exhibition of the Courtauld Fund purchases at the Tate Gallery in January 1926.
Critic unknown.

Some two years ago Mr. Samuel Courtauld gave £50,000 to the nation for the purchase of modern foreign paintings, mainly by French artists of the last half-century. The bulk of that sum has been spent, and the pictures acquired are now on view for a few months in Gallery X. at Millbank, after which they will be placed in the Modern Foreign Collection in the new Duveen Galleries, which will be opened probably in May or June.

One notable feature of Mr. Courtauld's generous gift is the provision made by him that pictures purchased out of his Fund may be sold or exchanged in cases where finer examples of the art of the painters represented become available or are bequeathed. This provision might in practice prove to be dangerous, as it actually empowers the Trustees to indulge in dealing to the possible detriment of the Fund. In this sense. Would a discarded painting be likely to realise as much as it cost? If such a case happened how could the deficit be made good?

Mr. Courtauld had apparently thought of this, for we understand that he intends to keep the Fund alive, and occasionally help to acquire works of outstanding importance. And nothing but pictures of this description should in future be considered if the nation is to reap the full benefit of Mr. Courtauld's wholly unsolicited bounty. By doing so there would be no necessity for later sale or exchange.

THREE VAN GOGHS

Those responsible for the administration of the Fund have not always acted discreetly in this respect. They have been too precipitate, no doubt impelled by competition which may be the life of the trade, and at the same time the death of art.

Take the case of Vincent Van Gogh. Three pictures by him are included among the sixteen purchased out of the £50,000; and not one of them is first rate. Sentiment is a fine thing, but what can be said for the sentimental gush which, in Eliza Cook fashion, 'embalmed,' the 'Yellow Chair' as a material and spiritual masterpiece, when shown at the Leicester Galleries in 1923. It is merely a schoolboy exercise, charming in colour and awry in perspective.

'Sunflowers' is inferior to another version of the same subject. Mawkish votaries of Van Gogh and alienists will doubtless prize the 'Landscape with Cypress Trees,' because of the wriggling forms that are supposed to indicate the incipient madness from which the artist died in 1890. Why buy three, or even one, of these works? With the moneys they represent a really splendid Van Gogh might in time have been added to the collection.

So, too, regarding Renoir. His alluring 'La Première Sortie' deserves

the praise we gave it at the Knoedler Exhibition, although it cannot compare with the glorious 'La Loge,' lent by Mr. Courtauld to the centenary exhibition at Norwich last October. 'Nu dans l'Eau' is in a completely different category. It is pleasing in colour, but fumbling in draughtsmanship, handling, and form.

We are told officially that 'La Baignade,' by George [sic] Seurat, 'has a special interest in the history of art, coming as it did on the watershed between impressionism and later developments.' As a contribution to art itself the picture does not greatly impress. The landscape part is well painted, but the picture as a whole is curiously barren of thought or emotion. 'La Baignade,' however, may have a firmer grip on our regard when seen in a larger room.

HIGH STANDARDS

We have dealt frankly and fairly with these particular paintings in the belief that neither Mr. Courtauld himself nor the Trustees would wish it otherwise. His own superb collection sets a high standard, which we feel sure the administrators of the Fund are anxious to reach, and can reach with a little patience and free thinking.

This is evident by the other pictures selected. They can be praised wholeheartedly, each from its own viewpoint. 'La Table,' by Bonnard, is brilliant if risky improvisation and colour.

Commendation has already been given to Cézanne's self-portrait, the merits of the landscape by him are minimised by our memory of Mr. Courtauld's perfect 'La Montagne Sainte Victoire.'

By Degas are two splendid examples of his accomplished eclecticism, 'Jeunes Spartiates s'exercant à La Lutte' and 'Miss Lola at the Cirque Fernando,' the one of classic formula, the other an exercise in technical skill.

Manet's 'La Servant [sic] de Bocks,' if a trifle congested on the left, is an admirable specimen of his robust style and faithful characterisation, Monet's Boudinesque, 'Plage de Trouville' very delightful, and Camille Pissarro's 'Boulevard des Italians [sic]' a most effective *effet de nuit*.

A SISLEY MASTERPIECE

The 'Rue du Tertre,' by Maurice Utrillo, is welcome. Previous to the exhibition at Lefevre's Galleries last November his work was almost unknown in London. Up to 1914 his art was of high promise; since then circumstances have prevented creative development. His subjects in the King-street Gallery were mainly long, grim-looking streets, lined with dilapidated houses and bare white walls, familiar to those who know Montmartre.

The Courtauld picture represents a narrow street that leads to the summit of that Bohemian haunt. With rare fidelity Utrillo sets before us the decaying beauty of old buildings.

But best of all the pictures is Alfred Sisley's 'L'Abreuvoir' in winter. Its charm is abiding. For subtlety of feeling, exquisite tone, and refined technique this little picture is unrivalled by any other painting of the Impressionist School. And Sisley was of English origin.

26 W. McCance, 'The Courtauld Collection', *Spectator*, 16 January 1926, p. 80

Review of the exhibition of the Courtauld Fund purchases at the Tate Gallery in January 1926.
W. McCance wrote art criticism for the *Spectator* from 1923–6.

The fifteen pictures acquired by the Trustees of the Courtauld Fund for the purchase of examples of modern foreign Art are being exhibited in

Gallery X of the Tate Gallery at Millbank. With a few exceptions these pictures are fairly representative of the work of the various artists, while their historical value is of unquestionable significance; for we have only to visit, say, the New English Art Club, the London Group, or even the Academy to see the far-reaching influence that these French painters have had on modern developments in painting. All of them in their time were considered to be revolutionaries in Art, but now the artistic creeds which they upheld have been accepted throughout the world in different degree. This lagging appreciation has its economic side; it accounts, in some measure, for the fact that any semi-official fund like that provided by Mr. Samuel Courtauld must almost be bound to become practically exhausted on the purchase of fifteen pictures that will be acceptable to the public instead of a hundred or so out of which fifty, perhaps, may find favour in the eyes of a discerning minority. But this speculative method of purchasing pictures is, after all, a function which probably belongs more rightly to the Contemporary Arts Society. In any case, although we may grumble a little at this uneconomic acquisition of pictures for the nation, we must, at the same time, admit that a National Collection is primarily concerned with historical values; and admitting this, also admit that history, whether of Art or any other branch, can rarely be assessed rightly until it has reached a certain remoteness. There is not one of these pictures at Millbank but what will take its place in the history of painting. Some of them have been criticized as not being typical examples of the artists' work; but surely, even an early work, although it may not be similar to that with which the artist is commonly associated, has, nevertheless, just as much significance and interest, besides having the added value of uniqueness: and this difficulty could well be overcome, at comparatively small expense, if a library, containing good reproductions of other characteristic paintings by the artists, were attached to the Gallery. The *Jeunes Spartiates s'exerçant à la lutte* of Degas does certainly produce a wrong impression of this artist's general tendency, but then the other example, *Miss Lola at the Cirque Farnando* [*sic*], would lead any interested spectator to seek further enlightenment, since it differs so vastly from the earlier work. Nor is the *Plage de Trouville* by Monet a typical example of the technique of Impressionism that would do justice to Monet as the originator of this movement. On the other hand, although the Cézannes are quite typical, both of them are inferior pictures to the example that has already been acquired by the Tate. The three Van Goghs differ from each other in their treatment, yet all of them represent very well defined phases of this impulsive artist's temperamental development; while the Seurat is not only a characteristic but also an exceptionally good example of the work of the precursor of Post-Impressionism. Probably one of the most important acquisitions of the collection is *La Servante de Bocks*, by Manet, for it is not only typical in its treatment, colour, and choice of subject matter, but also shows the artist's powerful sense of constructive design – a sense which most of the contemporary Impressionists lacked.

Besides the pictures already referred to, there are also characteristic works of Renoir, Pissarro, Sisley, Utrillo, and Bonnard.

---

27 Roger Fry, 'The Courtauld Fund', *Nation and Athenaeum*, 30 January 1926, pp. 613–14

Review of the exhibition of the Courtauld Fund purchases at the Tate Gallery in January 1926.

For Fry, see text no. 7.

In one of those small dark-rooms at the Tate Gallery so admirably suited for the development of photographic plates there are now exposed the pictures acquired under the terms of the Courtauld Fund and handed over by the donor to the nation.

At first I was puzzled to think why one of the most generous gifts of pictures which the nation has ever received should have been huddled away in this crypt-like gallery. A great deal of rehanging has taken place lately at the Tate, and many pictures are not on view. One would have supposed that it need not have passed the wit of man to clear one end of a properly lit gallery in order that the public might see and rejoice in its new acquisition. It was only gradually that it dawned on me that the Trustees and officials of the Tate Gallery had realized the dangerous precedent which Mr. Courtauld's gift might set. The fear that every week or two a cheque for £50,000 might arrive by post from some wealthy and patriotic citizen, stirred by emulation, naturally filled them with dread lest the smooth functioning of the Gallery administration might be seriously interfered with. It was no doubt well to discourage from the outset a habit that might so easily grow to unforeseen proportions.

But however much one sympathizes with these prudent considerations, one cannot help feeling that the authorities might have stretched a point and have cleared temporarily from this small gallery the large obstruction in the centre, a great show-case of drawings, which completely prevents any possibility of viewing these pictures at a proper distance – even if the light were adequate, as no doubt at certain very rare conjunctions of the weather it may be.

This applies especially to Seurat's Bathers, a picture of very large dimensions and monumental design, which can only be seen at a considerable distance and in a good light. This picture has now been in the Tate for a year or two, but it has never once been visible. As it is, I believe, one of the supreme masterpieces of European art of the last century or more, it is a pity that it has never been allowed even temporarily to replace on some well-lit wall a few of the many pictures in the Tate which no one could call masterpieces.

It is perhaps the finest of all Seurat's works, and Seurat is a centre of creative energy the full effects of which have not yet become manifest. Had he lived one cannot doubt that he would have dominated the whole art of the early twentieth century. He stands in strange isolation. There is no other figure comparable to him. He must have been one of the most intensely intellectual of artists, though his intellect was at the service of an extreme sensibility. With him the stages of perception, analysis, and synthesis were clearly separated, and each stage was carried through with a methodical precision and exactitude to which the history of art hardly affords a parallel. So perfectly were his sensational data reduced to method that in the end he was able to work as easily by night, and with very imperfect illumination, as he was by day. Every touch had been prearranged by his synthetic system. One has before such a work as the Bathers an almost uncanny feeling that not only is everything exactly right and inevitable, but that Seurat both felt this necessity and had understood it intellectually, that he felt it must be so and could have actually given a proof of why it must be so. In this respect a work like the Bathers comes nearer in spirit to the greatest work of the Italian Renaissance than anything else in the intervening centuries. At no other time can one feel this curious harmony between intellectual and sensitive perception of relations. In another respect also he stands alone in modern art and touches the Renaissance. Contour is for him a supreme method of expression – contour and not line, for even in his drawings there is never a line. Cézanne used line, but not contour, line being often used almost to avoid the dangerous statement of contour. But Seurat arrived at contour as the last word of his statement of volume and of the plasticity of the volume. It would, however, need a separate study to analyze fully this supreme work, and for that we must wait until it is made visible, as surely it one day must be.

The Cézannes are both of them masterpieces. The 'Paysage rocheux' was seen lately at the Leicester Galleries where even in that remarkable collection it was one of the most impressive pictures. It is an unusual colour scheme for Cézanne, in that the greys are more neutral and uniform, less broken up into blues, violets, and oranges, than was his wont. In fact, the synthesis seems to have been arrived at almost immediately and directly. It has almost the innocence and simplicity of a Corot. The little portrait head of himself is a great acquisition. Hardly any other work of his is more instructive for its evidence of his unique power of expressing form by means of colour. Precisely because the range of colour in the thing seen was so restricted we get a clearer idea of what richness of interplay he was able to create by his analysis of mere blacks, whites, and greys. In that respect this head is comparable to the marvellous little head of a saint by El Greco in the National Gallery.

Perhaps the greatest surprise of the collection is the little Monet of two ladies sitting under parasols on a sunlit beach. This shows Monet's extraordinary instinctive perception of values, and makes one regret that he ever abandoned so direct and effective a method for the quasi-scientific investigation of divided colour. One sees here how continuous the French tradition is. In a hundred years' time this may well be confused with some of Matisse's or Marquet's works. Degas has not fared well in this selection. 'Les Jeunes Spartiates' is one of those tiresome, almost pedantic constructions into which his youthful ambition betrayed him before he even began to explore his special sensibility. It shows what dangerous facility and competence he had to live down in the course of his long life.

'The Acrobat' is a much better work, with much of Degas's real feeling in the drawing of the figure, but one feels that it was a *tour de force*, and that Degas as well as the lady is hanging on by his teeth.

Van Gogh is adequately, perhaps a little too generously, represented. The sunflowers give him at his very best, with his passionate abandonment to certain colour sensations. Colour is with him an almost physiological excitement rather than as with Cézanne an aspect of formal design. He values certain colours almost in and by themselves, as children do when they talk of their favourite colour, and not as part of a necessary system of relations. But in the 'Sunflowers' there is an almost equally primitive and immediate apprehension of the life of the flowers and these two feelings happily harmonize and reinforce each other.

But more and more it becomes evident to what an extent Van Gogh was a 'literary' painter, and was moved by non-plastic qualities in nature. This comes out in the late work 'Landscape with Cypresses,' done whilst he was in the lunatic asylum at S. Remy. The appearances of nature have here acted merely as a stimulus to his exalted inner state, which he externalizes in a system of arbitrary and emphatic rhythm. This gives the design, no doubt, its singular unity and consistency, but also its too arbitrary and violent simplification. 'The Chair' adds little or nothing to what the other two examples afford.

Neither of the Renoirs is quite a masterpiece. 'La première sortie' is full of exquisite passages characteristic of Renoir at a very fortunate moment of his development, but is not altogether happy in its co-ordination of volumes. The nude also has passages of extreme beauty, but there is a certain lack of continuity in the treatment of the figure and the background.

The Sisley, though not one of his happiest compositions, is none the less a great addition to our collection by reason of its exquisitely subtle and fine colour. The Manet is curiously uneven. The head of the waitress is not only superbly painted, but is perhaps the most characteristic example of Manet's quality of anything in our public galleries. Unfortunately he seems never to have got clear about the figure in the foreground which is tentative and uninspired. Bonnard is seen almost at his very best in the picture of an interior by lamplight.

When one considers how late in the day Mr. Courtauld was able to come to the rescue of our national collection, in the hope of filling a gap which ought never to have existed, one cannot deny that on the whole the money has been well spent. At least as regards the older masters the evident masterpieces had long been snapped up. It is a matter for the greatest satisfaction that we should possess two first-rate Cézannes and perhaps the finest Seurat in the world. And these after all are the two great pioneers of modern art.

28 'The Courtauld Collection', *Truth*, 3 February 1926, pp. 200–1

Anonymous review of the exhibition of the Courtauld Fund purchases at the Tate Gallery in January 1926.

It has long been a reproach that though so far as the representation of 'Old Masters' is concerned, that is to say, roughly, up to the end of the eighteenth century, our National Gallery is second to none in the world, the subsequent phases of art outside England are practically ignored. From time to time a Corot or a Millet has been acquired, and Mr. J.C.J. Drucker, the Dutch banker, gave us a few valuable examples of the modern painters of his country. The British School from the end of the eighteenth century onward is provided for by the Tate Gallery, where contemporary representation is kept up more or less wisely by the annual purchases out of the Chantrey Bequest Fund and the occasional acquisitions of the Contemporary Art Society. The net result is—or has been—that a visitor to London from another planet might suppose that, except for the British School, the art of Europe ended somewhere about 1800. Even from the point of view of representing our own school this was a defect, because English painters of the nineteenth century and onward are not to be understood properly except with reference to phases of art on the Continent which influenced them and to which they themselves contributed.

The first considerable remedy for this defect was the bequest to the National Gallery of a number of nineteenth-century French pictures by the late Sir Hugh Lane. Then Sir Joseph Duveen, the son of the benefactor to whom we are indebted for the Turner Galleries at Millbank, offered to provide accommodation for the nucleus of a modern foreign collection thus formed; and the extension of the Tate Gallery given by him for the purpose is now nearing completion, together with the special gallery which he has provided to house the works of the late Mr. John Sargent. Sir Joseph Duveen's generous action was followed by that of Mr. Samuel Courtauld, who gave the handsome sum of £50,000 for the purchase of modern foreign paintings, chiefly by French artists of the last fifty years. When making his gift, Mr. Courtauld put in the wise provision that acquisitions out of it might be sold and exchanged in cases where finer examples of the painter became available or were bequeathed.

The bulk of the fund has now been expended by the Courtauld Trustees, and the pictures acquired—sixteen in number—are being exhibited as a unit for a few months in Gallery X. at Millbank, before being merged in the general Modern Foreign Collection—now with the Lane Bequest and pictures otherwise acquired, amounting to about 200 works—in the new galleries, which, together with the new Sargent gallery, will be formally opened in the early summer. In looking at these pictures it is well to make two reflections. One is that the function of a National Gallery is to represent, irrespective of whether the pictures exhibited are pleasing to the majority or not, painters who are of recognised importance in the history of art. Its function, in short, is similar to that of a public library: to provide adequate material for reference. The second reflection concerns the question of price.

At a first glance, sixteen pictures, three of them by living artists, may look like a poor return for nearly £50,000, and suggest that this kind of generosity is playing into the hands of the dealers. That a known demand for the work of a certain painter will send up its price is natural enough, but reflection shows that there is no way out of the difficulty. Only in very rare cases is the representative importance of an artist recognisable in his lifetime; still less frequently can it be judged at a time when, his reputation being still to make, his prices are low. The alternatives are to buy cheap from the 'unknown' artist on the strength of his promise – and this is done, in the main, with discrimination, through the Contemporary Art Society – with all the risks of backing the wrong horse, or to wait until his importance is beyond question, generally when he is dead, with the inevitable rise in his prices. In such a case as that of Mr. Courtauld's gift, with its expressed intentions, the latter alternative is the only one possible; and, considering the intrinsic quality of the pictures acquired and their representative importance, there is no reason whatever to suppose that any dealer has profited unduly by national requirements. Probably, from what we know about the purchase of Old Masters for the nation, investigation would show instances of patriotic abnegation. In one or two cases future advantage may well be taken of Mr. Courtauld's wise provision for sale or exchange, but looking at the collection as a whole, there can be no question that the money has been well and wisely spent.

Speaking broadly, the pictures represent the phase of French Impressionism and its later developments, and the artists, such as Manet, not immediately connected with it, who nevertheless made some contribution to what followed. Thus, with great variety in the individual works, the collection has a certain unity of meaning in the history of art. It may be said to 'bridge' Impressionism. Degas, Renoir, and Cézanne are represented by two pictures each; there are three by Van Gogh; and Manet, Monet, Pissarro, Sisley, Seurat, Bonnard, and Utrillo have one apiece. The last two, with Monet, are still alive. Taking everything into consideration, intrinsic quality and subject appeal as well as representative importance, the two most completely satisfying pictures are 'La Première Sortie,' a young girl at the theatre, by Renoir, and 'La Servante des Bocks,' a cabaret scene, by Manet; but the Cézanne landscape is a very fine example, and each of the other pictures has some good reason for its acquisition.

Sir Hugh Lane, and, more lately, Mr. Samuel Courtauld, and by individual gifts, bequests, and purchases, and for the further gift of a special gallery to contain the works by the late Mr. John Sargent, R.A., in the national possession.

Even for the proper understanding and appreciation of contemporary British art a representative modern foreign section is necessary, and it may be well to emphasize this point. The intention of the collection and its galleries is not so much to exalt foreign art at the possible expense of our own as to encourage in the public that broader view of art through which alone our native productions can be rightly appreciated. Comparison there must be, but it is of kind rather than quality. Nobody can pass through the British rooms at the Tate Gallery to the new foreign section without seeing that, allowing for the increasing cosmopolitanism of art throughout the world, British art has well-marked characters.

Broadly, and in landscape as well as figure painting, they amount to an emphasis upon subject interest. Whether or not these characters are 'artistic' is an idle question. They are ours; and if the opportunity for comparison afforded by the foreign section drives home the truth that, in the long run and allowing for changes due to the time spirit, British art gains when its characters are accepted and loses when they are self-consciously avoided a very useful purpose will be served. In any case the broader view cannot fail to stimulate interest in British art.

[...]

THE FOREIGN COLLECTION

This is hardly the occasion to discuss the pictures in detail – many of them have been already described – and it will be enough here to say that we have now a modern foreign collection which enables us to study the development of painting on the Continent from the end of the 18th century down to the present day. In gratitude, as well as to suggest opportunities for benevolence, it must not be ignored that many of the pictures in both the foreign and the Sargent collections are only on loan. These are separately catalogued with the names of their generous lenders. We are still weak in Cézanne, Gauguin, Monet, Matisse, and Matthew Maris, to name no others.

[...]

---

29 'Tate Gallery: The New Building: Opening To-Day by the King', *The Times*, 26 June 1926, p. 10

Announcement of the opening of the new modern foreign gallery at the Tate.

The King, who will be accompanied by the Queen, will open the new modern foreign and Sargent Galleries, erected by Sir Joseph Duveen at Millbank, to-day at noon. The National Gallery, Millbank, will be closed to the public until 2 p.m., after which the British section will be open. The new modern foreign galleries, however, will not be open to the general public until Monday. There will be a private view of the new modern foreign and Sargent galleries for members of the National Art-Collections Fund and Contemporary Art Society from 2 to 6 this afternoon.

With the opening of the new modern foreign section our reproach of seeming to ignore the more recent development of art outside these islands is removed, and a first duty is to thank Sir Joseph Duveen for providing adequate galleries for the display and study of the now considerable collection of modern foreign works of art made possible by the generosity of the late Mr. George Salting, Mr. J.C. Drucker, the late

30 'Private Art Collections: IV. – The Courtauld Pictures: Impressionism', *The Times*, 1 June 1928, pp. 15–16

Presumably by Charles Marriott (1869–1957), art critic of *The Times* from 1924–40, succeeding Arthur Clutton-Brock (see text no. 15). Marriott's many novels, published from 1901 to 1922, explore social and political issues, and his interest in modern art was influenced by similar concerns. His books included *Modern Movements in Painting* (1920) and *A Key to Modern Painting* (1938).

In discussing the private collection of pictures belonging to Mr. and Mrs. Samuel Courtauld at 20, Portman-square, it is impossible to avoid some reference to Mr. Courtauld's gift to the Tate Gallery of a fund of £50,000 for the acquisition of modern foreign pictures, particularly by French artists of the latter part of the 19th century.

This is not the place to enlarge upon the generosity of a gift the proceeds of which, added to bequests and gifts from Sir Hugh Lane, Mr. George Salting, and Mr. J.C. Drucker, in the place provided by Sir Joseph Duveen, have changed the Tate Gallery from a bad joke among the nations to a universally recognized shrine of modern European painting; our concern here is rather with its wisdom and discrimination, and, above all, with the personal preferences expressed in its terms. In the larger and longer view of things it is very doubtful if anybody can do much good to anybody else, publicly or privately, unless the action involves a gift of personality, and if Mr. Courtauld had not been confessing his own tastes in suggesting the kind of pictures to be acquired – giving himself, indeed – our gain, though real from the historical point of view in any case, would not have had the artistic value and importance that it undoubtedly has.

PICTURES FOR EVERY DAY

Officially and ostensibly there is no particular connexion between the Courtauld pictures at the Tate Gallery and the Courtauld collection at 20, Portman-square; in the larger and longer view of things indicated above the connexion is close and significant. Consisting almost exclusively of the kind of works, about 70 in all, indicated by the terms of the gift, the collection itself may be described as small, definite, consistent, and concentrated. In point of time it begins with Daumier and ends with Matisse, but the emphasis is put upon the central line of development between Impressionism and what is conveniently called Post-Impressionism rather than upon contributory influences or interesting side issues. In sporting language it keeps its eye very consistently 'on the ball.' As regards arrangement it is emphatically – or rather unemphatically – a domestic collection, disposed in the living rooms of the house for habitual enjoyment. It would be difficult to find a collection formed by one man that has so little the effect of a collection, that is so little worn 'on the sleeve,' so completely taken for granted as part of the everyday lives of the household.

This lack of emphasis is dwelt upon because it has its bearing upon the character of the pictures themselves. Not a few of them are the very pictures that created an uproar at the time of their first appearance. As we see them now we are struck chiefly by their effect of single-minded absorption in the business of painting or drawing on the part of the men who produced them. The differences between them, though they could be arranged in that progressive series which we mean when we speak about the historical 'development' of art, are seen to represent the irreducible minimum of difference between human beings completely absorbed in similar problems rather than any desire to make people 'sit up and take notice.' Several of the pictures were, so to speak, pivotal works in artistic 'movements,' but there never was a collection in which movements were so little obtruded. One thing brought home by the Courtauld collection is that, at any rate so far as the bigger men are concerned, the recognition and labelling of 'movements' proceeds less from the artists themselves than from excited onlookers.

Another thing brought home by the Courtauld collection, and it bears very closely on the educational value of foreign works of art in this country and the risks that all such values must have, is the comfortable effect of being 'at ease in Zion' which radiates from all genuine art of whatever nation or tendency. Of technical effort and conscious choice of subject or effect there is evidence, but there is no sign of that dissociation or suppression of part of the personality which is apt to limit our enjoyment of works produced by English artists who have, wisely enough, studied the modern Frenchmen. For practical reasons the French artist went into his studio, but he did not leave any of himself outside the door. Technically he was concentrated, but – possibly for that very reason – he was quite unguarded on the human side.

FRENCH AND ENGLISH

That French art is naturally less inclined to sentiment and less dominated by subject-interest than English art is true, but there is all the difference in the world between qualities which do not happen to be there and qualities which are, in the apt saying, 'conspicuous by their absence.' Something, of course, must be allowed for the natural austerity of youth, and something, too, for a protest against the humiliating history of English painting just before the turn of the century; but it would be well if in their study of the Frenchmen our younger artists penetrated below the surface of style and method and observed the engaging candour with which Manet, Monet, Renoir, and Cézanne unconsciously put all the cards of such human tastes and interests as they happened to possess on the table.

Of these general characters in the Courtauld collection we could not, after a glance at the Daumier – one of the several versions of 'Don Quixote,' in which, with a broad synthetic statement and a reckless disregard of mere probability in form, he anticipated the aims of a later day – find a better example than the very last picture to be added, 'Déjeuner sur l'Herbe,' by Manet, a smaller and earlier version of the picture now in the Louvre. That picture was rejected at the Salon, and at its exhibition elsewhere in 1863 caused a scandal. At this distance of time it is as difficult to understand what was said about the 'Luncheon' as it is to understand what Charles Dickens said about the 'Carpenter's Shop'; all that the picture suggests to us, apart from its purely artistic merits, is that Manet wanted to make a particular kind of composition of figures in landscape and that four of his friends, including a remarkably intelligent professional model, obliged. In the actual execution of the picture he was clearly trying to adapt to the chosen conditions, with further breadth and simplification of tones, what he had learnt from the great Spaniards, and the woody landscape is brushed in with more regard for tonal balance than naturalistic truth. The picture hardly needs description, but by way of a pretext for the composition the two men appear to be discussing some question of artistic truth, while the model gazes interestedly out of the canvas at what M. Manet is doing. A second lady, as if a little bored by the conversation, has wandered off to paddle in the stream. Between this and the Louvre version there are minor differences, and in freshness and directness of handling Mr. Courtauld's picture has the advantage.

A FAMOUS PAINTING

In the 'Bar des Folies-Bergère,' an equally famous if less notorious picture, first exhibited in 1882, Manet brings his artistic interests into closer accord with the probabilities of everyday life. So closely, indeed, that, in our pleasure at the nonchalant acceptance of whatever the subject contains of character and sentiment, we are tempted to make more of the subject than was intended, and to say that the barmaid realizes perfectly Henley's 'dove among the pots.' It is doubtful if Manet gave a second thought to her symbolical meaning; the point is that, by not taking the trouble to uglify her, he showed his real detachment, and so the contrast that resides in the subject for any person of a reflective turn comes through. What Manet was interested in, beyond the broad comparison in tone between the nearer and farther figures, appears to have been the sympathetic response of rounds and ovals and the sparkling relief of still life objects. Cover up the dark ribbon round the neck of the barmaid and you see how cunningly the apparently fortuitous collection is composed. Other works by Manet in the Courtauld collection are landscapes of 'Argenteuil,' painted in 1874, and 'Rue de Béarn,' [sic] showing to advantage his power of suggesting light without the division of tones.

Degas, who, like Manet, was somewhat outside Impressionism in the special meaning – though he warmly supported the Impressionists in their struggle for recognition – is well represented in the collection. Influenced by the Japanese in his designs, he was essentially a draughtsman, but with a grasp of three-dimensional form which is not always associated with the word. His powers in this respect are admirably shown in the pastel, 'Après le bain,' a woman drying herself, with its mastery of the relations in depth of armchair, figure, and bath, and its great beauty of colour. Other aspects of his art are shown in a picture of a woman seated at a window and a study of two dancers.

For sheer attractiveness, the complete and apparently effortless fusion of the charms of subject, colour, and substance, there is nothing in the collection to surpass 'La Loge,' by Auguste Renoir. The figures of the man and woman in the box are linked together by a sort of network of black, formed by the man's coat and the stripes of the woman's costume, and the group as a whole is framed by the disposition of the hands and arms, hers resting on the front of the box and his holding opera-glasses to his eyes. Within this frame Renoir seems to have expended all his enjoyment as a painter, comparing the face and breast of the woman in light with the face and shirt-front of the man in tone, as he tilts back in his chair, and extracting the last beauty of substance in the treatment of costume and flowers. Apart from its qualities as a painting the picture is an enchanting summary of a social period. Opinions are divided as to whether Renoir was at his best in such pictures or in later and more 'sculptural' compositions, such as 'Woman Dressing'; for ourselves, we cannot help feeling that a painter who so delighted in the substantial beauty of things lost more than he gained by simplification. Not that 'Woman Dressing' is 'dry,' but that the summary treatment of form and colour is felt to be at some cost to the natural instincts of the painter. Other works by Renoir in the collection are a portrait of a man and a spring landscape, in which, so to speak, 'all-overish' material of long grass and foliage is made coherent by the placing of figure and tree-trunks.

Toulouse-Lautrec, who, crippled by an accident in infancy, found compensation in a sort of half-envious, half-satirical treatment of the Parisian underworld, is represented by one of his most important paintings, 'Au Rat Mort,' in which the hectic gaiety of cabaret life is expressed with extraordinary intensity.

CLAUDE MONET

Claude Monet has been left until now, because–though he did not invent the name, which was a journalistic coinage from the title of one of his paintings in the exhibition of Salon-rejected works in 1863–he was the central figure of Impressionism as understood. He may be said to have painted solid objects only by implication, concentrating his powers on the exact rendering of the veil or envelope of light and air by which they are surrounded, obtaining the maximum of luminosity and vibration by placing touches of pure colour side by side, and following colour into the shadows. He is represented in the collection by several landscapes and by a large flower painting, in which the passage of light round and through the mass is realized with great skill and beauty of colour. With Monet, as nearest to him in aim, may be associated Camille Pissarro, represented by a painting of 'Rouen,' and Alfred Sisley, who was half-English, as is subtly apparent in his delightful landscape of a village road under snow.

From the extreme pre-occupation with general conditions, at the expense of form, into which Monet had carried painting, there was bound to come a reaction. It was led in one direction by Seurat, who combined a classical style of drawing with a more methodical system of 'dotting' than the Impressionists employed, enhancing the design as well as realizing the atmospheric effect. 'La Poudreuse' and 'Honfleur' are typical examples of his methods in figure and landscape composition, and there are several small paintings by him, very precious in quality. But it was Paul Cézanne who gave the most decided turn to

Impressionism, best described by his own statement that he wanted to make of Impressionism something solid and durable like the art of the museums. Retaining to a great extent the atmospheric gains of Impressionism, he insisted upon the fundamental structure of natural forms, establishing their relations in space by the coloured response of planes at a certain angle to light. With 'Man with a Pipe,' 'Madame Cézanne,' and 'Montagne de Ste. Victoire,' besides other landscapes–in oil and water-colour–and still life paintings, he may justly be called the hero of this collection–as he was the most important influence upon painting since Constable.

Gauguin, who reacted from Impressionism in a decorative direction, is represented by an early 'Harvesting in Brittany' and a late 'Tahitan' subject, 'Nevermore'; Van Gogh, whose aim was a passionate intensity of realization, by early and late landscapes in oil and drawings; and there is an interesting collection of drawings by Ingres, Signac, Segonzac, and Matisse, as well as by the artists whose oil paintings we have discussed. The crudity of words as applied to artistic intentions in painting must not lead the reader into supposing that either the artists represented or the Courtauld collection as a whole had or have didactic aims; all that is meant is that, by happy chance, the activities of the artists and the tastes and judgment of Mr. and Mrs. Courtauld coincide in securing from the accidents of time a singularly definite, consistent, and concentrated representation of the formative influences in painting of the later 19th century.

31 R.H. Wilenski, 'The Courtauld Collection', *Formes* (English edition), December 1930, pp. 16–17

Article on Samuel Courtauld's private collection.

R.H. Wilenski (1887–1975) trained as an artist in Paris (1907–9), and exhibited frequently at London exhibitions for some years after his return, but turned to art criticism and art history in the 1920s. He was art critic for the *Evening Standard* (1923–6), Special Lecturer on Art at Bristol University (1929–30), and Special Lecturer in the History of Art, Victoria University of Manchester (1933–46). His book of 1927, *The Modern Movement in Art*, established his position as a supporter of contemporary continental painting and aroused some controversy; this was followed by *The Meaning of Modern Sculpture* (1932) and *Modern French Painters* (1940), as well as works on the art of the past.

Mr. Samuel Courtauld, to whose generosity the British public owes many of the finest nineteenth century French pictures in the National Gallery of British Art, is himself the owner of the most important private collection of French pictures in London.

The pictures in Mr. Courtauld's own collection are lodged in the living rooms of his London house–an unspoiled Georgian mansion built and decorated by Robert Adam in 1764, and it is curious to see these pictures of a democratic age enshrined in a setting which is eminently aristocratic.

The collection consists of about thirty-five works most of which are celebrated landmarks in the history of painting between 1860 and 1900. It begins with one of Daumier's *Don Quixote* series. The early sixties are represented by Manet's large sketch for *Le Déjeuner sur l'herbe*; the early 'seventies by Renoir's *La Loge*, and one of Manet's early Impressionist pictures, *Woman and child by the bank of the river at Argenteuil*. From the later 'seventies Mr. Courtauld has Manet's *Les Paveurs de la rue de Berne*, Renoir's *La Place Clichy*, and *Deux Danseuses sur la scène* by Degas; from the 'eighties Manet's *Bar aux Folies-Bergère*, and a series of works by Seurat including *La Poudreuse*; and from the 'nineties two late works by Renoir, two by Gauguin, two by Van Gogh, *Jeanne Avril* by Toulouse-

Lautrec, *L'Octroi* by Douanier Rousseau, and an outstanding series by Cézanne.

All or nearly all these pictures look amazingly at home in their Georgian-Classic setting – the reason being, doubtless, that any form of art which has style will fraternise with any other which is imbued with this peculiar distinction. An eighteenth century picture of a 'classical' subject, however archaeologically correct and however much embellished with traditional ornament, would look out of place in Mr. Courtauld's Adam drawing-room if the artist who painted it had lacked the sense of style. Renoir's *La Loge* which now hangs there seems perfectly at ease. Renoir's man and woman squeezed into their uncomfortable box at the theatre represent a life which has lost the spaciousness in which wealth took its pleasures in the eighteenth century; but the painter's brush generalising the light and organising the pattern of the picture provides the element of distinction which was absent from the material with which he worked. In the same way Seurat's *La Poudreuse* fits without difficulty into these architectural surroundings. The sitter for this picture, a stout lady in corset and petticoat powdering her breast, is manifestly plebeian. But the goddess Reason has guided the artist's hand as she guided the hand of Robert Adam; no inchoate mob passion disturbed the one artist or the other as he worked out the balance of each line and tone and colour, no unfiltered enthusiasm induced Seurat or Robert Adam to break through their restraint. Van Gogh and Gauguin alone seem a little too emphatic and spontaneous for this environment. Van Gogh is represented by the vigorous landscape called *La Haie* – an enclosed orchard near Arles – and by the celebrated self-portrait with a bandaged head, painted after he had cut off his ear. Both pictures especially, of course, the portrait, seem to me more autobiographical outbursts than works of stylistic art. They break through the amenities of quiet life. The artist who painted them speaks with an emphasis which destroys the quiet drinking of a cup of tea and the smooth formalities of social intercourse. These pictures seem to me to demand a more austere, or perhaps I should say, a more negative environment. They would look their best on plain white-washed walls.

In a rather different way Gauguin also seems ill at ease in these surroundings. In spite of the decorative disposition in the recumbent nude called *Nevermore* I feel that the artist was really at bottom a romantic. This nude Tahitian girl is really an individual, far more an individual than the barmaid in Manet's *Bar des Folies-Bergère*, or than the nude in Manet's *Olympia* which Gauguin so much admired. I feel much the same thing in regarding Mr. Courtauld's second Gauguin known variously as *La Case* and *Le Repos* – a design which depicts two women with a child in a cradle, an animal (cat? or dog?) on the floor, and an apartment decorated with an erotic frieze. This picture looks *dépaysé* – partly because Gauguin's unit of scale is much larger than the unit of the surrounding decorations. But we must not forget that Gauguin fled from Paris to barbaric life and there is also this uneasiness to account for the pictures' refusal to 'fit in'.

Cézanne on the other hand – Cézanne whom the Academicians tell us was a clumsy fumbler – Cézanne fits into the polished eighteenth century setting with the same assurance as Renoir. Cézanne's faculty of dovetailing his physical subject into his mental image of that subject's plasticity brings his *L'Homme à la Pipe* and his *Les deux Joueurs de cartes* into the realm of essentially stylistic art. These rough peasants live happily in Mr. Courtauld's dining-room and feel at ease there though they have not had to don the silk breeches which Boucher thought necessary before the lower classes could be admitted to polite society. Cézanne's peasants have arrived in their everyday clothes and they keep their hats on even with ladies present – and yet the room and the company feel no more embarrassed than they do themselves.

When we get to Cézanne's landscapes in this collection we feel that Fragonard and Gainsborough would have painted their landscapes in just this way if Cézanne's conception of a landscape had ever entered their heads. For nothing could be more a distillation of an aspect of nature than *Le lac d'Annecy* where the foreground is so miraculously wedded to the distant hills, and nothing more controlled and reasoned than the architecture of *Les Grands Arbres*.

The twentieth-century Renaissance is hardly represented at all in Mr. Courtauld's collection. There are no works by Picasso or Matisse or Chirico. There is however one small picture by Pierre Roy. Is this I wonder the thin edge of the wedge? Will Mr. Courtauld, who is still on the right side of middle age, succumb to the fascination of the art of to-day as he has succumbed so heroically to the art of yesterday? For my own part I sincerely hope he will.

32 From 'The French Art Exhibition: Popular Appeal: First Notice', *The Times*, 2 January 1932, p. 11

Review of the exhibition of French art at the Royal Academy in 1932, presumably by Charles Marriott, then *The Times*'s art critic (see text no. 30).

It will be surprising if the Exhibition of French Art at the Royal Academy, which opens to the public on Monday, does not turn out to be the most generally popular of the series of similar exhibitions held at Burlington House. More than any it is calculated to afford 'the pleasures of painting.' Those who are specially interested in the Primitives will not find here the richness of material that there was in the Italian and Flemish exhibitions, and at no point does the aesthetic-emotional pitch rise to the height of some sections of the Italian and Dutch; but it offers a much more continuous round of pictures likely to please and interest the ordinary person. They are, too, in the majority, pictures which are self-contained in interest, not needing references to anything outside for their appreciation. There is, of course, a Primitive section, and the general characteristics of the Gothic period – in paintings, drawings, sculpture, tapestries, ivories, illuminated manuscripts, and works in precious metals – can be studied here to better advantage than in any of the other exhibitions, for Gothic art may be called a French invention; but even here the interest is artistic and human rather than ecclesiastical, and the works can be enjoyed without reference to their use. Of the exhibition as a whole, indeed, it may be said that its interest for students – as distinct from the general public – will be artistic and technical rather than historical or archaeological.

Though it covers the whole range of French art, from the twelfth to the end of the nineteenth century, this is preeminently an exhibition of painting. As already indicated, its great distinction is in the extent and splendour of the nineteenth-century contribution. This, in itself, should ensure popularity, for there can be no doubt that the majority of people prefer pictures which relate to something approaching their own times and circumstances. By the strictest artistic standards there is no falling off, and the general effect of the last two rooms is to make one wonder what all the fuss was about when the Impressionist and Post-Impressionist works were painted. Seen here they appear to be the natural evolution under the time spirit of tendencies implicit in French painting from the beginning; a working towards light and pure colour, and the emancipation of the picture as an object from social entanglements. The lesson to heretics about modern art should be very wholesome. What these two rooms – and the big room might be included – suggest more than anything is an ideal Academy exhibition, the sort of Academy exhibition one dreams about.

The effect of continuity in the exhibition, with a steady crescendo of artistic interest, is indeed remarkable. With continuity there is also great variety, nearly every century having its fresh infusion of character, such as the rather sophisticated Italianism of the sixteenth, expressed in the 'School of Fontainebleau'; the gravity, culminating in classical dignity, of the seventeenth; the gallantry of the eighteenth, with a sharp return at its close to 'the Greeks and Romans' under the Revolution; and then, with the nineteenth, after a preliminary tussle between the Classics and Romantics, a liberation of every kind of human interest, high or low, and a breaking in of the sun. For though, as was said, the French picture is remarkably self-contained and complete in itself, it does in sequence reflect with extraordinary vividness, and not only by subject matter, contemporary phases of life; and a person passing through the exhibition, without bothering about names or dates, would have a fair general idea of what may be called the atmospheric history of France.

[. . .]

33 From 'The French Art Exhibition: Second Notice', *The Times*, 4 January 1932, p. 10

See text no. 32.

It is no exaggeration to say that, apart from anything else, the Exhibition of French Art at Burlington House illustrates and elucidates the connexions between ancient and modern painting better than any exhibition we have ever seen before. What has often been claimed in argument is here seen to be a logical necessity—given the changes in general ideas. Just as in the first room we see French painting, as such, extricating itself from the linear bonds of the illuminated page and the flat patterns of tapestry, so in the ninth—the big room—we see French painting adapting itself to the new appreciation of light and atmospheric conditions; taking the responsibility from the object modelled in light and shade and putting it upon the patch of tone of the proper value.

Apparently, if not historically, the moment of change is between Courbet and Manet, and if, in the first room, the plastic instigation came from Italy, the tonal instigation, here, appears to have come from Spain. Between Manet's 'The Artist's Parents' (426), painted in 1861, and 'Boating at Argenteuil' (419), painted in 1874, you can almost see the thing happening. Immediately, too, as may be seen in 'Argenteuil' (422), but still more pointedly in 'Le Linge' (428), there is a substitution of colour values for tone values. The exact relationship between Manet and the more definite 'Impressionists' need not be discussed; it is clear that from henceforward the picture is going to be constructed in terms of coloured light. Some artists, like Degas, are more insistent upon form, while others, like Monet, push atmospheric diffusion to extremes. It is impossible to speak of all the fine paintings in the ninth room, but three in particular may be mentioned: 'Le Bon Bock' (396), by Manet, 'La Loge' (415), by Renoir, and 'La Vue de l'Ermitage pres Pontoise' (422), by Pissarro. This last is one of the few pictures in the exhibition that one feels ought to have been better placed.

A TRUE EVOLUTION

By the tenth room modern painting, as such, is fully established, with such lovely 'testaments' as 'The Thaw: Morning' (450) and 'Charing Cross Bridge' (455), by Monet; 'The Thames at Hampton Court' (463), by Sisley, and 'La Toilette' (469), by Berthe Morisot. If space allowed it would be possible to trace a dozen connexions between what is explicit in these and similar pictures and what is implicit in earlier French paintings; but it is enough to say that what can be observed is a true evolution, or unfolding, and that the line between Berthe Morisot and Fragonard is not only a family one. Nor is there any break when, in the last room, we come upon Seurat, Cézanne, and Gauguin. Each artist reinforced his picture in a different way: by architectural relations, by insistence upon volumes, by rhythm and pattern; but what had come into painting with Impressionism remained. It was a question of adjusting atmospheric to formal values—conditions to structure. Three at least of the Cézannes are magnificent: 'Le Pont' (500) and 'Le Lac d'Annecy' (505), in the last room, and 'The Mount of Sainte Victoire' (457), in the tenth. It is incredible that anybody, prepared by what has gone before, can look at these pictures and not see that they are the work of a great artist. For some of us Seurat remains a bit of a stumbling block—rather lawyer-like in his adjustment of conditions to structure—but 'La Parade' (552) is a welcome inclusion. Comparison of Gauguin's 'The Spirit Watches' (526) and 'Nevermore' (553), with their firm designs and splendid colour, with his other South Sea works suggests that—as, indeed, might be expected from his life—his risk was sentimentality.

[. . .]

34 From 'Art and Genius of France: Mr. Ormsby-Gore's Tribute: Refinement and Vitality', *The Times*, 9 January 1932, p. 12

Account of the British Government dinner held in connection with the exhibition of French art at the Royal Academy in 1932 (see texts nos 32–3), with speeches by the First Commissioner of Works, the President of the Royal Academy, and the French Ambassador.

A British Government dinner in honour of the French Ambassador and the members of the French committee associated with the Exhibition of French Art now being held at the Royal Academy, Burlington House, was given at Lancaster House last night. Mr. Ormsby-Gore, M.P., First Commissioner of Works, presided. The guests also included the President of the Royal Academy, private possessors and collectors in this country who had lent some of their pictures for the exhibition, and the directors of a number of provincial galleries and museums.

Sir William Llewellyn, President of the Royal Academy, in a message to the President of the French Republic, expressed on behalf of the Academy and the artists of Great Britain their appreciation of the generosity which had allowed so many of the rarest treasures of French art to be transferred to London and added that the presence of those masterpieces gave 'indubitable assurance of an active and confident friendship between France and Great Britain and increases our already high regard for the achievement of French artists.'

[. . .]

In submitting the toast of 'France and Success to the Exhibition,' the CHAIRMAN remarked that in recent years the winter exhibitions at the galleries of the Royal Academy of Arts had become historic events of real international importance. He recalled the exhibitions of Swedish and Spanish art, the display of Flemish painting organized by the Anglo-Belgian Union, and the remarkable collections of Dutch, Italian, and Persian art, and said that the numbers visiting the exhibitions, and the wealth of literary criticism and appreciation that they had evoked, had revealed the growing knowledge of, and enthusiasm for, works of art which was one of the characteristic features of the modern age. Great art had become not so much the hobby of the initiated few, but one of the chief delights in life of an ever-increasing number of people of all ages and classes. The work of the real artist was seen to be a revelation, rich in spiritual content, of the highest creative faculties of mankind.

It had been suggested, he thought wrongly, that these exhibitions had been in some way connected with politics. He was convinced that the cruder element which might be dubbed political advertising had throughout been absent; though not, perhaps, that better political intention, the greater understanding of the genius of a people and the diffusion of a greater knowledge of national character as exemplified by works of art. (Cheers.) There could be no doubt that these exhibitions had done much for peace and cooperation among nations in a still war-stricken world. It was, after all, through literature, through music, and through the plastic arts that they could learn so much regarding the soul of a nation at its best, and the more they knew of these the greater grew mutual understanding, respect, and admiration between civilized men, and the more surely the foundations of peace were laid.

[. . .]

THE MOST EXCITING CENTURY

The most exciting century, as far as painting was concerned, which they could study at Burlington House was the most recent, and he anticipated that what would remain the most abiding memory after this exhibition was closed would be the revelation, very largely new to many English people who had been unable to travel abroad, of French painting of the nineteenth century. France, with her humanity, her vitality, her vivid frankness, her love of true scholarship and fineness of actual workmanship and handling, her urbanity and ability to raise mankind to all those refinements of manners and feelings which constituted 'civilization' in the best meaning of that word, showed through her artists what she meant as a nation in true values to the world to-day. It had been left to French painters to transfigure landscape and scenes of every-day life to the level of religious art.

[. . .]

The FRENCH AMBASSADOR, M. de Fleuriau, read the speech which M. Petsche was to have delivered. M. Petsche stated that the works which to-day occupied the place of honour in Burlington House told the whole history of France: the treasure of Saint Denis and that of the Sainte Chapelle, Charlemagne's reliquary, the chalice of Anne, Queen of France, the armour worn by their Valois kings. Here they had the portrait of King John, and here the casket of Saint Louis. Near by they found the spirited horsemen of Poitiers and of Taillebourg, whom the fiery genius of Delacroix has called back to life in that very place. Those pages out of the history of France were also pages out of the history of Britain, since so much blood had to be shed that the union of the two countries might be sealed. Spiritual exchanges and peaceable victories had taken the place of armed invasions.

In the exhibition they gave a lion's share to the nineteenth century, of which they might now safely say that it would certainly rank among the greatest. The nineteenth century was an age of freedom, an age of victories in art as well as in the sciences and in social politics. It gave to the artist an all-embracing view of life. In the realm of painting, until then, the subject had been pre-eminent.

ARTISTS AND THE WORLD

If this exhibition went no farther than the end of the nineteenth century, it was not because our own century would not appear less important. In the strenuous watch which men kept over the peace of the world artists had their part to play. They could not foretell what would finally arise out of the great world struggle. But at the point which they had now reached, in proportion as the years which had elapsed made less vivid for them the horror of all the bloodshed for the freedom of the world, it was essential that artists, who were the children of one and the same spiritual family, should fight against everything that separated and for everything that united. They had worked together side by side and heart to heart. Even if the edifice they had raised were shortlived, the foundations would last, because they were built on the rock of friendship. Might that ceremony be a new pledge of the union of France and Britain, a union in which art must be in the future, as it was in the past, one of the safest warrants and one of the closest ties.

The PRESIDENT of the ROYAL ACADEMY, in reply, said that the exhibition unfolded the history of French art, more especially of French painting from the early centuries to 1900, though with a special consideration for the developments and movements of the nineteenth century, in which France had a special pride and which had no parallel in any other country or period, for it was claimed, and rightly so, that in modern times French art had touched and influenced the art of every other nation. The works of the nineteenth century occupied about a third of the space of the Galleries, and this section alone invested the exhibition with exceptional importance. It was a display of vitality, imagination, invention, and activity which should arouse interest and admiration.

[. . .]

35 Robert Anning Bell, 'The Functions of Art: Nature and Historic Truth: A Glance Back at the French Exhibition', letter to the editor, *The Times*, 14 March 1932, p. 15

Robert Anning Bell (1863–1933) was a painter, relief sculptor and designer in a variety of other media; an exhibitor at the Royal Academy from 1885, he was elected Associate in 1914 and Royal Academician in 1922. He was also a member of the New English Art Club (1892–1902) and other artists' organizations. He taught extensively, at Liverpool University from 1894, at the Glasgow School of Art from 1911, and at the Royal College of Art, as Professor of Design, from 1918–24.

Sir, – Mr. Furst must not be allowed to get away with his assertion that the inhabitants of these islands owe to the Cubists and Post-Impressionists the knowledge that a picture should be 'a whole on the wall,' as he neatly puts it. If his memory could carry him back to the eighties he would remember that this principle was professed and acted upon by Burne-Jones and his followers, as well as by Whistler and his. Indeed, it had been followed generally if often unconsciously all through the ages.

What we do owe to the Post-Impressionists and their friends is the decrepitude of French art, at any rate as represented in the exhibition at the Royal Academy which has just closed. They have evidently accepted the modern theory that pictures should be 'disentangled' (I thank the Art Critic of *The Times* for the word) from all associations or interests other than those purely aesthetic. A 'pietà' or 'Boors drinking' are indifferent as subjects to the artist, they are merely and solely arrangements in lines and colours; he would be going beyond his province should he touch the religious or convivial note! A landscape must not make you feel 'what a charming place,' but must interest you as pattern only.

This 'disentangled' art seems, however, to contain within itself the elements of decay. Its severe limitations are too narrow for the expression of human sympathies, and it, of course, ignores historic truth. For all great schools of art have arisen, surely, in answer to a demand for the aesthetic expression of these very sympathies. It repudiates the faithful study of Nature, logically enough, as aesthetic combinations obey other laws than those which govern natural forms; and therefore any distortion is permitted which falls in with an aesthetic formula. Exact knowledge declines; such subsidiary subjects as anatomy and perspective are derided; and as a result a fumbling execution replaces the precise statement of former times.

French painting in the Exhibition was seen as a living organism, admirably shown from the earliest to the latest stages in continuous evolution. It can well be compared to the growth and changes in the human body. That being so, the latest change is towards senile decay. There is the same contraction of interests, the same loss of power, and the same feebleness of hand and eye. It must be remembered that French art has been a great and vital one for many centuries, and therefore even in decay it shows traces of greatness still.

Fortunately there is not very much of this among English artists. The younger of them may express themselves in methods somewhat startling to an older generation; but they keep their minds unshackled and find their subjects wherever their sympathies lie, independent of pedantic theory, as their fathers did before them.

PSS. – When I say 'fathers' I must not be taken too literally! 'Les vieux ont toujours tort.'

We have lately been favoured by enterprising picture dealers with exhibitions of French art which has been 'produced,' as Euclid says, to the 'ga-ga' stage.

INDEX

The index includes names, picture titles and institutions mentioned in the essays and in the texts of the catalogue entries, together with the authors of the texts in the anthology of criticism. It does not include the provenance, exhibition history or literature sections of the catalogue entries, or the names mentioned within the texts included in the anthology of criticism.